SPECIAL EDUCATION

GARLAND REFERENCE LIBRARY
OF SOCIAL SCIENCE
(Vol. 375)

Source Books on Education

SPECIAL EDUCATION
A Source Book

Manny Sternlicht, Ph.D.

With the assistance of
Madeline Sternlicht, Ph.D.

GARLAND PUBLISHING, INC. · NEW YORK & LONDON
1987

Library of Congress Cataloging-in-Publication Data

Sternlicht, Manny.
   Special Education.

   (Garland Reference Library of Social Science;
vol. 375. Source Books on Education;7)
   Includes indexes.
   1. Special education literature—United States.
2. Exceptional children—Education—United States—
Bibliography.   3. Handicapped children—Education—
United States—Bibliography.   I. Title.   II. Series:
Garland Reference Library of Social Science; v. 375.
III. Series: Garland Reference Library of Social
Science.   Source Books on Education;7.

LC3969.S84   1987   016.3719   87-129
ISBN 0-8240-8524-8

Cover design by Valerie Mergentime

Printed on acid-free, 250-year-life paper
Manufactured in the United States of America

CONTENTS

INTRODUCTION

This annotated bibliography in the field of special education is designed for teachers of exceptional pupils and other educational personnel so that they may be aware of the research that exists in various areas and so that they may have a hand source book to which they can refer when necessary. The vast amount of research is both confusing and overwhelming to the teacher who must face the daily task of teaching students whose deviations are so marked. Exceptional pupils do not represent a homogeneous group requiring similar approaches, but instead manifest a diversity of etiology and behavior necessitating different methodologies. The need to classify and understand these differences is apparent. So, too, is the need to make order out of chaos. It is a difficult and time-consuming task for teachers to pore through all of the research, most of it in journals, to get at its essence, and then to combine the data into appropriate classifications for easy reference. The goal of this work was to provide such reference.

The division of the book into ten chapters, nine dealing with particular subgroups of special education and one with a technique common to all, was done both for clarity and for ease of reference. Although there are many ways to divide the various spheres of special education, we have elected to group them into the following four major categories:

1. Cognition (Mental Retardation and Giftedness).
2. Sensory and Neurological (Visual Impairments, Hearing Impairments, Learning Disabilities, and Brain Damage).
3. Physical Disabilities (Speech and Language Impairments, and Orthopedic and Other Physical Impairments).
4. Behavioral Disabilities (Emotional and Behavioral Impairments).

This grouping is primarily for ease of reference since there is always the problem of overlapping, oversimplification, and the consequent disregard of the complexity of individuals who defy single-category placement. We recognize

that negative aspects exist. For example, the area of learning disabilities is controversial and might just as easily
have been placed under cognitive functioning. Yet we adhere
to our scheme, not out of dogmatic conviction or mere stub-
bornness, but because of pragmatic considerations. We classify for convenience and coherence. To further pursue this
aim, an overview of all of these areas, detailing significant
highlights and pertinent background, is provided following a
broad, general introduction.

Special Education

     Although the words seem self-explanatory, it is necessary
to be precise in defining what we mean by "special education"
before proceeding to explore the various subgroupings that we
have already highlighted. Briefly stated, special education
is an educational program designated for children who are
"special" or "exceptional" because they deviate from the average or normal child in their mental characteristics, their
sensory abilities, their neurological or physical characteristics, their communication abilities, their emotional functioning, or because of their multiple and severe handicaps.
However, the problem with this and most other definitions is
that they seem to emphasize the child's limitations rather
than strengths. Usually the criteria incorporated into these
definitions focus on low mental and physical ability or deviant social behavior. Thus, by defining a child as exceptional
we label him/her as such, and a self-fulfilling prophecy may
very well occur in terms of teachers' expectations. Still,
definitions may be needed, if only to ensure the eligibility
of a child for special services regulated by laws enacted for
the exceptional population.
     Education for these children requires modifications,
since sufficient learning often cannot occur through the regular means of instruction. The fact that modifications currently exist should not obscure the fact that these gains are
only of relatively recent origin and that it was a struggle
to reach the point where educational access is now considered
a right to which all are entitled.
     In order to better understand the need for special edu-
cation, a brief review of its history is appropriate. In the
nineteenth and early twentieth centuries, when exceptional
children were first recognized as different or strange, the
majority of these children were either ignored, rejected, or
punished on account of their differences. During this time
(to about 1950), there were few, if any, psychological, social, or educational solutions to the difficulties encountered

by exceptional children and their families. Consequently, to receive any kind of help at all the parents and children were forced to find their own solutions. It was the general public's lack of knowledge, rather than its deliberate disregard of the exceptional child, that led to fear, superstitions, and a failure to provide meaningful program. Among the few that did exist were: the American Asylum for the Education and Instruction of the Deaf, established in 1817 in Hartford; the first special class for the mentally retarded, created in 1896 in Providence; a special class for the crippled in 1899 in Boston; and a class for the blind founded in 1900 in Chicago. Generally speaking, however, the early approaches either did virtually nothing, or placed the person in a residential center, or simply punished the individual because of his/her differences.

During this early period there were no special or specific curricula for the special child. The exceptional individual had to cope with the same instructional materials that were offered to everybody, and woe to the child who could not cope--exclusion or expulsion was his/her lot. Any training that was provided in the early 24-hour residential centers tended to focus upon the development of personal self-care skills, with very little emphasis placed upon social relations and adaptive behavior that would facilitate the individual's return to the outside community.

During these years as well, precious few professional personnel were initially involved in working with special children. There were no professional training programs, and those few individuals who were working intensively with these children were doing so primarily on a one-to-one basis. The first professionals to take an interest in the education of exceptional children were European physicians. The early list of practitioners included such luminaries as Jean Marc Gaspard, an ear specialist and expert on education the deaf; Itard, the inventer of instructional devices for the retarded and in some respects the father of special education for the mentally retarded; Maria Montessori, the first female doctor in Italy and a foremost educator of the retarded; and Sequin, another educator of the intellectually limited. In the United States, Samuel Gridley Howe was involved with the education of the handicapped.

During this early period in special education, very little emphasis was placed upon the development of special public school classes by parents and others. Because of the social stigma attendant upon having an exceptional child, many parents kept their children at home, often actually denying their very existence. Supportive or other services for these parents were unavailable, perhaps because no one knew what types of services might be helpful and appropriate.

Special children really had no place in the community prior to the 1950s, and, generally speaking, no community services were available; certainly not any that were especially designed for the exceptional child. Since the major emphasis at the time was upon the development of institutional training programs, there was no obvious need for communities to develop or to offer services. Thus, long-range planning for the development of community programs or professional training programs was virtually nonexistent. The growth of institutions was viewed as the answer for the problems of the exceptional child, his/her parents and siblings.

However, a period of rapid and dramatic growth took place between 1950 and 1980. During these three decades, the transition from almost total isolation, disregard, and rejection to toleration and inclusion in community programs began to occur. Yet, in spite of the community's new awareness of the need of the deviant child to be included in community programs, he/she was still segregated from the "normal" child. The movement of special children from residential settings into community settings was a slow and gradual process and was not the consequence of any drastic changes in public attitudes, but rather was primarily because of the demand for these services by parents and organized parent and professional groups. The parents and parent groups (and some groups of professionals) insisted that the exceptional child had as much right to the utilization of community services and programs as anyone else, and that special services should be provided by the community.

Since events do not occur in a vacuum, however, we should pause to consider what triggered the changes in attitudes and the increasing vociferousness of many parent and other groups. In 1958, actually preceding the height of the civil rights activism of the 1960s, P.L. 85-926 was enacted. Through this law, the federal government made an effort to insure a supply of especially trained personnel for the field of special education.

Fueled by the impetus of the Civil Rights movement, the courts began to examine injustices afflicting the handicapped. In 1974, the Parc decision established the rights of mentally retarded individuals (no longer called "children"), ages six-twenty-one, to obtain free, mandatory public education (designed to satisfy their needs). This was a key ruling inasmuch as it was the first such law to exist and it signalled a new attitude toward the developmentally disabled. Now the moving force was a desire to teach these children to function as effectively as they could, rather than to offer mere custodial care. The most famous ruling, however, came one year later. In 1975, Public Law 94-142 provided free mandatory public education in the least restrictive environment for all handicapped individuals. This was a landmark decision that ushered in many new and innovative educational programs and services designed to comply with the requirements of the law. Basically, there are three principles set aside by P.L. 94-142. They are: the right to due process procedures, the right of a student to be placed in the least restrictive environment, and the right to an individualized education program. The rights to due process procedures include the rights of parents to examine school records that involve the testing of their child. The parents may then obtain a second opinion from independent examiners. Parents must be notified in writing and in their native language whenever the school deems it necessary to evaluate the child or if the school wants to change the educational status of the child. If the parents refuse involvement or their whereabouts are unknown, surrogate parents must be appointed. Parents have the right to present complaints on anything relating to the evaluation, identification, or placement of the child. If after the school has held impartial hearings and found the parents not correct, the parents can pursue the matter through the civil courts.

The right to be educated in the least restrictive environment is not always simply implemented. What for one student may be considered the least restrictive environment may be very restrictive for another. Basically, the intention of this concept was to facilitate the interaction of handicapped students with their peers in regular education. For the mildly handicapped student, attempts should be made to mainstream the student as much as possible to the regular classroom, whereas for the profoundly retarded, a regular classroom may be one of the most restrictive environments.

The individualized education program, or the IEP as it is commonly known, is a plan of instruction based on short and long term objectives developed for the student by his special education teacher in cooperation with the other professionals involved, and the parents. One problem with the IEP is that it is sometimes viewed as strictly an administrative plan that consumes much valuable time. With the growing use of computers to handle time consuming paperwork, it is to be hoped that the full potential of the IEP will be realized.

A complete listing of all of the major highlights of P.L. 94-142 follows:

Highlights of PL 94-142
THE EDUCATION OF ALL HANDICAPPED CHILDREN ACT OF 1975

Education for All
Free and appropriate public education for all children with
 handicaps, ages 5-21 by September 1, 1978

Child-Find
Identification, location and evaluation of all children with
 handicaps

Priorities
First: "unserved" children, i.e., those not presently receiving an education
Second: children with the most severe handicaps not receiving
 an adequate education

Least Restrictive Environments
Education of handicapped children together with nonhandicapped children to the maximum extent
Special education and related services in the least
 restrictive environment commensurate with their needs

Pre-School Children
Additional $300/year to the State for every handicapped
 child served between ages 3-5

Parent Rights
Consultation, identification, evaluation, and placement
Participation in preparing and implementing educational plans
Examination of relevant records
Presentation of complaints
Right to a due process hearing

Professional Personnel
Appropriate pre-service preparation and training
In-service training for general and special educators
Equal employment of persons with handicaps

Educational Evaluation and Prescription
Written educational plan at the start of each school year
Annual goals
Short-term instructional objectives
Specific educational services
Degree of mainstream participation
Periodic evaluation
Participation in planning educational prescription by
 parents, teachers and, when appropriate, the child

Removing Architectural Barriers
Grants available to pay for part or all of the costs to
 remove physical barriers in educational facilities

How different things were in the days before this magnif-
icent piece of legislation! The early curricula and instructional materials were based upon the collective thinking of a
very few individuals who were working with exceptional children. Program development was almost entirely teacher-
oriented, with perhaps a small handful of curriculum "specialists" included. An attempt was made to adapt the regular
curriculum and instructive materials to the unique needs of
the special child. Early programs focused on the development
of manual skills, with occupational loci and arts and crafts
programs being emphasized almost to the exclusion of the development of suitable cognitive skills such as reading, writing, and arithmetic. Many of these programs stressed that
the educational goals for the exceptional child were the same
as the goals for the normal or regular class youngsters; however, a different type of curriculum had to be provided.
Even after the development of community programs for the exceptional child, professional training was generally similar
to the present concept of in-service training. There were
few books published pertaining to the exceptional child and
very few institutions of higher education preparing future
teachers and other professionals to work with exceptional
children. Early training had to be provided by those who had
worked with exceptional children, and the training was usually
provided on site.

Recruitment into the field of special education was a
very difficult task because of the lack of training that was
available, the small number of programs, and the limited future viewed for this field. Those people who were recruited
no doubt received training that focused on the needs of the
individual child. As programs became better established
within community settings, training programs grew somewhat
rapidly within the public schools and institutions of higher
education.

With the opening of community services to exceptional
children, many community agencies and individuals became involved in attempting to meet their needs. In more recent
years, these needs came to be recognized as more than custodial, and therefore professionals agreed that intensive and
comprehensive services were required if exceptional children
were to reach their potential.

The educational curriculum of today is beginning to place
a strong emphasis on the development of competencies of individuals. There is more emphasis on vocational and career
education for the exceptional child. The development and
implementation of values clarification is another rapidly
growing part of instructional programs for exceptional children. Further, the training of professionals--both regular

and special classroom teachers—focuses more than ever upon their abilities to understand and to meet adequately the individual needs of exceptional children.

An important question often raised by novice special education teachers is how they can effectively modify the educational program so as to meet each student's needs while at the same time fostering the development of the child's maximum potential. In preparing a special education curriculum, two important variables to consider are instructional modifications and adaptations and appropriate content changes. The special education teacher must adapt the instruction to meet the child's particular needs created by the handicap. (As the reader will find, the research literature abounds with specific illustrations as to how this can be accomplished.) In addition to instructional modifications, content changes, suitable skills training, and environmental changes also may be necessary in order to accomplish the goals of special education. Sometimes a prosthetic environment needs to be created. Often it is necessary to utilize consultant services or to modify the setting in which special education takes place, such as through the use of part-time special classes, special self-contained classes, special day schools, temporary residential facilities, and/or hospital and homebound teaching.

One needs to keep in mind, however, that the current philosophy of special education holds that exceptional children should be placed in the least restrictive educational environment, an environment that is as nearly as possible like that of the main body of children. Those children who warrant it are assigned to regular classes and, through mainstreaming, are the primary responsibility of the regular classroom teacher. Other children may be in regular grade classrooms, but are removed to a resource room for several periods of remedial work. In both of these cases the teachers receive supportive help from various consultants such as school psychologists, educational consultants, and school social workers who are available to them whenever they have questions about a child or whenever they may need advice concerning special educational materials or techniques of instruction. In addition, these consultants, as well as other special educational personnel such as speech pathologists and remedial reading teachers, may deal with special children on either an itinerant or as-needed basis. In any case, helping exceptional children is nearly always viewed as a cooperative venture.

The ultimate goal in the education of children, both handicapped and nonhandicapped, is to enable them to live productive, satisfying lives as fully participating members

of society. Since this goal requires a degree of independence, special educators must have practical, short-term and
medium-term objectives for exceptional children at various
points during their development. Perhaps one of the first
goals ought to be to continuously refine the means by which
special children are identified.

Improvement of educational services for exceptional children includes early identification of their problems in
health, adjustment, and learning. Professionals have hesi-
tated too long in identifying exceptional children at an early
age. This hesitation in order to "wait and see" can only
cause frustration on the part of children, parents, and teachers. Waiting until a child has continuously failed in the
regular school program in order to obtain diagnostic assessment data cannot help the progress of the child's self-
concept, nor can it enhance the relationship the child will
acquire toward learning and adjustment. Exceptional children
must be provided adequate and functional educational services
at an early age in order to prevent a significant loss of
human potential.

Once exceptional children have been identified, personnel
should then focus upon the development of quality educational
programs and related services, such as individualized remediation efforts, physical restorative services, and innovative
instruction in developing those necessary personal and social
skills needed in order to cope with our dynamic modern technological culture.

Placement in a special education class should never mean
that the child is destined to spend the remainder of the educational program within that special class setting. Our current educational philosophy is that exceptional children
should be placed in classes as close to normal class situations as is possible and feasible. As has already been mentioned, "mainstreaming" is the method whereby an exceptional
child spends most or part of the school day in a normal classroom setting with a regular teacher. The regular teacher
will usually have a support system for assistance in working
with these special children. Further, some teachers will
remove children on a relatively regular basis from their regular class for tutorial help as a form of supplementation to
the instruction offered by the students' regular classroom
teacher. This system is utilized mostly on a referral basis,
with the teacher normally initiating the referral. An itinerant teacher would usually bring this service to the students, as opposed to a resource room where extra group help
might be obtained.

Basically, the resource room is employed as an effort to
respond to criticisms of the special class approach, in order

to achieve a more fully integrated educational experience for
the student. Clearly, very close communication between regular classroom teachers and the resource room teacher is necessary. The resource teacher generally works with small groups
of pupils (or even with individuals), primarily with children
who are mildly handicapped. The emphasis is upon providing
supplemental materials to aid in their personalized instructional needs. The ultimate goal is to assist the student
sufficiently to become independent of the resource room situation. However, since the resource room is nearly always a
less restrictive environment than the regular classroom, children may continue in this setting through the eighth grade.

Should a resource room setting be insufficient, there is
also the part-time special class that is geared to children
who require more specific and more quantitative time than is
available in a resource room. There is usually one special
education teacher who spends up to half a day with each specified class. Moving up in intensity of educational involvement within the sphere of special education is the concept of
the self-contained special class, an idea that was in full
flower in the past. This is still the typical situation for
more severely handicapped children, wherein one teacher is
assigned the full-time responsibility for a special education
class.

There are also special day schools in existence whose
student bodies are composed entirely of exceptional children;
some are for one type of exceptional children only, while
others service a more heterogeneous population of special
children. Typically, students enrolled in such schools tend
to be especially severely handicapped. Parental involvements
in these settings usually are maximal. There also are residential schools or institutions that are either privately
operated or governmentally funded and operated. Although
there is a recent trend to build new facilities such as these
directly in the heart of population centers, most of the existing (older) residential institutions tend to be situated
in rural areas, making regular and frequent parental contacts
difficult, in some cases exceedingly so. There are at present
many negative feelings about this type of a setting where the
child is so separated from the mainstream of community living
and where the quality of the educational offerings may leave
something to be desired. Although this situation is
distinctly less appealing than any of the aforementioned alternatives, it is likely to continue in existence for some
time, particularly for those exceptional children who are
severely multiply handicapped and who are very difficult to
care for at home.

Generally speaking, however, special education should

not be apart from, but a part of regular education. Only after all other possible measures have been taken to provide an exceptional child with suitable and appropriate education in a close-to-regular setting should one resort to one or another of the various options mentioned above. Finally, satisfactorily educating parents to become significant con- tributors to their child's total overall development is an additional goal that all special educators ought to strive for. Parents should share fully the responsibility with the educators.

Educators must never allow their goals to become static. Exceptional children need a great deal of help in learning how to function satisfactorily in society. They need to de- velop sufficient skills so that they will be able to communi- cate, play, and work well with others, and also to be accepted by their peers. The teacher's instructional mandate must be coordinated to meet the three objectives of personal, eco- nomic, and social efficiency. Special education teachers must provide meaningful lessons to the students, always on a hands-on, practical basis. They must constantly remain aware that the essential difference between a special class and a regular class is not so much in the instructional didactic subject content areas as it is in the emphasis that needs to be placed upon the applications of the educational material to everyday life situations. Essentially, what special edu- cation means is a special kind of education, an addition to the ordinary education--one that is unique and that emphasizes learning practical skills through varied educational methods adapted to the special needs of these special students.

This relatively brief history of the background, philos- ophy, and principles of special education reveals the great strides that have been made in our perceptions of "special" children and in our ability to provide for their effective and individualized education.

One final note of caution should be made before conclud- ing this section and going on to the specific subgroupings in the field of special education. It is so fundamental that it is surprising that it was not accepted until rather recently. We refer to the fact that the emphasis on the differences of exceptional individuals has obscured the fact that they are basically the same as all other people, with the same human needs--to be loved, accepted, and allowed to develop their full potential. If their behavior is different, it may be in response to the frustrations over their handicap and also to the ways in which they have been treated by society at large. We can modify teaching techniques to take into account the particular disability, but our fundamental role is to provide the best learning climate that we can--one that is neither

patronizing nor supercilious, but rather one that approximates
the "normal" classroom setting as much as possible.

Since teachers' expectations influence children's learning, it is mandatory that teachers know and appreciate that
disability is not synonymous with limitation. The challenges
and the rewards are greater with exceptional children, and
the influence of the teacher is more critical. Knowing about
the limitations imposed by the handicap is essential in making
teaching more effective, just as long as that knowledge does
not subconsciously alter the teacher's expectations to a much
lower level.

Finally, the general statements about the following areas
of special education that have been researched in this book
are meant to help the teacher in formulating expectations
that are neither too high nor too low. The most important
role of any professional in the educational arena is to exude
a positive, accepting attitude, one that builds on success
and focuses on abilities rather than on failures and disabilities.

Special Education

CHAPTER I:
MENTAL RETARDATION

To commence, we must define what we mean when we use the term "mental retardation." According to the American Association on Mental Deficiency (and incorporated into PL 94-142), mental retardation refers to significantly subaverage general intellectual functioning resulting in or associated with concurrent impairments in adaptive behavior and manifested during the developmental period. Essentially, being mentally retarded means that a child's ability to learn new and novel material is slower or "retarded" as compared with the abilities of most children and that, perhaps as a consequence of this, some behavioral adjustment difficulties also may be in evidence.

An individual's level of cognitive functioning normally is determined via the administration of an intelligence test that will usually yield a consequent intelligence quotient (IQ). If the person attains an IQ that is more than two standard deviations below the mean, or an IQ of less than 70, then a finding of mental retardation is warranted. Although psychologists utilize a four-fold classification of the severity of retardation (profound, severe, moderate, and mild), most educators prefer to subclassify mentally retarded children into three categories--educable, trainable, and profound. (There also is another category that partially flirts with the very upper edge of retardation, and that is the category of "slow learner," but technically speaking such a child is not considered to be mentally retarded.)

The educable mentally retarded child (IQ 50-70) ordinarily is one who does not have sufficient intelligence to benefit from a program of regular classroom instruction, but who does have adequate cognitive resources to learn useful skills and to become capable of independent self-management. The educational goal for such an individual is adequate preparation for eventual total integration into society as an independently functioning person. The educable individual needs to be taught those skills necessary for getting along in the world. On the equivalent high school level, the educable (mildly) retarded adolescent will need to be taught not only the skills necessary for a specific job, but also those social skills necessary to maintain the job as well as the skills needed to transport himself/herself to and from the job.

The educational objectives for the trainable child (IQ 30-49) should be to assist the child to become as self-sufficient as possible. These children generally have a prognosis for some degree of economic self-sufficiency and acceptable social adjustment. Their educational curriculum needs to take into account the current developmental stage of the individual, the anticipated slower rate of development, and the ultimate level of development expected. Initially, habit training (e.g., personal hygiene, self-help skills) should be taught, followed by social interaction skills. The next level would be a refinement of these skills, followed, ideally, by learning a career skill. Virtually all trainable retarded persons are capable of some degree of employment, be it in the competitive arena or in a sheltered workshop setting.

Because all aspects of (physical and intellectual) growth and development tend to be interrelated, the profoundly retarded individual (IQ less than 25) also tends to have accompanying physical handicaps and stigmata. Such an individual, who may also require nursing care, can be expected to learn certain self-help practices, such as dressing and undressing, eating skills, communicating, and toileting. Most profoundly retarded persons will be unable to function with complete independence as adults and thus will frequently require placement in highly structured institution-like settings.

As has been demonstrated, the mentally retarded are a heterogeneous group with varying characteristics and varying abilities. Despite the differences in mental and physical ability and motor coordination and development, as a group mentally retarded children exhibit certain common characteristics. These include such things as limited memory and poor attention span, limited abstract ideation, delayed early developmental history (including delayed speech and language development), difficulty in associating cause and effect relationships, poor number concept and consequent difficulties in arithmetical problem solving, and relatively low frustration tolerance level. With few exceptions, mildly retarded children do not appear significantly physically different from their nonretarded peers and they often may excel in sports activities. The greatest difference lies in the ability to learn didactic materials, but even here the retarded individual has the potential to learn limited academic skills up to a 6th grade level, which is certainly enough to get by.

The causes of mental retardation, broadly considered, are primarily twofold: genetic-organic and cultural-familial.

The genetic-organic causes account for no more than twenty
percent of retardation, and usually individuals who are retarded on this account tend to be either trainable or profound.   Such causation includes children with Down's Syndrome,
PKU (phenylketonuria), organic brain damage, skull anomalies
(hydrocephaly and microcephaly), and retardation due to rubella, lead poisoning, and so forth.   The cultural-familial
origins of mental retardation, which account for the remaining
approximately eighty percent of retardation, are generally
unspecified and vague, but are thought to be the result of
lack of enrichment, nurturing, and stimulation often found in
children of families in the lower socio-economic bracket.

Whatever the cause, there are various and sundry techniques for dealing with the mentally retarded child in the
classroom, all taking into account the special skills and
needs of each child and the different teaching styles necessary to capitalize upon them.   Among those procedures that
have been found to be especially helpful are using concrete
objects rather than abstract ideas, providing sufficient opportunities for positive reinforcement, utilizing student
helper-tutors, explaining techniques and performing a maximum
of practice activities, and assigning work that is reading-
level appropriate.   Among the favored teaching modalities for
the retarded, especially for those of more limited intellectual functioning, is behavior modification.   This procedure
is based upon the simple principle that the positive reinforcement of a behavior will increase the probability that
that behavior will occur again.   The desired behavior or task,
however, must be consistently reinforced.

In short, while the three R's of regular education are
reading, 'riting, and 'rithmetic, the appropriate three R's
for the education of the retarded are routine, repetition,
and reinforcement (or reward).

1. Aloia, G.F.; R. Knutson; S.H. Minner; and M. Von Seggern.
       1980. Physical education teachers' initial perceptions
       of handicapped children. *Mental Retardation* 18:85–87.

           An attitude survey was conducted with fifty-seven
       regular class physical education teachers concerning
       their initial perceptions of handicapped children.
       Results indicated that significant differences existed
       among physical education teachers depending upon the
       labeled condition of the child. The authors conclude
       that considerable work at the preservice and inservice
       levels is needed for more effective involvement of
       physical education teachers in the total program of
       handicapped children.

2. Altman, R., and D. Feldman. 1985. Conceptual systems
       and teacher attitudes toward regular classroom place-
       ment of mildly mentally retarded students. *American
       Journal of Mental Deficiency* 89:345–51.

           The effects of a teacher personality construct
       (abstract vs. concrete conceptual system) and two pupil
       variables on 454 regular classroom teachers' attitudes
       toward mainstreaming were determined. Results revealed
       a significant main effect on the behavior variable and
       a significant personality x Race interaction on all
       inventory dimensions, suggesting that regular teachers
       perceived maladaptive behavior of mainstreamed retarded
       children as a threat to a conducive instructional at-
       mosphere and to the achievement of nonretarded stu-
       dents.

3. Arem, C.A., and B.J. Zimmerman. Vicarious effects on the
       creative behavior of retarded and nonretarded children.
       American Journal of Mental Deficiency 89:289–96.

           The effects of observing a model's overt display
       of a creative drawing response and hearing a descrip-
       tion of these actions were assessed with fifty-four
       retarded and sixty-eight nonretarded children (ten-
       twelve years old). The modeled creative strategy was
       designed to be high on the dimension of elaboration,
       as well as to determine transfer to tasks of varying
       degrees of similarity to the model's task and to cre-
       ative dimensions other than elaboration. The overt
       modeling of a creative strategy was most effective in

improving elaboration, although verbal descriptions also aided performance. Retarded children were less able than nonretarded children to discriminate the essential elements of the model's elaboration strategy but showed comparable gradients of transfer.

4. Ashman, A. 1982. Cognitive processes and perceived language performance of retarded persons. *Journal of Mental Deficiency Research* 26:131-41.

    In this research, a battery of tests was given to 88 mentally retarded persons with a mean age of 20.3 years. Among the tests were the Stanford-Binet, Raven Colored Progressive Matrices, a memory-for-designs tasks, a figure-copy task, an auditory recall test, the Digit Span from the WISC, and measures of expressive and receptive languages. Intercorrelations were computed between coding and language variables, and the simultaneous tests were analyzed. Discussion focused on coding and auditory-visual processing and the development of suitable language training programs for mentally retarded persons.

5. Baroody, A.J., and P.M. Snyder. 1984. A cognitive analysis of basic arithmetic abilities of TMR children. *Education and Training of the Mentally Retarded* 18: 253-59.

    The study assessed a range of basic arithmetic abilities of fifteen TMR students. Tasks were administered to the students individually over three sessions. The four-six year olds were capable of rule governed and other counting skills, and some could mentally compare numbers and choose the larger. Some subjects demonstrated a basic form of problem solving in that they used the addition identity and commutativity principles to shortcut computational effort.

6. Berkson, G., and T.J. Thompson. 1985. Stereotyped behavior of severely disabled children in classroom and free-play settings. *American Journal of Mental Deficiency* 89: 580-86.

    The relationships between stereotyped behavior, object manipulation, self-manipulation, teacher atten-

tion, and various developmental measures were examined
in 101 severely developmentally disabled children in
their classrooms and in a free-play setting. Partial
correlations showed that age, self-manipulation, and
developmental age shared unique variance with stereotyped behavior without objects.

7. Bilsky, L.H., and T. Judd. 1985. Sources of difficulty
in the solution of verbal arithmetic problems by mentally retarded and nonretarded individuals. *American
Journal of Mental Deficiency* 90: 395-402.

Effects of several logical (operational type and
amount of extraneous information) and memory (problem
text type) factors on verbal math problem-solving performance were assessed. Results of mildly retarded
were inferior to those of nonretarded fourth graders
in spite of comparable performance on computational
screening test. The possibly important role of comprehension in problem-solving was discussed. Retarded
individuals experience particular difficulty with subtraction.

8. Bos, C. and R. Tierney. 1984. Inferential reading abilities of mildly retarded and nonretarded students.
American Journal of Mental Deficiency 89: 75-82.

A study involving sixteen mildly retarded junior
high school students and sixteen nonretarded third
graders. The two groups were matched for reading comprehension level and their recall of what they read
was compared. There were as many inferences made by
the mentally retarded students as by the nonretarded;
however, they were qualitatively inferior.

9. Bricker, W.A. 1970. Identifying and modifying behavioral
deficiency. *American Journal of Mental Deficiency*
75:16-21.

This article proposes that the thrust of behavior
modification be aimed at instructional procedures
rather than at the learning process itself. It suggests changing the current behavior modification technology in dealing with developmental retardation and
specifies the changes necessary to maximize its effectiveness.

10. Brinker, R.P. 1985. Interactions between severely men-
     tally retarded students and other students in inte-
     grated and segregated public school settings. *Ameri-
     can Journal of Mental Deficiency* 89:587-94.

          In this study the subjects were 245 severely men-
     tally retarded students from fourteen school districts
     in nine states. They were observed in integrated and
     segregated social groups in 1981 and 1982. The social
     overtures by mentally retarded students to other stu-
     dents was significantly higher in integrated social
     groups than in segregated social groups. A higher
     rate of positive bids was directed by non-retarded
     students to severely retarded students in comparison
     to bids form other handicapped students in integrated
     groups. Non-retarded students responded to social
     bids from severely retarded students more frequently
     than did other retarded students. The implications
     of these results are discussed in terms of interaction
     opportunities and practice of social skills.

11. Burgess, J. 1981. Development of social spacing in
     normal and mentally retarded children. *Journal of
     Nonverbal Behavior* 6:89-95.

          This article discusses distances between closest
     playmates during free play in fifty mentally retarded
     and forty-eight normal children. The children were
     in grades one-three or four-six and were observed in
     a spacious playground environment. Younger students
     (one-three) kept closer distances than older ones
     (four-six). Two hypotheses resulted from this study.
     One hypothesis states that closer distances and in-
     creased teaching occur under conditions of social
     disturbance. The other hypothesis states that younger
     children may stay closer to a playmate because their
     cognitive development does not facilitate simultaneous
     interaction with many members in a group.

12. Calhoun, K.S., and P. Matherne. 1975. Effects of vary-
     ing schedules of time-out on aggressive behavior of a
     retarded girl. *Journal of Behavior Therapy and Exper-
     imental Psychiatry* 6:139-43.

          When a time-out procedure was used after two
     aggressive acts or after every act there were signif-

icant positive results. This study with a seven year-
old retarded girl showed that if the time-out procedure was used after every fifth act it was not effective. The article implies that the effectiveness of
time-out is proportionate to the percentage of the
target behavior it follows.

13. Carlton, M.B.; F.W. Litton; and S.A. Zinkgraf. 1985.
The effects of an interclass peer tutoring program on
the sight-word recognition ability of students who
are mildly mentally retarded. *Journal of Mental Retardation* 23:74-78.

This article examines the effects of an intra-
class peer tutoring program on the sight word recognition skills of students who are mildly mentally
retarded. Six classes consisting of a total of sev-
enty-four students ranging in age from eleven-thirteen
years received six weeks of peer tutoring instruction
and served as the experimental group. Six other
classes with a total of sixty-two students served as
the control group. Results indicated that the tutors
and the tutees had significantly higher score gains
than did the controls on both vocabulary and reading
subtests. A structured peer tutoring program is suggested as a valuable instructional technique for
teachers of students who are mildly mentally retarded.

14. Carroll, J.L.; D. Friedrich; and J. Hund. 1984. Academic self-concept and teachers' perceptions of normal, mentally retarded, and learning disabled elementary students. *Psychology in the Schools* 21:343-48.

Teachers completed an evaluation scale for
seventy-three educable mentally impaired students,
forty-five learning disabled students, and forty-five
students never served by special education (all aged
7.25-11.92 years). The results show that nonhandicapped subjects had better self-concepts than did
educable mentally impaired subjects. Teacher perceptions of self-concepts confirmed that nonhandicapped
subjects had better self-concepts than did handicapped
subjects. The article suggests that handicapped students as a group have lower self-concepts than nonhandicapped subjects. In conclusion, helping children
feel good about themselves and others should be an

integral part of a total education program.

15. Carter, J.L. 1975. Intelligence and reading achievement
     of EMR children in three educational settings. *Mental
     Retardation* 13:26-27.

          Describes a study with third grade children who
     are retarded. They are placed in regular classes,
     segregated self-contained classes, and Plan A main-
     stream classes. The three systems evidenced no sub-
     stantial differences in reading achievement, but Plan
     A provided considerable supportive resources.

16. Chasey, W.C., and W. Wannen. 1971. Effects of a physi-
     cal developmental program on psychomotor ability of
     retarded children. *American Journal of Mental Defi-
     ciency* 75:566-70.

          To determine effects of a concentrated physical
     developmental program on motor proficiency of insti-
     tutionalized educable mentally retarded children,
     experimental and control groups were established to
     measure and compare performance and improvement of
     subjects in each group. Subjects (N = 60, 30 experi-
     mental, 30 control: Ca 6-1 to 12-2; IQ 50 to 85) were
     chosen at random. Both groups were chosen at random.
     Both groups were under supervision of qualified female
     teachers and adult male and female dormitory attend-
     ants. Physical education majors worked with experi-
     mental subjects in groups of three or four in a vari-
     ety of physical education activities including gym-
     nastics, tumbling, conditioning exercises, distance
     running, ball skills, playground and individual games
     five days a week, an hour a day for fifteen weeks.
     Subjects in the control group received no formal phys-
     ical education program but participated in free play
     activities with subjects from the experimental group
     during recreational periods.
          The Oseretsky Motor Development Scale was admin-
     istered to both groups before and after the experi-
     mental period. The experimental group had made sig-
     nificant improvement in general static coordination
     as well as dynamic coordination in hands, in simul-
     taneous voluntary movement, and in the overall
     Oseretsky score.

17. Chess, S., and S. Korn. 1970. Temperament and behavior
     disorders in mentally retarded children. *Archives of
     General Psychiatry* 23:122-30.

         This study contends that temperament signifi-
     cantly influences the retarded child's ability to
     adapt. In the experiment involving mentally retarded
     children results indicate that certain temperament
     patterns intensify the stress to which the child is
     subjected. It suggests that parent involvement in
     managing the retarded child be positive so children
     will better adapt and so there will be a reduction in
     the probability of behavior disorders.

18. Cirrin, F.M., and C.M. Rowland. 1985. Communicative
     assessment of nonverbal youths with severe/profound
     mental retardation. *Mental Retardation* 23:52-62.

         Fifteen nonverbal youths with severe/profound
     mental retardation were the subjects of this study.
     Videotapes were coded for specific nonverbal communi-
     cative behaviors and the communicative functions for
     which these behaviors were used. All of the youths
     were able to communicate with adults nonverbally;
     however, they differed in accuracy and type of com-
     municative interactions. These findings suggest a
     need for careful and detailed assessment of expressive
     communication of this population. Conditions that
     increase occurrence of communicative behaviors in
     this population are described.

19. Crawford, C., and P. Siegel. 1982. Improving the visual
     discrimination of mentally retarded children: A train-
     ing strategy. *American Journal of Mental Deficiency*
     87: 294-301.

         In this research, eighty-two mentally retarded
     children ages six-eighteen years with IQs 33-69 were
     tested on the Peabody Picture Vocabulary Test. With-
     out being trained, these students had to give verbal
     answers and full feedback on a series of questions.
     Trained students showed total intradimensional trans-
     fer and it was therefore concluded that attention/
     retention theory of discrimination learning and dif-
     ferentiation relates to methodology and theory.

20. Crawley, S., and K. Chan. 1982. Developmental changes
     in free-play behavior of mildly and moderately re-
     tarded preschool-aged children. *Education & Training
     of the Mentally Retarded* 17:234-39.

         The study tells of two groups of ten mildly and
     moderately retarded preschoolers (aged 32-42 months
     and 49-73 months) being observed during free-play
     over four weeks. Both mildly and moderately retarded
     children spent less time in teacher-child interaction.
     As they grew older solitary and parallel play in-
     creased in both groups. However, peer interaction
     increased with age in the mildly retarded children,
     but not in the moderately retarded children, where it
     remained constant.

21. Crusco, A.H.; P. Carter; M. McGrath; E. Payne;
     T. Antonow; and S. O'Dell. 1986. Skill requirements
     for interactive video instructions of persons with
     mental retardation. *Mental Retardation* 24:99-105.

         This study was to determine the extent to which
     twenty individuals with various levels of mental re-
     tardation can exhibit, without training, the basic
     skills needed to use an interactive video system.
     Two basic tasks were presented via videotape to the
     subjects, pressing a button on command and discrimi-
     nating between two visual forms. Observers measured
     student's ability to sit through session and attend
     to screen. Data showed considerable individual vari-
     ability, which was generally correlated with tradi-
     tional measures of student's level of functioning.
     Results show that with no pretraining, interactive
     video cannot be assumed useful with this population.

22. Delprato, D.J.; P.A. Pappdardo; and P.A. Holmes. 1984.
     The role response-reinforcer relationship in discrim-
     ination learning of mentally retarded persons. *Ameri-
     can Journal of Mental Deficiency* 89: 267-74.

         In this study spatial relationship between target
     responses and reinforcers in the discrimination of
     mentally retarded persons was evaluated. Subjects
     were instructed to move hand operated manipulandum to
     a positive stimulus located at left or right end of a
     track. Correct response was followed by a light and

edible reinforcer. In control condition, light and
edible reinforcers were presented at single location
equidistant from ends of the track. In experimental
condition they were presented to the terminus of the
response at the end of manipulandum track correspond-
ing to location of correct stimulus. Results showed
discrimination performance was more favorable in experimental condition.

23. Diorio, M., and A. Edward. 1984. Evaluation of a method
    for teaching dressing skills to profoundly retarded
    persons. *American Journal of Mental Deficiency*
    89:307-9.

    A study involving the training of three pro-
    foundly retarded adults. Two of these attained the
    criterion for independent dressing. No residents
    reached this despite 108.2 hours of training. These
    results contrast with those of Azrin et al., whose
    subjects were successful in an average of twelve
    hours.

24. Donnellan, A.M., and P.L. Mirenda. 1983. A model for
    analyzing instructional components to facilitate gen-
    eralization for severely handicapped students *Journal
    of Special Education* 17:317-31.

    This article presents a model for analyzing the
    parts of instructional programs that are likely to
    affect generalization with severely handicapped chil-
    dren. There are natural vs. artificial environments,
    materials, cues and supplies. Suggestions for imple-
    mentation are 1) real materials or highly representa-
    tive photos, 2) multiple trainers, 3) natural effects,
    specifically those from peers--emphasizing reinforce-
    ment, and 4) a current task-presentation approach.
    There is room for further study among the parts of
    the approach itself and among the learners' traits.

25. Elliot, R.N. 1970. Meaningfulness in school tasks for
    LMR children. *Journal of Special Education* 4:189-197.

    This study deals with determining if the mean-
    ingfulness of tasks is relevant to acquisition and
    retention in EMR children and in normal children.

Students were matched in regard to CA and MA and given
meaningful tasks to learn. Follow-up learning and
retention after thirty days indicated that meaningfulness in tasks resulted in increased performance
for both groups. For retarded meaningfulness was
more important than for normal children. Educational
implications suggest that teachers should incorporate
familiar cues in tasks to be learned.

26. Fabry, B.D.; G.L. Mayhew; and A. Hanson. 1984. Inci-
     dental teaching of mentally retarded students within
     a token system. *American Journal of Mental Deficiency*
     89:29-36.

          Six moderately to severely mentally retarded
     students (aged 12.75-22.17 years) were taught to name
     sight words during token-exchange periods of the
     token-reinforcement system. Words appeared on twenty-
     five percent of the tokens, and a S was given 2 op-
     portunities to name a word written on a token before
     the token could be exchanged. Five of the six sub-
     jects acquired sight-word vocabularies. The data
     support the idea that token-exchange periods may be
     useful for educational purposes. The effectiveness
     of this approach may be related to each developmental
     level.

27. Fajardo, D.M., and D.G. McGourty. 1984. Promoting so-
     cial play in small groups of retarded adolescents.
     Education and Training of the Mentally Retarded
     18:300-307.

          A method for fading object rewards for super-
     ordinate prerequisites to social play simultaneously
     with socially rewarded training on specific play was
     effective in teaching games to fifteen institutional-
     ized retarded adolescents.

28. Filipp, M.D., and E.A. Zubensky. 1982. Study, general-
     ization and dissemination of progressive instruction
     methods in the school for mentally retarded children.
     Defektologiya 6:40-43.

          This article describes the methods of progressive
     instruction in a school for mentally retarded chil-

dren. There are twenty-nine tutors and teachers employed and sixteen have an education in defectology.
The results show that there are important and substantial changes to be seen from the school experience
and outside of it, too. The management of the school
controls the teaching and helps the teaching personnel. There are also four methodological groups within
the school. Recommendations are published, including
albums of photographs of the most excellent teachers
and descriptions of their own working experiences.

29. Fitzgibbon, W.C. 1965. A rationale for crafts for the
educable mentally retarded. *Exceptional Children*
32:243-46.

This article encourages the use of crafts to
increase a retarded child's concepts of truth, reality, and value. Crafts provide motor and sensory
experiences. The craft project can both help the
child develop concept of self and be used as a teaching implement.

30. Flynn, T.M. 1978. Ratings of educable mentally handicapped students by regular and special teachers.
Exceptional Children 44: 539-40.

This is a study to determine differences between
thirty-five regular and sixteen special class teachers' behavioral adjustment ratings of sixty-one educable mentally handicapped children (between the ages
of eight and fourteen years old). There were differences found in four items of the students' abilities
and these were attributed to the fact that the student
exhibited different behavior to the special class
teacher than to the regular class teacher.

31. Forness, S.R., and K.A. Kavale. 1985. Effects of class
size on attention, communication and disruption of
mildly mentally retarded children. *American Educational Research Journal* 22:403-12.

This study involved classroom behavior of 393
pupils in twenty-six educable mentally retarded classrooms. Although there were different numbers of students, approximately twelve, fifteen, or nineteen

pupils per classroom, the effect of the number of students per classroom was found in attention and communication, but not in disruptive behavior.

32. Forness, S.R., and K. Nihira. 1984. Relationship be-
     tween classroom behavior and adaptive behavior of
     institutionalized retarded children. *Education and
     Training of the Mentally Retarded* 19:222-27.

          Forty-seven students in eight trainable mentally
     retarded classrooms completed the Adaptive Behavior
     Scale. These ratings were compared with data from
     direct classroom observations. Findings showed rela-
     tionships between adaptive behavior in residential
     environments and actual observed behavior in classroom
     settings.

33. French, L.A. 1986. MR testing and evaluation: New di-
     mensions and old concerns. *Psychology in the Schools*
     23:64-76.

          This article deals with the role of IQ testing
     in the MR evaluation process, viewing this from both
     the historical and contemporary perspectives. The
     use of specific tests with the MR is discussed.

34. Gampel, D.H.; J. Gottlieb; and R.H. Harrison. 1974.
     Comparison of classroom behavior of special-class
     EMR, integrated EMR, low IQ and nonretarded children.
     American Journal of Mental Deficiency 79:16-22.

          Classroom behavior of twelve segregated and four-
     teen integrated EMR children who were all formerly
     segregated and then assigned randomly to class place-
     ment were compared to those of low IQ who were never
     identified for special-class placements and to an
     intellectually average group of children. Method was
     a time sampling observational one using twelve behav-
     ior categories. After four months, integrated EMR
     children behaved more like nonlabeled EMR children
     than their segregated peers. The results were dis-
     cussed in terms of appropriate peer models influencing
     classroom behavior of EMR children.

35. Gargiulo, R.M. 1984. Cognitive style and moral judgment
    ... of equal mental age. *British Journal of Developmental Psychology* 2:83–89.

    Using the Matching Familiar Figures Test and
    Piagetian measures forty-seven mentally handicapped
    children and forty-seven nonhandicapped children were
    tested for moral judgment. Results showed there was
    no difference between the 2 groups and were based on
    intention rather than consequence.

36. Goodman, J.F. 1976. The developmental class: Best of
    both worlds for the mentally retarded. *Psychology in
    the Schools* 13:257–65.

    Recommends school placement according to developmental level as opposed to chronological age or IQ.
    Implications include a more homogeneous classroom,
    elimination of negative teacher expectations, and
    enhancement of the retarded child's social position.
    Normal students would serve as models for the retardates.

37. Groden, A.; D. Dominque; and S. Pueschal. 1982.
    Behavioral/emotional problems in mentally retarded
    children and youth. *Psychological Reports* 51:143–46.

    A computer research study was done on 1,114 mentally retarded children and adolescents over a period
    of seven years to find out the prevalence of behavioral and emotional problems. Prevalence was found
    to be linked to both age and degree of retardation,
    but not to sex or economy.

38. Heath, C., and P. Obrzut. 1984. Comparison of three
    measures of adaptive behavior. *American Journal of
    Mental Deficiency* 89:205–8.

    Teachers and parents completed the Adaptive Behavior Scale-School Edition and the Adaptive Behavior
    Inventory for Children. Fifty-eight mildly retarded
    and slow-learning children completed the Children's
    Adaptive Behavior Scale. Results showed higher ratings for the slow-learners on all measures. Teachers
    rated students lower than did parents.

39. Herman, M., and C. Shantz. 1983. Social problem solving
     and mother-child interactions of educable mentally
     retarded children. *Journal of Applied Developmental
     Psychology* 4:217-26.

          In this research, mothers of ten retarded and
     nineteen nonretarded ten-year-olds were observed and
     video taped while interacting with these children.
     These children were from lower and lower middle
     classes. The Vineland Social Maturity Scale was used
     to test their problem-solving abilities. Results
     were that mothers who gave their children a chance to
     decide for themselves had children with higher
     problem-solving skills, whereas mothers who directed
     their children had children with lower problem-solving
     abilities. The conclusion is that problem-solving
     skills are related to social maturity.

40. Hickman, L.H. 1967. A formulation for the preparation
     of the educable child for the world of work. *Training
     School Bulletin* 64:39-44.

          A review of the philosophy behind a work training
     program for educable mentally retarded children at
     Bridgeton High School. Education, counseling, and
     attitude development are emphasized in this program.

41. Horgan, J. 1982. Comparison of mildly retarded and
     nonretarded children on a rotary pursuit task under
     optimal task conditions. *American Journal of Mental
     Deficiency* 87:316-24.

          Comparison was done on eighty mildly retarded
     and 133 nonretarded children to see if response-
     produced feedback by supplementary sensory feedback
     would enhance acquisition. All groups achieved acqui-
     sition under response-product and supplementary feed-
     back, but it was more pronounced in the mildly re-
     tarded groups who had additional feedback.

42. Karper, W.B., and T.J. Martinek. 1983. The differential influence of instructional factors on motor performance among handicapped and non-handicapped children in mainstreamed physical education classes. *Educational Research Quarterly* 8:43-44.

     This study tried to differentiate the relationships among teachers' perceptions of pupil effort, teacher expectation, grade, school, sex and handicapping/nonhandicapping conditions and their effect on gross motor performance. Twenty-eight handicapped and 104 nonhandicapped pupils from kindergarten through third grade were tested on motor performance and social behavior. The Body Coordinator Test tested motor performance. Grade had the strongest influence followed by teacher ratings of student expression of effort and teacher expectation on student overall physical skill performance and ability to reason.

43. Li, A.K.F. 1985. Toward more elaborate pretend play. *Mental Retardation* 23:131-36.

     Lowenfeld's World Technique was used as an assessment for the study of pretend play in twenty-five mildly retarded children aged five to seven years and twenty nonhandicapped children aged four to five years. The descriptive progressive levels of pretend play were observed--manipulative nonsymbolic play; symbolic play; play with a scene; play with a theme; and play with a story. Nonhandicapped children were found to have higher levels of pretend play than mentally retarded children of the same CA and two years older.

44. McEvoy, M.A.; V.M. Nordquist; and J.L. Cunningham. 1984. Regular and special education teachers' judgments about mentally retarded children in an integrated setting. *American Journal of Mental Deficiency* 89:167-173.

     The subjects of this study were fifteen regular education teachers and fifteen special education teachers on primary level. The purpose was to determine whether teachers' judgments about mentally retarded children would be related to characteristics of the children, characteristics of the teacher,

and/or characteristics of an integrated free-play
setting. Judgment ratings by regular education teachers were determined both by characteristics of target
child and the integration ratio in free play activity.
Special education teachers' judgments were influenced
by characteristics of child but not the integration
ratio.

45. McLeish, J., and G. Higgs. 1982. Musical ability and
mental subnormality: An experimental investigation.
British Journal of Educational Psychology 52:370-73.

This research is on 121 mentally retarded children (CAS eight-sixteen years; MAS five-twelve years)
completing a battery of measures of musical abilities.
The study shows that retardation in general ability
is linked to retardation in musical ability. Results
were also an extension of a 1968 finding on the musical capabilities of educationally subnormal children.

46. Meador, D. 1984. Effects of color on visual discrimination of geometric symbols by severely and profoundly
mentally retarded individuals. *American Journal of
Mental Deficiency* 89:275-86.

Twenty severe and profound mentally retarded
adults involved in three experiments showed that repeated color cues did not help visual discrimination.
Random colors and distinctive-feature training did.

47. Neisworth, J.T., and J.G. Greer. 1975. Functional similarities of learning disability and mild retardation.
Exceptional Children 42:17-21.

This article compares and contrasts educable
mentally retarded with learning disabled children.
It introduces the words "genotype" and "phenotype" to
conceptualize the differences between underlying condition and objectively assessed psycho-educational
repertoire. This study indicates considerable overlapping of educable and learning disabled classifications in regard to instructional objectives and intervention.

48. Nightingale, M.D. 1975. Special education for the
    mildly retarded: What are the alternatives? *Delta*
    17:32-41.

    This article discusses literature regarding spe-
    cial education for the mildly retarded and offers
    alternatives to approaches presently used. Its main
    suggestions are 1) mildly retarded children should
    remain in regular classes 2) ordinary classroom place-
    ment should be supplemented with a resource room.
    This article implies that current research does not
    reflect viable alternatives for decision making.

49. Ottenbacher, K., and R. Altman. 1984. Effects of vibra-
    tory, edible and social reinforcement of performance
    of institutionalized mentally retarded individuals.
    American Journal of Mental Deficiency 89:201-4.

    Sixty-six mentally retarded students were divided
    into high and low MA groups and assigned to reinforce-
    ment conditions. The purpose was to study the rela-
    tive effectiveness of verbal praise, vibration, and
    edible rewards as methods of enhancing and maintaining
    performance on perceptual motor tasks. Data revealed
    that response rates for the low MA students in verbal
    condition reinforcement and the non-reinforcement
    phases were significantly lower than the response
    rates for low MA students in any phase of the edible
    or vibratory condition. No significant differences
    in reinforcement effectiveness were observed across
    various phases for students in high MA groups.

50. Parashar, O.D. 1976. Disturbed classroom behaviour: A
    comparison between mentally retarded, learning-
    disabled and emotionally disturbed children. *Journal
    of Mental Deficiency Research* 20:109-20.

    The nature and prevalence of different types of
    disturbed classroom behavior were compared. The
    groups compared were fifty-six mentally retarded,
    fifty-one learning disabled, and sixty-five emotion-
    ally disturbed children. Their mean age was ten
    years. The Devereau Elementary School Behavior Rating
    Scale was used by teachers to rate the students on
    such behaviors as classroom disturbance, impatience,
    disrespect-defiance, and lack of creative initiative.

Intergroup differences were significant. The mentally
retarded exhibited more frequent comprehension disorders than the learning disabled or emotionally disturbed; the emotionally disturbed exhibited more frequent behaviors such as classroom disturbance and
achievement anxiety than the mentally retarded and
learning disabled.

51. Pipe, M.E. 1984. Social interactions of retarded chil-
     dren: Generalization from mainstream to special
     school. *Exceptional Child* 30:143-50.

Seven intellectually handicapped (IH) children
were integrated into a mainstream school on a part-
time basis over a period of eighteen weeks. Compared
to IH children in the special schools integrated children showed larger increases in associative play in
the special school free-play period but no differential changes in the classroom behavior.

52. Poddubnaya, N.G. 1980. Specificity of incidental memory
     processes in developmentally backward first-graders.
     Defektologiya 4:21-26.

Four experimental tests were done on forty-one
first grade retarded children and thirty third and
fourth grade normal children. The experiments were
to test their ability to memorize pictures and groups.
Results showed that the retarded children did poorer
than the normal ones because the retarded children
did not understand, follow directions, concentrate,
or act fast. Results indicate that retarded children
are not only slower, but also unique in characteristics.

53. Puskayeva, T. 1980. On studying structural specificity
     of cognitive activity in mentally backward children.
     Defeklotogija 3:10-18.

A study was done on the actual and potential
level of cognitive development in thirty normal and
thirty mentally retarded third grade students. In
order to determine their ability to classify, the
students were shown thirty-six pictures and had to
guess which ones the experimenter had mentally se-

lected. Those who failed to do so were helped by the
experimenter. Their failure to classify the objects
revealed low levels of cognitive development. That
they were later able to classify the objects with
help proved that training enhances potential development level.

54. Roos, P. 1970. Trends and issues in special education
     for the mentally retarded. *Education and Training of
     Mentally Retarded* 5:51-61.

     This paper both reviews progress in special edu-
     cation for the mentally retarded and documents further
     needs. Major areas of agreement among professionals
     are identified and some key unresolved issues are
     discussed. The author concludes that theoretical and
     methodological innovations have been disappointing,
     but that application of operant conditioning princi-
     ples is an encouraging recent development.

55. Russell, A.T., and S.R. Forness. 1985. Behavioral dis-
     turbance in mentally retarded children in TMR and EMR
     classrooms. *American Journal of Mental Deficiency*
     89:338-44.

     Disruptive behavior of 646 subjects in TMR and
     EMR classrooms was observed over a four day period.
     Although mean disruptive behavior occurred in rela-
     tively low levels, considerable variability appeared
     with some differences in the nature of disruptive
     behavior of TMR and EMR subjects. Further examination
     within a sub-sample of high and low disrupters was
     also made.

56. Schilling, R.F.; S.P. Schinke; B.J. Blythe; and R.P.
     Barth. 1982. Child maltreatment and mentally re-
     tarded parents: Is there a relationship? *Mental Re-
     tardation* 20:201-9.

     A review of child protection and mental retarda-
     tion literature suggests a relationship between par-
     ents' intelligence and maltreatment of children.
     Findings and differences in studies of mentally re-
     tarded parents and maltreating parents are high-
     lighted. Further investigation of the relationship

between mentally retarded parents and child maltreat-
ment, studies on how mentally retarded parents care
for children, and evaluation of approaches to helping
such parents are suggested.

57. Silberstein, A.B.; L.B. Pearson; B.A. Kelbert; W.J.
     Cordeiro; J.L. Marwin; and M.J. Nakaji. 1982. Cog-
     nitive development of severely and profoundly mentally
     retarded individuals. *American Journal of Mental
     Deficiency* 87:347-50.

         After studying seventy-one severely and pro-
     foundly mentally retarded individuals (mean age 19.62
     yrs; mean IQ 19.65) for five years for object perma-
     nence and spatial relationship, it was noted that
     gains were smaller but significant for both. Gain
     was more so in spatial relationships than object per-
     manence. This led to the belief that cognitive devel-
     opment continues throughout childhood, even though
     special programs were not designed to promote such
     development.

58. Singh, J., and N.N. Singh. 1985. Comparison of word
     supply and word analysis error correction procedures
     on oral reading by mentally retarded children. *Amer-
     ican Journal of Mental Deficiency* 90:64-70.

         Alternating treatment design was used to measure
     the differential effects of two error correction pro-
     cedures (word supply and word analysis) and a no
     training control condition on the number of oral read-
     ing errors made by four mentally retarded children.
     The correction procedures greatly reduced the number
     of errors (word analysis significantly more effective
     than word supply). The number of self-corrections of
     errors increased under both conditions when compared
     to the baseline and no training control conditions.

59. Siperstein, G.N., and J.J. Bak. 1985. Effects of social
     behavior on children's attitudes toward their mildly
     and mentally retarded peers. *American Journal of
     Mental Deficiency* 90:319-27.

         The subjects of this study were 191 non-retarded
     fourth through sixth grade boys and girls. This group

viewed a videotape of either a non-retarded, mildly
retarded or moderately retarded target child who was
reading. Then they were read a story that depicted
the target as either socially competent, withdrawn,
or aggressive. On three measures, children in general
responded favorably toward retarded target children
who were socially competent, neutrally to withdrawn
targets, and negatively to aggressive targets. They
were most positive to the non-retarded, socially competent targets and most negative to the non-retarded,
aggressive targets. Pro-social behavior attributes
had a positive effect on children's attitudes and
behavioral intentions toward targets.

60. Stapley, V.J.; M.A.H. Smith; J.B. Bittle; F.E. Andrews;
     and L.J. Nuckolls. 1984. Food and nutrition educa-
     tion for children who are mentally retarded. *Mental
     Retardation* 22:289-93.

     The development and evaluation of a food-
nutrition program for mildly retarded and nonretarded
children of the same mental age was the purpose of
this study. Lessons taught by a nutritionist and
taking the Four Food Group approach were followed by
pre- and post-testing program evaluation. Significant
differences were not found in group performance on
tests. Results supported the hypothesis that children
with mental retardation can increase knowledge of
nutrition through educational activities designed for
their level as well as retain knowledge, if appropriate reinforcement is given.

61. Sternlicht, M., and A. Hurwitz. 1981. *Games Children
     play: Instructive and creative play activities for
     the mentally retarded and developmentally disabled
     child.* New York: Van Nostrand Reinhold.

     This is the first book of games designed specif-
ically to stimulate the psychological and developmental growth of mentally retarded and learning disabled
children. It contains both individual and group games
that are organized around the areas of functioning
covered in standard IQ tests and that provide direct
experiences in the utilization of children's sensory
facilities and the increasing of their learning ca-
pacities.

62.   Sternlicht, M., and L. Martinez. 1985. *Psychological testing and assessment of the mentally retarded: A handbook*. New York: Garland Publishing.

      Literature on the testing and assessment of the mentally retarded is the subject of this compendium. A general introduction discusses in depth the history of the mental testing movement and 10 shorter essays introduce the chapters. Tests and their original sources are also listed.

63.   Sternlicht, M., and G. Windholz. 1984. *Social behavior of the mentally retarded*. New York: Garland Publishing.

      Approximately 600 entries describe books, articles, and dissertations on mentally retarded individuals' social development, family and peer interaction, emotional disturbances, adjustments in institutional settings, and play and leisure time activities. An introductory essay discusses the problems a mentally retarded person faces as he/she comes of age in a complex society whose challenges often discourage even the most able of its members.

64.   Stratford, B., and J.A. Metcalfe. 1982. Recognition and recall in children with Down's Syndrome. *Australia & New Zealand Journal of Developmental Disabilities* 8:125-32.

      A discrimination task was given to 108 mentally handicapped students and 123 normal ones to match three cards of different sizes in six trials from memory. After the six trials the mentally handicapped students could match only one card, whereas the normal ones matched all cards. This study reveals that mentally handicapped individuals with Down's Syndrome cannot recognize, reproduce, or recall.

65.   Taylor, Z., and C. Sherrill. 1969. Development of a core curriculum in health and safety education for trainable mentally retarded children. *Journal of School Health* 39:153-58.

      This study of nine ten-fourteen year olds over

ten weeks tested through participation in a core curriculum in health and safety that the mentally retarded will progress toward self-realization, human
relationships, and economic efficiency, as well as
civic responsibility. The results indicate that students made progress toward economic usefulness. Self-
realization encouraged individuals to be more responsible.

66. Thurman, R.L.; L.I. Richardson; and O.C. Bassler. 1982.
An analysis of teacher rating differences between
first-grade and mentally retarded children: Were ex-
pectancy biases involved? *Educational Research Quarterly* 7:7-14.

Forty-five teachers of educable mentally retarded
children and thirty-four first-grade teachers rated
their pupils' mathematical abilities. There were 175
educable mentally retarded and 737 first grade children. The ratings of the teachers were compared both
by individual and overall scores. Findings showed
that the teachers of the mentally retarded rated their
students lower than the first grade teachers did.

67. Thurman, S.K. 1976. Environmental maintenance of retarded behavior: A behavioral perspective. *Education*
97:121-25.

There is an indication that a retarded child's
behavior is maintained by environmental factors.
Factors such as positive reinforcement, avoidance
behavior, and contingency schedules contribute to the
maintenance of these behaviors. Maintenance effects
are presented.

68. Tymitz-Wolf, B. 1984. An analysis of EMR children's
worries about mainstreaming. *Education and Training
of the Mentally Retarded* 19:157-68.

A study comparing the responses of EMR students
awaiting placement to the responses of EMR students
assigned part-time to regular classrooms. Data showed
a wide range of worries related to academic performance and social interactions. Significant differences
between the groups were noted.

69. Wagner, P., and M. Sternlicht. 1975. Retarded persons
     as "teachers": Retarded adolescents tutoring retarded
     children. *American Journal of Mental Deficiency*
     79:674-79.

         Retarded adolescents in a residential school
     were trained to act as tutors for younger retarded
     children who were deficient in dressing and eating
     skills. The tutors received thirty hours of training
     in each of the skills to be taught. The statistically
     significant overall success of the trainees supports
     the view that retarded persons can successfully in-
     struct other retarded individuals. Educational and
     economic implications of the findings are discussed.

70. Wehman, P. 1976. Imitation as a facilitator of treat-
     ment for the mentally retarded. *Rehabilitation Lit-
     erature* 37:41-48.

         This article presents an overview of theories
     and research studies that rely on modeling to imple-
     ment a change in behavior in the retarded individual.
     It suggests that modeling used in self-management
     skills focus on issues and discusses further uses of
     imitative learning with the mentally retarded.

71. Weisen, A.E.; G. Harley; C. Richardson; and A. Roske.
     1967. Retarded child as a reinforcing agent. *Journal
     of Experimental Child Psychology* 5:109-13.

         This study explores social interaction among
     retarded children. Three pairs of children with the
     least interaction were formed and a "generosity" re-
     sponse was generated whereby candy was given to the
     partner and reinforced by E. The reinforcement con-
     tingency increases the moments of interaction.

72. Westling, D.L. 1985. Similarities and differences in
     instructional tactics used by teachers of TMR and PMR
     students. *Education and Training of the Mentally
     Retarded* 20:254-59.

         A survey was made of TMR and PMR teachers and
     their common and unique preservice and inservice needs
     are discussed. PMR teachers need to use more unique

and highly specialized behavioral management techniques.

73. Wilson, M.G., and T.L. Glynn. 1983. Increasing self-
selection and self-location of words by mildly retarded children during story writing. *Exceptional
Child* 30:210-20.

Sentence writing behavior, including the use of
words self-selected and self-located independently of
teacher modeling, was established with eight mildly
retarded children (aged 6.9-9.6, Stanford-Binet Intelligence Scale IQs 51-71) in a special class. The
procedure comprised three parts: 1) provision of word
lists, 2) praise for self-selecting and self-locating
words from supplied word lists, and 3) response cost
for responses dependent on teacher modeling. The
latter were termed "Words Shown" and "Words Told,"
while self-selected and self-located responses were
termed "Words Found." Words Shown decreased with the
introduction of response cost for responses dependent
on teacher modeling. Also, Words Found increased
substantially above levels in all phases and Words
Shown decreased to zero frequency. These changes
within sentence-writing behavior are discussed in
terms of the need for accurate discrimination of and
selective attention to positive and negative instances
in the acquisition of self-regulation.

74. Winters, J., and D. Hoats. 1984. Effects of isolation
by color on mentally retarded and nonretarded persons'
recall of printed words. *American Journal of Mental
Deficiency* 89:310-12.

Eighteen mentally retarded and nonretarded children of equal mental age read lists of nine nouns
that were presented simultaneously in a horizontal
format. Results were the same in both groups: recall
of items when isolated was higher than when not isolated.

CHAPTER II:
GIFTEDNESS

On the other side of the spectrum of cognitive functioning (two standard deviations above the mean) are the gifted
and talented children (IQs above 130) who are blessed with
special abilities, but who are frequently overlooked when it
comes time to provide special classes. The overall misconcep-
tion is that gifted or exceptionally creative children can
progress and develop on their own. This is no more true for
these children than it is for any other group of children.
The gifted are considered exceptional children because regular
classroom instruction fails to satisfy their needs to fulfill
their potential. They are in need of additional services,
programs that are enriched, creative, and advanced. The
gifted frequently are not viewed as handicapped or exceptional, which may explain why some administrators fail to
provide specialized programs for the gifted within their district. Then, too, giftedness is not limited only to academic
achievement per se; children can be creatively gifted, psychosocially gifted, and kinesthetically gifted.

For purposes of federal funding, giftedness is defined
in PL 91-230 as follows: Gifted and talented children are
those identified by professionally qualified persons who, by
virtue of outstanding abilities, are capable of high performance. These are children who require differentiated educational programs and/or services beyond those normally provided
by the regular school program in order to realize their con-
tribution to self and society. Children capable of high performance include those with demonstrated achievement and/or
potential ability in any of the following areas, singly or in
combination: general intellectual ability, specific academic
aptitude, creative productive thinking, leadership ability,
visual and performing arts, psychomotor ability. It is difficult to determine the exact percentage of children who are
gifted. Owing to the lack of programs for the gifted, many
such children go unnoticed and many talents remain undevel-
oped. Our best guesstimate of prevalence is that the gifted
constitute two to four percent of the total school population.

Some intellectually gifted children may have cognitive affinity for most subject areas, while others may be under-achievers in specific content areas and may therefore not be classified as gifted. This may be due to their all-consuming interest in a specific field, such as science or language. Still other gifted children may reveal outstanding abilities in other areas such as resourceful thinking and perception and logical reasoning and curiosity. Some teachers may find that these children are difficult to deal with in class, since they often surpass their teachers in spheres of competence.

Despite prevalent stereotypes, gifted children are not automatically physical, emotional, or social misfits. In fact, the exact opposite is more often the case. However, if gifted individuals are frequently accelerated in school, they may have problems physically and socially because of the great age differences with their classmates. If they are exposed to additional pressures at home to excel and to accelerate, then this factor might create additional problems. Generally, however, gifted children do not present emotional problems per se.

As a group, though, the gifted do exhibit certain behavioral characteristics. They are especially verbally proficient for their age or grade level, self-motivated, intellectually curious, self-confident, often creative, and somewhat domineering. They tend to excel in studies requiring abstract thinking, and they are physically superior and enjoy better health. Their early developmental history tends to be one of acceleration, and they are more productive than their average colleagues. The creatively gifted exhibit superior creative or productive thinking, come up with new and novel ideas, and include authors and composers. The psychosocially gifted are those with outstanding leadership potential, while the kines-thetically gifted are those individuals who display excellent levels of psychomotor skills, such as artists, musicians, and dancers.

Giftedness, if present, must be nurtured and developed. Many people still maintain that the gifted will succeed in any kind of educational environment. This is a fallacy. If placed in an inadequate or inappropriate learning situation, gifted children often will become discipline problems, will appear bored in class, and may even drop out of school. As a first step, therefore, it is very important to determine which children are gifted. Because such identification is not an easy task, it is usually best made by a combination of methods using the team approach. Individualized intelligence and achievement tests, group assessment procedures, and teacher, parent, and peer observations are among the currently recom-mended techniques for the selection and identification of the

gifted. Classification should never be made on the basis of
any single criterion or routine test. Some attention is now
being directed to certain subgroups of intellectually gifted
children who have their own unique sets of characteristics
and educational problems, including the gifted underachiever
and the gifted child who is culturally different.

Scientific inquiry into giftedness began in 1874 with
Sir Francis Galton, who divided all people into sixteen categories ranging form idiot (profoundly retarded) to genius
(intellectually gifted). He recognized genius among those
adults who had a reputation for accomplishing what few others
could in their generation. His insights into people who had
earned renown in science led him to the conclusion that they
were endowed with superior intellectual ability, tremendous
energy, good physical health, a sense of independence and
purposefulness, and exceptional dedication to their fields of
productivity. The traits he saw were very similar to the
traits discovered through psychometric methods in subsequent
research in the field, and that we continue to hold true today. Additional characteristics often seen in gifted children
include a sense of humor, a sense of justice and fairness, a
search for the truth, and a very self-critical attitude. Not
all of these personality traits are found in all gifted children; however, the presence of some of them are cues to possible giftedness.

Since gifted students are special, special programs must
be designed for them. Early school admission is one possibility. Others are acceleration programs, advanced study,
and independent study. The most important fact to remember
is that whatever program we decide to use for these students,
it must be uniquely suited to them. The three basic ways in
which to modify the educational program for gifted children
involve changes in curriculum content, in the application of
learning skills, and in learning environments. Changes in
content focus on emphasizing the structure and basic concepts
of subject matter fields. Interest also has been shown in
adding special areas, such as the teaching of ethics and values. Skills instruction for the gifted emphasizes stimulation
of their productive thinking and creative skills. The focus
is upon those learning processes by which one solves problems,
such as the scientific method or the sequence of steps in the
creative process itself. Modifications in the learning environment often vary from community to community and may include special classes, special schools, resource rooms, and
differential forms of acceleration.

In essence, the instructional curriculum for gifted students should be sufficiently flexible so as to allow for independent and guided explorations into many diverse fields of

interest and, when the child is ready, large amounts of independent work. Gifted children should be provided with opportunities to develop leadership abilities, while also allowing
for private time. They need to work along with other children
of similar capabilities, while still maintaining contact with
their peers of average ability and talents. Through all of
this one must keep in mind that they are still children, even
if on many occasions they may sound like adults. Like all
children, the gifted require love, acceptance, and security--
physically, psychologically, and socially.

Finally, what of the teachers of the gifted? In order
to help gifted pupils to succeed, the teacher of the gifted
ought at least to have the following attributes: to possess a
positive attitude toward the gifted; to recognize the gifted
student and to accept him/her as an individual; to have an
in-depth knowledge of the subject matter being taught; to be
able to create an enriched, flexible atmosphere within the
classroom; to teach research and thinking approaches; to be
willing to become a learner along with the students; to be
capable of acting as a resource guide for the students; and
to be able to promote the love of learning within the children.

75. Alexander, P. 1985. Gifted and nongifted students'
     perceptions of intelligence. *Gifted Child Quarterly*
     29:137-43.

     The purpose of this study was to examine gifted
     and nongifted students' perceptions of intelligence.
     To this end gifted and nongifted students answered
     questions on a questionnaire. Gifted students defined
     intelligence in terms of cognitive processes whereas
     nongifted did so in terms of social and academic at-
     tributes. Gifted students had a more realistic self-
     assessment than did nongifted students and perceived
     the importance of mental rather than physical behav-
     ior. However, both groups viewed intelligence as
     arising from hard work and good attitudes.

76. Anderson, M.; N. Tollefson; and E. Gilbert. 1985.
     Giftedness and reading: A cross-sectional view of
     differences in reading attitudes and behavior. *Gifted
     Child Quarterly* 29:186-88.

     It was reported that the gifted student reads an
     average of nine books per month. Personal choice was
     the primary reason for reading. Gifted students enjoy
     reading and consider it easy. They select their ma-
     terials from both the school and public libraries.
     The authors suggest that school librarians and the
     regular classroom teachers work as a team to develop
     a comprehensive reading program using the highest
     quality literature possible.

77. Baer, D.S. 1972. A talking typewriter for young gifted
     children: Joys and headaches. *Gifted Child Quarterly*
     16:41-47.

     Discussed are disadvantages and advantages of
     using a talking typewriter program with preschool and
     primary grade children to teach reading and spelling.
     Such a program is found to be time consuming and
     costly, but advantages are high student interest in
     using the machine with resulting gains in concept
     formation ability, incentive behavior, and ability to
     find embedded figures in a picture. Unforeseen prob-
     lems include the children's tendency to jam the type-
     writer and the difficulty young children have in re-
     turning manual carriages.

78. Baldwin, A.Y.   1981.   Effect of process oriented instruc-
     tion on thought processes in gifted students.   *Excep-
     tional Children* 47:326-30.

          A process oriented instructional strategy to
     develop higher levels of thought processes in gifted
     students was studied to determine whether gifted stu-
     dents in the experimental group would advance more in
     this area than students in the average ability and
     treatment groups. A total of 312 seventh grade stu-
     dents from widely differing geographic areas and eth-
     nic groups took part in the study. Results showed
     that under research conditions gifted students in the
     experimental population did significantly better than
     average students in the experimental and control
     groups. Although there was a mean difference in the
     scores of the experimental and control gifted classes,
     this difference was not significant at the .01 level.
     The evaluative comments of the students and teachers
     and the data from the Classroom Activities Question-
     naire provided insight into the processes being used
     and the effect of lower level thought processes on
     developing higher level thought processes.

79. Ballering, L., and A. Koch.   1984.   Family relations
     when a child is gifted.   *Gifted Child Quarterly*
     28:140-43.

          This study focused on the perception of gifted
     and nongifted children of the emotional relationships
     among members of their families. Twenty families of
     middle and upper socioeconomic status containing at
     least one gifted (IQ above 130 or higher) and one
     nongifted child were studied. The FRT was used by
     the children to assign positive and negative effect
     to his relationships with all family members in a
     play situation. It was found that nongifted children
     perceived their relationships with other children in
     the family more positively than did gifted children.

80. Barell, J.   1984.   Reflective thinking and education for
     the gifted.   *Roeper Review* 6:194-96.

          Taking as its impetus questions asked by a gifted
     12th grade girl during an American history class, the
     article defines reflective thinking as a search for

meaning that involves imaginative as well as critical and logical thought processes. The author suggests that such thinking is regarded as essentially poetic in nature. Implications for the education of gifted persons are included in terms educational planning, teacher's knowledge and skill, student awareness, and perception of giftedness.

81. Barnett, L., and J. Fiscellas. 1985. A child by any other name...Comparison of the playfulness of gifted and nongifted children. *Gifted Child Quarterly* 29:61-66.

Thirty-five preschool children (fifteen of whom scored above 130 on the Stanford-Binet and the remainder of whom scored within average range) were interviewed in a classroom and observed and rated on degree of playfulness and play styles. The gifted children were more developmentally advanced in play styles, more creative, unique, and imaginative. In terms of enthusiasm, exuberance, joy or sense of humor, there was no difference between the two groups.

82. Bellanca, J. 1984. Can quality circles work in classrooms of the gifted? *Roeper Review* 6:100-200.

The advantages of the quality circle problem solving method when working with gifted students is discussed with the emphasis on the development of responsibility and leadership skills. The strategy that is stressed is utilizing analytic thought, task oriented group process, school and community concerns, and the development of an action plan with evaluation of results.

83. Berger, G. 1980. *The gifted and talented*. New York: Franklin Watts.

The gifted and talented are defined as those "who show outstanding ability in one or more areas, including academic achievement, intellectual capacity, creative or productive thinking, leadership, or special talent in the performing or visual arts." This book emphasizes how the needs of these people are to be fulfilled by the society in which they live,

through the educational facilities, and by the individuals themselves. Berger feels that the gifted and
talented are a valuable resource to society and that
they must be educated in order to develop properly.

84. Bleedorn, B.B. 1982. Humor as an indicator of gifted-
     ness. *Roeper Review* 4:33-34.

     Argues that the mental processes of humor and
     creativity are inseparable and that integrating the
     study of humor in the classroom is one method of rec-
     ognizing and developing creative talent. Observation
     of both the origination of and the response to humor
     will provide teachers with clues to high level cre-
     ative thinking talents.

85. Brown, S. 1984. The use of WISC-R subtest scatter in
     the identification of intellectually gifted handi-
     capped children: An inappropriate task? *Roeper Review*
     7:20-23.

     The purpose of this paper is to discuss issues
     involved in identifying handicapped children who are
     gifted. The author reviews several research studies,
     attempting to define a specific configuration of
     Wechsler Intelligence Scale for Children-Revised sub-
     test scores indicative of handicapped children who
     are intellectually gifted. The conclusion of the
     paper is that profiles and scatter are not clinically
     significant enough to identify handicapped children
     who are gifted using the WISC-R subtests.

86. Carr, K.S. 1984. What gifted readers need from reading
     instruction. *Reading Teacher* 38:144-46.

     The writer of this article contends that although
     gifted students have characteristics that suggest
     superior reading ability such as high verbal abstract
     ability, not all gifted students become capable read-
     ers. An outline of factors leading to hindered read-
     ing ability in gifted children is presented along
     with suggestions for altering teaching programs in
     terms of content, method, and pacing to help gifted
     children reach their potential in reading.

87. Carter, K.R., and J.E. Ormrod. 1982. Acquisition of formal operations by intellectually gifted children. *Gifted Child Quarterly* 26:110-15.

Research indicates that gifted, average, and retarded children all follow the same patterns in terms of stage progression. The sequence of their development through the stages seems to be the same regardless of intellectual ability. The present study was designed to investigate differences between gifted and normal children during the transition to, and progression through, the stage of formal operations. The results of the study showed a positive relationship between cognitive development and age for both intellectually gifted and normal children in late concrete operations and through formal operations. Within both gifted and normal groups, children at higher age levels scored higher than children at lower age levels. Thus the hypothesis that stage progression is invariant was supported.

88. Chang, L. 1984. Who are the mathematically gifted? *Exceptional Child* 31:231-34.

This article examines the definition of mathematically gifted and calls for identification procedures that include the compiling of qualitative information concerning students' higher-order reasoning skills. Most achievement tests, including standardized tests it is found, are not designed to measure the ability to solve problems, to engage in high level reasoning, or to handle sophisticated content. Qualitative information about a child's thinking can best be determined through the careful construction and presentation of interview protocols.

89. Chauvin, J., and F.A. Karnes. 1984. Perceptions of leadership characteristics by gifted elementary students. *Roeper Review* 6:238-40.

The purpose of this study was to examine the responses of gifted children and compare their own leadership capabilities with those of their images of ideal leaders. This analysis of checklist responses by 122 gifted elementary students indicated that they see themselves as possessing the same traits they

attribute to their views of the ideal leader and in
fact see no significant differences between themselves
and their ideal leader model.

90.   Chelelat, F.J. 1981. Visual arts education for the
      gifted elementary level art student. *Gifted Child
      Quarterly* 25:154-58.

         Guidelines for implementing an elementary school
      gifted visual arts program are outlined by the author.
      A station learning experience is one of the strategies
      described. Also, the benefits of a yearly art exhi-
      bition or art celebration are pointed out, and char-
      acteristics of the successful art teacher are men-
      tioned.

91.   Cioffi, D. 1984. Writing is a thinking process: A back
      to basics model for the gifted. *Gifted Creative Tal-
      ented Children* 34:13-14.

         This article points out that special attention
      should be given to developing writing skills in gifted
      students. Four approaches to the thinking-writing
      process are briefly compared. Learning activities
      such as community problem solving, seminars, and com-
      munity based mentorships are considered.

92.   Clark, W., and N. Hankins. 1985. Giftedness and con-
      flict. *Roeper Review* 8:50-53.

         This research involved analysis of a question-
      naire completed by 162 pairs of gifted-nongifted stu-
      dents, ages 6-10 years. It revealed that gifted stu-
      dents read the newspaper more, attend more to world
      and national news items, and are more concerned about
      war. Differences were also found in concern over
      educational matters and attention to governmental
      differences between the U.S. and other countries.

93. Colangelo, N., and K. Kelly. 1983. A study of student, parent, and teacher attitudes toward gifted programs and gifted students. *Gifted Child Quarterly* 27:107-10.

Thirty-one students from a gifted/talented program, 204 students from a general studies program, twelve teachers, and fifty-two parents completed a questionnaire on school activities for the purpose of assessing student, teacher, and parent attitudes toward gifted students and programs. The questionnaire assessed the importance of each school activity and the attitudes of students towards other students already participating in each activity. Results show that the gifted/talented program was viewed as being just as valuable as other academically oriented programs. However, other academic programs were not seen as valuable to the school. General studies students' attitudes toward gifted students was neutral. Gifted students expressed more favorable attitudes toward the gifted program and toward fellow students than did general studies students.

94. Coleman, D. 1983. Effects of the use of a writing scale by gifted primary students. *Gifted Child Quarterly* 27:114-121.

The article summarizes a study carried out among sixty-one second and third graders who showed evidence of intellectual giftedness. The study was designed to assess the effects of using the Sager Writing Scale (SWS) as an instructional tool for the gifted, and to investigate whether the use of the SWS would effect change in students' attitudes regarding creative writing. Students participated in three forty-five minute creative writing sessions and were administered the Test of Written Language. Results showed that the SWS was a valuable instructional tool.

95. Coleman, J.M., and B.A. Fults. 1982. Self-concept and the gifted classroom: The role of social comparisons. *Gifted Child Quarterly* 26:116-20.

This study investigated the influence of instructional environments on the self-concepts of highly intelligent children. The self-concepts of fourth,

fifth, and sixth grade gifted children who participated in a one-day-per-week segregated program were
compared to those of high achievers who remained in
regular classes. Two specific hypotheses derived
from social comparison theory were tested: (1) partially segregated gifted children residing, at times,
in a more homogeneous environment where the capabilities of all individuals were roughly comparable would
have lower self-concepts than high achieving children
who remained solely in regular classes where the range
of student ability was far greater, and (2) these
effects would be transitive, with gifted children
increasing in self-concept upon return to the regular
classroom program. The results indicated that when
academically talented children, regardless of giftedness, view their abilities in relationship to a comparison group that is generally less capable, positive
self-concept results. If the composition of the comparison group is restructured so that most individuals
are of equivalent ability, self-concept diminishes.

96. Cooley, D.; J. Chauvin; and F.A. Karnes. 1984. Gifted
     females: A comparison of attitudes by male and female
     teachers. *Roeper Review* 6:164-67.

     The researchers administered a survey to 162
     teachers, 84% female, 15% male, and 1% unidentified
     by sex. All were teachers of the gifted. The purpose
     of the survey was to determine male and female teacher
     attitudes toward gifted female students. The results
     show that the male teachers viewed gifted females in
     a more traditional manner than the female teachers,
     but that they did see gifted females in occupations
     and professions previously closed to women. Male
     teachers also perceived of the female gifted student
     as more emotional, high-strung, and gullible than the
     female teachers' perceptions. Both male and female
     teachers viewed male gifted students as more competent
     in critical/logical thinking skills.

97. Cordell, A., and T. Cannon. 1985. Gifted kids can't
     always spell. *Academic Therapy* 21:143-52.

     Case studies of three learning disabled gifted
     students are offered to illustrate apparently contra-
     dictory characteristics and neuropsychological func-

tioning patterns as demonstrated on the Wechsler Intelligence Scale for Children-Revised. Techniques
are suggested, including avoiding open-ended activities, providing enrichment alternatives along with
remediation, and limiting choices, materials and completion time.

98. Crittender, N.; M. Kaplan; and J. Heim. 1984. Developing effective study skills and self-confidence in
academically able young adolescents. *Gifted Child
Quarterly* 28:25-33.

The authors studied early adolescents who had
succeeded in elementary schools, still scored high on
standardized and IQ tests, but performed below the
level they and/or others wanted. The pilot study
sought to determine whether a short course providing
monitored practice in advanced study and written language skills, presented systematically by a teacher
who modeled desired behaviors and encouraged active
student participation would lead to a better knowledge
of study skills, improved written language proficiency, and enhanced self-concepts as measured by
pre- and post-tests. The findings indicated that the
above did occur. However, boys seemed to make greater
gains from short term intervention than girls did and
younger students made a greater improvement in terms
of rated gain than did older ones.

99. Daniels, R., and P. Parks. 1984. Administrators assessments of programs for the gifted. *Creative Child &
Adult Quarterly* 9:82-87.

The purpose of this study was to determine administrators' levels of support for programs for the
gifted in their schools. A survey of 101 administrators of school programs for the gifted was conducted.
Findings indicate that administrators generally had
favorable attitudes about gifted education, but had
mixed feelings about the overall effect of the programs. Critical thinking, research, and creativity
were emphasized as meriting special focus in programs
for the gifted; however, affective development, academic strategies, and psychomotor experiences were
seen as being of less significance.
Findings indicate a great disparity among admin-

istrators in knowledge of and attitudes toward gifted
education, and implications for program unity and
implementation are discussed in this context.

100. Davidman, L. 1982. Expressive encounters and the un-
      leashing of creative potential. *Gifted Child Quar-
      terly* 26:57-62.

         This article is intended primarily for the reg-
      ular classroom teacher and discusses developing mate-
      rial for the gifted--Types I and II Creative Teaching
      Sequences. Type I focuses on problem solving skills,
      emphasizing a positive attitude toward inquiry.
      Type II builds on that attitude for advanced creative
      problem solving.

101. Deschamp, P., and G. Robson. 1984. Identifying gifted
      disadvantaged students: Issues pertinent to system-
      level screening procedures for the identification of
      gifted children. *Gifted Education International*
      2:92-99.

         This paper describes four ways of conceptualiz-
      ing gifted disadvantaged students and proposes iden-
      tification procedures appropriate to each concept.
      The implications of adopting these identification
      procedures in relation to system-level screening for
      the identification of gifted students are also dis-
      cussed.

102. Dirkes, M. 1977. Learning through creative thinking.
      Gifted Child Quarterly 21:526-37.

         Discussed are the relationship between learning
      and divergent production and implications for the
      development of academic abilities. Research studies
      and examples are given to explain how construction
      and invention transform reality into products through
      cognition, convergent production, and divergent pro-
      duction or through a combination of these operations
      interspersed with evaluation.

103. Dole, J., and P. Adams. 1983. Reading curriculum for gifted readers: A survey. *Gifted Child Quarterly* 27:64-72.

    The results of a survey of ninety-nine national and state leaders in the fields of education for the gifted and reading education indicate three major findings: 1. A reading curriculum for gifted readers is not so different from a developmental reading curriculum. 2. Gifted educators and reading educators basically agree on the reading curriculum components needed by both gifted and non-gifted students. 3. Teachers of gifted students need assistance in gaining more effectiveness in their reading instruction.

104. Dorhout, A. 1984. The symposium for the arts: An activity for students in the visual and performing arts. *Roeper Review* 6:218-20.

    Gifted students (N=155) in grades 6-12 participated in the Symposium for the Arts, a model program allowing hands-on experiences with professional artists. Significant positive attitude changes toward the arts were revealed, and student evaluations of the symposium were overwhelmingly favorable.

105. Dover, A. 1983. Computers and the gifted: Past, present, and future. *Gifted Child Quarterly* 27:81-85.

    This article discusses the use of computers in the education of the gifted. Working with computers appears to nurture self-confidence and curiosity, encourage exploratory behavior, and foster positive attitudes towards learning. Also, there is a significant cost reduction afforded by computer instruction that would justify its widespread application in gifted/talented education.

106. Dowdall, C., and N. Colangelo. 1982. Underachieving gifted students: Review and implications. *Gifted Child Quarterly* 26:179-84.

    The authors review findings from research on definition, identification, characteristics, courses,

and intervention programs for 150 underachieving
gifted elementary school students. The notable conclusion cited is the need for a more commonly accepted and functional definition of underachievement
and for the realization that it is a pattern typically set in the elementary years.

107.   Dunn, R.S. and G.E. Price. 1980. Learning style char-
       acteristics of gifted students. *Gifted Child Quar-
       terly* 24:33-36.

       Previous investigations comparing low and high
       achievers, males and females, students with varying
       levels of self-concept and of various age levels
       indicate that certain learning style characteristics
       are highly visible within selected populations,
       whereas others appear to be individual, rather than
       group, traits. This study was undertaken (1) to
       provide data concerning whether gifted youngsters
       tend to reflect clustered, rather than individual-
       ized, learning style characteristics; and (2) to
       test another method for identifying the gifted (New
       York State Education Department, 1978). The results
       indicate that gifted elementary students are somewhat
       different from non-gifted elementary students on six
       of the eighteen learning style variables. Additional
       investigations need to be conducted to determine the
       relationship(s) between learning style and achieve-
       ment.

108.   Evans, E.D., and D. Marken. 1982. Multiple outcome
       assessment of special class placement for gifted
       students: A comparative study. *Gifted Child Quar-
       terly* 26:126-32.

       The main objective of this study was to assess
       the cumulative impact of special class placement for
       gifted children in a public school setting. Subjects
       were from grades six, seven, and eight who were eli-
       gible for special class placement. Control subjects
       were gifted students who proceeded with regular age-
       grade placement. The special class placement program
       was functioning three years prior to the introduction
       of any formal evaluation research activity. The
       results showed no main effects of special class
       placement across any of the composite dependent var-

iable measures. As a group, females reported
stronger intellectual achievement responsibility
than did males. Overall, females showed the most
positive school orientation. Sex differences are
also apparent for intellectual achievement responsibility, again in favor of females who seem more certain about their attribution of personal causation
for academic performance.

109. Feldhusen, J. 1981. Teaching gifted, creative, and
talented students in an individualized classroom.
Gifted Child Quarterly 25:108-11.

The author describes her efforts to individual-
ize classroom instruction to meet the needs of
gifted, creative, and high-ability children. The
program is centered around the establishment of
learning centers in various parts of the classroom.

110. Feldhusen, J. 1982. Myth: Gifted education means having a program! Meeting the needs of gifted students
through differentiated programming. *Gifted Child
Quarterly* 26:37-41.

Educational programs for the gifted should be
designed to meet their diverse needs. Gifted students differ widely in the types and levels of their
talents and abilities. There is no single model
program that could service all gifted children and
their needs.

111. Feldman, D. 1984. A follow-up of subjects scoring
above 180 IQ in Terman's 'genetic studies of genius.'
Exceptional Children 50:518-23.

Using the Terman files, twenty-six students with
IQs above 180 were compared with twenty-six randomly
selected subjects from Terman's sample (IQ above
150). In extent of education and careers some margin
of benefit seemed to be derived from the extra IQ
points of the 180 group, yet this was not uniformly
so. Furthermore, while 180 IQ suggests the ability
to do academic work with relative ease, it does not
signify a qualitatively different organization of

mind such as the presence of "genius" in its common meaning.

112. Fox, A.E. 1971. Kindergarten: Forgotten year for the gifted? *Gifted Child Quarterly* 15:42-48.

The author deals with the problem of the gifted underachiever at the kindergarten level and stresses the importance of completely altering the present program. Examples illustrate how kindergarten tends to stifle children's creativity and initiative. The place of the kindergarten in today's educational system is discussed and the need to stress its diagnostic function is pointed out. The author identifies some of the central problems of the kindergarten as being its lack of content and student performance rigidity.

113. Freedman, P. 1984. Identifying the leadership gifted: Self, peer or teacher nomination. *Roeper Review* 7:91-94.

The purpose of this study was to show that students who were nominated by themselves, their peers, and their teachers for leadership ability scored higher in a three part leadership task than students who were self nominated. The students who were self nominated scored high too, but not as high as those nominated by the three groups.

114. Frith, G.H., and A.A. Mims. 1984. Teaching gifted students to make verbal presentations. *Gifted Child Quarterly* 28:45-47.

This article identifies and describes selected procedures gifted students can use to make effective verbal presentations. A list of questions for classroom discussion and suggested activities is included.

115. Gang, M.A. 1984. Reading acceleration and enrichment in the elementary grades. *Reading Teacher* 37:372-76.

This survey of 116 elementary school teachers in a large suburban Minnesota school district as-

sessed attitudes and practices concerning reading
acceleration and enrichment. Reading acceleration
was defined as using a reading textbook designed for
a higher grade level. The terms gifted readers and
high ability readers were used to mean those readers
well above the average for the grade.

The teachers who responded to the questionnaires
did not all agree that acceleration was the best
method to meet the needs of gifted readers; however,
all agreed that enrichment activities were necessary.
The author concludes that research supports the use
of acceleration as one way to meet the needs of
gifted readers and suggests that teachers should
determine on an individualized basis whether acceleration is an appropriate method of reading instruction.

116. Gear, G.H. 1984. Providing services for rural gifted
children. *Exceptional Children* 50:326-31.

Small numbers of gifted children in rural areas
inhibit programming by special classes or hiring of
additional staff. Inadequate financial resources do
not allow for the development of comprehensive programs. The article suggests some changes that can
be implemented without great efforts and resources.
Cooperative programs with higher education institutions allow gifted students to benefit from advanced
instruction. Curricular compression allows a quick
learner to accomplish the curricula offered in a
three year period within a two year span. Cooperative work/study programs with community businesses
and agencies is an option that should be explored.
These options do not require a wealth of extra funding, but rather an innovative staff and use of existing community resources.

117. Granzin, K.L., and W.J. Granzin. 1969. Peer group
choice as a device for screening intellectually
gifted children. *Gifted Child Quarterly* 13:189-94.

Fourth-graders were asked to distinguish among
fifteen traits pertaining primarily to gifted children and fifteen traits pertaining to children in
general. They were later asked to name those of
their peers possessing the fifteen gifted traits.

Analysis of results showed both gifted and non-gifted
pupils able to distinguish traits of giftedness,
although the former group performed significantly
better. Peer group choice of gifted pupils agreed
significantly with teacher rankings, although no
superior performance by gifted pupils themselves was
noted on this task. These results suggest the value
of peer group choice as an additional method for
screening potentially gifted children.

118. Griggs, S.A., and R.S. Dunn. 1984. Selected case
      studies of the learning style preferences of gifted
      students. *Gifted Child Quarterly* 28:115-19.

      This study discusses the characteristics of the
      learning styles of the gifted and talented student.
      The learning style preferences among the gifted
      stress independence, persistence, non-conformity,
      strong self-motivation and a reliance on individual
      perception.

119. Griggs, S.A., and G.E. Price. 1982. A comparison be-
      tween the learning styles of gifted versus average
      suburban junior high school students. *Creative Child
      and Adult Quarterly* 7:39-42.

      Five factors were found to discriminate between
      the learning style preferences of gifted versus av-
      erage junior high students. Gifted students were
      more persistent, tolerated the presence of sound,
      and preferred learning alone, whereas average stu-
      dents had higher auditory preferences and greater
      dependency on teacher motivation.

120. Guilford, A.M. 1981. Aspects of language development
      in the gifted. *Gifted Child Quarterly* 25:159-63.

      This study investigated receptive and expressive
      language skills in eleven preschool gifted children
      and concluded that as a group the gifted students
      did not have a better selection of deep structure
      and transformation rules than normal students.

121. Hagen, E. 1980. *Identification of the gifted*. New
     York: Teachers College Press.

     This book focuses on the methods available for
     identifying the gifted and the problems that must be
     resolved in making these identifications. The term
     gifted is used for individuals who have exceptional
     ability in academic areas and the term talented is
     used for individuals who have exceptional ability in
     art, music, or drawing. Standardized tests, ratings,
     questionnaires, and observations are used when iden-
     tifying those who are gifted.

122. Hall, E.G. 1979. Simulation gaming—A device for al-
     tering attitudes about sex roles. *Gifted Child Quar-
     terly* 23:356-61.

     The value of simulation gaming for changing
     attitudes of gifted students concerning sex roles is
     explored in this article. Simulation gaming has
     considerable potential for reducing, altering, and
     changing attitudes concerning sex limitations. Gam-
     ing involves devising plans and motivating appeals
     as well as role playing, negotiating, bargaining,
     and decision making.

123. Halpin, W.G.; D.A. Payne; and C.D. Ellert. 1974. In
     search of the creative personality among gifted
     groups. *Gifted Child Quarterly* 18:31-33.

     The concept of giftedness has been widened to
     include not only those individuals with a high intel-
     ligence quotient, but also those who score high on
     measures of creativity. The relationship between
     creativity and giftedness has already been noted.
     However, knowledge concerning the differences in
     creativity among individuals gifted in various aca-
     demic and artistic areas is limited. It is the pur-
     pose of this study to determine if adolescents gifted
     in the areas of mathematics, science, English, for-
     eign language, social science, drama, music, and art
     do differ in their creative personalities. The re-
     sults of this study support the assumption that in-
     dividuals gifted in different areas are also differ-
     entially creative.

124. Hanson, I. 1984. A comparison between parent identi-
      fication of young bright children and subsequent
      testing. *Roeper Review* 7:44-45.

           Test results of eighty gifted four-six year
      olds confirmed the accuracy of parent recommendation,
      the high ability and achievement levels of the chil-
      dren, and their variability within achievement.
      Program adaptations included more mathematics teach-
      ing, individualized instruction, parent meetings,
      and allowance for inadequate handwriting skills and
      emotional and social variability.

125. Hanson, I. 1984. Research on the roles of intuition
      and feeling. *Roeper Review* 6:167-70.

           A survey was conducted for the purpose of de-
      termining if intuition and feeling played an impor-
      tant role in student processing of information. A
      survey was conducted on two populations of third,
      fourth, and fifth graders based on the typology of
      C.G. Jung. The findings showed that gifted students
      are predominantly intuitors. In decision making,
      there is a surprisingly high degree of feeling in-
      volved.

126. Harris, D.G., and S.S. Blank. 1983. A comparative
      study: Two approaches to enhance creative problem-
      solving in grade five students. *B.C. Journal of
      Special Education* 7:171-80.

           In an examination of a school-based program to
      develop creative thinking skills of gifted children,
      in the beginning intermediate grades few differences
      were found in curricular achievement between gifted
      children in segregated homogeneous classes and those
      in heterogeneous classes.

127. Hay, C.A. 1984. One more time: What do I do all day?
      Gifted Child Quarterly 28:17-20.

           This article relates the experiences of a gifted
      facilitator for junior high school students. The
      author describes her role in providing direct serv-
      ices including teaching academic course content and

higher level thinking skills and indirect services
such as consulting with parents, teachers, and mentors. Included is a presentation of a case example
of a gifted seventh grader who is interested in ar-
chitecture.

128. Henegar, L.E. 1984. Nurturing the creative promise in
      gifted disadvantaged youth. *Journal of Creative
      Behavior* 18:109-116.

      The purpose of this study was to identify ap-
      proaches in the literature that would add to the
      strengths of gifted disadvantaged youths. Among
      such approaches are creative problem solving, art
      activities, dramatics, story telling, and creative
      writing.

129. Hermelin, R., and N. O'Connor. 1980. Perceptual, mo-
      tor, and decision speeds in specifically and gener-
      ally gifted children. *Gifted Child Quarterly* 24:180-
      85.

      Work on the psychological processes that might
      be specific to highly gifted children has tended to
      be dominated by the concept of the IQ. This predom-
      inance has been only marginally affected by research
      on creativity. One difficulty has been that measures
      of intelligence and creativity tend to be positively
      correlated. In this experiment one group of high IQ
      children and two groups of lower IQ children had to
      judge pairs of words or pictures. One of the lower
      IQ groups contained only children with high musical
      ability. The other lower IQ group was the control.
      Reaction times to pairs of pictures or words were
      compared, and three types of judgments had to be
      made by the children. Although all groups needed an
      equal time to identify words, the control group
      needed significantly less time than the two others
      for the identification of pictures. While the musi-
      cally gifted and highly intelligent children required
      equal exposure time for words and pictures, controls
      needed significantly shorter exposures for pictures
      than they needed for words. There was a clear trend
      in the data on picture-pair judgments that suggested
      that the musically gifted children were fastest and
      the controls slowest on this task, but the group

differences were not significant. The control group
did in fact need a shorter exposure time to identify
pictures than the other subjects. It would appear
from the results of this experiment that the respec-
tive speeds of motor responses, perceptual identification, and discriminative judgments are distinct
and unrelated.

130. Hershey, M. 1981. An approach to mainstreaming for
     gifted children. *Roeper Review* 4:27-28.

         This article suggests program provisions for
     gifted students under the direct jurisdiction of
     special education for funding purposes but without
     the need to differentiate publicly degrees of service
     using labels. It cautions school districts and edu-
     cators that although program provisions for gifted
     students need the protection of the "special educa-
     tion umbrella," they should not be forced to operate
     under the regulatory processes appropriate for other
     special education programs.
         The article further suggests a comprehensive
     screening process to nominate students, a three stage
     method of streaming the target population, and vari-
     ous educational options ranging from limited enrich-
     ment within the regular classroom environment to
     options such as seminars, mentorship provisions, and
     flexible "pull-out" programs. The need for gifted
     education personnel to work closely with regular
     classroom teachers to provide an important link with
     special education is stressed along with the need to
     monitor and assess the implementation of meaningful
     programs for the gifted. The "least restrictive
     environment" of the mainstreaming movement should
     not be allowed to take on an inverse connotation
     when applied to gifted students, for whom a regular
     classroom may constitute a "restrictive environment."

131. Hershey, M., and P. Kearns. 1979. Effect of guided
     fantasy in the creative thinking and writing ability
     of gifted students. *Gifted Child Quarterly* 23:71-77.

         There are few studies in the literature that
     examine fantasy as a process of tapping a reservoir
     of acquired sensory or perceptual information for
     the purpose of enhancing creativity in an educational

setting. This study made the following hypotheses:
(1) Students who participate in sessions emphasizing
relaxation techniques and guided fantasy will produce
higher fluency, flexibility, and originality scores
on the Torrance Tests of Creative Thinking than students who participate in arithmetical exercises during concurrent sessions; (2) Students who participate in sessions emphasizing relaxation techniques
and guided fantasy will receive higher fluency,
flexibility and originality ratings on a writing
exercise than students who participate in arithmetical exercises during concurrent sessions. This study
demonstrated some important findings relevant to
classroom application of guided fantasy techniques.
A randomly assigned group of intermediate-age students who were exposed to a total of four hours of
guided fantasy in eight weekly sessions scored significantly higher on tests of divergent thinking
than did their randomly assigned counterparts who
received four hours of placebo exercises in the form
of arithmetic recreational exercises.

132. Hester, J.P. 1982. The gifted: An enrichment curricu-
      lum. *Creative Child and Adult Quarterly* 7:43-48.

      The author describes the resurgence of the
gifted education movement. He urges that an enrichment curriculum be developed to promote self-develop-
ment, rational thinking, and ethical awareness in
gifted students.

133. Hollinger, C., and E. Fleming. 1984. Internal barriers
      to the realization of potential: Correlates and in-
      terrelationships among gifted and talented female
      adolescents. *Gifted Child Quarterly* 28:135-38.

      Women are underrepresented in careers in math
and science and the authors feel that this is a result of four internal barriers--the protection of a
feminine self-image, non-assertiveness, fear of success, and self perception of social competence and
self-esteem. 284 female adolescents identified as
gifted and talented were given a comprehensive career
battery (including WFOS, TSBI and PAQ). The results
of this study were inconclusive.

134. Hollinger, C., and S. Kosek. 1985. Early identifica-
      tion of the gifted and talented. *Gifted Child Quar-
      terly* 29:168-71.

      The Star IQ test was found to be a good tool
      when used in the initial screening for children who
      are candidates for gifted programs. Because it has
      limitations as well as advantages, it should not be
      used as the sole screening instrument. In the eval-
      uation process, it should be used with other readi-
      ness measures, such as parent and teacher question-
      naires. Overall, the Star was found to make a valu-
      able contribution when identifying the gifted and
      talented younger child.

135. House, E.R. 1972. Whose goals? Whose values? Whose
      kids? *National Elementary Principal* 51:56-61.

      An interview with a gifted seven-year-old boy
      about a special science class for sixteen gifted
      boys in grades two through five introduces the de-
      scription and evaluation of the weekly one hour long,
      special program. The boy is seen to illustrate the
      problems of special education for the gifted in his
      intellectual ability, curiosity, and developing snob-
      bery. Also included is an interview with the teacher
      of the special class that stresses the importance of
      bringing the boys together to stimulate each other
      and the positive contribution of the class to student
      growth. The program is evaluated by criteria such
      as student involvement and enthusiasm, and encourage-
      ment of independence. The author emphasizes that
      putting gifted children in average classes denies
      them a stimulating intellectual climate, though rigid
      tracking systems often stigmatize children in the
      lower tracks.

136. Houtz, J.C.; S. Rosenfield; and T.J. Tetenbaum. 1978.
      Creative thinking in gifted elementary school chil-
      dren. *Gifted Child Quarterly* 22:513-19.

      A variety of creative thinking and problem solv-
      ing tasks were administered to 233 intellectually
      gifted second to sixth graders at a special school
      for the gifted in New York City. The tasks were
      selected to represent conceptual stages of a total

creative problem-solving model. Intelligence, achievement, and personality data were also gathered. Findings indicated interesting patterns of growth in creative problem solving abilities.

On creative thinking tasks a plateau in perform-ance appeared from the fourth grade on, but on the problem solving tasks, growth continued through the sixth grade. Individual variation within the sets of creative thinking and problem solving tasks was great, suggesting the need for training in creative thinking and problem solving skills for the gifted.

137. Humes, C.W., 2nd, and R.D. Campbell. 1980. Gifted students: A 15-year longitudinal study. *Gifted Child Quarterly* 24:129-31.

This study was undertaken to determine the im-pact of the gifted program on the attitudes of its former students since their participation. The sub-jects were from Greenwich (Connecticut) Public Schools, 1961-62 through 1969-70. The study was intended not only to assess past effectiveness, but also to chart a direction for future efforts in a mature program. The hypothesis was that program participation would be viewed positively by former participants. The results support the hypothesis that a longitudinal study of gifted students would establish effectiveness of the program, and would have a positive impact on the lives and attitudes of the participants.

138. Issacs, A.F. 1978. The gifted, talented, and creative: A two decade comparison of needs. *Creative Child and Adult Quarterly* 3:15-30.

The author discusses the current pressures on gifted, talented, and creative youth and suggests ways in which individuals and groups can serve these pupils.

139. Janos, P. 1985. Friendship patterns in highly intel-ligent children. *Roeper Review* 8:46-49.

Responses of high IQ students and moderate IQ students to a set of questions about friendships

were compared. Students preferred friends of their
own sex. More high IQ students reported their
friends to be older than themselves, that they did
not have enough friends, and that being smart made
it harder to make friends.

140.   Janos, P.; H. Fung; and N. Robinson. 1985. Self-
       concept, self-esteem and peer relations among gifted
       children who feel different. *Gifted Child Quarterly*
       29:78-81.

            271 high IQ elementary school children completed
       an extensive battery on social and emotional develop-
       ment. 37% conceptualized themselves as differing
       from their peers. They generally described differ-
       ences in a positive fashion and their self-esteem
       was above the mean quoted for a large normative
       sample. However, their self-esteem was lower than
       that of high IQ children who did not consider them-
       selves different.

141.   Juncture, J. 1979. Project REACH: A teacher training
       program for developing creative thinking skills in
       students. *Gifted Child Quarterly* 23:461-71.

            Project development activities centered on the
       following: teacher in-service, classroom activities,
       curriculum materials, parent/community involvement,
       and student evaluation. After three years of opera-
       tion, test scores showed increasingly superior per-
       formance in creative thinking on the part of the
       students.

142.   Juncture, J. 1982. Myth: The gifted constitutes a
       single homogeneous group! *Gifted Child Quarterly*
       26:9-10.

            The myth that gifted students comprise a single
       homogeneous group is refuted by the author. She
       cites the wide variety of characteristics and notes
       the influence of environment upon the individual.
       All of this supports the need for multicomponent
       programs.

143. Kaiser, C., and S. Berndt. 1985. Predictors of lone-
liness in the gifted adolescent. *Gifted Child Quarterly* 29:74-76.

     This research examined loneliness among gifted
     adolescents. 175 junior and senior high school stu-
     dents at or above the top 5% of their class as mea-
     sured by standardized achievement tests were used
     for this study. Slightly more depression, stress,
     loneliness, and anger are reported by gifted adoles-
     cents than by their adolescent peers. However, the
     degree of loneliness reported was found to be a func-
     tion of anger and depression, suggesting a possible
     success depression in certain gifted adolescents.

144. Kamer, P.P. 1984. Conceptual level of development as
it relates to student participation in gifted programs. *Gifted Child Quarterly* 28:89-91.

     This study assessed the conceptual levels of
     130 secondary students identified as gifted and 131
     students from schools without gifted programs.
     Gifted students scored significantly higher, suggest-
     ing that such a measure of cognitive complexity may
     be useful in the identification of gifted students.

145. Kanevsky, L. 1985. Computer-based math for gifted
students: Comparison of cooperative and competitive
strategies. *Journal for the Education of the Gifted*
8:239-55.

     This study assessed effective math skills of
     forty gifted third and fourth graders. Both computer
     assisted instruction and flashcard presentation were
     effective. Gifted students working on the computer
     preferred more competitive than cooperative activi-
     ties.

146. Karnes, F.A., and N. Wherry. 1981. Wishes of fourth-
through seventh-grade gifted students. *Psychology
in the Schools* 18:235-39.

     Three wishes and primary wishes of fourth-
     through seventh-grade gifted students who took part
     in a residential program for the gifted were col-

lected and categorized. The results indicate that
males wished for material things more often than did
females. With the exception of fourth graders, subjects made altruistic wishes more frequently than
any other wish.

147. Karnes, M.B.; A.M. Schwedel; and G.F. Lewis. 1983.
      Short-term effects of early programming for the young
      gifted handicapped child. *Exceptional Children*
      50:103-9.

          The article compares young, gifted, handicapped
      pre-school children who were part of a model program
      called RAPHYT (Retrieval and Acceleration of Promis-
      ing Young Handicapped and Talented), with a compari-
      son group of children who did not qualify for the
      program. Significant treatment effects on the chil-
      dren who participated in RAPHYT were found in talent-
      area functioning, creative functioning, and school-
      related task performance.

148. Kelly, K., and N. Colangelo. 1984. Academic and social
      concepts of gifted, general and special students.
      Exceptional Children 50:551-54.

          This study hypothesizes that academic ability
      is positively related to both academic and social
      self-concepts. The sample consists of 145 male and
      121 female students from grades seven-nine who were
      divided by ability level based on GPA, and ratings
      by parents, teachers, fellow students and self-
      evaluation into gifted, special learning needs, and
      general students groups. The Tennessee Self-Concept
      Scale and the Academic Self-Concept Scale were admin-
      istered to all students. The results of the study
      indicate that the gifted students held significantly
      higher academic and social concepts compared to non-
      gifted students in the same grade. Males with spe-
      cial learning needs scored significantly lower than
      other males on all scales.

149. Kontos, S.; L.H. Swanson; and C.T. Frazer. 1984.
     Memory-metamemory connection in intellectually gifted
     and normal children. *Psychological Review* 54:930.

     In this study twenty-seven children (thirteen
     intellectually gifted, fourteen intellectually nor-
     mal) with a mean age of 13.3 years were administered
     a metamemory interview and recall tasks. No signif-
     icant difference between the two groups was apparent.
     There were several significant correlations between
     metamemory and memory; however, the expected superi-
     ority of gifted subjects on both metamemory and mem-
     ory was not supported.

150. Kulm, G. 1984. Geometry enrichment for mathematically
     gifted students. *Roeper Review* 6:150-51.

     This article describes a summer program for
     mathematically gifted eighth graders. Pretests
     showed that the students had mastered geometric
     terms, but not axiomatic approaches. A problem-
     solving approach was used to develop abilities to
     hypothesize. The students worked best independently.
     Geometry is shown to provide an excellent context
     for developing intuition, rational thinking, and
     deductive reasoning abilities.

151. Lazar, A.L.; J. Gensley; and J. Gowan. 1972. Develop-
     ing positive attitudes through curriculum planning
     for young gifted children. *Gifted Child Quarterly*
     16:27-31.

     Described is an enrichment activity included in
     a social studies curriculum on creative Americans
     that is designed to teach gifted elementary school
     children positive attitudes toward handicapped per-
     sons. During a four-week workshop, the children
     studied the accomplishments of selected famous people
     throughout United States history and listened to
     guest speakers describe their creative activities.
     It was then pointed out that each individual experi-
     enced some sort of handicap. Results indicated that
     realistic and systematic curriculum planning can
     help to develop positive attitudes in gifted chil-
     dren.

152. Lehman, E.B., and C.J. Erdwins. 1981. The social and
      emotional adjustment of young, intellectually-gifted
      children. *Gifted Child Quarterly* 25:134-37.

          Through administration of a battery of tests,
      this study examined the similarities in social and
      emotional aspects of gifted children to their mental
      age peers. Subjects included sixteen gifted third
      graders, sixteen nongifted third graders, and six
      average IQ sixth graders. Findings suggested that
      gifted children do vary significantly on several
      scales but do not vary consistently in manner from
      their same age peers.

153. Lewis, C. 1984. Alternatives to acceleration for the
      highly gifted child. *Roeper Review* 6:133-36.

          The author contends that acceleration is not
      the most effective way of meeting the needs of the
      highly gifted child. Flexible scheduling and indi-
      vidual counseling are required for these special
      students.

154. Lindsey, M. 1980. *Training teachers of the gifted and
      talented*. New York: Teachers College Press.

          The author feels that the principles that guide
      the educational programs for developing the poten-
      tials of gifted children should also guide the pro-
      grams that educate their teachers. A teacher of the
      gifted should understand, respect, expect trust, be
      sensitive to others, be flexible, be creative, be
      intuitive, have perception, be committed to excel-
      lence, have a desire to learn, increase knowledge,
      and be enthusiastic.

155. Lowery, J. 1982. Developing creativity in gifted chil-
      dren. *Gifted Child Quarterly* 26:133-39.

          This study proved that twelve students, grades
      three-five, in a music and imagery training program
      scored higher on indices of figural originality,
      figural fluency, figural flexibility, and figural
      elaboration than gifted students in two packaged
      treatment programs. These programs are: New Direc-

tions in Creatively Basic and New Directions in Creatively Enhanced.

156. Ludlow, B.L., and D.T. Woodrum. 1982. Problem-solving strategies of gifted and average learners on a multiple discrimination task. *Gifted Child Quarterly* 26:99-104.

Twenty gifted learners (eleven years old) demonstrated performance superior to twenty average age matched learners on problem solving tasks related to memory and attention, but not on all measures related to performance efficiency and strategy selection. Average learners used significantly more advanced strategies when continued access to feedback was permitted.

157. Ludwig, G., and D. Cullinan. 1984. Behavior problems of gifted and nongifted elementary school girls and boys. *Gifted Child Quarterly* 28:37-39.

Comparison of the personal and social adjustments of 124 gifted elementary school students and 124 nongifted controls revealed that gifted students showed fewer behavior problems. Boys of both gifted and nongifted groups demonstrated greater conduct disorder problems.

158. Lupskowski, A. 1984. Gifted students in small rural schools do not have to move to the city. *Roeper Review* 7:13-16.

The purpose of this study was to point out that gifted students do not need to live or go to urban area schools in order to have their greatest potential cultivated. This article points out learning strategies that can be used for gifted students in many small rural schools. The strategies mentioned are cooperative programs, community resources, and challenging courses.

159. Maddux, C.D.; L.M. Scheiber; and J.E. Bass. 1982.
      Self-concept and social distance in gifted children.
      Gifted Child Quarterly 26:77-81.

          This investigation explored self-concept and
      sociometric variables among fifth- and sixth-grade
      gifted children who receive their schooling in a
      totally segregated program, a partially segregated
      program, and the regular school program. The present
      study was designed to determine whether a gifted
      program in general, and a totally segregated gifted
      program in particular, might produce lower self-
      concept and peer acceptance scores in participating
      gifted children than in normal children in the stan-
      dardization sample, or in non-participating gifted
      children in the regular program. The results show
      that no evidence was found to suggest that identifi-
      cation or placement in segregated or integrated pro-
      grams might result in less favorable peer ratings at
      the fifth-grade level only.

160. Maker, J.C., and S.W. Schiever. 1984. Excellence for
      the future. *Gifted Child Quarterly* 28:6-8.

          This article provides a comparative discussion
      between the report by the National Commission on
      Excellence in Education (1983)--"A Nation at Risk"--
      and the "Action for Excellence" report developed by
      the Task Force on Education for Economic Growth as
      they relate to the education of the gifted. The
      writers caution that a literal interpretation of "A
      Nation at Risk" may be damaging to the future of
      gifted education and that the recommendations by the
      ECS Task Force more closely parallel the aims of
      education for the gifted including the development
      of higher-order reasoning skills, the practice of
      problem solving, the development of skills in com-
      munication to various audiences, and the development
      of an understanding of concepts and principles that
      cut across the lines of traditional disciplines.
      The writers share their hope that programs for the
      gifted will generate a quality of excellence in edu-
      cating children in the general population.

161. Maltby, F. 1984. Teacher-pupil and teacher-gifted
      pupil interaction in first and middle schools.
      Gifted Education International 2:11-18.

          The purpose of this study was to identify the
      amount of interaction gifted students have with their
      teachers. Thirty-nine gifted children were observed.
      The quantity of teacher-pupil contact time would
      make it disadvantageous for gifted students to be in
      a class with nongifted students. The demands on
      teacher time by gifted students would be so great
      that it would make it inadvisable to put gifted and
      nongifted together in the same class.

162. Master, D. 1983. Writing and the gifted child. *Gifted
      Child Quarterly* 27:162-68.

          The author describes a developmental program
      designed to improve and develop the writing skills
      of gifted children grades three-five. Pretests were
      used to determine specific needs. Teacher and stu-
      dents built on the base of skills by stressing vari-
      ety in sentence structure, research skills, note
      taking, and vocabulary. Post-testing, as well as
      teacher and student evaluation, indicated that im-
      provement had occurred in some areas of need.

163. Mathews, F.N. 1981. Influencing parents' attitudes
      toward gifted education. *Exceptional Children*
      48:140-45.

          The purpose of this study was to examine the
      influence of a parent awareness meeting on parental
      attitudes toward gifted children and the programs
      that serve these children. Parents of 360 gifted
      and nongifted children who attend grades kindergarten
      through six in a small-town western Massachusetts
      school district involved in the initial stages of
      designing a program for gifted students were randomly
      assigned to one of two parent education meetings and
      invited to attend on the evening specified by group
      membership. The parental attitudes were measured by
      the Wiener Attitude Scale. Results indicated that
      the attitudes of the parents varied significantly
      based on attendance or nonattendance at the meeting
      and were directly related to the relative level of

their desires to support educational programs for the gifted. The study suggests that parent education meetings may be beneficial in encouraging awareness and support for educational programs that serve gifted and talented students.

164. Meyers, E. 1984. A study of concerns of classroom teachers regarding a resource room program for the gifted. *Roeper Review* 7:32-36.

    The purpose of this study was to analyze the concerns of teachers when gifted students are taught in a resource room setting. A survey of teacher attitudes was taken in a pull-out program in one school district. The concerns of the teachers are categorized as ownership of and responsibility for the program through involvement, concerns about communication, criteria for selection, scheduling, fragmentation, and how all these factors have an impact on pupil performance.

165. Milgram, R., and N. Milgram. 1976. Personality characteristics of gifted Israeli children. *Journal of Genetic Psychology* 129:185-94.

    This study of 182 gifted and 310 nongifted Israeli children in grades four to eight examined the differences in their personal and social adjustment. It was found that gifted girls were at least as well adjusted as gifted boys, that gifted children showed a more positive self concept (except physical self concept), and more internal locus of control. The results of the study indicated that children who solve problems more effectively experience less anxiety.

166. Miller, M. 1983. Analysis of gifted students' attitudes toward the handicapped. *Journal for Special Educators* 19:14-21.

    This study analyzed the attitudes of gifted children toward handicapped children. The survey included eighty-two gifted children from grades kindergarten to twelve and the results were positive. The students showed greatest acceptance toward learn-

ing disabled children. The gifted students also
responded favorably toward handicapped children when
they initiated interaction.

167. Mitchell, B. 1984. An update on gifted/talented education in the U.S. *Roeper Review* 6:161-63.

The article reports the findings of the third
annual survey on gifted and talented education in
the United States. Funding for programs did not
decrease, and the ratio of state funded programs
increased. There is attention focused on the development of creative thinking skills. Only four states
made reference to computer learning programs for the
gifted. Little progress had been made on the initiation of special requirements for teachers of the
gifted and talented.

168. Navarre, J. 1979. Incubation as fostering the creative
process. *Gifted Child Quarterly* 23:792-800.

The author stresses that because creative production most often takes place after reflection on
inspiration, educators must recognize this and provide situations conducive to preparation and incubation.

169. Nicely, R.F., Jr.; J.D. Small; and R.L. Furman. 1980.
Teachers' attitudes toward gifted children and pro-
grams--Implications for instructional leadership.
Education 101:12-15.

This study assessed teachers' attitudes toward
gifted students and programs by developing and administering a survey to kindergarten-twelfth grade
teachers. The results indicate that the more teachers know about gifted students and gifted programs,
the more likely it is that they will be positively
disposed to having students removed from their classrooms to participate in such programs.

170. Obrzut, A.; R.B. Nelson; and J.E. Obrzut. 1984. Early
      school entrance for intellectually superior children:
      An analysis. *Psychology in the Schools* 21:71-77.

            This study was a four year follow-up comparing
      sixty-eight gifted children admitted early to school
      and nongifted children admitted at the regular time.
      Many variables are discussed including promotion,
      retention, achievement scores, and emotional adjust-
      ment. Results indicated no significance regarding
      the variables that contribute to school progress.

171. Oglesby, K., and J. Gallagher. 1983. Teacher-pupil
      ratios, instructional time and expenditure estimates
      for three administrative strategies for educating
      gifted students. *Gifted Child Quarterly* 27:57-63.

            This article presents the results of a survey
      in which ninety-five directors of programs for the
      gifted were questioned concerning program cost, per-
      sonal use, and staff-student ratios for three of the
      most popular administrative models for gifted educa-
      tion: the special class, the teacher consultant, and
      the resource room. In the use of personnel, the
      highest teacher-pupil ratio was reported in the re-
      source room, while the special class had the lowest.
      In time spent per student, the least attention per
      student was provided under the teacher consultant
      model, while the most attention was provided under
      the special class model. In terms of cost, the me-
      dian cost of the three models fell between 15-30%
      above the cost of the average pupil's education.
      This was due to the employment of additional trained
      personnel to implement special programs.

172. Okabayash, H., and E.P. Torrance. 1984. Role of style
      of learning and thinking and self-directed learning
      readiness in the achievement of gifted students.
      Journal of Learning Disabilities 17:104-7.

            This study explores relationships between mea-
      sures of style of information processing and readi-
      ness for self-directed study and failure of identi-
      fied gifted students to achieve at a level equal to
      their measured intellectual abilities. The subjects
      were 148 identified gifted students, grades four

through seven, classified by their teachers according
to achievement level (below expectations, at expec-
tation level, above expectations). The subjects
were administered Torrance and McCarthy's "Your Style
of Learning and Thinking" and Guglielmino's "Readiness for Self-Directed Learning." Three-way analyses
of variance revealed a significant role for style of
learning and thinking and self-directed learning
readiness in the achievement of gifted students.

173. Park, B. 1983. Use of self-instructional materials
with gifted primary-age students. *Gifted Child Quarterly* 27:29-34.

This study finds that self-instructional techniques and materials are effective in teaching high
achieving students, and can serve either to enrich
the curriculum or to accelerate the child. Goals
and objectives are written and evaluations assess
the progress made by the child in meeting the levels
of mastery.

174. Pesickas, B., and B. Lane. 1985. Stimulating with
simulations. *Science and Children* 22:28-29.

The authors report on a program for gifted and
high-achieving students in which participants learn
through involvement in real-life situations. Students are required to work together and organize
information, make decisions and arrive at realistic,
responsible decisions. A certain amount of structure
and guidance is needed but students have demonstrated
that they can make wise choices, learn to take risks,
work willingly as members of a group, and improve
their ability to solve problems as they learn from
their experiences.

175. Powell, P., and T. Haden. 1984. The intellectual and
psychosocial nature of extreme giftedness. *Roeper
Review* 6:131-33.

The authors contend that the highly gifted person creates structure, generates ideas, and effi-
ciently processes information in ways that are qualitatively superior to the ways in which moderately

gifted and average ability persons operate. In addition, the adult academic and occupational achievements of highly gifted persons are also superior.

176. Quisenberry, N.L. 1974. Developing language fluency
      in the gifted culturally different child. *Gifted
      Child Quarterly* 18:175-79.

         Culturally different gifted children need con-
      tinuing opportunities to develop oral language flu-
      ency. Educators should be aware of normal stages in
      the child's language development (such as temporary
      tendencies to overgeneralize irregular nouns and
      verbs) and should not expend undue effort correcting
      apparently ungrammatical dialectal forms that are
      used by adults in the child's home environment.

177. Raina, M.K. 1968. A study into the effect of competi-
      tion on creativity. *Gifted Child Quarterly* 12:217-
      20.

         This investigation was designed to study the
      effect of competition on ideational fluency and
      flexibility. A sample of forty students, twenty in
      the experimental and twenty in the control group
      were matched for intelligence, age, class, and cre-
      ativity. Both groups were administered Test of Imag-
      ination (Product Improvement and Unusual Uses). The
      results showed that the experimental competitive
      group scored significantly higher in number of ideas
      and flexibility of ideas than the group where compe-
      tition was not a factor.

178. Reis, S.M., and M. Cellerina. 1983. Guiding gifted
      children through independent study. *Teaching Excep-
      tional Children* 15:136-139.

         Guidelines are offered for facilitating indepen-
      dent or small group investigations by gifted and
      talented students. Steps include exploring student
      interest, developing the chosen topic, using the
      management plan, implementing and monitoring the
      project, and helping students with evaluation.

179. Renfrow, M.J. 1983. Accurate drawing as a function of training of gifted children in copying and perception. *Educational Research Quarterly* 8:27-32.

This investigation's goal was to establish evidence that trained gifted children, ages eight-eleven, would draw more realistically than untrained gifted children. Eighteen lessons in perception and drawing were presented over nine weeks to the experimental group, while the control group received eighteen lessons in a traditional art program. An analysis of variance compared the mean scores of the experimental and control groups and indicated a significant difference between the two groups.

180. Renzulli, J.S., and R.K. Gable. 1976. A factorial study of the attitudes of gifted students toward independent study. *Gifted Child Quarterly* 20:91-99.

Although independent study has been a relatively popular method of programming for gifted and talented students, few systematic attempts have been made to evaluate the attitudes of students toward this particular approach to learning. The two-fold purpose of this study was (1) to develop a valid and reliable instrument for evaluating independent study programs and (2) to use the instrument to assess the attitudes of gifted students who have enrolled in an independent study program. A sixty-five-item scale was initially developed and piloted on 109 students enrolled in an independent study program. After some revision, the test was then administered to 196 students. The results indicate that student attitudes toward the program were highly positive.

181. Ritchie, A.C.; J.M. Bernard; and B.E. Shertza. 1982. Comparison of academically talented children and academically average children on interpersonal sensitivity. *Gifted Child Quarterly* 26:105-9.

This study sought to investigate the interpersonal sensitivity of academically average ten-year-olds, academically talented ten-year-olds, and academically average twelve-year-olds. The children were tested in their interpersonal sensitivity to three interaction groups: adult/adult, adult/child,

and child/child. Results of this study confirmed
that research should be conducted on specific components of gifted children's emotional and social adjustment. The results do not support statements in
the literature regarding the superior interpersonal
sensitivity of gifted children. The most clear-cut
implication of this research is that interpersonal
sensitivity appears to be developmental in nature.
The results suggest that as children grow older,
they become more perceptive of the interpersonal
dynamics between others.

182. Roedell, W. 1984. Vulnerabilities of highly gifted
      children. *Roeper Review* 6:127-30.

      This work examines the unique vulnerabilities
to which gifted children are prone such as uneven
development, perfectionism, adult expectations, in-
tense sensitivity, alienation, inappropriate environments, and role conflicts. Problems arise from the
discrepancy between the level of development and the
expectations of society. As information about the
needs of highly gifted children becomes more widespread and society's expectations become more attuned
to reality, the degree of vulnerability will diminish. Educating highly gifted children requires a
parallel commitment to building support systems to
help them come to terms with their abilities.

183. Ross, A., and M. Parker. 1980. Academic and social
      concepts of the academically gifted. *Exceptional
      Children* 47:6-10.

      The purpose of this study was to ascertain
whether or not there is a discrepancy between gifted
students' academic and social self-concepts. The
Sears Self-Control Inventory was administered to 147
fifth through eighth grade intellectually gifted
students. The responses indicated that these gifted
students possess significantly higher academic than
social self-concepts.

184. Rubenzer, R. 1986. Stress: Causes and cures in gifted kids. *Gifted Children's Monthly* 7:1-3.

Gifted children are susceptible to stress and burnout. Stress is the energy that helps to motivate us, that enables us to concentrate and to attain our goals. This is the positive form of stress. However, there is the negative form of stress to which the gifted child is highly susceptible. This leads to burnout. The gifted child must learn to cope successfully with stress. Relaxation training is helpful when dealing with stress and burnout. It can be accomplished by taking the holistic approach in dealing with attitudes, behaviors, and circumstances causing the problem.

185. Saltzer, R.T. 1984. Early reading and giftedness-- Some observations and questions. *Gifted Child Quarterly* 28:95-96.

After interviewing parents of children who were early readers and observing reading performance in informal settings, it became apparent that a number of characteristics were shared by these children including an early interest in alphabet letters and regular viewing of "Sesame Street."

186. Schlechter, C. 1981. The multiple talent approach in mainstream and gifted programs. *Exceptional Children* 48:144-48.

The multiple talent approach to providing enrichment for all: students in regular class programs and for gifted students in special programs is the subject of this article. The use of the model in regular programs that include gifted students is also discussed. Implications for more effective identification and enrichment of gifted children are discussed.

187. Schwartz, L., and R. Lickman. 1984. Integrating the potentially able and the exceptionally able. *Gifted Child Quarterly* 28:130-34.

Thirty students, half of them identifiably

gifted and half potentially gifted (the latter being selected by questionnaires given to music, art, and gym teachers plus librarians, peers, and the students themselves) were given an enrichment program at Penn State University. The program was taught by faculty members and several students enrolled in special education courses were available as nonacademic resource aides and ultimately as "buddies" to the youngsters. In all phases of the project identified gifted and potentially gifted interacted well. The potentially gifted were successful in the academic activities. The interaction with college students proved rewarding for both sets of students. Most reported increases in self-esteem and the potentially able reported at a follow-up interview that their grades, school behavior, and aspirations had improved. More formal measurement techniques are needed for this study.

188. Scobee, J., and W.R. Nash. 1983. A survey of highly successful space scientists concerning education for gifted and talented students. *Gifted Child Quarterly* 27:147-51.

The article reports on the results of a survey given to fifty-six outstanding space scientists. It indicates that they were influenced by opportunities to learn from teachers and parents and from peer interaction. Determination, perseverance, and curiosity helped them attain success and influenced their career choices. They recommended that problem-solving skills, creativity, understanding, and discipline should be nurtured among gifted students.

189. Scruggs, T., and S. Cohn. 1983. Learning characteristics of verbally gifted students. *Gifted Child Quarterly* 27:169-72.

This comparative study analyzed learning styles and effectiveness in verbally gifted children and nongifted children. Twenty-nine children between the ages of nine and fourteen were used. Qualification standards were scoring at least 370 on the verbal section of the Scholastic Aptitude Test. The procedure used was paired associate learning tasks. The results revealed no significant evidence that

verbally gifted children learn differently from the
typical individual. It did find that gifted students
do in fact use the same strategies as their normal
age peers.

190. Shaw, G. 1985. The use of imagery by intelligent and
by creative schoolchildren. *Journal of General Psychology* 112:153-71.

These studies addressed themselves to the question of creativity and intelligence. In study I,
ethnographic observation testing with problem-solving
interviews were used in a regular classroom. In
study II, testing procedures and problem-solving
interviews were completed with thirty children in a
gifted program. Both studies produced evidence sup-
porting the link between imaging abilities and creative thinking.

191. Silvernail, D. 1980. Gifted education for the 80's
and beyond: A futuristic curriculum model for the
gifted child. *Roeper Review* 2:16-18.

The author advocates the development of a varied
curriculum for future studies to meet the needs of
the gifted. Components of a "futuristic curriculum"
include the basic skills extended to incorporate new
skills such as cross-disciplinary understandings,
skill in human processes computer language, research
skills, anticipatory skills of observing relationships and taking action on evaluated data, skills
based on cross-cultural and multi-ethnic insights,
and skills to deal with a changing world. Additional
suggestions for future studies programs for the
gifted are a study of the future that would include
an examination of the past and emerging issues and
the development of creative plans for action, and
exploration and planning for personal futures.

192. Sisk, D.A. 1980. The relationship between self-concept
and creative thinking of elementary school children:
An experimental investigation. *GATE: Gifted and
Talented Education* 2:47-49.

Three units were formed from a group of 400

sixth graders: those participating in writings and
discussions on topics that encourage self-knowledge;
those participating in writings and discussions of
topics that were more generalized; and those who
were tested on creative thinking and self-concept
without the benefit of intervening treatment. After
a five-week testing period, results showed that ability was related to flexibility and originality, but
not fluency. High self-concept, however, was related
to flexibility and fluency.

193. Spina, D., and C. Crealock. 1985. Identification of
      and programming for the gifted student and the gifted
      underachiever: A survey of the current situation in
      Ontario's schools. *Canadian Journal for Exceptional
      Children* 2:8-13.

          Results of questionnaires completed by eighty-
      eight Ontario school boards revealed that most boards
      have programs for both gifted and gifted underachiev-
      ing students and that most used a variety of identi-
      fication criteria and programing alternatives. A
      majority specifically identified and programed for
      gifted underachievers although they tended to treat
      them primarily as gifted students.

194. Starr, C. 1979. Simulation: A teaching strategy for
      the gifted and talented. *Gifted Child Quarterly*
      23:269-87.

          This article discusses the use of simulation
      games in teaching gifted children. The activity is
      one in which participants interact within an artifi-
      cially produced environment that recreates some as-
      pect of social reality.

195. Stewart, E.D. 1981. Learning styles among gifted/tal-
      ented students: Instructional technique preferences.
      Exceptional Children 48:134-37.

          The findings of this study indicate that gifted
      students differ from students of the general popula-
      tion in their preferred styles of learning. Gifted/-
      talented students apparently preferred instructional
      methods that foster independence, such as independent

study and discussion, while students of the general population preferred more structured activities, such as lectures. These findings support the opinion that special educational services must be provided for the gifted population. In addition, curriculum planning and teacher training must be adapted when dealing with education of the gifted.

196. Stoddard, E.P., and J.S. Renzulli. 1983. Improving the writing skills of talent pool students. *Gifted Child Quarterly* 27:21-27.

This study examined whether or not specific training experiences in selected writing skills could result in products that achieve higher levels of quality. The study also compared the writing samples of talented students who took part in special pull-out sessions seems to be a matter that can be determined either by teacher preference or by practical considerations.

197. Subotnik, R. 1984. Emphasis on the creative dimension: Social studies curriculum modification for gifted intermediate and secondary students. *Roeper Review* 7:7-10.

The purpose of this study was to research and recommend a successful technique for modifying social studies curriculums for gifted students. The curriculum in social studies should be modified for the gifted intermediate and secondary students by including techniques that would have as their outgrowth creative thinking. These strategies include brainstorming, attribute listing, morphological synthesis, reverse historical chronology, webbing, consequence charts, and guided fantasies. This study includes examples of these strategies.

198. Switzer, C., and M.L. Mourse. 1979. Reading instruction for the gifted child in first grade. *Gifted Child Quarterly* 23:323-31.

The article discusses the role of the first-grade teacher in implementing special programs for gifted children and providing appropriate environ-

ments for the development of students' full potential. The author suggests instructional practices
that may be used with the gifted reader.

199. Tannenbaum, A.J. 1972. A backward and forward glance
      at the gifted. *National Elementary Principal* 51:14-
      23.

         A review of trends in the education of the
      gifted reveals periods of emphasis alternating with
      periods of declining interest, and it appears that
      special programs for the gifted are once again in
      style. Special educational provisions have, however,
      consistently been seen as luxuries to be discontinued
      when budgetary pressures are increased. A sign of
      revived interest is the inclusion of the gifted among
      those benefitted by federal acts such as the Elemen-
      tary and Secondary Education Act. A look at the
      youth culture of today leads one to the conclusion
      that the current revival must not be as dehumanizing
      and science oriented as that of the Sputnik era.
      Young people see themselves and their society in a
      holistic way and the gifted, particularly, are con-
      cerned with social values. For an educational pro-
      gram to survive when the current interest in the
      gifted has faded, it must emphasize social concern
      as the context for all studies.

200. Tan-Willman, C., and D. Gutteridge. 1981. Creative
      thinking and moral reasoning of academically gifted
      secondary school adolescents. *Gifted Child Quarterly*
      25:149-53.

         This study assessed the creative thinking and
      moral reasoning of 115 academically gifted adoles-
      cents who completed a seven-year program in a six-
      year accelerated program. The Torrance Tests of
      Creative Thinking and the Defining Issues Test were
      administered. The results indicate that although
      their performance on the Defining Issues Test was
      better than that of average adolescents, their cre-
      ative thinking abilities were considered under-
      developed. The subjects were functioning mostly on
      the conventional level of moral judgement similar to
      adolescents of the general population.

201. Taylor, I.A. 1970. Creative production in gifted young (almost) adults through simultaneous sensory stimulation. *Gifted Child Quarterly* 14:46-55.

> To induce creative openness and to determine the effects of intensive simultaneous sensory stimulation on drawing production, twenty-seven gifted students (IQ mean of 158, age seventeen years) were tested before and after stimulation and their drawings judged with the AC Test of Creative Ability. The size and the openness of the drawings increased significantly after stimulation over a five-week period, and their esthetic quality was judged higher. The results were interpreted to indicate that openness is an essential part of creativity and that simultaneous sensory stimulation may practically induce openness.

202. Thomason, J. 1981. Education of the gifted: A challenge and a promise. *Exceptional Children* 48:101-3.

> While we are committed to the education of all individuals, particularly those who differ from the general population, we tend to neglect the needs of a group of individuals who have not been receiving the proper educational program designed to facilitate maximum growth--the gifted and talented. Some advances in this area have been made over the past ten-fifteen years. In the 1970s, there was a vast increase in the number of gifted and talented students who had been identified and were reported as receiving some type of special service. In addition, funding of gifted/talented programs has increased 112% over the past five years. Federal legislation, in the form of the Gifted and Talented Children's Education Act of 1978 set forth the federal definition of gifted and talented children.

203. Tomlinson, S. 1986. Career awareness for the future. *Gifted Children's Monthly* 7:22-23.

> Career education for the gifted child should begin in the upper elementary and middle school levels. Self-awareness gives the child an opportunity to explore, analyze, and assess the interests, abilities, and personality characteristics that are nec-

essary in the selection of various careers.

204. Torrance, E.P. 1969. Curiosity of gifted children and
      performance on timed and untimed tests of creativity.
      Gifted Child Quarterly 13:155–58.

      This experiment was designed to test the hypoth-
      esis that an untimed test of creative thinking will
      work more to the advantage of highly curious gifted
      children than it will to gifted children low in cu-
      riosity. The subject population was seventy-five
      highly gifted sixth grade children (IQ 130 or
      higher), and teachers were asked to nominate from
      each class the five most curious and the five least
      curious children. The test task was to produce un-
      usual questions about ice, questions that would make
      people think about ice in new ways. The results
      suggest that among gifted preadolescents the level
      of curiosity makes a difference in performance on
      creativity tests.

205. Torrance, E.P. 1971. Identity: The gifted child's
      major problem. *Gifted Child Quarterly* 15:147–55.

      Three response patterns of conformity, rebel-
      lion, and creative individuality that were found to
      characterize gifted children's resolve in the search
      for their identity were illustrated by brief case
      studies of six gifted young people. The gifted young
      persons were viewed first during the seventh to
      twelfth grade period and second during the ages of
      twenty-five to thirty. It was found that gifted
      children needed freedom to wander, to experiment, to
      risk, and to discover their individual limits, which
      ultimately enabled them to find their identity. The
      lives of the six young people described were said to
      reveal the duality of the unique and universal.
      Each was said to seek his unique identity and yet,
      seeking identity was characterized as a universal
      phenomenon. The author advocates that gifted chil-
      dren should receive supporting adult guidance in the
      quests for their identity.

206. Torrance, E.P. 1974. Ways gifted children can study
the future. *Gifted Child Quarterly* 18:65-71.

It is important that educators of the gifted
foster study of the future since it is today's gifted
children who must solve the problems of the future.
Children can be taught to use imaginative role playing as a vocational guidance technique, sociodrama
as a problem solving technique, and curriculum materials designed to let students see aspects of a future problem by elaborating on it through drawings
and other visual representations.

207. Torrance, E.P. 1980. Educating the gifted in the
1980s: Removing limits on learning. *Journal for
the Education of the Gifted* 4:43-49.

The writer considers limits to the learning of
gifted students and offers fifteen guidelines for
identifying gifted children in the 1980s. He also
discusses the identification processes. The article
focuses on the need for an exciting image of the
future in gifted education.

208. Tremaine, C.D. 1979. Do gifted programs make a difference? *Gifted Child Quarterly* 23:500-517.

This two-part study was designed to test common
criticisms of gifted programs. A comparison of student transcripts revealed higher GPA and SAT scores
for the enrolled. The enrolled elected many more
challenging classes in high school and won three
times as many scholarships. This contrasts with the
sometimes expressed opinion that gifted programs
harm academic standing. This study also measured
the validity of common socially-based criticisms of
gifted programs. It revealed that the enrolled
gifted students had higher educational goals and
more regard for high school and teachers. They were
more involved in school activities and as involved
in community projects as the unenrolled. They had
numerous and varied friends and voiced equal respect
for their peers. The study provided no data to support the contention that gifted programs breed elit-
ism, snobbery, indifference, conceit, or any other
negative quality. Thus, the results show that gifted

programs do make a difference and that difference
makes program development and participating vitally
worthwhile.

209. Van Tassel-Besker, J. 1984. The talent search as an
     identification model. *Gifted Child Quarterly* 28:172-
     76.

     The author discusses the Talent Search Identi-
     fication Model as a standard approach on a national
     basis for screening, verifying, and placing gifted
     children. It uses the SAT as a second level test to
     determine verbal and mathematical ability. He feels
     that its advantage is that it allows for score dis-
     crimination among gifted population. On the basis
     of scores received on this test gifted students could
     be assigned to varying programs.

210. Vare, J.W. 1979. Moral education for the gifted: A
     confluent model. *Gifted Child Quarterly* 23:487-99.

     The author feels that both cognitive and affec-
     tive goals may be achieved through choice of instruc-
     tional strategies in any particular subject area.
     Some of these strategies include: peer discussions
     of problems, values clarification techniques, role
     playing, simulation and games, and creative dramat-
     ics.

211. Waldorf, D. 1984. Enrichment as a part of gifted edu-
     cation. *Special Education in Canada* 58:139-40.

     The program described in this article shows how
     enrichment and gifted education can be combined to
     maximize learning experiences for bright and gifted
     students. The article also describes four pilot
     programs.

212. Washbourne, M. 1984. A school-based programme for
     gifted and talented students. *Gifted Education In-
     ternational* 2:134-37.

     This paper describes secondary science curricu-
     lum extension programs. Individual extension proj-

ects are developed from the core of the school curriculum and then extended into broader, more unusual
areas based on the students' particular interests.
Students are required to discuss their intended
goals, develop a plan of action, and contract to
complete the task.

213. Whitmore, J. 1981. Gifted children with handicapping
conditions: A new frontier. *Exceptional Children*
48:106-14.

The purpose of the article is to generate further interest and professional involvement and commitment in the identification and appropriate programming of gifted students with handicapping conditions. The author indicates that strategies and
programs developed for the handicapped have tended
to assume cognitive limits and often fail to provide
opportunities for self-directed learning, creative
self-expression, and exploration of the sciences and
the arts that are areas of critical programming for
gifted learners. The focus on educating gifted and
talented handicapped students has been on problems
rather than abilities. The article stresses that
more accurate means of identifying and developing
their abilities should be utilized as well as strategies for overcoming handicaps.

214. Wright, D., and S. DeMers. 1982. Comparison of the
relationship between two measures of visual-motor
coordination and academic achievement. *Psychology
in the Schools* 19:473-77.

This study involved a group of eighty-six elementary students. Their scores from a scoring system
for the Bender-Gestalt and Beery's Developmental
Test of Visual-Motor Integration were correlated
with Wide Range Achievement Test scores, controlling
for WISC-R IQ. Results suggested that visual-motor
ability may not contribute to the prediction of
achievement.

215. Yadusky-Holahan, M., and W. Hohahan. 1983. The effect
      of academic stress upon the anxiety and depression
      levels of gifted high-school students. *Gifted Child
      Quarterly* 1:42-46.

      The scores of sixty gifted twelfth graders on
      scales of anxiety and depression supported the hy-
      potheses that depression was significantly higher
      during the second testing than during baseline.
      Students in single rooms reported more age specific
      problems. Implications include the need to promote
      greater social interaction in residence halls.

216. Yarborough, B., and R. Johnson. 1983. Identifying the
      gifted: A theory practice gap. *Gifted Child Quar-
      terly* 27:135-38.

      Identifying the gifted child often arouses neg-
      ative feelings and charges of elitism. Thus far,
      the identification of the gifted child combines IQ
      tests, achievement tests, and behavioral checklists.
      Until there is a clearer operational definition de-
      veloped and applied as to who are the gifted in the
      schools, support for programs for the gifted will
      lag and will not be popularly endorsed.

217. Yewchuk, C. 1984. Learning disabilities among gifted
      children. *Special Education in Canada* 58:95-96.

      The purpose of this article was to state the
      importance of identifying the gifted child who is
      also learning disabled. Examples are given to show
      the need for detecting both conditions. When pro-
      gramming for this group, special attention should be
      paid to reducing external pressures on the child and
      maximizing opportunities for independent activity.

218. Zabel, M.K.; P.D. Dettmer; and R.H. Zabel. 1984. Fac-
      tors of emotional exhaustion, depersonalization, and
      sense of accomplishment among teachers of the gifted.
      Gifted Child Quarterly 28:65-69.

      Teachers of various types of exceptional stu-
      dents (LD, ED, SD, MS, HI, and Gifted) were given
      the Maslach Burnout Inventory (MBI) to measure fac-

tors involved in the experience of burnout. It was found that teachers of the gifted appeared at higher risk for emotional exhaustion than teachers in all other exceptionalities but emotionally disturbed and hearing impaired. However, depersonalization was relatively low among teachers of the gifted and teachers of the gifted rated highest on a sense of personal accomplishment.

CHAPTER III:
VISUAL IMPAIRMENTS

Impairment in the sense of vision often results in the individual's having a poor self-image. The disability itself is not as significant as the reactions of others. It is thus important for the teacher to recognize the child's strengths (as well as his/her limitations) in order to assist the child in gaining acceptance and achieving his/her potential.

Children who are visually impaired have received a formal education in this country since 1829, beginning with the incorporation of the New England Asylum for the Blind in Watertown, Massachusetts. The first public school for the teaching of Braille opened in Chicago in 1900, while the first public school for partially seeing children was opened in Boston in 1913. Today, in order to qualify for educational benefits, the visually impaired (handicapped) are defined as follows: Visually handicapped means a visual impairment which, even with correction, adversely affects a child's educational performance. The term includes both partially seeing and blind children.

Visually impaired children are placed in classes according to their academic ability. Children with 20/200 vision or less are placed in self-contained classes for the blind. Children with 20/200 and upward, but less than 20/70, are considered partially blind. Classes for the partially blind are not found today. Children who are partially blind retain little residual vision and can read very large print under very special conditions. The incidence of blindness and partial blindness is one of the lowest among the other disabilities. The incidence of mild defects, however, is high. Based on the definition, one in every 3000 children is blind, and one in every 500 children is partially blind.

Heredity appears to be the major cause of blindness, but accidents and disease also play a role. In the 1940s and 1950s, retrolental fibroplasia accounted for over half of all blindness in preschool children. It was found that incubators were sealed air-tight, resulting in the administration of an excessive amount of oxygen and causing this blinding disorder.

89

German measles epidemics resulted in the increase of multiple handicaps that included visual impairments. A vaccine for this has eliminated the problem to great extent.

Visually impaired children exhibit certain characteristics. A totally blind child will lack facial expression, may have disfigured eyes, and may be awkward handling himself in space. The partially blind child wearing thick lenses will hold objects or materials extremely close so that he can see them.

For fear of injury, the visually impaired are not encouraged to be mobile. Restriction and overprotection can be harmful, however, resulting in the development of undesirable social behavior such as rocking of the body, rolling of the head, moving fingers in front of the eyes, and poking oneself.

With the absence of the visual sense, auditory acuity becomes "sharper," helping the visually impaired child to listen to clues about his environment. Because learning cannot take place by visual cues or by imitation, it must occur through the other senses and through the use of concrete objects.

Since 1960, major changes have occurred in the education of the visually impaired. The majority of these children attend local schools and are placed in classes according to their achievement level. Services are administered through the resource room and by itinerant teachers. Teaching procedures and instructional materials are modified to meet the needs of the students, but educational goals remain the same as those for normal students.

Visually impaired children learn through active participation, and learning situations must include the use of the senses. Children must be taught spatial comprehension and relationships. They must learn the schoolroom setting including the locations of the teacher's desk, the clothes closet, and the wastepaper basket. Only in this way can these children function as other children do in the classroom.

Braille, a system of touch reading that makes use of embossed characters, must be taught to the visually handicapped. Games using braille can be included. Typing, which eliminates the problem of writing down the written word by hand, is also included in the curriculum in elementary school. Audio aids such as tapes, records, and talking books must be made part of the school materials and equipment. For the teaching of math, an abacus must be used and even a talking calculator. Maps must be embossed so that the child can learn geography and map reading by tactile means. For the visually impaired pupil, teaching must emphasize the auditory and tactile senses.

Despite its severity, blindness does not preclude learn-

ing or economic independence. However, modifications in the
regular school program must be made beforehand for the blind
child. There are different degrees of useful vision and skill
with respect to learning in the classroom and moving safely
through one's surroundings. Blind children constitute the
smallest group of exceptional learners. The content and methods of instruction for the blind and partially seeing are
essentially the same as those used with seeing children; only
the media differ--braille, audio materials, and large bold
type.

Visual impairments often result in a lack of control of
the environment and a minimal chance to acclimate oneself to
a new environment (without moving one's position). It is
thus not surprising that the visually impaired were among the
first to receive special educational services. Intelligence
and achievement tests reveal only slight, if at all, retardation for the visually impaired, albeit some evidence exists
of subtle cognitive differences in understanding abstract
ideas.

The effects of visual impairment on the individual vary
according to the age of onset, severity, and other environmental factors. In general, however, because of experiential
limitations, all pedagogical practices must be of a very concrete nature. Oftentimes extensive readiness programs may be
needed to train this group, so as to improve their fine and
gross motor skills, cognitive development, self-concept, and
social and self-help skills.

At rock bottom, the very best way to teach visually impaired children to accept and manage their handicaps is by
example. If the teachers and staff treat it matter-of-factly,
so will the children. Some emphasis is currently being placed
on parent education to aid in the early development of those
skills and attitudes crucial to later adaptation. Special
methods of training residual vision also have been, and are
being, developed.

Finally, progress in the education of the visually impaired is revealed by the fact that they are now being educated in local mainstreamed day school classes with the services of resource rooms and itinerant special teachers.

219.   Abang, T.B.   1985.   Blindism: Likely causes and preven-
       tive measures. *Journal of Visual Impairment & Blind-
       ness* 79:400-401.

              The article discusses why the phenomenon of
       blindism occurs in blind children.   Blindism is char-
       acterized by rocking back and forth or rolling the
       eyes for extended periods of time.   The two control
       groups used in a study of this phenomenon were chil-
       dren from Nigeria and from England--apparently in an
       effort to adequately represent both industrial and
       non-industrial countries.   The children of Nigeria
       demonstrated *less* of both behaviors based upon the
       test results.   This was believed to be due to the
       warmer, more intimate family structure.   The author
       also feels that lessened behavior is "... a result
       of being ill at ease in using gestures or moving,
       for fear of knocking something over or appearing
       awkward."   Blindism can be amended if detected early.

220.   Anderson, D.W.   1984.   Mental imagery in congenitally
       blind children. *Journal of Visual Impairment &
       Blindness* 78:206-9.

              A comparison was made in this study between the
       mental images of blind children and the mental images
       of sighted children.   Ten blind children and ten
       sighted children were interviewed and asked to de-
       scribe certain objects.   The author was attempting
       to find out if blind children could acquire as good
       a mental picture through their other senses as
       sighted children would through their vision.   His
       conclusion was that blind children seem to be able
       to construct their concepts of things through their
       experience just as sighted children would.   Many
       times in the experiment the children in both groups
       spoke about the same attributes of certain items.
       The author concluded that blind and sighted children
       should be able to communicate about mutually experi-
       enced objects on an equal basis.

221.   Arensman, D.   1975.   The role of the teacher for visu-
       ally handicapped in vision assessment. *Education
       for the Visually Handicapped* 7:5-8.

              The purpose of this article is to identify and

organize procedures and materials helpful to the
teacher of visually impaired children in assessing
students referred by such sources as the regular
classroom teacher, school nurse, principal, etc.

222. Awad, M.M., and J.L. Wise. 1984. Mainstreaming visually handicapped students in mathematics classes.
Mathematics Teacher 77:438-41.

The authors of this article believe that visually handicapped children should be mainstreamed in
regular classes and they offer certain suggestions
that they believe will help achieve this goal.
1. Blind students should have basically the same
responsibilities as other members of the class.
2. Teachers should be very descriptive and avoid
using words such as "this" and "that." For example,
do not allow students to confuse $x+y^2$ and $(x+y)^2$.
3. Allow blind students to explain their work and
not be required to write on the chalkboard.
4. Allow visually impaired students to take oral
exams.
5. Obtain an abacus and other valuable graphic aids.

223. Barton, L.E., and S.J. Lagrow. 1985. Reduction of
stereotypic responding in three visually impaired
children. *Education of the Visually Handicapped*
16:1-4.

It is common for people with visual impairment
to develop different kinds of repetitious, unnecessary motions. This study attempted to find out if
these behaviors could be eliminated through the use
of momentary restraint and differential reinforcement. One particular child exhibited head weaving.
When this would occur, his head would be held still
for three seconds. When the behavior did not occur
for a certain set amount of time, he was given a
particular reward that he had previously seemed to
enjoy. The experiment was performed with three children who had exhibited different nonfunctional movements. The rate at which the behavior occurred
dropped for all three children as a result of the
procedure. The test showed that these unnecessary
behaviors can, apparently, be controlled. It would
be most interesting to attempt a similar experiment

using only one treatment instead of two, conclude
the authors.

224. Bauer-Dibble, F.J. 1984. Focus on the hands: A beginning approach to teaching typing to visually impaired, multiply handicapped students. *Journal of
Visual Impairment & Blindness* 10:345-48.

In this article, the author gives her rationale
for a good typing curriculum. Typing is a skill
that visually impaired and multiply handicapped students need, and finger and hand exercises increase
dexterity and strength of such beginning typing students. She describes the students' abilities before
and after typing instruction, and the hand and finger
exercises she used to motivate students to become
skilled in writing with the typewriter.

225. Bekiares, S.E. 1984. Technology for the handicapped:
Selection and evaluation of aids and devices for the
visually impaired. *Library Hi Tech* 2:57-61.

This article provides a bibliographic essay on
recent books and articles dealing with problems of
providing library services to the disabled, particularly the visually impaired, and to sources that
describe technological equipment in detail. It also
suggests ways to identify libraries that use special
equipment such as large type and reading machines.

226. Berla, E.P., and L.H. Butterfield, Jr. 1975. Teachers'
views on tactile maps for blind students: Problems
and needs. *Education of the Visually Handicapped*
7:116-18.

The use of tactile maps with blind students has
presented problems for the classroom teacher and
consequently teachers do not use them to any great
extent in the classroom. As a result blind students
have little experience with maps and do not develop
map reading skills, knowledge of maps, or geographi-
cal concepts. An open-ended questionnaire survey
was undertaken to determine the nature of the problems. The responses were classified and presented
in four categories: conceptual and experiential pre-

requisites to map reading; materials; map symbology; and design, inspection and use of tactile maps.

227. Bernstein, G.B. 1979. Integration of vision stimulation in the classroom I: Individual programming. *Education of the Visually Handicapped* 11:14-17.

This is the first of three articles written to share ideas about vision stimulation for multiply handicapped blind children. Descriptions of selected children at Upsal Day School are provided, along with the medical and educational information needed to understand this population. Necessary changes made in their programs to facilitate enhanced visual functioning are detailed.

228. Bernstein, G.B. 1979. Integration of vision stimulation in the classroom II: Group programming. *Education of the Visually Handicapped* 11:39-47.

In this article the author describes specific classroom activities and materials that can be used with visually impaired, multihandicapped children who are functioning at a level high enough to be taught in a group. Objectives and areas of development are presented for each group of activities. In addition, specific suggestions are made for modifications to meet individual needs.

229. Bernstein, G.B. 1979. Integration of vision stimulation in the classroom III: A total approach. *Education of the Visually Handicapped* 11:80-84.

Integrating vision into a visually impaired child's activities is an important factor to consider when planning the child's educational program. This final article in the series (see entries 227 and 228) discusses a program developed cooperatively by a vision stimulation specialist and a classroom teacher at the Upsal Day School in Philadelphia. Classroom goals are stated and activities described that include visual behaviors as a focal part of each activity.

230. Brothers, R.J. 1974. Classroom use of the Braille
      Code Recognition materials. *Education of the Visu-
      ally Handicapped* 6:6-13.

          The primary purpose of this project was to de-
      velop an instructional kit that would prepare teach-
      ers to use the Braille Code Recognition (BCR) mate-
      rials developed and validated by Umsted (1970) and
      Henderson (1967). Subsequent evaluations were to
      determine the effectiveness of the teacher instruc-
      tions and the effect of the use of these materials
      on the Braille reading skills of visually handicapped
      students. The present account has focused on the
      use of the materials in the classroom.

231. Bryan, W.H., and D.L. Jeffrey. 1982. Education of
      visually handicapped students in the regular class-
      room. *Texas Technical Journal of Education* 9:125-31.

          Problems the visually handicapped child is
      likely to encounter in a regular mainstream classroom
      are discussed in this study. Suggestions are then
      presented as to educational modes and methods teach-
      ers can use to meet the special needs of the visually
      impaired student in the regular classroom. The stu-
      dents' special needs are met while still maintaining
      the focus on learning activities for all classroom
      students.

232. Cetera, M. 1983. Laboratory adaptations for visually
      impaired students: Thirty years in review. *Journal
      of College Science Teaching* 12:384-393.

          This study presents a critical review of the
      laboratory adaptations developed over the past thirty
      years for visually impaired students in general
      science, biology, chemistry, and physics. It also
      addresses learning models used by these students and
      ways in which students benefit working independently
      in a science laboratory.

233. Champion, R.R. 1976. The talking calculator used with
      blind youth. *Education of the Visually Handicapped*
      8:102-6.

          This study demonstrated that blind children in
      grades three through eight were able to achieve
      greater speed and accuracy in mathematics computation
      using a talking calculator after one hour of indi-
      vidualized instruction and three weeks of informal
      practice. Implications for modifications in opera-
      tional procedures are also discussed.

234. Civelli, E. 1983. Verbalism in young blind children.
      Journal of Visual Impairment & Blindness 77:61-63.

          This study reviews the literature regarding the
      development of verbal language by sighted and blind
      children. The study concludes that there are no
      gross differences in the language of intellectually
      normal sighted and blind people when they become
      adolescents.

235. Clayton, I. 1983. Career preparation and the visually
      handicapped student. *Education of the Visually
      Handicapped* 14:115-20.

          The high school program should include career
      preparation for blind and visually handicapped stu-
      dents. The teacher should emphasize preparation
      skills that include work skills, basic skills, and
      awareness of aptitudes, interests, and family or
      peer influences. The preparation phase ends with
      the placement of the visually impaired student in
      further education, training, or full-time employment.

236. Corn, A.L. 1985. An independence matrix for visually
      handicapped learners. *Education of the Visually
      Handicapped* 17:3-10.

          The author of this article is concerned that
      visually handicapped students develop the indepen-
      dence to function in society. She gives an example
      of a fourth grade student who has to go to the lunch-
      room. One approach would be to allow the child to
      go a few minutes early by himself to avoid the

crowds. This, however, causes the student to be separated from his classmates and appear different or privileged. A better way, according to the author, is to develop within the student the ability to take care of himself. The student should identify the possible ways to get to the lunchroom, e.g., use a cane, walk independently, use a sighted guide, or hold a friend's hand. The student should then be encouraged to make his own decision as to the best way to get to the lunchroom. This approach teaches independence and problem solving to the youngster which is very important for his future life.

237. Corn, A.L., and V.E. Bishop. 1984. Acquisition of practical knowledge by blind and visually impaired students in grades 8-12. *Journal of Visual Impairment & Blindness* 10:352-55.

   In this study, 116 blind and visually impaired adolescents in public and residential schools in Texas were tested to measure their acquisition of practical knowledge. Most of the demographic variables were found to have little or no relationship to acquired practical knowledge. However, it was found that legally blind, visually impaired students had more difficulty in acquiring practical knowledge than did their totally blind peers.

238. Couvillon, L.A., and P.E. Tait. 1982. A sensory experience model for teaching measurement. *Journal of Visual Impairment & Blindness* 76:262-68.

   This teaching model for the visually impaired student addresses teaching the concepts of area, temperature, capacity, weight, volume, angles, and money or value. It was developed for children in Grades kindergarten through eight.

239. Cunningham, D. 1983. Educating the visually impaired, severely-to-profoundly retarded child: A long range perspective. *Education of the Visually Handicapped* 15:95-100.

   Developments in the education of the visually impaired, severely-to-profoundly retarded population

are examined in this article. Current trends using
functional curricula, particularly with the adolescent, are explained. The article concludes by pro-
posing a framework for the future by narrowing the
range and scope of individual programs dealing with
life goals.

240.   Daugherty, K.M., and M.F. Moran. 1982. Neuro-
       psychological, learning and developmental character-
       istics of the low vision child. *Journal of Visual
       Impairment & Blindness* 76:398-406.

            This study administered the Halstead-Reitan
       Neuropsychological Tests, Stephen's Piagetian Battery
       of Reasoning Assessments, and Standardized Achieve-
       ment tests to fifty low vision children, aged seven
       to eighteen years. The author used the case study
       method on 143 variables. The results indicated that
       there were significant delays in cognitive and psy-
       chomotor development and academic achievement with
       these visually impaired children.

241.   Davis, P.A. 1984. Helping the visually impaired child
       succeed in school. *Exceptional Parent* 14:35-38.

            The author provides the parents of visually
       impaired children with suggestions for helping to
       make school a success. Guidelines begin with infancy
       and deal with topics related to the preschool period
       such as providing special experiences and teaching
       social skills. They include the school-age period
       and important decisions such as school placement.

242.   Doorlag, D. 1983. Cassette Braille: A new communica-
       tion tool for blind people. *Journal of Visual Im-
       pairment & Blindness* 77:158-61.

            In this article, the author discusses the advan-
       tages of using the Versa Braille System over the
       standard mechanical Braille. The Versa Braille Sys-
       tem incorporates cassettes with Braille that resulted
       in promoting reading and writing rates in the San
       Diego unified school district. It was also more
       easily and quietly operated than the mechanical
       Brailler.

243. Douglas, S., and S. Mangold. 1975. Precision teaching of visually impaired students. *Education of the Visually Handicapped* 7:48-52.

This article discusses precision teaching, a tool designed to supplement a teacher's existing program. Precision teaching is a technique for measuring a student's improvement in basic skills. Any subject matter ranging from reading and math to appropriate classroom behavior can be precision taught. This article discusses the five parts of this technique and the mastery level established for many subskills.

244. Efron, M., and G.H. Lackey, Jr. 1982. Arithmetic test performance of low vision adolescents using two modes of magnification. *Journal for Special Education* 18: 76-82.

The findings of this study suggest the potential uses of a special device for visually impaired or low vision students. It was discovered that the Visolett, a small magnification device, was as effective as large print materials for forty-five visually handicapped adolescents performing arithmetic tasks. The device is intended to be a supplement to large print materials.

245. Ferry, D. 1981. Don't spoil the child. *Education of the Visually Handicapped* 13:25-30.

The article discusses how attempting to change behaviors in a visually impaired student takes more than a braille writer, braille books, or large print materials. It takes that special someone, a teacher who will go beyond the definition of teacher to provide the missing eighty-five percent of visual learning that the visually impaired child is lacking.

246. Franks, F.L., and R. Glass. 1985. Microslide cassette programs for low vision students. *Education of the Visually Handicapped* 17:11-16.

The authors of this article examined something called the microslide viewer to find out if it would

be useful to visually impaired students who have
some residual vision. It would be used for the same
purpose that a fully sighted student would use a
microscope. The conclusion was that the microslide
viewer is very valuable for visually impaired students. Audio tapes were developed to be used in
concert with the slides. The researchers found that
these tapes enabled students to concentrate on the
slides without being distracted by having to shift
to braille pages. It was also found that completely
blind students benefited from these audio tapes.

247. Gardner, L.R. 1985. Low vision enhancement: The use
      of figure-ground reversals with visually impaired
      children. *Journal of Visual Impairment & Blindness*
      79:64-68.

         Printed material usually comes with black words
      on a white background. This study was an attempt to
      find out if figure-ground reversals--putting white
      or yellow words against a black background--would
      help a visually impaired reader. The results of the
      experiment indicated no evidence to suggest that
      figure-ground reversals would be effective in helping
      a visually impaired person. The major factor that
      should be considered when processing materials for
      the visually impaired is the luminance contrast--how
      dark are the letters in comparison to the background,
      or how dark is the background in comparison to the
      print.

248. Goodrich, G. 1984. Applications of microcomputers by
      visually impaired persons. *Journal of Visual Impair-
      ment & Blindness* 78:408-14.

         The uses of microcomputers by sighted, blind,
      and visually impaired individuals is the subject of
      this article. The strengths and weaknesses of adap-
      tive aids and their specific applications are dis-
      cussed. Also examined in this article is the need
      for additional resources for training and equipping
      visually impaired computer users. The author calls
      for efforts to ensure equal computer access.

249. Griffin, H.C., and P.J. Gerber. 1982. Tactual development and its implications for the education of blind children. *Education of the Visually Handicapped* 13:116-23.

    The purpose of this article is to explore and provide practical application for the developmental aspects of tactual modality. This system was developed based on the concept that the key to tactual modality rests upon knowledge of tactual development synthesized with activities for appropriate stimulation and skill acquisition.

250. Hall, A. 1983. Methods of equivalence grouping by congenitally blind children: Implications for education. *Journal of Visual Impairment & Blindness* 77:172-74.

    In this study, the author discusses ways in which congenitally blind children group objects and words. Different groupings can give us an idea of the level of cognitive development of the child. The author also discusses the implication of these findings for the education of this population.

251. Head, D.N. 1980. The stability of self-concept scores in visually impaired adolescents. *Education of the Visually Handicapped* 12:66-74.

    The stability of self-concept from junior to senior high school was examined for sixty-two blind and low vision adolescents in residential, resource room, and itinerant class placements. While no significant differences for this group were determined as a function of grade level or visual loss, a significant interaction effect between these variables did occur. A further analysis of the data showed a notable increase in self-concept scores for the low vision subjects (N=39) as a function of their grade-level placement.

252. Hill, E.W.; D.A. Guth; and M.M. Hill. 1985. Spatial
      concept instruction for children with low vision.
      Education of the Visually Handicapped 16:6-9.

          The authors of this article point out the im-
      portance of teaching spatial concepts to children
      with low vision. These concepts (near, far, next
      to, etc.) are learned automatically by children with
      normal vision. They are very important for all chil-
      dren because as soon as a child gets to school, he
      can be told to sign at the "top" of the paper or go
      the "back" of the line. This vocabulary is obviously
      important for children with low vision. The article
      ends by saying that we should research the best ways
      to teach these ideas to low sight children and not
      assume that they will know them by themselves.

253. Hill, E.W., and M.M. Hill. 1982. The use of the Dis-
      crepancy Evaluation Model in evaluating educational
      programs for visually handicapped persons. *Education
      of the Visually Handicapped* 14:2-11.

          The purpose of this article was to provide a
      brief rationale for the importance of evaluating
      educational programs and to describe in detail a
      widely used program evaluation model--The Discrepancy
      Evaluation Model. An application for this model was
      provided using an orientation and mobility program
      at a hypothetical residential school for the visually
      handicapped.

254. Hodgson, A. 1985. How to integrate the visually im-
      paired. *British Journal of Special Education* 12:35-
      37.

          Examined in this article are the types of plan-
      ning and school and classroom organization necessary
      to mainstream visually impaired students. Many gen-
      eral teaching techniques and adaptations and modifi-
      cations to the traditional classroom are suggested.

255.   Hubbard, C.L. 1983. Reverse mainstreaming sighted
       children into a visually impaired special day class.
       Journal of Visual Impairment & Blindness 77:193-95.

            This article talks about the academic and social
       benefits to both groups of mainstreaming sighted
       children into a visually impaired special class.

256.   Jackson, R.M. 1983. Early educational use of optical
       aids. A cautionary note. *Education of the Visually
       Handicapped* 15:20-29.

            In this study the author traces the change from
       the sight conservation era to the one advocating
       maximum use of remaining vision. Some caution re-
       garding the early educational uses of optical aids
       with visually impaired children is indicated.

257.   Kirkman, R.E. 1983. Career awareness and the visually
       impaired student. *Education of the Visually Handi-
       capped* 15:105-14.

            This article discusses thirteen different career
       awareness and career exploration modules that were
       developed for use in regular class settings. These
       modules were adopted for blind and visually impaired
       elementary and secondary students during 1981 and
       1982.

258.   Koenig, M.S.; C.G. Mack; W.A. Schenk; and S.C. Ashcroft.
       1985. Developing writing and word processing skills
       with visually impaired children: A beginning. *Jour-
       nal of Visual Impairment & Blindness* 79:308-12.

            Visually impaired children face certain problems
       as they try to develop basic skills. Reading is
       difficult for them because the process of reading
       braille is much slower than reading the printed word.
       Writing is difficult for them to master because it
       is very hard for them to correct and revise something
       printed in braille. It is also difficult for teach-
       ers to provide feedback on what has been written.
       With a braille word processor, a blind student can
       revise and correct his work by himself. He can also
       learn the skill of writing in a manner similar to

the sighted public. This new technology is a big
step towards normalizing the education of visually
impaired people.

259. Kornswiet, D.K., and G.D. Yarnall. 1981. Increasing
attending to tasks and completion of tasks with an
easily distracted, visually impaired eleven-year-
old. *Education of the Visually Handicapped* 13:84-90.

The author presents a case study of an eleven-
year-old visually impaired child in an elementary
school. The on-task behavior of the child increased
from forty-nine percent to ninety-six percent over a
nine-week period when the child received tokens and
social reinforcement for on-task behavior and assign-
ment completion. Positive reinforcement contributed
to behavior modification.

260. Kronheim, J.K. 1985. Home grown toys: The learning
pillows. *Journal of Visual Impairment & Blindness*
79:158-59.

This article describes the learning pillow, a
special toy for visually impaired children. The
pillow has various textures that are designed to
stimulate the child's imagination. Children will be
able to learn spatial concepts, directionality, and
many other concepts while having a good time with
these learning pillows.

261. Lagrow, S.J. 1981. Effects of training on CCTV reading
rates of visually impaired students. *Journal of Visual Impairment & Blindness* 75:368-73.

Lagrow presents his investigative findings on
the effects of a closed circuit television (CCTV)
system on the reading rates of six visually impaired,
college-bound students aged sixteen to eighteen years
old. Systematic instruction in the use of closed
circuit television was administered to the students.
The results reveal that the reading rates of all the
students increased, regardless of the direction of
change exhibited in the preceding phase.

262. LaSasso, C.J., and T.W. Jones. 1984. A survey of approaches to teaching reading to visually impaired students in residential schools. *Journal of Visual Impairment & Blindness* 78:263-64.

A survey was conducted to determine which approach to teaching reading was most widely used at residential schools for the blind. Fifty-four percent of the responding schools were using basal readers, thirteen percent were using the programmed approach, eleven percent the language experience approach, and ten percent the individualized approach. Basal readers are common because they form a structured approach that systematically develops vocabulary and other vital skills.

263. Loeschke, M. 1977. Mime: A movement program for the visually handicapped. *Journal of Visual Impairment & Blindness* 71:337-45.

Describes an experimental study with two groups of subjects to determine whether mime techniques are useful for teaching movement to the visually handicapped. Includes class and subject descriptions, evaluation methods developed, and detailed observations of selected subjects.

264. Lowenfeld, B. 1982. In search of better ways. *Education of the Visually Handicapped* 14:69-77.

This article reviews the history of education for visually handicapped students in the twentieth century. The intent is to make the teacher of visually impaired students aware of educational trends, student placement, and visually handicapped mobility. Noted are the establishment of residential schools for the visually impaired, gradual integration into public school classes, appearances of "talking books," and beginning efforts in orientation and mobility.

265. Maddux, C.D.; D. Cates; and V. Sowell. 1984. Finger-
     math for the visually impaired: An intrasubject de-
     sign. *Journal of Visual Impairment & Blindness*
     78:7-9.

     The authors of this study attempted to find out
     whether fingermath is a good alternative to the aba-
     cus as a means of teaching arithmetic to visually
     impaired children. The advantages of fingermath are
     that no extra materials are needed, no outside help
     is necessary, and it is more concrete for the chil-
     dren than an abacus. The study found that children
     were able to master fingermath very quickly and that,
     after an expected slow beginning, the test scores
     when fingermath was used were very high.

266. Malone, L., and L. DeLucchi. 1979. Life science for
     visually impaired students. *Science & Children*
     16:29-31.

     Life science activities for visually impaired
     elementary school students are explored in this ar-
     ticle. The researchers describe such science educa-
     tion activities for the blind or visually handicapped
     student as aquarium studies, plant germination,
     classroom animals, and outdoor activities. All these
     educational activities are designed with a multi-
     sensory approach.

267. McConnel, J. 1984. Integration of visually handicapped
     students in industrial education classes: An over-
     view. *Journal of Visual Impairment & Blindness*
     78:319-20; 322; 324.

     Visually impaired secondary students can be
     successfully mainstreamed into industrial education
     classes as long as careful selection, placement, and
     planning decisions have been made. This article
     concerns techniques for teaching machine-tool opera-
     tions along with the use of aids developed specifi-
     cally for visually impaired students.

268. McCrimmon, S. 1974. Programmed instruction as a means of teaching blind children addition and subtraction on the abacus. *Education of the Visually Handicapped* 6:72-79.

    The abacus, an ancient device almost as old as the number system itself, has been adapted for and used by blind students. This study demonstrated that for some blind children programmed instruction was an effective means of teaching basic abacus skills. The program contains a large number of systematically sequenced calculation items written with specific reference to the principles of abacus calculation.

269. McIntire, J.C. 1985. The future of residential schools for visually impaired students. *Journal of Visual Impairment & Blindness* 79:161-63.

    This article reviews the role of residential schools for the visually impaired in the past and gives a prediction as to their role in the future. At one time, residential schools were very popular for visually impaired students. However, for a number of reasons these students soon began attending public schools. Among other things, the residential schools caused segregation between the blind and sighted children, the blind children were not able to live at home with their families, and the graduates of the residential schools did not impress people with their skills. Now, with the Education for All Handicapped Children Act (P.L. 94-142) which states that handicapped children are to be educated in the least restrictive way possible, public schools are even more popular for visually impaired students. The author concludes that the future of residential schools lies in educating multiply handicapped children. These students with a variety of problems would not do well in a public school setting and would be best served by residential schools.

270. Merbler, J.B., and T.A. Wood. 1984. Predicting orien-
     tation and mobility proficiency in mentally retarded
     visually impaired children. *Education and Training
     of the Mentally Retarded* 19:228-30.

          The mobility skills of thirty-seven mentally
     retarded visually impaired children in the elementary
     and secondary schools were examined to see if there
     exists a relationship between chronological age,
     social age, motor, sensory, and concept skills, and
     mobility skills. Results of this study revealed a
     strong relationship between developmental levels in
     the areas of motor, sensory, and concept skills, and
     mobility proficiency.

271. Miller, J.W. 1982. Development of an audio-tutorial
     system for teaching basic geographic concepts. *Edu-
     cation of the Visually Handicapped* 13:109-15.

          In an attempt to teach visually impaired stu-
     dents on the elementary and secondary level, an in-
     structional system was developed in which visually
     impaired students listen to audio cassettes or Dobbie
     tapes to learn basic geographic terms and concepts.
     The program includes tapes, land form models, and a
     teacher's manual.

272. Moore, S.B. 1982. Student-Use educational materials
     developed for the multihandicapped, visually im-
     paired. *Journal of Special Education Technology*
     5:26-27.

          This study reviews new materials developed for
     young, multihandicapped, visually impaired students
     by the Educational Research Department of the Ameri-
     can Printing House for the Blind. They include sen-
     sory stimulation art, prevocational materials, low-
     vision stimulation materials, and a home based media
     program for developing critical skills in young blind
     children.

273.   Moore, S.B. 1984. The need for programs and services
        for visually handicapped infants. *Education of the
        Visually Handicapped* 16:7-9.

             This article underlines the importance of early
        intervention in the education of visually impaired
        children. Studies are quoted that show that children
        who received early help were much more likely to be
        self-supportive by the age of twenty-one. The best
        place for this early intervention is the home because
        the child needs to develop in his/her natural envi-
        ronment. Therefore, teachers must be prepared to
        work together with parents and set up certain ground
        rules governing the home environment when the ses-
        sions are in progress.

274.   Morris, O.F. 1981. Teacher assessment of visual func-
        tioning. *Education of the Visually Handicapped*
        13:42-50.

             A dilemma occurs when the teacher of a visually
        handicapped student attempts to formulate a statement
        of current level of performance for an I.E.P. (Indi-
        vidualized Educational Program) based solely on a
        report from an eye specialist. The author describes
        a group of teacher-made activities that can be used
        to assess visual functioning, outlines various types
        of activities, suggests samples of each, and shows
        ways to organize material and record observations.

275.   Morrison, R., and D. Lunney. 1984. The microcomputer
        as a laboratory aid for visually impaired science
        students. *Journal of Visual Impairment & Blindness*
        78:418-25.

             The importance of instruments in science and
        technology are discussed in this article. The devel-
        opment, operations, uses, and software of the Uni-
        versal Laboratory Training and Research Aid (ULTRA)
        are outlined. ULTRA is a portable talking laboratory
        computer that enables visually impaired students to
        perform independently important instrumental measure-
        ments and other laboratory experiments.

276. Nater, P. 1982. An electronic teaching device for
      blind students. *Journal of Visual Impairment &
      Blindness* 76:274-78.

          This author's research was done in the early
      seventies, and addresses the comparative efficiency
      of an electronic teaching system for programmed in-
      struction and a conventional brailled book program
      for teaching seventh and eighth grade blind students
      to spell.

277. Nolan, C.Y., and J.E. Morris. 1969. Learning by blind
      students through active and passive listening. *Ex-
      ceptional Children* 36:173-81.

          Studies were conducted comparing learning
      achieved by blind students at different grade levels
      for three types of material presented at normal and
      compressed rates under conditions of active and pas-
      sive listening. Findings support the theory that
      active participation in the listening process results
      in greater learning.

278. Olson, M.R. 1977. Teaching faster braille reading in
      the primary grades. *Journal of Visual Impairment
      & Blindness* 71:122-24.

          Recent studies have reported considerable suc-
      cess in teaching the visually handicapped techniques
      of rapid reading. Most of the braille readers par-
      ticipating in these studies had been reading for
      several years. Little if any efforts in the past
      had been made toward application of rapid reading
      principles in the primary grades. This article iden-
      tifies twelve rapid reading principles and discusses
      their implementation by itinerant or resource teach-
      ers of beginning braille readers.

279. Olson, M.R. 1981. Writing a visual assessment report.
      Education of the Visually Handicapped 13:21-23.

          The purpose of this paper is to present guide-
      lines on writing a visual assessment report on visu-
      ally handicapped students for purposes of evaluation
      or for writing an individualized education program.

Topics to be covered as well as steps in preparing and writing the report are discussed. Such an assessment is designed to aid the classroom teacher in administering the proper program for the visually impaired child.

280. Orlansky, M.D. 1982. Education of visually impaired children in the U.S.A.; Current issues in service delivery. *Exceptional Child* 29:13-20.

The paper discusses current issues in the education of visually handicapped children with emphasis on appropriate educational placement. A review of the literature suggests that a dichotomy exists between advocates of public school and residential school programs, with differing interpretations of how P.L. 94-142 (The Education for All Handicapped Children Act) will affect educational placement of the visually impaired. The author concludes that both public school and residential programs will continue to operate and that cooperation between them may increase thus creating a favorable climate for the provision of a continuum of appropriate educational services for visually impaired children.

281. Ricker, K.S., and N.C. Rodgers. 1981. Modifying instructional materials for use with visually impaired students. *American Biology Teacher* 43:490-92; 501.

Various ways to adapt commercially or teacher-prepared educational aids are illustrated in this study. The instructional needs of the visually impaired students are accommodated while retaining useability by sighted students. The authors focus on tactile changes involving cutout figures, raised surfaces, and punched holes. This is especially relevant for the secondary school science teacher.

282. Roessler, R.T., and S.E. Boone. 1979. Locus of control, self-esteem, and hope for individuals with visual impairments. *Rehabilitation Counseling Bulletin* 22:448-50.

Visually impaired students in a facility for the visually handicapped were administered the

Rotter's Scale of Beliefs, Rosenberg's Self-Esteem
Scale, and Cantril's Self-Anchoring Striving Scale.
The study confirms the prediction that external locus
of control was related to low self-esteem. Neither
of the variables was related to hope.

283. Rogow, S.M. 1981. Appreciation of riddles by blind
and visually handicapped children. *Education of the
Visually Handicapped* 13:4-10.

This study supports the hypothesis that visually
handicapped children are able to recognize and resolve riddles at the same age as sighted children.
The study used two groups—one sighted and one visually handicapped. Both groups were seven to eight
years of age.

284. Rogow, S.M. 1984. Uses of social routines to facilitate communication in visually impaired and multi-
handicapped children. *Topics in Early Childhood
Special Education* 3:64-70.

Communicative skills were developed by using
social routines based on rhyming verses presented by
adults to visually impaired young children with additional handicaps. The fields of interaction,
games, and social development were all part of this
study on communicative responses.

285. Roscoe, B., and K.L. Peterson. 1983. Teacher attitudes
toward material availability for teaching visually
impaired students. *Reading Improvements* 20:239-44.

This study reports that regular classroom teachers with visually impaired students believed that
preservice and inservice training would be useful in
teaching the handicapped. These teachers also felt
that specialized materials were needed to teach such
students. The study concerns visually impaired students in both the elementary and secondary schools.
The article concludes with the fact that although
the teachers felt that training and materials would
be beneficial, they thought that they were not available.

286. Rossi, P. 1980. Closed circuit television--A method
      of reading. *Education of the Visually Handicapped*
      12:90-94.

          This article discusses how two relatively new
      possibilities can now be added to the five accepted
      methods of reading for students with visual impair-
      ments. The five accepted methods are: regular print,
      large print, braille, tape, and reader service. The
      two relatively new possibilities are: paperless
      braille and closed circuit television. The author
      discusses the technical aspects, versatility, and
      economics of reading with closed circuit television.

287. Rouse, M.W., and J.B. Ryan. 1984. Teacher's guide to
      vision problems. *Reading Teacher* 38:306-17.

          Problems in the areas of visual acuity, visual
      skills efficiency, and visual perceptual-motor devel-
      opment are looked at in depth by the authors. They
      point out symptoms that children may exhibit and
      offer suggestions for what teachers can do to help.
      The teacher must first accurately identify the visual
      impairment and then plan an effective management
      program. Charts dealing with the visual impairment
      and corresponding classroom management are presented.

288. School, G.T. 1983. Bridges from research to practice
      in education of visually handicapped people. *Journal
      of Visual Impairment & Blindness* 77:340-44.

          Five dissemination models that may ensure that
      research findings are translated into practice are
      described in this article. Current research findings
      in seven areas (such as technology, curriculum, and
      early intervention) related to education for visually
      handicapped people are summarized, together with
      recommended dissemination procedures.

289. Schwartz, T.J. 1983. Social cognition in visually
      impaired and sighted children. *Journal of Visual
      Impairment & Blindness* 77:377-81.

          This article discusses findings on the compari-
      son of spatial role taking, social role taking, and

referential communication in fifty-six congenitally
visually impaired and sighted children (seven to
nine years old) that revealed that visually impaired
students need not differ from sighted students in
cognitive social functioning if they have had significant verbal interaction with others.

290. Sloane, S. 1983. Teaching the handicapped imagination.
     Education of the Visually Handicapped 15:88-94.

This article describes a series of exercises in
drama and creative writing that the author feels
will broaden the imagination of visually handicapped
children. The article suggests that teachers write
stories and poems with nonvisual imagery in mind,
and that they present them to a visually handicapped
class with the purpose of inspiring the class to
write their own stories and poems. (Examples of
stories and poems are included.)

291. Steele, A.L., and C. Crawford. 1982. Music therapy
     for the visually impaired. *Education of the Visually
     Handicapped* 14:56-62.

The article discusses the development and implementation of a music therapy program to achieve behavioral changes in visually impaired children and
adolescents. Goals targeted by a music therapist
include altering unusual body movements, poor posture, and other mannerisms often associated with
visual impairments.

292. Sullivan, F. 1984. The Retinitis Pigmentosa student:
     Selected aspects. *Education of the Visually Handi-
     capped* 16:30-35.

The characteristic features of RP (Retinitis
Pigmentosa--an untreatable condition usually resulting in night blindness) are discussed. Functioning
considerations in the classroom that include the use
of protective devices and mobility aids are outlined.
Classroom modifications such as darklined paper and
black pens are suggested.

293. Swanson, H.L. 1977. Effect of positive reinforcement on visual academic performance with a partially sighted child. *Education of the Visually Handicapped* 9:72-76.

    A multiple baseline design was used to assess the effects of positive reinforcement on a partially sighted child's visual academic performance. Tasks of matching and counting number sets without teacher or tactual cues were assessed under conditions of primary reinforcement (M&M's) and primary reinforcement paired with social praise. Academic accuracy increased from a baseline rate of approximately forty-five percent for both behaviors to an overall treatment rate of eighty-five percent. Pairing primary reinforcement with praise in the classroom setting had the most pronounced effect upon academic behavior. Follow-up procedures indicated that visual academic behavior was maintained at an accuracy level above eighty percent. Implications for teachers are discussed.

294. Tait, P.E., and M.B. Ward. 1984. The comprehension of verbal humor by visually impaired children. *Journal of Visual Impairment & Blindness* 76:144-47.

    The purpose of this study was to compare the ability of fifty-one visually impaired and fifty-one sighted children, aged seven to fifteen, to comprehend verbal humor in the form of jokes. The results indicate that visually impaired children can comprehend humor as well as do their sighted peers.

295. Terrell, L.W. 1981. Children's attitudes toward visual impairment: The effects of a teaching unit. *Education of the Visually Handicapped* 13:68-76.

    This paper discusses a study conducted to consider the effects of a short-term teaching unit in correcting misinformation and increasing positive attitudes toward visually impaired persons on the part of sighted elementary school children. Twenty-seven fifth grade children were exposed to a three-session teaching unit related to visual impairment. An attitude questionnaire was administered in a pretest post-test format. The increase in positive re-

sponse following the teaching unit suggests that
such a unit could be useful in helping sighted children develop realistic and positive attitudes toward
visually impaired persons.

296. Thomas, J.E. 1979. Factors influencing the integration
      of visually impaired children. *Journal of Visual
      Impairment & Blindness* 73:359-64.

          Research findings are presented on the integra-
      tion of sixty-one visually handicapped children,
      ranging in age from eight years to twenty-two years
      old. The effects of age, grade placement, visual
      acuity, sex, arithmetic, and reading achievement
      were factors under investigation. The success fac-
      tors of these visually handicapped children inte-
      grated into the mainstream are presented in this
      article.

297. Thurman, D. 1983. Career education and teacher atti-
      tudes. *Education of the Visually Handicapped* 14:133-
      39.

          This article surveys teachers' views at two
      North American schools for the blind concerning occu-
      pations appropriate for visually impaired print and
      braille readers. The teachers tended to hold the
      stereotyped ideas that blind people are good musi-
      cians, are good with their hands, or should be in a
      profession.

298. Traun, M.B. 1984. Starting right: Selecting the opti-
      mum beginning placement for visually impaired chil-
      dren. *Topics in Early Childhood Special Education*
      3:71-77.

          The author discusses the full range of educa-
      tional supports required for complete services to
      visually impaired students entering school. The
      article also describes key characteristics of young
      blind children and presents guidelines for assessing
      school-age visually impaired children for purposes
      of proper student placement.

299. Trevelyan, S. 1984. Handmade multi-textured maps. *Journal of Visual Impairment & Blindness* 78:75.

    Tactile maps with raised lines can be made by the teacher with relative ease for visually impaired students. The materials are not difficult to obtain or make. First, lines are drawn with an aqueous adhesive solution, and then dusted with a thermo-engraving powder. Lastly, the map is exposed to a source of intense heat, such as a microwave oven. A raised line map results.

300. Vander Kolk, C.J. 1979. A school-community agency project for visually handicapped children. *Journal of Visual Impairment & Blindness* 73:140-43.

    A model public school and community project for visually impaired children is described in this article. The project, involving community agencies and workshops, provides assessment and supportive services for mainstreaming visually handicapped children. All the actively participating ancillary services, public community agencies, and school community programs are mentioned in this article.

301. Wagener, E.H. 1979. Drama: Key to history for the visually impaired child. *Education of the Visually Handicapped* 9:45-46.

    This article describes a method for the use of dramatic improvisation as an appropriate approach to the teaching of history to visually impaired children. Emphasis is upon inducing pupils' projections of the personalities, feelings, and thought processes of major historical figures.

302. Williams, J.M. 1984. Technology and the handicapped. *American Education* 20:27-30.

    With the development of synthetic speech and talking computers there are exciting new opportunities for visually impaired people. The terminals are able to produce sixty-four different phonemes and a microprocessor converts these sounds into language. This gives visually impaired people an equal

opportunity in math, spelling, writing, computer
literacy, as well as many other fields.

303. Wilson, L.D., and S.J. Pine. 1985. The word test:
     Language assessment of elementary age visually im-
     paired children. *Journal of Visual Impairment &*
     Blindness 79:289-92.

     "The word test" is a commercial language-
     assessment test. It is used to identify language
     disorders in elementary school age children in areas
     such as vocabulary and verbal reasoning. This study
     was an attempt to find out if the word test is a
     fair test for visually impaired students. This par-
     ticular test was chosen for the study because it
     uses no visual stimulus during the exam. The con-
     clusion of the researchers was that the word test is
     not discriminatory in assessing language skills of
     visually impaired children since no visual stimuli
     are needed and the test is not timed.

304. Wohl, A., and S. Eshet. 1985. Building a learning
     readiness program for the mainstream visually im-
     paired children of Israel. *Journal of Visual Impair-*
     ment & Blindness 79:312-16.

     The author talks about the developmental stages
     that would aid the blind child in reading braille.
     He notes that auditory perception is the basis of
     concept formation, and may be the greatest aid to
     reading readiness. Tactile, or touch, perception is
     also very important to prepare the reader. Further-
     more, physical stamina, as well as correct posture
     when sitting at a desk are aids to pre-reading.
     Last discussed is body image. A sighted child sees
     his body as an entire entity, separated from the
     mother, whereas the blind child sees his body only
     in parts.

305. Wurster, M.V. 1983. Where we've been and where we
     are. *Education of the Visually Handicapped* 14:99-
     104.

     The purpose of this article is to stress that
     daily living skills and academic and vocational

skills such as career education and training for
life's roles must become better integrated for visually impaired children during the early educational
years.

306. Zendel, I.H., and R.O. Pihl. 1983. Visual and auditory
      matching in learning disabled and normal children.
      Journal of Learning Disabilities 16:158-60.

      The purpose of this article was to point out
      that visually learning disabled elementary school
      children did more poorly than normal children at
      tasks involving intersensory and intrasensory
      matches. However, the psychological processes re-
      lated to performance were, with one exception, simi-
      lar in both groups.

CHAPTER IV:
HEARING IMPAIRMENTS

Children who are hearing impaired can be either deaf or hard of hearing. Children who have no hearing at all in either ear are termed "deaf."

According to the definition formulated by the Conference of Executives of American Schools for the Deaf:

> A deaf person is one whose hearing is disabled to an extent (usually 70 dB ISO or greater) that precludes the understanding of speech through the ear alone, with or without the use of a hearing aid;
> A hard of hearing person is one whose hearing is disabled to an extent (usually 35 to 69 dB ISO) that makes difficult, but does not preclude the understanding of speech through the ear alone, with or without a hearing aid.

Children with slight hearing loss are those with losses of 27 to 40 decibels. These children need to be placed into special seats and may require special services because hearing from a distance may be difficult for them.

A moderate hearing loss may affect the child's ability to hear class conversation. His hearing range may be no farther than five feet. A hearing aid or a special course in lip reading would be helpful for this type of child.

A marked or moderately severe hearing loss will limit the child's ability to hear loud sounds. A specialized program needs to be formulated for this type of hearing loss.

The severe hearing loss (71 to 90 decibels) means that loud sounds cannot be heard at a close distance. A hearing aid, lip reading, speech and language training must be included in a specialized program.

Those with extreme or profound hearing losses (91 decibels) on the ANSI standard are classified as deaf. These children can hear only vibrations. Vision is relied upon to process information. If an intensive speech and language instruction program is not implemented, speech may never develop. Hearing impairments may be caused by heredity, mater-

nal rubella, premature births, RH incompatibility, and menin-
gitis. Some causes are unknown.

By the very nature of this condition, the child is likely
to have problems that will affect his total development. The
individual's hearing impairment will usually create a language
and speech deficit as well. Approximately five percent of
school age children have difficulties with their hearing. As
is true of visual impairments, there are many factors that
influence the extent to which this disorder can be a handicap,
including such variables as the age at onset, extent of the
loss, the intelligence of the person, and at what point in
the child's life the problem was ascertained and dealt with.

Children with severe and profound hearing losses are
found to be from two to five years below their chronological
age in educational achievements. There are several traits
affected by the hearing defect--primarily speech development,
but also language development, reading, and spelling. A child
who is totally deaf would probably be placed in a special
school or class for the deaf. If he is integrated in a regular class, he may be offered intensive tutorial services.
Special education teachers must use channels of communication
other than hearing in teaching this type of child. A child
who suffers from total deafness will have difficulty with
communication skills and therefore have greater problems in
developing interpersonal relationships. This prevents normal
social maturity from occurring and causes the child to have
greater problems in adjusting.

In speech development, language development, and other
school subjects, a hard of hearing child is not as retarded
as a totally deaf child. Due to the fact that he/she has a
lower degree of disability, fewer special educational services
are warranted. A hard of hearing child can remain in the
regular classroom and still receive special instructions in
speech and auditory training to assist him or her in coping
with the regular curriculum. The identification and diagnosis
of hearing impairment in children include (a) preliminary
screening of children through threshold testing, (b) otologi-
cal and other medical examinations, (c) audiological and
hearing-aid evaluation, and (d) psychological and educational
assessment.

Specialized programs must be implemented for the hearing
impaired, and there are three primary approaches to such programs. The oral/aural approach emphasizes auditory training
(learning to listen), oral training (learning to speak), and
speech reading (learning to read lips). The second approach,
the manual approach, includes teaching finger spelling or
some form of sign language as the primary mode of communication. The third approach, a total communication approach,

combines the oral/aural and manual methods to meet the needs of the individual child.

Children must be taught the use of hearing aids, speech reading (lip reading), speech remediation, language development including finger spelling, and sign language. Reading and other academic subjects must also be included in the curriculum.

There exists a controversy in the field of education for the deaf over whether to use oralism or manualism. Oralism requires communication through lip reading and speech without relying on signs or gestures. The manual method uses an alphabet with fixed positions of fingers and hand to represent letters. Most schools use both methods, but there are some that use exclusively one or the other. Children themselves often communicate by the manual method. Abstract language skills are hard to develop and must be systematically taught to deaf children.

Finally, teaching hearing impaired children involves great use of visual cues, captioned films, and proper seating. Nonimpaired children can be taught tolerance, understanding, and compassion by working with their handicapped classmates. They can help copy notes, since the hearing impaired child's eyes must always be on the teacher. They also can learn to better appreciate the various parts of their body that they take for granted.

307. Allen, M. 1975. Education through music--An innovative program for hearing impaired children. *Volta Review* 77:381-83.

   Allen adapted an education/music program for her hearing impaired students. Recognizing that the rhythmic patterns of familiar songs closely follow those of spoken language, Mrs. Allen began to apply the principles of Mary Helen Richard's "Education Through Music" program in the teaching of a class of five severely hearing impaired children. Her techniques resulted in increased motivation and enjoyment of learning for the children as well as in improved linguistic, perceptual, social, and motor skills.

308. Anita, S.D. 1982. Social interaction of partially mainstreamed hearing impaired children. *American Annals of the Deaf* 127:18-25.

   The study examined social interaction of partially mainstreamed elementary grade children with hearing (N=84) and their hearing impaired (N=32) peers. It was found that hearing impaired children interacted less frequently with peers and more frequently with teachers than did hearing children. Hearing impaired students interacted more frequently with hearing impaired peers. Mode of communication did not appear to affect frequency of interaction. It was concluded that physical proximity was necessary but not a solely sufficient condition for interaction and that opportunities for social interaction between hearing and hearing impaired students needed to be carefully planned by teachers.

309. Arnold, D. 1978. The deaf child's written English-- Can we measure its quality. *Teacher Deaf* 2:196-200.

   A crucial skill that deaf children must acquire for everyday life is writing. However, writing good English is often a problem. This article reiterates major attempts to measure writing quality in word meaning, syntax, and semantics. The psychological and educational basis of deviant written language is investigated.

310. Arnold, D., and A. Tremblay. 1979. Interaction of
      deaf and hearing preschool children. *Journal of
      Communication Disorders* 12:245-51.

          Hearing and hearing impaired children attending
      an integrated preschool were observed in a free play
      situation. The objective was to discern how hearing
      and deaf children interacted and modified their com-
      munication skills as a function of hearing status.
      The indications were that hearing children interact
      more with other hearing children, whereas deaf chil-
      dren showed no preference in a number of interac-
      tions, though they did tend to approach other deaf
      children somewhat more. The results are consistent
      with other research on such groups as the mentally
      retarded in showing that while hearing impaired chil-
      dren showed no peer preference, they were least pre-
      ferred by normal peers.

311. Baldwin, R.C. 1975. Characteristics of quality pro-
      grams for hearing impaired children. *Volta Review*
      77:436-39.

          Quality programs for hearing impaired children
      have six common characteristics: leadership, esprit
      de corps, curriculum, centralization, systematic use
      of amplification-speech and language instruction,
      and a high expectation level for children. The
      reader is offered twelve questions to use as a guide
      in evaluating a program.

312. Beggs, W.D.A., and P.I. Breslaw. 1982. Reading clumsi-
      ness and the deaf child. *American Annals of the
      Deaf* 127:12-17.

          The experiments reported on in this article
      were undertaken in order to investigate the relation-
      ship between clumsiness and retardation in reading
      ability in the deaf, including those with no blatant
      vestibular or neural damage. Tests used failed to
      differentiate between deaf and hearing children.
      The usual relationship between low reading ability
      and clumsiness was confirmed in the hearing popula-
      tion but not in the deaf. Previous research sug-
      gesting clumsiness in the deaf was criticized, and
      the failure to link degree of clumsiness and reading

ability was related to the research showing that reading age in the deaf means something different from reading age in the hearing.

313. Belenky, M.F. 1984. The role of deafness and education in the moral development of hearing-impaired children and adolescents. *Educational Resources Information Center* 20:1-29.

Belenky takes an in depth look at the research on moral development done by such noted people as Piaget and Kohlberg, and proceeds to extract from it a foundation for her own views on the moral development of hearing-impaired children and adolescents. She agrees that the three processes vital to moral development are 1) cognitive growth, 2) liberation from adult constraint, and 3) social interaction. The third process forms the heart of her paper. It is her opinion that because deaf people all too often are not taught sign language at very young ages and thus are denied the opportunity to communicate they are socially isolated and stagnate morally. She also points out that they are dominated by parents and teachers alike and are not given the opportunity to initiate activity that would spawn independence and the opportunity to reason on a moral level.

314. Bentler, R.; J. Elfenbein; and R. Schum. 1984. Identical deaf triplets: Audiological, speech-language, and psychological characteristics. *American Annals of the Deaf* 129:466-80.

Deaf male triplets were followed in this study from ages two and one-half to six years. The test results have shown that the boys demonstrated almost identical auditory, speech articulation, language, developmental, and intellectual abilities. However, they displayed very different personality characteristics. At first, the triplets were acquiring essentially the same levels of communication skill. Towards the end of the study the most interactive and attentive triplet was acquiring vocabulary skills more rapidly than his brothers. The general conclusion drawn from these findings is that communication and psychological development have an interactive effect.

315. Bernstein, H.W. 1974. Special approaches in learning
      processes for the deaf. *Volta Review* 76:42-50.

            Effective teaching of deaf children requires
      more than adherence to one specific method or one
      approach to communication. Each child or group of
      children will react in an individual way to a given
      educational experience. Educators must therefore be
      flexible and willing to consider innovative tech-
      niques and new ideas.

316. Blair, J. 1985. The effects of mild sensorineural
      hearing loss on academic performance of young school-
      age children. *Volta Review* 87:87-93.

            A comparison study of twenty-four mildly hearing
      impaired students and twenty-four hearing students
      indicated that hearing loss at young ages results in
      poor academic achievement. Some data suggests that
      the negative results increase with age.

317. Blake, R.S. 1984. Discovery versus expository instruc-
      tional strategies and their implications for instruc-
      tion of hearing-impaired post-secondary students.
      Educational Resources Information Center 20:1-49.

            One of the mental frameworks that leads to rac-
      ism is dichotomy. People are short or tall, skinny
      or fat, smart or stupid. In general, people seem to
      be uncomfortable with middle ground which is the
      arena where most things reside. The author recapit-
      ulates the research on expository vs. discovery
      teaching and comes to the conclusion that a blend of
      the two is the most logical way to teach and learn.
      Perhaps he feels that way because the research on
      which is the better way is inconclusive and ambiguous
      as indicated in this document.

318. Bonham, S.J. 1963. *Predicting achievement for deaf
      children*. Ohio State Department of Education: Colum-
      bus, Ohio.

            This study was done to determine the predictive
      value of individual and group achievement tests when
      used to evaluate deaf children. The thirty-six chil-

dren selected for this study were in grades two,
four, and six in the Kennedy School in Dayton, Ohio.
All had severe auditory handicaps and were ten to
sixteen years old. Four psychologists administered
a variety of tests. Results indicated that 1. The
leiter IQ score was fifteen to twenty points lower
than the WISC performance IQ score. 2. The group
appeared to be three years overage for their actual
grade placement based on their MAT scores. The
Pearson product moment coefficient of correlation
revealed significant correlations between a. leiter
and group reading tests, b. knox cube, with individual reading scores, c. leiter and WISC performance,
and d. WISC performance scale and individual reading.

319. Bornstein, H., and K.L. Sailnier. 1981. Signed En-
     glish, a brief follow-up to the first evaluation.
     American Annals of the Deaf 126:69-72.

     A study was conducted on how children are able
     to use the Signed English System. The Signed English
     System is a way to represent English words over the
     many and varied forms they may take within sentences
     (adding 's, etc.). The problem is that it is time
     consuming and that in English there are many excep-
     tions. Deaf children seemed to have an especially
     slow progress in this.

320. Bowman, E. 1973. A resource room program for hearing
     impaired students. *Volta Review* 75:208-13.

     A resource room located within a regular public
     school provides a setting where integrated hearing
     impaired students can receive tutoring and support
     from a trained teacher of the deaf to supplement
     their daily participation in regular classes. The
     children who are in these specialized resource rooms
     benefit from the individualized assistance and com-
     panionship at the opening and close of the day and
     for one additional fifty minute period of daily in-
     struction.

321. Bragman, R. 1982. Review of research on test instruc-
      tion for deaf children. *American Annals of the Deaf*
      127:337-46.

            Although special tests have been developed for
      hearing-impaired students, the most common problem
      that occurs is in the communication of test instruc-
      tions. Most modifications have dealt with reinforc-
      ing responses, omitting verbal items, adding printed
      or signed words, practicing test type items, elimi-
      nating time limits, and demonstrating strategies.
      There is a fear that altering the instructions will
      alter the reliability of evaluating the students'
      process, but as this study has shown there is no
      conclusive evidence that that happens.

322. Braverman, B.B. 1977. Review of literature in instruc-
      tional television: Implications for deaf learners.
      American Annals of the Deaf 122:395-402.

            This article examines how useful instructional
      television is for deaf learners. Research designs
      for determining the effect of instructional tele-
      vision and certain media variables that have been
      studied are reviewed. Characteristics of deaf stu-
      dents as learners that would allow them to interact
      with media variables are mentioned. Further research
      is recommended.

323. Brenza, B. 1981. Comprehension and production of basic
      semantic concepts by older hearing-impaired children.
      Journal of Speech and Hearing Research 24:414-19.

            The Boehm Test of Basic Concepts was used to
      evaluate the comprehension of semantic concepts.
      The fifteen children studied, aged thirteen and four-
      teen, were orally trained and severely to profoundly
      hearing impaired. They were required to construct
      written sentences using these same semantic concepts.
      The teachers completed a questionnaire of their ex-
      pectations for each child on the BTBC. The majority
      of the children scored in the lowest percentiles for
      second grade hearing children. Over half of the
      sentences written contained semantic and/or syntactic
      errors. As well, the teachers were able to correctly

predict each child's scores. The implications of
these findings are discussed.

324. Brooks, R.W.; F. Hudson; and L.E. Reisberg. 1981. The
effectiveness of unimodal versus bimodal presentations of material to be learned by hearing-impaired
students. *American Annals of the Deaf* 126:835-39.

Seven different methods of input upon the learning rate of hearing-impaired students were examined
to determine their effectiveness. Different combinations of unimodal and bimodal methods were used to
teach Spanish number words. Results showed that
bimodal presentations are more effective than unimodal.

325. Browns, F. 1979. Beginning reading instruction with
hearing impaired children. *Volta Review* 81:100-108.

Describes two studies of beginning reading instruction with severely to profoundly hearing impaired children. One study intended to establish a
minimum language level prerequisite for beginning
reading with hearing impaired children. It showed
children were reading at a language level below the
generally accepted prerequisite level. The second
study showed that a commercially available program
could be adapted and used successfully with hearing
impaired children. The conclusion was that commercial language scores cannot be the sole determinant
of readiness to begin a reading program.

326. Bryans, B.N. 1979. Breaking the sentence barrier in
language and reading instruction. *Volta Review*
81:421-30.

Many deaf students fail to attain a level of
reading proficiency that enables them to comprehend
high school texts. Low levels of reading achievement
in the deaf reflect a lack of attention to the characteristics of continuous discourse. This study
describes some of these characteristics and shows
how they may be taught in the context of questions
on a reading passage.

327. Casby, M.W. 1985. Symbolic play and early communica-
      tion development in hearing impaired children. *Jour-
      nal of Communication Disorders* 18:67-78.

          The relationship between symbolic play and lan-
      guage development in twenty young hearing impaired
      children was investigated in this study. The results
      indicated a significant difference in symbolic play
      in two oradinal communication levels. Moreover, a
      strong positive relationship was observed between
      the variables of symbolic play and early communica-
      tion development.

328. Cherry, R. 1985. A three-dimensional language acquisi-
      tion program for hearing impaired preschoolers.
      Volta Review 87:155-64.

          As part of an auditory-verbal habilitation pro-
      gram for four hearing impaired preschoolers, a three-
      dimensional approach to language acquisition was
      instituted. Results indicated that the children
      were developing verbal language skills paralleling
      normally developing children with hearing, but at a
      later age.

329. Cole, E., and M. Shade. 1985. Social-emotional adjust-
      ment of integrated hearing impaired adolescents.
      A.C.E.H.I. Journal 11:82-91.

          The social-emotional adjustment patterns of
      eight mainstreamed hearing impaired adolescents were
      compared with a matched group of eight normally hear-
      ing adolescents. No statistically significant dif-
      ferences were found between the two groups. The
      authors conclude that the social and emotional well-
      being was similar for both the hearing impaired and
      hearing adolescents.

330. Coley, J.D., and P.R. Bockmiller. 1980. Teaching read-
      ing to the deaf: An examination of teacher prepared-
      ness and practices. *American Annals for the Deaf*
      125:19.

          This study shows that the data analyzed indicate
      rather convincingly that teachers use techniques

that make them feel well prepared. The fact that
teachers of the deaf have by their own evaluation
inadequate training in reading is reflected in their
overwhelming reliance on one approach to the teaching
of reading. There is nothing wrong with a basal
reader as one instructional technique, but it certainly has shortcomings when used as the only method
of teaching reading to hearing-impaired children.

331. Culross, R. 1985. Adaptation of the Pictoral Self-
Concept Scale to measure self-concept in young hear-
ing impaired children. *Language, Speech, and Hearing
Services in the Schools* 16:132-34.

The results of the Pictoral Self-Concept Scale
(PSCS), which was developed and field-tested with
255 hearing impaired students (grades four to eight),
suggest that the PSCS is valid and reliable and requires little dependence on verbal facility.

332. Deal, R., and R. Thornton. 1985. An exploratory investigation of comprehension of English through Sign
English (Siglish) and Seeing Essential English (SEE
1). *Language, Speech, and Hearing Services in the
Schools* 16:267-79.

This study explored the comprehension levels of
deaf children for English stories through Seeing
Essential English and Signed English. Eleven deaf
children using SEE and eleven using Siglish visually
received the first of three narrative passages and
accompanying questions in manual form from the Durell
Analysis of Reading Difficulty Listening Comprehension subtest. The data indicated that subjects
trained in SEE were generally superior in comprehension to those trained in Siglish. Further investigation is needed of the hypothesis that a manual communication system representing English structures
provides better comprehension than sign systems not
similarly based.

333. Decker, N., and B. Montandon. 1984. Captioned media
      in the classroom. *Educational Resources Information
      Center* 20:1-48.

           This research was done to promote the effective
      use of captioned media in the education of hearing-
      impaired students. It takes a theoretical and his-
      torical look at captioning but does not stop there.
      It also reviews major issues in the field such as
      edited vs. verbatim captioning, and even offers in-
      structional ideas for using captioned media to teach
      decoding skills, word meaning, grammar, and story
      structure.

334. Delaney, M.; E. Stuckless; and G. Walter. 1984. Total
      communication effects--a longitudinal study of a
      school for the deaf in transition. *American Annals
      of the Deaf* 129:481-86.

           A ten-year evaluation of the effects of intro-
      ducing total communication into a previously oral/
      aural school focused on student achievement levels
      and communication skills. The effects on academic
      achievement, speech development, speech-reading,
      reading, and writing were evaluated. Three groups
      were studied. The groups consisted of students hav-
      ing all education in total communication, none in
      total communication, and a mixed group. Staff per-
      ceptions test results indicated important changes in
      both achievement and communication skills when total
      communication was introduced. However, some of these
      changes may have been due to direct intervention,
      legislative aspects, and greater community involve-
      ment.

335. Dowaliby, F. 1985. The relationship between student,
      course, and instructor characteristics. *Volta Review*
      87:77-86.

           Research indicates that student characteristics,
      in combination with teacher characteristics, result
      in particular course choices for students and in
      certain behavioral patterns for teachers.

336. D'Zamko, M. 1985. Personnel preparation for multi-
      handicapped hearing impaired students. *American
      Annals of the Deaf* 130:9-14.

          From a review of the literature the author con-
      cludes that 1) hearing impairments and additional
      handicaps result in a multihandicap, 2) one-third of
      all hearing impaired students are multihandicapped,
      and 3) appropriate school programs are lacking.

337. Ewoldt, C. 1978. Reading for the hearing or hearing
      impaired: A single process. *American Annals of the
      Deaf* 123: 945-48.

          A study of the reading strategies of four pro-
      foundly prelingually deafened children ranging in
      age from seven to seventeen revealed that they were
      using tactics similar to those that hearing readers
      use. Predicting, chunking, use of their own dialect,
      using peripheral field of information, developing
      concepts through reading, and retelling stories ef-
      fectively all show evidence of refined reading strat-
      egies. Implications for the reading instruction of
      the deaf are discussed.

338. Ewoldt, C. 1985. A descriptive study of the developing
      literacy of young hearing-impaired children. *Volta
      Review* 87:109-26.

          This study was the first attempt to document
      the literacy development of ten hearing impaired
      preschoolers. These children had varying degrees of
      hearing loss and of preschool experience. The re-
      sults address organizational features, generative-
      ness, intentionality, socialization, demonstrations,
      text, context, risk, and spelling. Some develop-
      mental progression in writing was noted, but the
      children's individual styles sometimes obscured that
      progression.

339. Farrugia, D.L. 1982. Deaf high school students' voca-
      tional interest, and attitudes. *American Annals of
      the Deaf* 127:753-62.

          This study examined the differences in voca-
      tional interests and attitudes of deaf persons and
      hearing persons between the ages of sixteen and nine-
      teen using the Wide Range Interest and Opinion Test.
      Results showed that deaf people had less interest in
      educational and cultural vocations and favored manual
      over verbal activities. Deaf students also had lower
      ambitions.

340. Farrugia, D.L., and G.F. Austin. 1980. A study of
      social-emotional adjustment patterns of hearing im-
      paired students in different educational settings.
      American Annals of the Deaf 125:535-41.

          The purpose of the study was to examine the
      social-emotional adjustment patterns among hearing
      impaired students in different educational settings.
      200 subjects ages ten to fifteen were divided into
      four groups. Deaf students in public school, deaf
      students in residential schools, hard of hearing
      students in public school, and hearing students in
      public school. Results showed that deaf students in
      residential schools and hearing students in public
      school were similar in all areas of development.
      Hard of hearing and deaf students in public school
      showed lower levels of self-esteem than other stu-
      dents. Deaf students in public school also showed
      lower levels of social, emotional, and mature behav-
      iors.

341. Fitch, J.L. 1982. Orientation to hearing loss for
      educational personnel. *Language, Speech, and Hearing
      Services in Schools* 13:252-57.

          When hearing impaired children are in a regular
      education program, their success or failure may be
      affected by information conveyed to educational per-
      sonnel. Educational programs should provide work-
      shops to increase staff awareness of characteristics
      and needs of hearing impaired children. The speech-
      language pathologist is often the staff member most
      capable in terms of background to organize such a

workshop. This article outlines a workshop on hearing impairment that can be presented by a speech-
language pathologist to regular educators.

342. Fletchi, J.D., and C.M. Stauffer. 1973. Learning language by computer. *Volta Review* 75:302-11.

The design of computer-assisted instruction
(CAI) is discussed with reference to a specific cur-
riculum--language arts for the deaf. The four general objectives of such a CAI curriculum are that
students should: a) recognize specified grammatical
categories, b) recognize and supply various forms of
given grammatical structures, c) select appropriate
grammatical units to complete a specified structure,
and d) perform specified transformations on given
grammatical structures. These goals do not define a
comprehensive curriculum in language arts, and the
essential and integral role of teachers in the design
of CAI is strongly emphasized. Major advances for
CAI design during the seventies are anticipated in
instructional dialogue, optimization of instruction,
simulation, and computer administration of tests.

343. Frankmann, J.P.; S.E. Herman; K.S. MacKain; and H.S.
Oyer. 1979. Methods of training deaf children to
comprehend the passive voice. *Journal of Speech and
Hearing Research* 22:247-58.

Four variations on a programmed filmstrip were
shown to deaf children to improve comprehension of
the passive voice. The design included two training
strategies that treated the passive voice as a uni-
tary structure or as a control to the active voice.
Within strategies, two orders of training were compared for the various types of passive sentences:
nonreversible, reversible, agent-deleted; and
agent-deleted, nonreversible, reversible. Evaluations were given before, immediately after, and following three months of training. Scores on these
tests were much higher after the three-month period.
Highest scores were achieved on nonreversible pas-
sives followed by reversible and agent-deleted pas-
sives.

344. Gaines, R. 1981. Immediate and delayed story recall
     by hearing and deaf children. *Journal of Speech and
     Hearing Research* 24:463-69.

         This study involved twelve orally trained, con-
     genitally, profoundly deaf children, aged fourteen
     to fifteen years, and a group of hearing children.
     Its purpose was to assess their reading comprehension
     and retention of stories. Each group read one normal
     and two experimentally confused stories. They were
     then tested for recall immediately after and one
     week later. The amount recalled of the normal story
     was the same for both groups, but the deaf children
     recalled more of both confused stories. However,
     these children also made more distortions in their
     recall than did the hearing group. This finding may
     be due to the strategies used for lip-reading where
     guessing and reconstructive activities are needed.

345. Gardner, J., and J. Zorfass. 1983. From sign to
     speech: The language development of a hearing-
     impaired child. *American Annals of the Deaf* 128:20-
     23.

         The case study of a boy with a bilateral, severe
     to profound sensory neural hearing loss is presented.
     Separate examinations of his spoken and signed lan-
     guage were made and the related change in progress
     of each was noted. At fifteen months he used signs
     exclusively. Eight months later he relied on expres-
     sive language only using signs for unfamiliar terms.
     By three his oral language equaled that of a hearing
     child of the same age. The authors conclude that
     signs are a vehicle to assigning meaning to sounds.

346. Gormley, K.A. 1981. On the influence of familiarity
     on deaf students' text recall. *American Annals of
     the Deaf* 127:18-24.

         Third grade deaf students were examined for
     their reading comprehension based on the influence
     of prior knowledge. Fifteen students comprising a
     younger and an older group were studied. Each was
     given three paragraphs of familiar topics and three
     of unfamiliar topics. Students then retold the para-
     graphs and were asked probing questions. Results

for both groups found the rate of recall to be significantly higher on the familiar topics. Conclusion
was that familiarity of material has a direct correlation to deaf students' understanding of written
texts.

347. Gormley, K.A. 1982. The importance of familiarity in
      hearing impaired reader's comprehension of text.
      Volta Review 84:71-79.

      The purpose of this study was to examine the
      influence of familiarity on older and younger second
      grade-level hearing impaired students' memory of the
      text. Students silently read familiar and unfamiliar
      paragraphs that were structurally equivalent. After
      each silent reading, students retold the selection
      and answered probe questions. Students recalled
      familiar paragraphs noticeably better than unfamiliar
      ones.

348. Grammatico, L.F. 1975. The development of listening
      skills. *Volta Review* 77:303-8.

      Development of listening skills in hearing im-
      paired students is a continuous process to be empha-
      sized during the child's entire working day. Selec-
      tion of appropriate amplification is crucial in de-
      veloping the child's residual hearing. Educational
      intervention that organizes teaching and learning
      experiences in a sequential way is necessary. The
      basic factors contributing to development of sophis-
      ticated listening skills are sound awareness, dis-
      crimination, localization, intonational patterns,
      and memory. With concerted effort on the part of
      the teacher to provide appropriate amplification and
      continuous auditory stimulation, deaf children can
      develop oral communication skills.

349. Green, K.W.; W.B. Green; and D.W. Holmes. 1981. Speed-
      reading skills of young normal hearing and deaf chil-
      dren. *American Annals of the Deaf* 126:505-9.

      This study compared the speedreading performance
      of deaf children to that of normal hearing children.
      Performance was assessed across word, phrase, and

sentences. Results revealed significantly better
performance by normal hearing children on all stimuli. Both groups did better on word than the other
stimuli. Normal hearing children seemed to have
been assisted by the visible aspects of words while
the deaf seemed to be influenced solely by language
structure.

350. Gregory, J.F.; T. Shanahan; and H.J. Walberg. 1984.
     Mainstreamed hearing-impaired high school seniors: A
     re-analysis of a national survey. *American Annals
     of the Deaf* 129:11-16.

        A previous study showed that 514 of 26,146 high
     school seniors claimed to have hearing problems.
     This group was compared to hearing peers in demo-
     graphic characteristics, academic achievement, and
     motivation. Results showed that in terms of percent-
     age fewer black students were mainstreamed. In gen-
     eral, scores on academic achievement and motivation
     were significantly lower than for the hearing group.
     These results indicate a need for more support serv-
     ices for the hearing impaired.

351. Hamilton, H. 1984. Linguistic encoding in short-term
     memory: An overview. *Educational Resources Informa-
     tion Center* 20 1:1-22.

        The author examines the history of research on
     linguistic encoding and focuses in particular on the
     multi-store model vs. levels of processing model.
     The two theories converge in the acceptance of sen-
     sory memory—both short-term and long-term. Hamilton
     believes that by investigating the coding bases for
     linguistic material, the organization and representa-
     tion of language in memory may be more clearly de-
     fined and described. In his research on short-term
     memory he finds for the most part that hearing chil-
     dren use a phonological encoding system and that
     deaf children use a cherological or sign encoding
     system. The big question that he finds is whether
     encoding is related to level of hearing, early lin-
     guistic experiences, total linguistic experiences,
     or a combination of these factors.

352. Hasentab, M.S. 1979. The neglected component in teaching language to hearing impaired children. *Journal of Speech and Hearing Association* 20:12-15.

   Present attempts to teach and develop language abilities in hearing impaired children have emphasized syntactic development and phonological proficiency. The author suggests instead that teachers and clinicians develop specifically semantic categories with hearing impaired children and progressively refine these categories into adult syntactic forms.

353. Hawkins, R. 1984. Primary mentoring as a teaching strategy. *Educational Resources Information Center* 20 2:1-47.

   This paper is divided into two sections. The first section reviews historical aspects of the reintroduction of mentors in modern education. In the second section a mentorship experiment underway for the past ten years at Empire State College is reviewed. Finally the author makes recommendations for designing and establishing a mentor position at the National Technical Institute for the deaf. He feels that mentoring would both lessen the isolated feeling of hearing impaired students and enable them to live a more full life by integrating them into a world that is at least in the beginning not made in their own image.

354. Higginbotham, J.D., and B.M. Baker. 1981. Social participation and cognitive play differences in hearing-impaired and normally hearing preschoolers. *Volta Review* 83:135-149.

   The free play of seven severe-to-profoundly hearing impaired children attending a preschool for the hearing impaired and seven normally hearing children attending a non-specialized preschool were assessed using a social cognitive play classification. Each subject was observed in his/her classroom setting for fifteen consecutive days. The hearing impaired children demonstrated much more non-interactive constructive activities and less cooperative and dramatic activities than their hearing peers. Results are discussed in light of the hypothesis that hearing impaired children are unable to sustain the complex social and cognitive play patterns that need verbal and social interaction skills, and that the resulting free-play deficiencies may further restrict language acquisition by limiting opportunities for social interaction.

355. Howell, R.F. 1984. Maternal reports of vocabulary development in four-year-old deaf children. *American Annals of the Deaf* 129:459-65.

This study examined vocabulary development of two deaf children of deaf parents and two deaf children of hearing parents having conversational sign skills. Data indicated that vocabulary development occurs in a similar fashion for young deaf children whether they have deaf or hearing parents, as long as fluent communication is established. Additional research is needed with more children and parents.

356. Innes, J., and C. Rohr-Redding. 1984. Can thinking skills be incorporated into a curriculum? *Educational Resources Information Center* 20 1:1-10.

Seventeen hearing impaired students participated in a program to improve thinking skills via the Instructional Enrichment approach that focuses on concepts by suggesting alternative strategies by which the learner can arrive at the objective. These students were adolescents who might have been very narrow in their thinking. As a result of this program there was an increase in student motivation in problem solving tasks, more peer cooperation, and greater interest in process over product.

357. Iran-Nejad, A.; A. Ortony; and R.K. Rittenhouse. 1981. The comprehension of metaphorical uses of English by deaf children. *Journal of Speech and Hearing Research* 24:551-56.

The results of the two experiments that were examined revealed that deaf children do not have a particular problem in understanding metaphorical uses of natural language as is often suggested by

educators of and researchers on the deaf. The two
experiments used profoundly deaf subjects from two
different residential schools. It was found that
the ability to understand the metaphorical uses of
language was present, but that deaf children rarely
interpret it as such spontaneously. This suggests
that more experience with metaphorical language might
increase spontaneous metaphorical interpretations of
language. It was concluded that the problem of understanding metaphorical language is probably not a
deep-seated one.

358.   James, P. 1980. The benefits of art for mainstreamed
       hearing impaired children. *Volta Review* 82:103-8.

           Hearing impaired children live in a world where
       the spoken word is the primary means of communica-
       tion. These children are at a disadvantage in school
       subjects that rely on discussion and explanation.
       Art is the subject area in which verbal communication
       is not of primary importance, and vision rather than
       hearing is the vital sense.

359.   Jones, T. 1984. Behavior modification studies with
       hearing-impaired students: A review. *American Annals
       of the Deaf* 129:451-58.

           Thirty-four studies were identified in which
       behavior modification was used with hearing impaired
       students. These were analyzed according to students
       involved, setting, procedures, target behaviors,
       accommodations for hearing impairment, evaluation,
       and place of publication. Comparison of the studies
       supported the conclusions that, although frequent
       behavior modifications have not been specifically
       adapted for hearing impaired students, they have
       been used successfully with that population. Behav-
       ior modification also was used to teach these stu-
       dents a variety of skills, both academic and social.
       More studies are suggested to research the use of
       behavior modification to teach specific academic
       skills and complex procedures.

360. Jordan, I.K.; G. Gustafson; and R. Rosen. 1976. Current communication trends at programs for the deaf. *American Annals of the Deaf* 121:527-32.

A survey was done of communication modes presently used in schools and classes for the hearing impaired to determine frequency of use of various modes, both as the primary mode of communication and as a supplementary mode in special situations. Any recent change was reported as previous mode, present mode, class level affected, and year of change. The 796 responses indicate a large and continuing trend, with more than sixty-four percent of the reporting classes now using total communication. Questions were also asked about the provision of classes to teach sign language, the sign language book considered the primary reference, and whether standardization of signs was considered within the program.

361. Kaiser-Grodecka, I., and A. Knobloch-Gala. 1984. Developing symbolic thinking in hearing-impaired children. *Educational Resources Information Center* 20:1-27.

The authors studies thirty hearing-impaired students (eleven-fourteen years old) in order to ascertain which of three methods of teaching classificatory principles is best. Analysis of mistakes made by students revealed that in each case the use of iconic signs guaranteed better results than either demonstration techniques or verbal labels. Iconic signs allowed for a more precise definition and a better separation of a part from a larger whole than did verbal signs. Iconic signs are also more easily memorized and more operational than the verbal ones. The symbolic sign may make natural sign languages useless as a device of symbolic thinking.

362. King, C.M. 1984. National survey of language methods used with hearing-impaired students in the United States. *American Annals of the Deaf* 129:311-316.

To determine language methods and philosophies about teaching language, a national survey was taken. Results showed that teachers of hearing impaired students used a combination of many different methods rather than sticking to one. The type of symbol system used varied considerably. Symbol systems are used to produce grammatical sentences, analyze them, and correct them.

363. Kluwin, T., and M. Lindsay. 1984. The effects of the teacher's behavior on deaf students' perception of the organizational environment of the classroom. *American Annals of the Deaf* 129:386-91.

The way in which the teacher structures the classroom often dictates the behavior of deaf students in it. An observational study was made on the effects of the teaching behavior of both deaf and hearing teachers on deaf students' perception of the classroom environment. The results showed that a positive class attitude was associated with moderated control of the students, together with an overt and task oriented reward system. Persistance with students who did not understand the task was also a positive aspect.

364. Kluwin, T., and D.F. Moores. 1985. The effects of integration on the mathematics achievement of hearing impaired adolescents. *Exceptional Children* 52:155-60.

Mathematics achievement of thirty-six students in mainstreamed classes was compared with that of forty-four students in self-contained classes. Analysis showed that integrated students performed significantly better than self-contained students. The differences were accounted for by higher expectations, exposure to greater quantities of demanding material, availability of individual support, and training in academic content for regular mathematics teachers.

365. Knight, M.S., and L. Rosenblatt. 1983. The effects of bimodal (sound-light) stimulus presentation on selective responding of deaf-blind multi-handicapped children. *American Annals of the Deaf* 128:397-401.

Eight severely multi-handicapped, deaf and partially blind children were tested to ascertain the value of light reinforcement techniques for determining hearing assessments. The first experiment showed poorer discriminative performance under the light reinforced condition. A second experiment assessed the effects of an auditory-visual stimulus. Both findings showed poorer selectivity but increased general activity.

366. Kyle, J.G.; R. Conrad; M.G. McKenzie; A.J.M. Morris; and B.C. Weiskrantz. 1978. Language abilities in deaf school leavers. *Journal of British Association of Teachers of the Deaf* 2:38-42.

Over a three year period, the performance of all deaf school leavers in England and Wales was assessed on a number of basic tests of language ability. As a whole, measured ability was lower than would be expected at the end of a child's education. Degree of hearing loss and intelligence were important factors, but an additional significant factor of internal speech emerged, especially related to reading. This is interpreted as a cognitive development at the representational level that is crucial to normal language performance.

367. Ladd, G.W.; H.L. Munson; and J.K. Miller. 1984. Social integration of deaf adolescents in secondary level mainstreamed programs. *Exceptional Children* 50:420-28.

This study explored the social interaction of forty-eight deaf adolescents attending two-year occupational education programs with normal hearing peers. Classroom interactions between deaf and hearing students and classmates' perceptions of mainstreamed peers were assessed for students entering the program during three consecutive academic years. Results indicated that a climate conducive to integrated interaction and friendships did emerge in the mainstreamed program.

368. Lang, H.G. 1979. Metric education for deaf and hard of hearing children. *American Annals of the Deaf* 124:358-65.

       A diagnostic test of metric measurement skills was administered to 283 summer Vestibule Program students in 1978 at the National Technical Institute for the Deaf. Results indicated that the majority of deaf students lacked an understanding of the information needed for metric living. Suggestions are provided for teachers of the deaf to implement metric in their curricula.

369. LaSasso, C.J. 1985. Visual matching test-taking strategies used by deaf readers. *Journal of Speech and Hearing Research* 28:2-7.

       This study used fifty profoundly deaf and fifty hearing students to learn if visual matching test-taking strategies were used, what they consisted of, and if they related to the overall test performance of deaf readers. Also, it investigated if there were differences between the strategies used by deaf and hearing readers. The results involving the fourteen-eighteen year old students indicated extensive use of these strategies by deaf students, but not by hearing students. The extent of strategy use was not related to the deaf students' overall performance on the look-back test. Nine variations of strategy were described and implications were discussed.

370. Lewis, S.; L. Higham; and D. Cherry. 1985. Development of an exercise program to improve the static and dynamic balance of profoundly hearing-impaired children. *American Annals of the Deaf* 130:278-81.

       Since hearing impaired children have decreased balance abilities, a study was done to assess possible ways of remediation. Sixteen hearing impaired children, aged 6-10 years, participated in a six week posture and body awareness activity program. The eleven children in the experimental group participated in a weekly activity during their physical education class at school and the control group followed its normal physical education routine. Pre- and post-tests showed that the balance of the experi-

mental group subjects improved, while the control
group's balance did not. This suggests that further
investigation is needed regarding the decreased balance skills of hearing impaired children.

371. Lynas, W.A. 1979. Integration and the education of
      hearing impaired children. *Teacher Deaf* 3:7-15.

           Various aspects of the term integration are
      discussed as they relate to educating hearing im-
      paired children. Among those aspects are handicapped
      status, assimilation, normalization, adaptation,
      integration, the deaf as a subculture, segregation
      and isolation, and equality of opportunity. These
      issues are discussed in relation to their ramifica-
      tions for deaf education, and the numerous questions
      raised reaffirm the complexities of integration.

372. Marschark, M., and S. West. 1985. Creative language
      abilities of deaf children. *Journal of Speech and
      Hearing Research* 28:73-78.

           This study investigated language flexibility
      and creativity of deaf children. They were video-
      taped and examined for nonliteral communication while
      generating stories on experimenter-supplied themes.
      Analysis of the videotapes of the four deaf and four
      hearing 12-15 year olds revealed that deaf subjects
      showed considerable use of creative language devices
      when evaluated in sign rather than vocal language.
      Deaf subjects produced traditional types of figura-
      tive language equal in rate to the hearing children.
      These findings were discussed in terms of cognitive
      skills and common assumptions concerning deaf chil-
      dren.

373. Masserly, C.L., and D.M. Abram. 1980. Academic
      achievement of hearing impaired students of hearing
      parents and of hearing impaired parents: Another
      look. *Volta Review* 82:25-31.

           Academic achievement was compared between
      matched groups of high school level hearing-impaired
      students of hearing-impaired parents and of hearing
      parents. In no instance did the hearing-impaired

students of hearing impaired parents surpass those
of hearing parents. Hearing impaired students of
hearing parents were found to perform above the
hearing-impaired students of hearing-impaired parents
on the standard achievement tests of vocabulary,
language, science, and mathematical concepts. Reading comprehension, mathematical application, social
science, spelling and mathematical comprehension
failed to differentiate between the two groups, although reading comprehension and mathematical application approached significance in favor of the
hearing-impaired students of hearing parents.

374. Maxwell, M.M. 1979. A model for curriculum development
     at the middle and upper school levels in programs
     for the deaf. *American Annals of the Deaf* 124:425-
     32.

        What do the deaf need? They need to learn Eng-
     lish and to learn how to take care of themselves.
     With these two ideas in mind, teachers from the var-
     ious disciplines must coordinate their efforts. The
     curriculum offered should be decompartmentalized.
     For those that have not mastered English, the curric-
     ulum must fit together. The study describes a struc-
     ture developed by teachers at the Arizona State
     School for the Deaf and the Blind.

375. McKee, B.G., and H.G. Lang. 1982. A comparison of
     deaf students' performance on true and false and
     multiple choice items. *American Annals of the Deaf*
     127:49-54.

        Previous studies have reported on vocabulary
     and syntactical structures that cause difficulty for
     hearing-impaired students. This study has focused
     on the item format used on the evaluation instrument.
     A hundred-item final with 6 true and false, multiple
     choice questions was given to students in a physics
     class at a deaf institute. Results indicated that
     format alone can affect deaf students and that dif-
     ferent conclusions may be possible concerning spe-
     cific course objectives mastered.

376. Moores, D.F.; K.L. Weiss; and M.W. Goodwin. 1978.
      Early education programs for hearing impaired chil-
      dren: Major findings. *American Annals of the Deaf*
      123:925-36.

             Seven early education programs cooperated in a
      six-year evaluation. Methods were developed to as-
      sess receptive and expressive communication, academic
      achievement, cognitive function, psycholinguistic
      abilities, classroom structure, and communication in
      the classroom. A cognitive academic stress was found
      to be more beneficial than traditional preschool
      socialization oriented programs. Oral-manual commu-
      nication was more effective than oral only. Total
      communication and the Rochester method were not found
      to differ in results. Class placement did not appear
      to have a significant effect on communication
      achievement. Normal development was noted in cogni-
      tive skills and visual motor functioning. The neces-
      sary use of residual hearing was not effectively
      trained in most programs. Strength was found in
      pre-reading skills, but there were serious problems
      in English and arithmetic. The acoupedic or auditory
      based program that stressed social integration was
      found to be least effective.

377. Mullen, Y. 1984. A psychologist looks at mainstream-
      ing. *Educational Resources Information Center* 20:1-
      14.

             Although this article is on the broad topic of
      mainstreaming, it focuses to a large degree on main-
      streaming of hearing-impaired students. Research on
      six student variables (audiological factors, commu-
      nication skills, intelligence, achievement, personal-
      ity, and age factors) and five environmental vari-
      ables (classroom teacher's skills and attitudes,
      administrative support, direct support services,
      physical environment, and family support) is re-
      viewed. The author concludes that the relative re-
      strictiveness of a placement lies not in the setting
      itself, but in the closeness of the match between
      programing and student needs.

378. Nelson, K.E., and P.M. Prinz. 1984. A child-computer-
      teacher interactive method for teaching reading to
      young deaf children. *Educational Resources Informa-
      tion Center* 20:1-29.

          Twelve hearing-impaired children (2-5 years
      old) were trained to use a new interactive micro-
      computer system with a special interface word key-
      board that builds in perceptual salience, individual-
      ized vocabulary, animation, and color graphics in a
      two-person-plus computer communication system. Stu-
      dents were taught to press keys with words and short
      statements drawn from their own central interests
      and favorite expressions. In using this system the
      students learned not only to read but also a special
      form of "writing"--creating his/her own printed mes-
      sages on a TV. Results have demonstrated significant
      gains in word recognition and reading comprehension.

379. Newton, L. 1985. Linguistic environment of the deaf
      child: A focus on teachers' use of nonliteral lan-
      guage. *Journal of Speech and Hearing Research*
      28:336-44.

          Teachers' communication with deaf and hearing
      children was compared to assess the differences in
      two types of nonliteral language used by the teach-
      ers. The study observed one group of teachers of
      the deaf who used oral language and another who used
      total communication. A third group consisted of
      teachers of normal hearing children. The findings
      revealed no differences in the teachers' use of non-
      literal language. Reduced use of idiomatic language
      occurred in both oral and signed communication only
      when total communication was used.

380. Novelli-Olmstead, T., and D. Ling. 1984. Speech pro-
      duction and speech discrimination by hearing-impaired
      children. *Volta Review* 86:72-80.

          The relationship between speech production and
      speech perception was studied in seven matched pairs
      of profoundly hearing-impaired children between the
      ages of 5 and 7 years. The pairs were matched as
      closely as possible on the basis of age, gender,
      hearing levels, and pretest measures of phonetic

level, phonologic speech skills, and auditory discrimination. Subjects were then randomly assigned
to one of two groups, speakers and listeners. The
speaking subject of each pair orally imitated and
rehearsed one of two or three given speech "targets"
(vowels or consonants in syllables, and words), while
the listening subject of each pair was required to
discriminate between these same speech targets and
respond by pointing to objects representing them.
All subjects received training twice daily for fifteen minutes until thirty sessions were completed.
Results revealed that the speaking subjects made
highly significant gains both in speech production
and in auditory discrimination, whereas the listening
subjects only showed some gains in speech production
and no gains in auditory discrimination. The major
implication of the study was that combined speech
and auditory training is more effective than auditory
training alone.

381. Osguthorpe, R.T. 1984. Tutoring special students.
Educational Resource Information Center 20:1-38.

This article reviews studies assessing the effects of tutoring on both tutors and tutees in three
broad areas: academic performance, personal/social
adjustment, and moral development. It also reviews
the major types of tutoring (adult-child, peer, and
cross-age tutoring). Among the conclusions formed
are: 1) tutoring is one of the most effective methods
of instruction available, and 2) that tutors can improve social behaviors, adjustment, and self-esteem
as well. The author suggests that hearing-impaired
students should benefit greatly from tutoring experience.

382. Panara, R.F. 1979. On teaching poetry to the deaf
(or: let the student be the poem!). *American Annals
of the Deaf* 124:825-28.

Notes that poetry is one of the best means of
developing concepts or ideas, enlarging a vocabulary,
and improving overall skills of communication. It
helps stimulate creativity and self-expression, and
it encourages the development of a student's intellectual faculties, imagination, thinking, and inter-

pretation. Finally, as in exposure to acting or
dancing, it makes students react emotionally and
sensitively to the concept of expression.

383. Perman, B.Z. 1978. Reading attainment in hearing impaired children: A comparison of higher and lower
achievers. *Journal of Communication Disorders*
11:227-35.

　　　Studied hearing impaired children with higher
and lower reading attainment in order to suggest why
some of these children achieve greater competency
than others. Sixteen children ages eight to seventeen from two oral schools for the hearing impaired
in Britain were given two tests of reading comprehension. These tests revealed both pronounced differences in the reading levels of the children and a
relationship between the test scores and the schools
the children attended. Differences were also found
in oral language and reading comprehension levels,
though these were seen as a result of early language
experiences that the children had had. Insights are
offered to explain how one school fostered the growth
of reading skills where other schools had not succeeded.

384. Pflaster, G. 1980. A factor analysis of variables
related to academic performance of hearing impaired
children in regular classes. *Volta Review* 82:71-84.

　　　Identifies and describes thirteen intrinsic
uncorrelated factors related to academic performance
of hearing impaired children integrated into regular
classes. Intrinsic factors pertain to communicative
and linguistic ability, aptitudes, personality
traits, and confidence. Extrinsic factors deal with
parental and professional attitudes, support, and
expectations. Discusses each factor in terms of its
implications for determining the value of a mainstream setting for a particular hearing impaired
child.

385. Pitchers, B.J.   1978.   Forward trends--three areas of
      forward movement. *Teacher Deaf* 2:155-8.

            Discusses forward movements in the areas of
      assessment, parental involvement, and curriculum in
      the education of the hearing impaired. Stresses
      assessment as a continuous review of progress and
      change. Discusses parental needs, and the importance
      of parents and teachers working together. Curriculum
      should include such areas as developing powers of
      communication, providing opportunities for self ex-
      pression, understanding the world, physical develop-
      ment, and spiritual experiences.

386. Polk, S.   1985.   The attributional beliefs of hearing
      impaired students concerning academic success and
      failure. *American Annals of the Deaf* 130:32-38.

            Patterns of academic attributions, developed by
      225 hearing impaired college students to explain
      success or failure, closely resembled those of hear-
      ing students. The internal factors of ability and
      effort received the strongest ratings for success,
      whereas luck received the weakest rating.

387. Power, D.J.   1971.   Characteristics of successful
      student-teachers of the deaf. *Volta Review* 73:529-
      37.

            Through a battery of tests and records it was
      found that two factors determined who was a success-
      ful student teacher of the deaf: initial college
      academic record and intelligence. The pattern of
      results differed considerably for men and women.
      Student teaching success and academic excellence
      were related for the men in this group, but not for
      the women. Women were seen to be more "intuitive"
      in their approach to teaching, in contrast to the
      more "intellectualized" approach of men. Previous
      full-time teaching experience with hearing children
      was related to better performance in student teaching
      of the deaf. Few personality and attitude scale
      measures were correlated with either student teaching
      or academic success.

388. Reber, R., and C. Sherrill. 1981. Creative thinking
      and dance/movement skills of hearing-impaired youth:
      An experimental study. *American Annals of the Deaf*
      126: 1004-9.

          Changes in creative thinking and dance/movement
      skills were examined in two groups of deaf children
      aged nine to fourteen. The experimental group was
      given twenty creative dance lessons over a ten-week
      period where the control group adhered to a regular
      schedule. Results showed the experimental group had
      improved in originality, elaboration, total thinking
      creativity score, and dance/movement skills.

389. Rittenhouse, R.K., and K. Stearns. 1982. Teaching
      metaphor to deaf children. *American Annals of the
      Deaf* 127:12-17.

          Described in this article is a research based
      program for teaching metaphorical language to deaf
      children. Research that led up to the program of
      instruction is presented in detail. Deaf children
      as young as ten years old were found to be able to
      understand idiomatic expression consistently. In
      addition, with the use of appropriate instruction,
      deaf children showed improved performance on meta-
      phorical tasks. These instructional procedures are
      detailed in this article as part of the teaching
      program.

390. Rodger, I.A. 1979. Curriculum evaluation, humour and
      the teaching of the deaf. *Teacher Deaf* 3:21-24.

          Sets out to illustrate how recent developments
      in the field of curriculum evaluation may be applied
      to the teaching of the deaf. Describes a model
      called Illuminative Evaluation and its application
      in the teaching of profoundly deaf and partially
      hearing children. The study suggests that humour
      can play a vital role in the relationship between
      the teacher and the deaf pupils. A final suggestion
      is that humour can be a deliberate tool of educa-
      tional policy.

391. Rose, S., and M. Wabdron. 1984. Microcomputer use in programs for hearing-impaired children: a national survey. 129:333–42.

This article presents the results of a survey taken to identify computer equipment software and training, and the rate of growth of their uses in the education of deaf students. Eighty-two percent of the 342 programs surveyed responded, and fifty-one percent used microcomputers as an instructional tool. Results showed a further need for software development and in service training together with information-sharing programs.

392. Rupp, R.R., and M. Mikulas. 1973. Some thoughts on handling the communication needs of the very young child with impaired hearing. *Volta Review* 75:288–94.

There are three well-established approaches to teaching language to deaf children: the manual, the oral/aural multisensory, and the oral/aural unisensory. The authors favor this last approach, based as it is on a normal human communications system, and they provide reasons for choosing it, four basic principles, and eight guidelines for its use.

393. Sarachan-Deily, A. 1985. Written narratives of deaf and hearing students: Story recall and inference. *Journal of Speech and Hearing Research* 28:151–59.

This study examined the ability of deaf high school students to recall propositions and inferences from prose and compared their abilities to those of hearing students. When asked to read and write a given story, twenty hearing students recalled significantly larger numbers of propositions than twenty deaf high school students. However, both deaf and hearing students recalled similar numbers of story inferences in their written narratives. The interaction between the deaf students' reading comprehension levels and their narratives revealed that better readers more accurately recalled explicit, rather than implicit, propositional information. Implications of this finding are discussed.

394. Schirmer, B. 1985. An analysis of the language of young hearing-impaired children in terms of syntax, semantics, and use. *American Annals of the Deaf* 130:15-19.

   The language acquisition of young hearing-impaired children is the focus of this study. Twenty 3 to 5 year old children were videotaped and then interacted with the investigator who used stimulus material. Such components of language as syntax, semantics, and use were measured, and the results showed that hearing-impaired children developed in the same way in all areas as hearing children but just at later chronological ages. The best way to describe their language development is to say that it is delayed.

395. Schmidt, S., and J.M. Dunn. 1980. Physical education for the hearing impaired: A system of movement symbols. *Teaching Exceptional Children* 12:99-102.

   Discusses the responsibility of physical education teachers to become increasingly sensitive to instructional methodology appropriate to hearing impaired children. Attention must be given to communication symbols that may be used in the physical education setting. A practical symbol system is illustrated.

396. Schwartz, J.I. 1979. Reading readiness for the hearing impaired. *Academic Therapy* 15:65-75.

   States that proficiency in reading requires competence in both receptive and expressive language, selective perception, and a rich experiential background. Discusses how these three requirements should constitute the core of a reading readiness program for the hearing impaired child.

397. Shafer, D., and J. Lynch. 1981. Emergent language of six prelingually deaf children. *Teacher of the Deaf* 5:94-111.

   Six prelingually hearing impaired children between the ages of fifteen and thirty-four months

with severe to profound losses were studied as expressive language emerged. The subjects were trained
in oral, aural, or total communication. The data
indicated that single word utterances were used for
an extended length of time and semantic intentions
expressed surpassed early function forms. All the
subjects learned to encode the same general semantic
intentions, using the same words, as normal hearing
children. However, the deaf children showed an overall decreased linguistic output and rate of linguistic development.

398.   Sisco, F.H.; P.H. Kranz; N.L. Lund; and G.C. Schwartz.
       1979. Developmental and compensatory play: A means
       of facilitating social, emotional, cognitive, and
       linguistic growth in deaf children. *American Annals
       of the Deaf* 124:850-57.

            Examines the role that developmental and com-
       pensatory play can serve in bringing about social,
       emotional, cognitive, and linguistic growth of deaf
       children. Literature is cited on the etiology of
       maladaptive behavior in the deaf population and the
       article discusses the importance of play as a tool
       for early intervention and developmental growth in
       hearing children. Research reports dealing with the
       use of play as a therapeutic and developmental tool
       for deaf children are incorporated into the study.

399.   Stoefen-Fisher, J. 1985. Reading interests of hearing
       and hearing-impaired children. *American Annals of
       the Deaf* 130:291-96.

            A reading interest inventory was administered
       to 115 hearing impaired students and seventy-two
       hearing students between the ages of nine and twelve.
       The items were grouped into five clusters depending
       on the type of reading passage. The hearing impaired
       students had a broader base of interests than their
       hearing peers. Sex was a significant factor affect-
       ing hearing students' cluster choices, but was not
       as influential for the hearing impaired students.

400. Stoker, R.G., and W.N. Lape. 1980. Analysis of some non-articulatory aspects of the speech of hearing-impaired children. *Volta Review* 82:137-47.

Sixteen measures thought to be related to the intelligibility of speech of hearing-impaired children were examined. Forty-two children ranging in ages four to nineteen were the subjects of the study. Results indicated that intelligibility of speech was highly connected to several factors not conventionally used in speech assessment, i.e., breath control and lip-reading. Hearing acuity was also sensitive as an indicator of speech intelligibility. Hearing aid usage and tactile perception were found to be unrelated to speech intelligibility in the subjects studied.

401. Stone, P. 1983. Auditory learning in a school setting: Procedures and results. *Volta Review* 85:7-13.

This study examined the effectiveness of using maximal amounts of unisensory instruction within self-contained classrooms. Twenty-one hearing-impaired children who had received unisensory instruction for at least three years were administered a series of syllable reception tests. Students in this study showed more improvement when audition was added to visual reception than has been shown in previous studies of children educated in multisensory settings.

402. Suchman, R.G. 1968. Visual impairment among deaf children--frequency and educational consequences. *Volta Review* 70:31-37.

An ophthalmologist and a psychologist tested 103 deaf children, aged four through twelve for four aspects of visual function including acuity, muscle balance, depth perception and general physical status of the eye. Results showed that only forty-three percent had normal vision while the remaining fifty-eight percent had some visual abnormality. Out of fifty-four children with correctable vision forty-seven had received no treatment.

403. Sunal, D.W., and D. Birch. 1982. School science pro-
      grams for the hearing impaired student. *American
      Annals of the Deaf* 127:411-17.

          The purpose of this study was to survey the
      state of science programs for the deaf in the
      schools. Forty-seven schools for the deaf were sam-
      pled to obtain a description of materials being used
      for students ages two to fourteen. Of the schools
      studied, more than twenty percent had no planned
      science program. Much of the material being taught
      was not modified to meet the needs of the deaf stu-
      dents. On this basis, it was concluded that the
      majority of sampled residential schools were not
      providing adequate science programs that met the
      needs and capabilities of deaf students.

404. Tate, M. 1979. A measure of readability for the class-
      room. *Teacher Deaf* 3:16-20.

          Discusses the need for a readability measure
      for the classroom, and puts forward Mugford's Read-
      ability Chart as a possible solution. Describes the
      Chart and compares it with three other measures.
      The results show that the Chart is a feasible method
      for evaluating books and providing the teacher with
      a valuable tool for the coordination of a variety of
      books into a cohesive reading scheme.

405. Watts, W.J. 1979. Some problems in the teaching of
      mathematics to deaf children. *Teacher Deaf* 3:2-6.

          Considers the effectiveness of teaching mathe-
      matics to deaf children and such aspects as individ-
      ual approaches, modern mathematics, tables, revers-
      ibility, structuring of learning, logic of childhood,
      progressive steps, intervention, language, and speech
      accuracy. The deaf child's development of mathe-
      matical concepts needs to be clothed with language,
      and when this occurs symbolization and computation
      become secondary to thinking and communication. The
      study provides a philosophy for those involved in
      the teaching of mathematics to the deaf.

406. Wilson, J.J. 1981. Notetaking: A necessary support
      service for hearing impaired students. *Teaching
      Exceptional Children* 14:38-40.

           Notetaking and tutoring have been noted as re-
      quired support services for mainstreamed hearing
      impaired students. Provision can be supplied by
      peers, paraprofessionals, adults, volunteers, and
      professionals, but the crucial factor for success is
      training and management. Notes are beneficial for
      teachers, students, and resource personnel, and they
      can meet many needs of students whose needs are spe-
      cial.

407. Witters-Churchill, L.J.; R.R. Kelly; and L.A. Witters.
      1983. Hearing-impaired students' perception of liq-
      uid horizontality: An examination of the effects of
      gender, development, and training. *Volta Review*
      85:211-225.

           Sixty-four deaf students were compared to gifted
      hearing students in their ability to perceive and
      understand that liquid remains invariantly horizon-
      tal. The effects of gender, development and training
      were especially of interest. Significant results
      concerning the deaf students were found for training
      on the most difficult bottle positions (oblique ro-
      tations) regardless of gender. Furthermore, the
      hearing impaired do not show any differences between
      male and females. In addition, hearing-impaired
      students' overall performance appeared to be equal
      to that of the gifted, while the hearing-impaired
      females actually performed better than the gifted
      hearing females on the pretest for the oblique bottle
      positions.

408. Yoshinaga-Itano, C., and L. Snyder. 1985. Form and
      meaning in the written language of hearing impaired
      children. *Volta Review* 87:75-90.

           Semantic discourse features of written narra-
      tives of forty-nine hearing impaired children were
      examined. An analysis was made of the relationship
      between form and meaning in the writings of both
      hearing and hearing impaired children aged 10-15
      years old. Syntactic and semantic written language

growth between 10-14 years appear to be qualitatively and quantitatively different in the groups. The two groups also exhibit a different peak on semantic written langauge variables. This study may help understand how and why hearing impaired children have trouble achieving higher language development levels.

CHAPTER V:
LEARNING DISABILITIES

The area of specific learning disabilities has generated
more parental involvement, government legislation, and professional interest than almost any of the areas of exceptionality. Learning disabled children represent a major challenge
to educators and parents because the reasons for their learning problems are not as clear as those for other handicapping
conditions. Moreover, these youngsters are considered to
have average or superior intelligence despite their handicap,
yet they are unable to achieve academically. Some of the
world's greatest achievers had learning problems. If we look
at Albert Einstein, we see that before he reached the age of
seven, he found his schoolwork laborious had trouble formulating the simplest sentence. Among other distinguished individuals who had learning problems were Thomas Edison, Woodrow
Wilson, Auguste Rodin, and Nelson Rockefeller. It is evident
that the subject of learning disabilities is an enigmatic one.
The difficulty in formulating a description for learning
problems lies in the fact that many disciplines are involved
in defining the disorder. PL 94-142 states that "specific
learning disability" means a disorder in one or more of the
psychological processes involved in understanding or in using
language, spoken or written, which manifests itself in an
imperfect ability to listen, speak, think, read, write, spell,
or do mathematical calculations. The term includes such conditions as perceptual handicaps, brain injury, minimal brain
dysfunction, dyslexia, and developmental aphasia. The term
does not include children who have learning problems which
are primarily the result of visual, hearing, or motor handicaps, of mental retardation, of emotional disturbances, or of
environmental, cultural, economic disadvantage.
Furthermore, the law states that a multidisciplinary
team may determine that a child has a specific learning disability if:
(1) The child does not achieve commensurate with his or
her age and ability levels in one or more of seven specific
areas when provided with learning experiences appropriate for

the child's age and ability levels.

(2) The team finds that a child has a severe discrepancy between achievement and intellectual ability in one or more of the following areas:

    a. Oral expression
    b. Listening comprehension
    c. Written expression
    d. Basic reading skill
    e. Reading comprehension
    f. Mathematics calculation
    g. Mathematics reasoning.

The term learning disabilities was introduced in 1963 when a small group of concerned parents and educators met in Chicago to organize a cohesive entity out of separate and isolated parent groups using different names for the children-- i.e., perceptually handicapped, brain-injured, neurologically impaired.

The cooperative efforts of many professions have brought a distinctly multidisciplinary approach to the field. In many cases, however, the neurological component involved is difficult, if not impossible, to detect by medical examination; often therefore, the medical diagnosis is presumed or inferred and is necessarily made through observation of be- havior. In educational circles, the tendency is to de- emphasize the presumed pathological aspects and stress the behavioral. The medical field has begun to use more behav- ioral terminology, suggesting that the term "attention deficit disorder" be used.

The recently developed "clinical teaching method," as opposed to traditional methods of teaching in the classroom, is suggested as an approach to use with the learning disabled youngster. The goal of the clinical teaching method is to tailor learning experiences to the unique needs of a partic- ular child. Continuous diagnosis and treatment is required; the teacher modifies teaching procedures and plans as new needs become apparent. The method can be applied in various settings, and it requires that the teacher be flexible. Clin- ical teaching implies, as Janet Lerner maintains, that the teacher be aware of the individual student's "learning style, interests, shortcomings, areas of strength, levels of develop- ment and tolerance in many areas, feelings and adjustment to the world."

Remedial approaches for the learning disabled can be narrowed down to three educational strategies: *task training* which simplifies a particular task to be learned by breaking it down into several sub-skills; *ability training* where reme- diation focuses on a specific disability; and *ability or process task training* in which the first two approaches are combined.

After the child has been properly diagnosed and a remediation program has been planned, the least restrictive environment must be provided. Within the classroom, alternative
teaching techniques should be introduced to help the L.D.
student with his handicap. For example, for students with
poor visual memory, remembering facts which are written on
the board will be difficult. Class lessons should be taped
so that the students can listen to the lesson after class
making it easier for them to learn the material. A typewriter
should be available for the students who have difficulty with
fine motor skills. If in the later grades of elementary
school handwriting is illegible, typing should be included in
the students' programs. For the students with poor auditory
perception, visual aids should be included as part of the
lesson. Testing should be administered orally if necessary
to the students with poor visual perception.

Regardless of whether the learning disabled child has
reading problems, math problems, language problems, or organizational problems, there are a host of alternative educational strategies that are both available and effective.
These include such procedures as a very highly structured
classroom environment with orderly, clear rules and expectations; learning centers for variety of experiences in needed
skills mastery; constant and consistent appraisal and feedback; and ubiquitous rewards and reinforcement. Varying presentation and assessment approaches are a desideratum, as are
varying amounts and difficulty of homework and appropriate
sequencing from the concrete to the abstract and from fact to
inference.

In any case, a major responsibility remains with educators to structure the most effective learning experiences
possible for the learning disabled in our schools. During
the last 15 years, public school programs have expanded for
the learning disabled, but because of our budget problems,
the quality of the services varies widely. If there remains
a limit as to the size of the population to be designated as
learning disabled, then only the children with severe learning
disabilities will be eligible for service; the remaining children will either have to be served by specialists or receive
no special services.

409. Ackerman, P.T. 1977. Teenage status of hyperactive and nonhyperactive learning disabled boys. *American Journal of Orthopsychiatry* 47:557-96.

   In this study three groups of L.D. boys (twenty-three hyperactives, twenty-five normoactives, and fourteen hypoactives) were studied in grade school and reevaluated at age fourteen. At the followup, all three groups remained at disadvantage as to controls on academic and cognitive measures and on complex reaction time. Half of the hyperactives had experienced major conflicts with authority, and over a third of the hypoactives exhibited psychologically disturbing behaviors.

410. Adelman, H.S., and L. Taylor. 1983. Classifying students by inferred motivation to learn. *Learning Disability Quarterly* 6:201-6.

   A plan for categorizing learning disabled students was devised. Their level of motivation, degree of misbehavior, and degree of learning disability were tested. Thirty-seven students (ages nine to eighteen), who were diagnosed as learning disabled, participated.

411. Adler, S. 1982. Nutrition and language learning development in preschool programs for children with learning disabilities. *Journal of Learning Disabilities* 15:323-25.

   Do's and don't's regarding appropriate nutrition based on a program used at the Pediatric Language Laboratory.

412. Algozzine, B. 1977. The effects of labels and behavior on teacher expectations. *Exceptional Child* 44:131-32.

   This study investigated the effects of labeling children as L.D. or E.D. The assessment based on studying 128 students in four case studies was that behaviors of emotionally disturbed children were more disturbing and less accepted when they were thought to be exhibited by an L.D. child than by an E.D. child.

413. Amerikaner, M., and M. Summerlin. 1982. Group counseling with learning disabled children: Effects of social skills and relaxation training on self-concept and classroom behavior. *Journal of Learning Disabilities* 15:340-41.

   This study examined the effects of two group-counseling approaches, social skills and relaxation training, on L.D. children's self concept and on their in-class behavior as assessed by their teachers. The social skills group had more positive social self-concept scores than the other groups, though there was no difference on personal or intellectual self, while the relaxation training group was perceived by teachers as exhibiting less acting out and less distractibility than the other group.

414. Ames, L.B. 1983. Learning disability: Truth or trap? *Journal of Learning Disabilities* 16:16-18.

   Diagnosis of learning disability is made too loosely. Psychologists and educators should pursue the possibility of poor school adjustment and unreadiness for the work of the grade.

415. Anderson, P. 1982. A preliminary study of syntax in the written expression of learning disabled children. *Journal of Learning Disabilities* 15:359-62.

   The purpose of this study was to evaluate the arrangement of words and phrases in the written expression of five normal and five learning disabled fourth grade students. The results showed that the syntax of the learning disabled group was significantly inadequate when compared to that of the children in the normal group.

416. Argulewicz, E.N. 1982. Effects of an instructional
      program designed to improve attending behaviors of
      learning disabled students. *Journal of Learning
      Disabilities* 15:23-27.

          The study was undertaken to determine the ef-
      fects of a program designed to improve the attending
      behavior of individuals. Third grade learning dis-
      abled students were divided into two treatment
      groups: an experimental group and a control group.
      The results showed that the group which received the
      instructional program did a better job on two out of
      three tasks involving attending behaviors.

417. Argulewicz, E.N. 1983. Effects of ethnic membership,
      socioeconomic status and home language on LD, EMR,
      and EH placements. *Learning Disability Quarterly*
      6:195-200.

          A study was conducted to examine the proportions
      of special education placements. The subjects were
      Anglo, Black, and Hispanic elementary school children
      from a large school in the Southwest. Of three cate-
      gories, educable mentally retarded, emotionally hand-
      icapped, and learning disabled, the latter was the
      most frequently assigned placement.

418. Atkinson, B., and O. Seunath. 1973. The effect of
      stimulus change on attending behavior in normal chil-
      dren and children with learning disorders. *Journal
      of Learning Disabilities* 6:569-73.

          Eighteen boys, ten to eleven years old, with
      learning disorders were compared with normally
      achieving boys on an attention demanding task under
      the conditions of constant stimulation and stimulus
      change. Boys with learning problems did not perform
      as well under the change condition as the normal
      controls, but did perform as well under the constant
      stimulus condition. Data suggests that children
      with learning disorders are more influenced by stim-
      ulus change than are normally achieving children.

419. Axelrod, L. 1982. Social perception in learning dis-
     abled adolescents. *Journal of Learning Disabilities*
     15:610-13.

     A study was done to examine non-verbal social
     perception in adolescents with learning disabilities.
     Two separate groups of fifty-four learning disabled
     and normal eighth and ninth grade students were com-
     pared. Included in this evaluation were standard-
     ized tests on non-verbal communication and social
     intelligence tests. The results show that the L.D.
     adolescents were much lower in non-verbal social
     perception and communication skills than the control
     group of normal children.

420. Bangs, T.E. 1968. *Language and Learning disorders of
     the pre-academic child*. New York: Appleton-Century-
     Crofts.

     Parent goals, language, avenues of learning,
     assessment, and pre-academic training are discussed;
     communication, oral language, speech, written lan-
     guage, and intelligence are operationally defined.
     Assessment tools are described for language skills,
     avenues of learning, and diagnostic teaching. Devel-
     oping a pre-academic program must take into consid-
     eration many things, including educational philos-
     ophy, school policy, and the curriculum guide. Pre-
     academic curriculum is given for various levels.

421. Barsch, R.M. 1965. *A movigenic curriculum*. Madison,
     Wisconsin: Wisconsin Department of Public Instruc-
     tion.

     The impetus behind this experimental curriculum
     was a physiological approach to the education of
     children with special learning difficulties. The
     learner was seen as a space-oriented being with a
     physiological makeup designed to travel through edu-
     cational space, processing information to his advan-
     tage. Eight constructs serve as a nucleus for a
     theory of movement and special activities programmed
     in each area are detailed. The movigenic curriculum
     is a supplement to the existing curriculum. Two
     groups of elementary grade normal ability children

with learning problems were in the program for one
year.

422. Barsch, R.M., and N.D. Bryant. 1966. *The education of
      children with learning disabilities.* New Brunswick,
      New Jersey: Rutgers University Press.

      A perspective on learning disability and the
      concept of movement efficiency are the subjects here.
      Barsch suggests classes for special learning disabil-
      ities by part-time units that prepare the children
      for return to other classes. An experimental class-
      room is described. Bryant used the dyslexic child as
      learning disabled and used the following guiding
      principles: start with the most basic element that
      the child has trouble with, making the steps small
      enough (ninety percent correct responses), and avoid
      negative learning and confusion. The child should
      make noticeable improvement at every lesson. Over-
      learning and reviews will help keep retention high.

423. Battle, J., and I. Blowers. 1982. A longitudinal com-
      parative study of the self-esteem of students in
      regular and special education classes. *Journal of
      Learning Disabilities* 15:100-102.

      The purpose of this study was to examine changes
      in the self-esteem and perceptual ability of regular
      children and learning disabled children over a period
      of three years. The authors examined seventy-five
      children. The results showed that sixty-eight chil-
      dren who were learning disabled and in special educa-
      tion classes had greater gains in self-esteem and
      perception than the children in regular classes.

424. Becker, L., and M. Snider. 1979. Teachers' ratings
      and predicting special class placement. *Journal of
      Learning Disabilities* 12:37-40.

      This study focused on determining the validity
      of kindergarten and first grade teachers' ratings
      and predictions about future special education place-
      ment for learning disabilities in those children who
      experienced behavioral and academic problems in their

classes. The results showed that educationally handicapped boys were identified by more kindergarten
and first grade teachers as being immature, insecure,
and having short attention spans than normal boys
the same age. This kind of data supports the use of
teacher ratings as part of an early screening process
for learning disabilities. The results of this study
also appear to suggest that educationally handicapped
students are not ready to learn in kindergarten and
fail later on because they lack many of the academic
readiness skills (e.g., working independently, paying
attention, interacting well with others). In view
of this, the researchers suggest that early childhood
programs should focus on developing these readiness
skills before attempting to teach academic skills.

425.   Beery, K.E. 1967. *Preschool prediction and prevention
       of learning disabilities*. San Rafael, California:
       Marin County Superintendent School Office, San Rafael
       City Schools.

          This is a report on the initial screening phase
       of a four-year longitudinal study designed to predict
       and prevent learning disabilities in a general school
       population. Children (three and one-half to five
       and one-half) of an entire school district were
       tested intensively and rescreened annually. How the
       children were assigned and what the screening and
       tests were is described. Results from the experi-
       mental children were forwarded to their future
       schools and doctors with suggestions for preventative
       guidance. It was found that boys did as well as
       girls (contrary to the more usual findings). The
       younger children performed at a higher level (rela-
       tive to their age) than the older children did.
       Test patterns revealed nearly twice as many visual-
       motor deficits as there were auditory-vocal deficits
       and almost twice as many association, encoding, and
       sequencing deficits as there were decoding deficits
       in both experimental and control groups.

426.   Bernstein, B. 1967. *Everyday problems and the child
       with learning difficulties*. New York: John Day.

          The problems that daily living may present to
       children who experience learning difficulties are

discussed, and the need for the teacher to develop a
method for dealing with the children's problems is
described. The environmental problems explored in
this book are put into three categories--as situation
problems, as concept problems, and as applied information problems. The bulk of the book consists of
thirty-eight problems and suggested solutions. Some
examples of situation problems are: how to open a
can or jar, which tool to use, and why paint things.
Concept problems include: what do colors mean and
what do arrows tell you to do. Applied information
problems are: how do you send for things or find
your favorite television program or what should you
know about yourself in an emergency.

427. Bingham, G. 1978. Career attitudes among boys with
and without specific learning disabilities. *Exceptional Children* 44:341-42.

In this study the Career Maturity Index was
administered to 120 boys in two groups consisting of
thirty boys with S.L.D. and thirty with N.L.D. of
preadolescent and adolescent ages. The results seem
to imply that boys with L.D. at both age levels were
less mature in responses to demands associated with
career choice and would need planned experiences and
activities to accommodate developmental differences.

428. Bos, C.S., and D. Filip. 1984. Comprehension monitoring in learning disabled and average students. *Journal of Learning Disabilities* 17:229-32.

This study examined the comprehension monitoring
skills of learning disabled and average seventh grade
students. The students were given expository passages with text inconsistencies using standard and
cued conditions to read. The results suggested that
although the learning disabled students had an inability to adopt task appropriate strategies spontaneously, the students could be activated to produce
these task appropriate strategies with relatively
minimal training or cuing.

429. Breen, M.J. 1984. The temporal stability of the Woodcock-Johnson Tests of Cognitive Ability for elementary-age learning disabled children. *Journal of Psychoeducational Assessment* 2:257-61.

     An investigation of the stability of the Woodcock-Johnson Tests of Cognitive Ability for elementary aged learning disabled was made. The Woodcock-Johnson test was administered to fifty-seven learning disabled students in grades two to five and again six months later. Results show that only the Full Scale Index and the Verbal and Oral Language cluster scales demonstrate adequate stability over six months. Small but significant gains in mean standard score performance occurred for all measures from one W-J test to the other. These findings have diagnostic implications in terms of initial enrollment in and/or termination from a learning disabilities program.

430. Bruininks, R.H., and V.L. Bruininks. 1977. Motor proficiency of learning disabled and nondisabled students. *Perceptual and Motor Skills* 44:1131-37.

     In this study the motor proficiency of fifty-five L.D. students and fifty-five nondisabled students, average age nine years, was compared on a comprehensive battery of motor skills tests. It was found that L.D. students performed significantly lower than non-L.D. students on measures of fine motor skills and on gross motor skills. Findings therefore suggest the need for structured motor training for learning disabled children.

431. Bruininks, V.L. 1978. Actual and perceived peer status of learning disabled students in mainstream programs. *Journal of Special Education* 12:51-58.

     This study investigated the peer status of sixteen L.D. children, all of elementary school age and in regular classrooms and the accuracy with which they perceived themselves in the classes' social structure. Then all the students rated each child in the classroom on a peer acceptance scale. The results showed that L.D. children were both less socially accepted in the mainstreamed class and less accurate than the normal children in assessing their personal status in the group.

432. Bruno, R. 1981. Interpretation of pictorially presented social situations by learning disabled and
normal children. *Journal of Learning Disabilities*
14:350-52.

The purpose of this study was to focus on the
interpretation of pictorially presented social settings. Two groups consisting of twenty learning
disabled and twenty normal children ranging in age
from nine to eleven years old were selected. The
reactions of the forty students to a social inference
task were recorded. After careful examination, it
was determined that the learning disabled children
expressed a significant deficit in interpreting a
situation properly and predicting its consequences.
However, there were no differences found between the
two groups as far as understanding the order of
events.

433. Bryan, J.H., and T.H. Bryan. 1978. Social interactions
of learning disabled children. *Learning Disabilities
Quarterly* 1:33-38.

In this study an investigation was made using
twenty-five L.D. children, grades four to five, as
to verbal communication both among themselves and
with their peers. The results showed that L.D. children were less popular than their peers, and that
their communication habits were a major cause of
their social rejection.

434. Bryan, J.H.; L.J. Sonnefeld; and B. Grabowski. 1983.
The relationship between fear of failure and learning
disabilities. *Learning Disability Quarterly* 6:217-
22.

The Test Anxiety Scale for Children (TASC) and
the Lie Scale for Children (LSC) were given to sixty
children for the purpose of determining if there is
a difference in the amount of test anxiety experienced between students in regular classes and students who have been identified as learning disabled.

Half of these students had been identified as having
learning disabilities. An analysis of the data indicated that the children who were learning disabled
were more anxious than the other children, and that
a large portion of this anxiety was significantly
related to reading and mathematics achievement
scores. The researchers also discussed possible
reasons for the additional anxiety experienced by
the students who were learning disabled. Although
the causality was unclear, the researchers did offer
possibilities and suggest the need for further research.

435.   Bryant, S.; C.W. McIntyre; M.E. Murray; and S.L.
       Blackwell. 1983. Rate of visual information pick-
       up in learning disabled and normal boys. *Learning
       Disability Quarterly* 6:166-71.

       In this study, a "span-of-apprehension" (re-
       flecting the amount of information a person can ex-
       tract or process from a brief visual display) task
       and a "backward masking" technique were combined in
       order to measure the apprehension span of learning
       disabled and "normal" boys at various time intervals
       after a stimulus had been presented. The rates of
       pick-up and comparisons of said rates are discussed.
       The results revealed that the students who were
       learning disabled had a slower rate of information
       pick-up. Also, implications of eye movement training
       programs are discussed.

436.   Byrne, B., and B. Schneider. 1985. Factorial validity
       of Stephen's Social Behavior Assessment. *Journal of
       Consulting & Clinical Psychology* 53:259-60.

       Teacher ratings of elementary school pupils
       from regular classes, of learning disabled students,
       and of emotionally disturbed children were used in a
       factor and item analysis of the Social Behavior As-
       sessment. Factors obtained from item analysis ex-
       plained more of the variance than factors based on
       subcategory scores. A revised instrument is proposed
       that consists of seventy-one items based on four
       underlying factors--Social Participation/Conversa-
       tion, Self-Control, Consideration for Others, and
       Academic Responsibility. This revised Social Behav-

ior Assessment discriminated between the sample in
regular classes and those enrolled in special education programs.

437. Caplan, P. 1977. Sex, age, behavior, and school subject as determinants of report of learning problems.
Journal of Learning Disabilities 10:314-16.

A group of 280 college students were asked to
make priorities for assigning tutorial help to children who were failing in school. The students were
asked to rate the children on the basis of various
combinations of sex, age, type of problems, and the
subject of school difficulty. Top priority were
boys, the older child, acting out behavior, and difficulty in reading. The lowest priority were girls,
the younger child, withdrawn behavior, and difficulty
in arithmetic. The child's sex interacted with behavior in such a way that withdrawn boys and acting
out girls were considered to need more help than
children whose behavior conformed to the norm of
their sex.

438. Cartledge, G.; T. Frew; and J. Zaharias. 1985. Social
skill needs of mainstreamed students: Peer and
teacher perceptions. *Learning Disability Quarterly*
8:132-40.

Two studies were conducted on social skills
that mainstreamed students needed; peer and teacher
perceptions were studied. In study I, fourth and
fifth graders viewed a videotape that featured children labeled as normal or learning disabled, and
then answered a questionnaire on their perceptions
of the children. Items of inquiry were academics,
kindness, communication, friendship, and play behaviors. Only the responses to the kindness item favored the L.D. children. In study II, fourteen
teachers rated 136 social skills that were most important for L.D. children mainstreamed into the regular classroom. Teachers placed emphasis on task and
order-related behaviors. The article discusses the
discrepancy between the two groups' social skills
focus, and social skills instruction for the mainstreamed L.D. student.

439. Ceci, S. 1984. A developmental study of learning dis-
      abilities and memory. *Journal of Experimental Psy-
      chology* 38:352-71.

          This study was designed to assess the develop-
      mental course of automatic semantic processing and
      purposive semantic processing. Seven, ten and thir-
      teen year old L.D. and non-L.D. (NORM) children were
      presented structured lists of thirty-eight words
      each. Each list contained four semantically related
      words. Two of the four were presented consecutively
      on the list while the other two were spaced. All
      children disproportionately recalled more of the
      adjacent words. Spaced words were less likely remem-
      bered by young than old children and by L.D. than
      NORMs. Findings reveal NORMs' memory processes are
      governed by purposive semantic processing more so
      than L.D. subjects. No group or age difference is
      reported in automatic semantic processing. The study
      suggests that weak purposive semantic processing is
      a causal factor in L.D. difficulties.

440. Clarizio, H., and S. Phillips. 1986. Sex bias in the
      diagnosis of learning disabled students. *Psychology
      in the Schools* 23:44-52.

          The purpose of this investigation was to deter-
      mine if the sex of a student is a factor in the ini-
      tial diagnosis and placement into L.D. programs by
      multidisciplinary teams. Data was gathered on 235
      L.D. students. The discrepancy between expected
      achievement and actual achievement was examined.
      Other factors such as intelligence, social/economic
      status, and reason for referral were taken into ac-
      count. No evidence was found to indicate sex bias
      in diagnostic and placement practices.

441. Clinkert, R.J. 1978. Language competency, dyslexia
      and learning disabilities. *Bulletin of the Orton
      Society* 28:208-16.

          Three hundred and ninety-seven first graders
      were given the Peabody Picture Vocabulary Test, the
      Purdue Perceptual Motor Survey, and the Preschool
      Language Scale in order to test the hypothesis that
      language competence is a better differentiator be-

tween normal and learning disabled children than
perceptual-motor-memory competence. The results from
these tests showed that the learning disabled children did not perform as well as the normal children
and had poorer vocabulary repertories as well. Performance on the language tests was better correlated
to the learning disabled children than their performance on the perceptual-motor-memory tests.

442. Coleman, M. 1984. Mothers' predictions of the self
concept of their normal or learning disabled children. *Journal of Learning Disabilities* 17:214-17.

The self-concepts of fifty-four regular classroom children, forty-eight learning disabled (L.D.)
children, and twenty-two students referred for special education were assessed. Mothers were then
asked to rate their child's self-concept. Results
revealed minimal differences between self-concept
scores of L.D. and regular classroom children. However, mothers of the L.D. students predicted lower
self-concepts than their children.

443. Coleman, M. 1985. Achievement level, social class,
and the self-concepts of mildly handicapped children.
Journal of Learning Disabilities 18:26-30.

In this study self-concept scores were examined.
169 elementary students ranging in age from five to
twelve who spend half their school day in special
classes and half in education mainstream classes
were selected. Based on the self-concept scores,
results show that children who come from high socioeconomic status levels, are mildly handicapped, and
are inadequate academically have much lower self-
concepts when compared to normal children.

444. Cooks, S.; T. Scruggs; M. Mastropieri; and G. Castro.
1985-86. Handicapped students as tutors. *Journal
of Special Education* 19:483-90.

A meta-analysis was conducted on available research documenting effectiveness of handicapped students as tutors of other students. Studies were
included in this analysis only if the authors of the

study identified the tutors as either L.D., B.D., or intellectually handicapped. Results indicated that tutoring programs were generally effective. Results also showed tutees for the most part gained more than tutors. Tutor and tutee gains on self-concept and socio-metric ratings were small, while gains on attitude measures were larger.

445. Copeland, A.P.; E. Reiner; and A. Jirkovsky. 1984. Examining a premise underlying self-instructional techniques. *Cognitive Therapy & Research* 8:619-29.

Twenty learning disabled children, ages six and one-half to nine years old, took the Matching Familiar Figures Test and then played alone in a room while their behavior and private speech were video-taped. Tapes were coded according to activity level and the amount and type of private speech used during play. Results showed that the sample used more fantasy/role-playing speech than affective or regulatory speech. The speech of ten children diagnosed hyperactive was generally similar to that of the rest of the sample, although high activity level during play was accompanied by more private speech. The less active sample used fantasy/role playing speech more than the impulsive sample did. The findings supported the premise that high active L.D. children show differences in their private speech as compared to less active children, and that they can benefit from techniques designed to modify self-directed speech.

446. Copeland, A. P., and S. Weissbrod. 1983. Cognitive strategies used by learning disabled children: Does hyperactivity always make things worse? *Journal of Learning Disabilities* 16:473-76.

Maturity and style of problem solving of learning disabled children were compared to those of children not learning disabled. Results indicated that L.D. children performed less well than the non-L.D. children on tasks requiring internal strategies or plans. Hyperactive L.D. children used a less mature strategy than the non-hyperactive L.D. children. Children with more behavioral problems also were children who used less mature cognitive strategies.

447. Corman, C. 1978. Let's do it again--please! *Academic Therapy* 14:91-94.

Pointed out in this study are the benefits of using games in instructing learning disabled students. Some games that can be played with a deck of learning cards are outlined to illustrate several methods that can be used with a single set of materials. The study concludes that within the setting of play, children with learning disabilities can forget their fears about new tasks with confidence and therefore find that learning can be fun.

448. Cornelius, P.L., and M. Semmel. 1982. Effects of summer instruction on reading achievement regression of learning disabled students. *Journal of Learning Disabilities* 15:409-13.

This study was done to examine the effects of long-term breaks from school as far as reading is concerned. Pre- and post-test scores were evaluated from learning disabled children. The results revealed L.D. students show a significant decline in their reading skills when they experience an eight-week summer break from an educational setting. Studies show that a five-week reading program given at the beginning or end of the summer can prevent this regression from occurring.

449. Darch, C., and R. Gersten. 1985. The effects of teacher presentation rate and praise on LD students' oral reading performance. *The British Journal of Educational Psychology* 55:295-303.

This study assessed the effects that the rate of instructional presentation and the frequency of praise had on student on-task behavior. The components' effects were measured individually and cooperatively in a study involving four L.D. students for twenty-five days. Praise proved to be more powerful than the presentation rate in affecting the overall performance of the child. The combination of the two components has a most powerful effect. The study demonstrates that application of two simple teaching skills can increase how much students learn.

450. De Chiara, E. 1982. Visual arts program for enhance-
      ment of the body image. *Journal of Learning Disabil-
      ities* 15:33-37.

          The purpose of the study was to determine
      whether a visual arts program related to the human
      figure would enhance the body image of children with
      learning disabilities. It was found that imaging
      and representation are important processes because
      they give the child access to memories. Art experi-
      ences were found not only to allow the child to ex-
      press what he knows about the body but also to extend
      and enhance his knowledge.

451. Decker, L.A., and R.J. Decker. 1977. Mainstreaming
      the L.D. child: A cautionary note. *Academic Therapy*
      12:353-56.

          This article deals with reasons for advocating
      caution in mainstreaming L.D. students. Among six
      reasons cited are lowered self concepts in main-
      streamed students due to competition with their nor-
      mal peers, lack of individual attention, and possibly
      inadequate teacher preparation.

452. Delamater, A., and B. Lahey. 1983. Physiological cor-
      relates of conduct problems and anxiety in hyper-
      active and learning disabled children. *Journal of
      Abnormal Child Psychology* 11:85-100.

          In this study thirty-six learning disabled chil-
      dren (twenty-one of whom were also classified as
      hyperactive) were subgrouped according to teacher
      ratings of tension/anxiety and conduct problems and
      then compared on measures of tonic and phasic auto-
      nomic arousal. Findings uphold the idea that hyper-
      active and learning disabled children are heteroge-
      neous at a physiological level. The authors suggest
      that physiological differences previously attributed
      to hyperactivity may actually be correlates of the
      conduct problem area.

453. Deno, S.L. 1979. An experimental analysis of the na-
     ture of reversal errors in children with severe
     learning disabilities. *Learning Disability Quarterly*
     2:40-45.

         The nature of reversal errors in letter identi-
     fication was studied with five severely learning
     disabled elementary school children. The children
     were presented with the task of naming lower case
     letters, "b," "d," "p," and "q" in thirty second
     trials and in untimed trials. A multiple baseline
     across students was used in an experiment to deter-
     mine the extent to which changes occur in the incen-
     tive conditions. The results showed that reversal
     errors decreased quickly when incentives were intro-
     duced.

454. Derr, A.M. 1985. Conservation and mathematics achieve-
     ment in the learning disabled child. *Journal of
     Learning Disabilities* 18:333-36.

         This study investigates the development of the
     cognitive stage of concrete operations, conservation,
     in twenty-two L.D. children, ages nine to twelve
     years, who had deficits in mathematics achievement,
     and in eighteen age-matched controls with average
     achievement in math. The children were given tests
     of conservation in six areas. Significant differ-
     ences appeared; many L.D. students (fifty percent)
     had not yet developed the concept of conservation,
     even in the upper elementary school grades. The
     study suggests that this type of lag in cognitive
     development may constrict the ability of L.D. chil-
     dren to understand mathematics as it is taught today.

455. Derr, A.M. 1986. How learning disabled adolescent
     boys make moral judgments. *Journal of Learning Dis-
     abilities* 19:160-63.

         This investigation studied the formulation of
     moral judgments in learning disabled boys as compared
     to average achieving adolescents. The learning dis-
     abled group were less able to see moral situations
     from a social or community point of view and exhib-
     ited a strong focus on the needs of the self. The
     keystone to mature moral reasoning is the acceptance

of a social perspective. This study therefore suggests that special educators also teach social perception and moral reasoning.

456. Dixon, N. 1982. An alternative framework for consider-
     ing learning disabilities in a more positive light.
     Journal of Learning Disabilities 15:390-92.

     The author presents an alternative framework
     that defines learning disabilities as a product of
     conflicting relationships between symbol perceiving
     ability and response to feedback.

457. Donahue, M., and T. Bryan. 1984. Communicative skills
     and peer relations of learning disabled adolescents.
     Topics in Language Disorders 4:10-21.

     This article concerns itself with the communi-
     cative ability of the learning disabled adolescent
     and how it affects his/her acceptance by peers. The
     research indicated difficulties in social perception,
     oral language, and social experience. It concludes
     with suggestions for enhancing the communication
     skills by using group reinforcements and by exposing
     L.D. students to normal adolescents.

458. Doyhle, W. 1982. The effectiveness of color coded
     cues in remediating reversals. *Journal of Learning
     Disabilities* 15:326-30.

     This paper explores the effectiveness of the
     color-coding technique in remediating reversals.
     Plain old-fashioned practice seems to win out over
     color-coded practice of equal duration. The hypoth-
     esis was not valid.

459. Dykman, R.A.; T. Ackerman; J. Holcomb; and Y. Boudrequ.
     1983. Physiological manifestations of learning dis-
     ability. *Journal of Learning Disabilities* 16:46-49.

     The article reviews the physiological studies
     that have been done on non-hyperactive learning dis-
     abled youngsters. The evidence reviewed indicates
     some degree of attentional deficit in L.D. children,

but does not necessarily imply brain damage or brain dysfunction.

460. Elbert, J.C. 1984. Short-term memory encoding and memory search in the word recognition of learning disabled children. *Journal of Learning Disabilities* 17:342-45.

This study was designed to analyze the abilities of L.D. children to employ two essential tasks necessary for effective word recognition and decoding skills: encoding and memory search. The subjects were sixteen learning disabled children with word recognition deficits and sixteen control children of equal age, grade, and intelligence. The results indicate that although the L.D. subjects did not differ from the control subjects at the initial encoding stage of their word recognition task, they did require significantly more processing time for memory scanning. This delay in short-term memory searching was especially apparent when the input word was visually, rather than auditorally, presented.

461. Elliott, J.L., and J.R. Gentile. 1986. The efficacy of a mnemonic technique for learning disabled and nondisabled adolescents. *Journal of Learning Disabilities* 19:237-40.

Sixty junior high school students participated in a replication of a study that was done by Bugelski. One-half of these students were "normal" while one-half were learning disabled. Half of the students learned four lists of words linked to mnemonic devices. The others, serving as controls, learned the lists of words in any manner they chose. Retention tests were given immediately following the learning of the last list, then again one week later, and five months later. The memorability in both the learning disabled and "normal" groups was greater than that of control groups. The results indicated that the mnemonic devices aided not only on the tests given immediately, but also at the intervals that followed.

462.   Epstein, L. 1978. The effects of interclass peer tu-
       toring on the vocabulary development of learning dis-
       abled children. *Journal of Learning Disabilities*
       11:518-21.

           In this study the effects of interclass peer
       tutoring on vocabulary development were studied in
       primary level learning disabled children. Some of
       the results were that the peer tutoring-reading group
       did better on criterion test reading than did the
       peer tutoring-math, self instructional, teacher in-
       structed, and control groups. The study also found
       that the peer tutoring-reading groups covered a sig-
       nificantly greater number of words than did the
       teacher instructed group.

463.   Epstein, M.; W. Bursuck; and D. Cullinan. 1985. Pat-
       terns of behavior problems among the learning dis-
       abled: Boys aged 12-18, girls aged 6-11, and girls
       aged 12-18. *Learning Disability Quarterly* 8:123-29.

           The purpose of this study was to examine behav-
       ior problem patterns among the learning disabled.
       Behavior Problem Checklists were completed by fifty-
       seven special education teachers on 302 females and
       316 male learning disabled students. Two broad di-
       mensions of psychopathology were found--environmental
       conflict and personal disturbance. The factor struc-
       tures differed between the groups. The factors were
       labeled Conduct Problem, Socialized Delinquency,
       Anxiety-Withdrawal, and Inadequacy-Immaturity for
       twelve to eighteen year old males. Both groups of
       girls showed alternative factors labeled Attention
       Deficit, while the younger group showed a factor
       labeled Social Incompetence and the older group one
       labeled Aggression Delinquency. Results are consist-
       ent with previous factor analytic studies, and also
       suggest age may interact more strongly with behavior
       problems than sex.

464.   Epstein, M.; D. Cullinan; and G. Nieminen. 1984. So-
       cial behavior problems of learning disabled and nor-
       mal girls. *Journal of Learning Disabilities* 17:609-
       11.

           This study compared social behavior problems of

learning disabled and normal girls. Teacher ratings
of 150 L.D. and non-L.D. females, grouped at three
age levels, seven to eight, ten to eleven, and thirteen to fourteen years, on school emotional and behavior problems as measured by the Behavior Problem
Checklist, were compared. Personality Problem was
the only factor that differentiated L.D. from non-
L.D., and these differences were not apparent at
every age level. For normal females, the number of
problems increase with age, but older and younger
L.D. females showed higher levels of problem behaviors than L.D. females in the middle age group. The
findings support results of previous studies that
indicate the existence of personal behavior and social problems in L.D. students.

465. Evans, J.R., and L.J. Smith. 1977. Common behavioral
      s.l.d. characteristics. *Academic Therapy* 12:425-27.

          In this study children's behavior characteris-
      tics as reported by the parents of sixty clients
      (six to thirteen years old) who had been evaluated
      for special learning disabilities were examined.
      The study found that there occurred a high incidence
      of sensitivity to criticism and easy discouragement.
      This finding supports the assumption that with con-
      tinued school failure experiences, these children
      tend to become anxious and generally emotionally
      disturbed, further handicapping them in school.

466. Faerstein, L. 1986. Coping and defense mechanisms of
      mothers of learning disabled children. *Journal of
      Learning Disabilities* 19:8-11.

          This study investigated the ways in which
      twenty-four mothers of learning disabled children
      cope with and defend against the diagnosis and mani-
      festations of their child's problem. Results indi-
      cated that the mothers usually showed coping mecha-
      nisms when involved with medical, social, or educa-
      tional agencies, and were able to appropriately ob-
      tain services for their child. However, in direct
      confrontation with the child coping functions broke
      down and gave way to more defensive mechanisms such
      as projection, denial of the problem, and displace-
      ment of anger on the child. Mothers, contrary to

traditional attitudes, experienced relief at receiving a diagnosis confirming their suspicions rather than experiencing shock or grief.

467. Feagans, L., and E.J. Short. 1986. Referential communicative and reading performances in learning disabled children over a three year period. *Developmental Psychology* 22:177-83.

      The authors wanted to learn the differences between learning disabled children and normal children in following a given set of instructions. They gave thirty normal and thirty learning disabled children a task that could only be performed in an exact sequence and specific instructions on how to perform the task. Their results showed that the normal children were significantly superior to the learning disabled group in the areas tested.

468. Fisher, E.; J. Miller-White; and J. Fisher. 1984. Teaching figurative language. *Academic Therapy* 19:403-7.

      This paper offers an approach to teaching L.D. students figurative language, an important element in developing good reading and communication skills. Many L.D. students draw conclusions based upon perceptual information rather than analytical skills and therefore, a special approach to teaching this skill is needed. First, the student must develop an understanding of the difference between a literal and a figurative statement. This is done by carefully dissecting the figurative statement. For example, in dissecting the statement, "you drive me up a wall," the student and teacher try to act out each word to see if this action is really physically possible. (Can a person really take a car and drive it right up the wall?) The student eventually begins to understand by seeing how foolish and impossible these statements can be when dissected and analyzed in this manner. After this skill is mastered, practice is the next step to success. Understanding figurative language can help provide a basis for developing cognitive skills in other subjects, as well. Using this approach L.D. adolescents have been successful in identifying figurative statements within a few short months.

469. Fleisher, L.S.; L.C. Soodak; and M.A. Jelin. 1984. Selective attention deficits in learning disabled children: Analysis of the data base. *Exceptional Children* 51:136-41.

New data in the area of special education suggest that attention deficits are a distinguishing characteristic of learning disabled children. An analysis of existing data supported the theory of selective attention deficits in learning disabled children. Concepts and methodologies used in interpreting findings were explored. The results suggest that the evidence of selective attention deficits is inconclusive and should not be used as a basis for classification.

470. Foster, G.G., and J.E. Yaseldyke. 1978. Bias in teachers' observations of emotionally disturbed and learning disabled children. *Exceptional Children* 44:613-15.

In this study it was found that when asked to rate the expected behavior of a hypothetical child assigned to all three labeling groups, N.L.D., L.D., and E.D., seventy-five elementary teachers differentially responded to labels. Students rated a videotaped fourth grader more negatively when he was labeled L.D. or E.D. than when he was labeled N.L.D.

471. Fowler, S.A. 1986. Peer-monitoring and self-monitoring: Alternatives to traditional teaching management. *Exceptional Children* 52:573-81.

A peer-monitoring procedure and a self-monitoring procedure were developed and researched in an effort to determine if these interventions would decrease disruption and non-participation by children with behavior and/or learning problems during transition activities. A group of ten children attending a special kindergarten class took part in the study. The children were divided into teams. Student captains were assigned during the peer-

monitoring portion of the study. They monitored
children's activities and awarded points to those
who had followed instructions during four transition
activities. A substantial reduction of inappropriate
behavior was noted after which a self-monitoring
procedure was introduced. The children were still
assigned to teams, but each child was responsible
for awarding his own points at the end of the transition activities. Improvements obtained during the
peer-monitoring procedure were for the most part
maintained during the self-monitoring procedure.
Study results suggest that the achievement of better
classroom management may be obtained when peer-
managed or self-managed points are awarded for compliance with the routine.

472. Freides, D., and C.A. Messina. 1986. Memory improve-
      ment via motor encoding in learning disabled chil-
      dren. *Journal of Learning Disabilities* 19:113-15.

          The effect of motor enactment to improve verbal
      memory was studied in children with learning dis-
      abilities, with or without motor impairment. The
      children, fifty male students, were told active sen-
      tences. They repeated the sentences twice and then
      did an enactment of them. The results showed that
      by acting out the sentences the children were able
      to remember the sentences told to them.

473. Gaskins, I.W. 1982. Let's end the reading disabil-
      ities/learning disabilities debate. *Journal of
      Learning Disabilities* 15:81-82.

          Experts do not agree on a definitive way to
      decide whether a poor reader should be labeled read-
      ing or learning disabled. Author suggests that
      fields should merge and provides recommendations for
      creating this merger.

474. Gaskins, I.W. 1984. There's more to a reading problem
      than poor reading. *Journal of Learning Disabilities*
      17:467-71.

          A study was done to evaluate an academic envi-
      ronment and to identify characteristics that would

explain why 321 high I.Q. elementary students were
doing poorly in reading. The results of the study
revealed that teacher should stop dealing with reading problems in isolation.

475. Gelzheiser, L. 1984. Generalizations from categorical
memory tasks to prose by learning disabled adolescents. *Journal of Educational Psychology* 76:1128-38.

This study investigated how sixty learning disabled and twenty nondisabled, ages twelve to fourteen
and one-half, transfer the use of four study rules
from instructed materials to a prose recall task.
Over a three-week period four phases were involved:
pre-test, informational phase, individualized training, and post-test. Results showed that on the prose
task, a majority of the learning disabled demonstrated transfer of the instructed rules. As a group
the learning disabled did not differ observably from
the nondisabled in recall or in the strategies they
used to study and to retrieve. The clinical view
that L.D. are characterized by failure to generalize
was not supported by these findings.

476. Gelzheiser, L.; R. Solar; M. Shepherd; and R. Wozniak.
1983. Teaching learning disabled children to memorize: A rationale for plans and practice. *Journal
of Learning Disabilities* 16:421-24.

This study discussed the process by which we
memorize and how learning disabled children must be
trained in memorizing techniques. Several steps to
memorizing are discussed and great emphasis is placed
on the need to practice these skills until they become automatic.

477. German, D.J.; B. Johnson; and M. Schneider. 1985.
Learning disability vs. reading disability: A survey
of practitioners' diagnostic populations and test
instruments. *Learning Disability Quarterly* 8:141-57.

The study compared diagnostic practices among
three professional groups: 141 resource learning
disabilities specialists, 74 self-contained learning
disabilities specialists, and 118 reading resource

specialists. The areas looked at were diagnostic
tests employed, informational sources utilized, diagnostic populations serviced, and diagnostic factors
considered in typical assessments of reading disorders. The groups differed with respect to each of
these issues; however, all groups identified language
deficits as a characteristic of their diagnostic
population. All groups considered causality,
strengths, weaknesses, and language deficits to be
important in the diagnosis of reading disorders and
all utilized tests of reading potential and reading
skills.

478. Gillespie, J. 1982. The "pushouts": Academic skills
and learning disabilities in continuation high school
students. *Journal of Learning Disabilities* 15:539-
41.

Although students from California high schools
are sent to continuation schools because of attend-
ance and behavior problems, assessment measures suggest the presence of a number of unidentified learning disabled students. Although the staff deny that
they work with handicapped children, continuation
schools appear to use a number of procedures associated with effective learning disability instruction.

479. Gillet, P. 1986. Mainstreaming techniques for learning
disabled students. *Academic Therapy* 21:389-400.

Mainstreaming learning disabled children is a
problem encountered in all schools that have normal
children and learning disabled children. This article describes techniques that teachers of special
education can offer to the teachers of the mainstream
class. It also describes what the teacher of special
education can do to help the children being mainstreamed. Such help should be in accord with the
specific problems of the individual children involved.

480. Gordon, M. 1984. Do children with constitutional delay
      really have more learning problems? *Journal of
      Learning Disabilities* 17:291-93.

           The purpose of this study was to see if children
      with constitutional delay really have a lot more
      problems learning things. A study looked at the
      scores of twenty-four children of short stature on
      academic, intellectual, and visual motor skills and
      compared them to twenty-three subjects of normal
      height for age, socioeconomic level, and sex. The
      results showed that short and control groups were
      the same on all aspects tested.

481. Graybill, D. 1984. Remediation of impulsivity in
      learning disabled children by special education re-
      source teachers using verbal self-instruction. *Psy-
      chology in the Schools* 21:252-54.

           Special education resource teachers trained
      impulsive learning disabled children to use Verbal
      Self-Instruction (VSI) to decrease the children's
      impulsivity. The students trained with VSI showed
      reductions in impulsivity on the Matching Familiar
      Figures test, but were not rated as less impulsive
      by regular classroom teachers.

482. Hagin, R. 1984. Effects on first-grade promotion prac-
      tices of a program for the prevention of learning
      disabilities. *Psychology in the Schools* 21:471-76.

           The article examines a program in an inner-city
      school for the prevention of learning disabilities
      over a twelve-year period and its impact upon promo-
      tion practices. This program was the cooperative
      venture of a community school district and a medical
      center. It provided services to identify children
      vulnerable to learning disabilities, to diagnose the
      causes of their vulnerabilities, and to intervene
      educationally. Educational intervention resulted in
      a decrease in nonpromotion rate to five percent or
      less. 217 children in intervention and in no treat-
      ment control groups were evaluated; the intervention
      group attained superior performance on the Woodcock
      Reading Mastery Test at the end of the first and

second grade, and on a measure of reading comprehension at the end of second grade.

483. Haman, T.; D. Isaacson; and G. Powell. 1985. Insuring classroom success for the LD adolescent. *Academic Therapy* 20:517-24.

Eleven secondary classroom teachers, who were perceived by teachers of the L.D. to be highly effective in teaching L.D. students, were surveyed. The purpose was to identify sources of assistance to them in expanding their knowledge of how to instruct L.D. students, and to identify teaching strategies they used when instructing L.D. students. The sample represented ten academic areas: business, home economics, mathematics, English, industrial arts, science, music, physical education, social studies, and vocational education. The sources of assistance and teaching strategies that are seen to be most valuable are outlined on a table. The source that received the highest rating by all of the sample was teaching experience. The strategy that received the highest rating was positive reinforcement. The article suggests that secondary L.D. students can experience success in a regular classroom only when the teacher is able to meet their individual needs.

484. Hiroshige-Nulman, J., and M. Gerber. 1984. Improving spelling performance by imitating a child's errors. *Journal of Learning Disabilities* 17:328-32.

Normally achieving learners form effective attack strategies for spelling over a period of time with repeated attempts. The information gained can be stored and utilized at some future point when these strategies are needed again to manage similar tasks. L.D. students seem to formulate their attack strategies based on insufficient or incorrect recall techniques. As a result, they fail to spell correctly, repeatedly. This particular study focused on increasing the number of correctly spelled words and improving the quality of errors of elementary learning disabled students when a contingent imitation and modeling approach was used. Each student's misspelled word was reviewed with the teacher and approached in the following manner--"This is how you

spelled the word...now here is the correct way to
spell this word." The child is then required to
write the word correctly. If the child spelled a
word correctly the first time, he was rewarded with
reinforcers such as candy or games. Repeated trials
using this technique resulted in faster acquisition
and a higher percentage of correct spellings for
L.D. students. Although this study proved to be
successful, caution is advised in using this procedure due to the fact that some students may view
imitation and modeling as a punishment.

485. Holmes, B.C. 1985. The effects of a strategy and se-
quenced materials on the inferential comprehension
of disabled readers. *Journal of Learning Disabilities* 18:542-46.

The researcher wished to determine if teaching
disabled readers through a structured inferencing
strategy utilizing materials that were arranged from
easy to more difficult would increase the children's
abilities to answer inferential questions. The subjects were fourth and fifth grade students who had
been attending remedial reading classes. The researcher split the group into four segments—strategy
plus materials, strategy only, materials only, and
control. An analysis showed that the group that had
been given strategy plus materials scored significantly better than the three other groups in answer
to inferential questioning presented by the researcher. Also, the strategy plus materials group
and the materials only group both scored significantly higher than the control group on a standardized reading test. Results indicated that disabled
readers problems may arise from their difficulty in
finding a strategy to attack problems. This difficulty may, according to the researcher, be eased
through the use of specially prepared materials.

486. Horn, W., and T. Packard. 1985. Early identification
of learning problems: A meta-analysis. *Journal of
Educational Psychology* 77:597-607.

This study summarized data on the early prediction of learning problems. A meta-analysis was conducted on fifty-eight studies that reported correla-

tions between measures administered in kindergarten
or first grade and reading achievement later on in
elementary school. Results showed a great deal of
overlap in the distributions of the various
predictor-criterion correlations. The best predictors of achievement during the elementary school
years were found to be attention-distractibility,
internalizing behavior problems, and language variables. Measures less directly related to reading
skills, such as sensory tasks, were generally weaker
predictors of achievement.

487. Horowitz, R.S. 1970. Teaching mathematics to students
     with learning disabilities. *Academic Therapy* 6:17-
     35.

          This study provides teachers with techniques
     for teaching math to children who do not respond to
     traditional teaching methods. Author lists what he
     considers errors in traditional approaches to teach-
     ing math to students with learning disabilities. He
     then describes a tutorial program designed to inter-
     est the students that is based on games, hobbies,
     crafts, and self-stimulating media.

488. Hubert, B.; B. Wong; and M. Hunter. 1983. Affective
     influences on learning disabled adolescents. *Learn-
     ing Disability Quarterly* 5:334-44.

          The researchers studied (1) differences between
     learning disabled and adolescents achieving at a
     normal rate regarding academic expectations;
     (2) teacher perception of and academic expectations
     for children identified learning disabled and those
     classified "normal"; (3) parent academic expectations
     for both student groups mentioned above; and (4) pa-
     rental stress. Results indicated that the adoles-
     cents who have learning disabilities had considerably
     lower academic expectations than normally achieving
     adolescents. Also, parents of the learning disabled
     adolescents had lower academic expectations for these
     children as compared with the expectations of the
     parents of the normally achieving children. Stress
     levels did not differentiate between the parents of
     either of the groups.

489. Ivarie, J.; D. Hogue; and A.R. Brulle. 1984. An investigation of mainstream teacher time spent with students labeled learning disabled. *Exceptional Children* 51:142-49.

Two naturalistic observation experiments were conducted to ascertain the extent to which mainstream teachers spent differing amounts of time with students labeled as L.D. and with nonlabeled students. The first experiment was conducted across an eight-week period in a secondary setting, and the second experiment was conducted across a ten-week period in an elementary setting. The results of both experiments showed that teachers do not spend significantly more time assisting students labeled as L.D. Two opposing viewpoints were suggested--1) that mainstreaming students labeled as L.D. does not require significantly more effort on the part of the regular classroom teacher, and 2) that regular classroom teachers are simply not responding to the special needs of the students identified as L.D. in their classrooms.

490. Kavale, K.A. 1982. A comparison of learning disabled and normal children on the Boehm Test of Basic Concepts. *Journal of Learning Disabilities* 15:160-65.

The performance of learning disabled children was compared with that of normal children on the Boehm Test of Basic Concepts. The L.D. children were found to have a lower level as well as greater variability in their understanding of basic concepts of quantity, space, etc. The author concludes that L.D. children do not possess the same degree of understanding of basic concepts as normal children.

491. Kavale, K.A., and E. Andreassen. 1984. Factors in diagnosing the learning disabled: Analysis of judgemental (sic) policies. *Journal of Learning Disabilities* 17:273-78.

This study examined the decision-making processes of fifteen administrators, twenty-two psychologists, twenty-eight teachers, and fifteen nurses in judgments about the learning disabled. Results indicated that judges did in fact differ with respect

to the weights assigned specific cues, but were similar in their ratings of severity level and recommended educational placement.

492. Kerchner, K. 1984. Language processing/word process-
      ing: Written expression, computers and learning dis-
      abled students. *Learning Disability Quarterly* 7:329-
      35.

      Learning disabled junior high school students
      participated in a study. A holistic method that
      combined the process approach to writing with the
      word processor capabilities of the microcomputer was
      used. Results indicated that writing skills on the
      computer improved and that paper and pencil writing
      improved also.

493. Korhonen, T. 1984. A follow-up study of Finnish chil-
      dren with specific learning disabilities. *Acta
      Paedopsychiatrica* 50:255-63.

      A four- to five-year follow-up study was per-
      formed on the scholastic and behavioral status of
      thirty-eight Finnish children with specific learning
      disabilities and thirty-eight matched controls with
      no learning disabilities. The children were first
      studied at eight to nine years and followed up at
      thirteen to fourteen years. At follow-up, children
      were administered a self-rating scale and parents
      and teachers were given short rating scales. These
      rating scales indicated sixty-five percent of the
      L.D. children still had learning problems and fifty
      percent had behavioral problems. The article dis-
      cusses the impact of learning disabilities on per-
      sonality development.

494. Krupski, A. 1985. Variations in attention as a func-
      tion of classroom task demands in learning handi-
      capped and CA-matched non-handicapped children.
      Exceptional Children 52:52-56.

      This study was initiated to compare the behav-
      iors reflecting attention between handicapped and
      non-handicapped as they worked on tasks of varying
      cognitive difficulty. Observations were made within

the classroom settings. The study reveals that non-handicapped children spent eighty percent of the observed time on task regardless of the cognitive demand. However, their learning handicapped peers worked on task as a function of the cognitive difficulty of the task. As the cognitive demand of the task increased, the percentage of time they were observed on task decreased.

495. Larson, B.L., and B.B. Roberts. 1986. The computer as a catalyst for mutual support and empowerment among learning disabled students. *Journal of Learning Disabilities* 19:52-55.

The first author met with a small group of five learning disabled high school students around the computer once a week over a period of four months to investigate the uses of the computer that promote social skills and esteem. Most of the computer work was in the LOGO language, which was chosen because of its ability to interest the students. At first it was assumed that by modeling socially supportive behavior at the computer, the experimenter could help foster its development in the students. Objective and subjective testing measures were used to provide a composite picture of the development of supportive skills and esteem. The most positive results occurred when the students were given a chance to share their computer skills with other students through a tutoring program.

496. Lawson, J., and J. Inglis. 1985. Learning disabilities and intelligence test results: A model based on a principal components analysis of the WISC-R. *British Journal of Psychology* 76:35-48.

The study suggests that the principal components analysis of the WISC-R normative data from 2,200 children yields a bipolar factor that corresponds to a verbal/nonverbal continuum of test material. A review of previously published WISC-R and WISC data from L.D. children shows that the amount of deficit shown by these children is closely proportional to the degree of verbal content. Two defects in the majority of the published studies of the WISC and WISC-R results for L.D. children are discussed.

They fail to report actual subtest results and they
do not separate the test results by sex. A search
for homogeneous groups of subtest in the data for
L.D. children is likely to be unsuccessful; a continuum of subtests comprising different proportions
of verbal and nonverbal content is likely to exist.

497. Levin, E.K.; N. Zigmond; and J.W. Birch. 1985. A
      follow-up study of 52 learning disabled adolescents.
      Journal of Learning Disabilities 18:2-7.

         This study assessed the progress of fifty-two
      learning disabled adolescents four years after they
      entered a special education program in the ninth
      grade. The adolescents were administered the Peabody
      Individual Achievement Test, the WISC-R, the Piers-
      Harris children's Self-Concept Scale, and mathematics
      and reading achievement tests at the start of the
      program. Theoretically, the adolescents should have
      been in the twelfth grade at the time of follow-up.
      In fact, sixteen were still enrolled in a special
      education high school program, seven were still in
      high school, twenty-four had stopped attending
      school, and five could not be located. Thirty-four
      were retested on academic skills, and the results
      indicated impressive gains for all students. The
      dropouts tested were also interviewed about their
      reasons for leaving school. Data available to the
      school district at the time of placement into the
      special education program were used in a discriminant
      analysis or predicting status at the follow-up. The
      analysis was poor at identifying students who would
      leave school.

498. Levy, G. 1984. Learning disabled and non-learning
      disabled children at play. *Remedial and Special
      Education* 5:43-50.

         Thirty-four learning disabled and normal chil-
      dren were observed in a playground. Although there
      were few differences in the learning disabled group,
      sociometric questionnaires showed that the learning
      disabled had a lower status.

499. Lewis, R.B., and C.E. Kass. 1982. Labeling and recall in learning disabled students. *Journal of Learning Disabilities* 15:238-241.

The purpose of this study was to observe the labeling and recall in learning disabled students. The authors observed forty-four learning disabled students and forty-four average students, four to nine years of age. The students had to label pictures and objects, recall the labels, and relabel common objects in their own language. The results showed that the students who were learning disabled were qualitatively different in language and memory.

500. Licht, B.; J. Kistner; T. Ozkaragoz; S. Shapiro; and L. Clausen. 1985. Causal attributions of learning disabled children: Individual differences and their implications for persistence. *Journal of Educational Psychology* 77:208-16.

The study was designed to compare learning disabled students and non-learning disabled students with respect to their tendencies to attribute their academic difficulties to insufficient effort, insufficient ability, and external factors. Results indicate that L.D. girls are more likely than their non-L.D. peers to attribute failure to poor ability; no difference was noted in blaming external factors. On the other hand, L.D. boys are more likely than their non-L.D. peers to blame failures on external factors; no difference was noted in tendency to attribute difficulties to insufficient ability. L.D. in general are less likely to attribute failure to insufficient effort. The study suggests that children are affected differently by academic failure and an examination of factors must take place for each child.

501. Lindsey, J.D. 1983. The experience of learning disability: A qualitative time series study. *Journal for Special Educators* 19:29-38.

A time series study of sixty individuals in elementary through postsecondary levels who had been labeled L.D. in the public schools. Their likes were revealed, such as sports and field trips. The

majority of their dislikes were related to formal
reading. They specified what could have made a difference in their learning experiences.

502. Lovdahl, K.; A.S. Brown; C.W. McIntyre; and A.J. North.
      1986. Picture-word interference in learning disabled
      and normal children. *Journal of Learning Disabili-
      ties* 19:294-300.

      The responses of learning disabled and normal
      control boys were compared on a picture-word inter-
      ference task. A series of pictures (line drawings)
      with words in the center was presented. The words
      either named the picture, were from the same category
      as the picture, or were from a different category
      than the picture upon which it had been imbedded.
      In separate trials, the child's task was to (1) name
      the word, (2) name the picture, (3) categorize the
      word, or (4) categorize the picture. Both groups
      exhibited greater interference effects (longer re-
      sponse latencies) when naming pictures as opposed to
      naming words and when categorizing words versus cate-
      gorizing pictures. Also, the learning disabled boys
      experienced more interference than the control boys
      when any irrelevant stimuli were presented.

503. Lovitt, T., and D. DeMier. 1984. An evaluation of the
      Slingerland method with L.D. youngsters. *Journal of
      Learning Disabilities* 17:267-72.

      The purpose of this study was to evaluate the
      Slingerland method of reading. Seven children with
      learning disabilities were studied in classes that
      used the Slingerland approach. Some of these chil-
      dren participated in the Sullivan reading approach.
      The children were six to nine years of age. The
      Slingerland approach concentrated on group multi-
      sensory activities. The Sullivan approach was an
      individualized approach to reading. The results
      showed equal improvements in different areas.

504. Maher, C. 1982. Learning disabled adolescents in the
     regular classroom: Evaluation of a mainstreaming
     procedure. *Learning Disability Quarterly* 5:82-84.

        This study describes the effects of the Goal-
     Oriented Approach to Learning (GOAL), a technique to
     actively involve mainstreamed learning disabled pu-
     pils in determining which instructional approach
     within the regular classroom will work best for them.
     The GOAL approach consists of 4 steps:
     1) *Goal setting* - during this phase the regular
     classroom teacher and pupil meet to establish an
     instructional goal for that marking period.
     2) *Goal attainment* - after establishing the instruc-
     tional goal, the teacher and student develop a goal
     attainment scale. This scale ranges from a score of
     70, as the "most favorable outcome," gradually moving
     down to a score of 40, as the "least desirable out-
     come."
     3) *Selection of classroom instructional strategy* -
     at weekly meetings the teacher and student discuss
     academic progress. Based upon classroom factors
     that appear to be enhancing or retarding learning,
     an instructional plan is proposed for the week.
     4) *Evaluation of goal attainment* - at the end of the
     marking period progress is evaluated and the teacher
     and pupil begin the GOAL procedure all over again
     for the next marking period.

        Positive results were obtained using the GOAL
     approach. Students appeared to benefit from actively
     participating in the decision making process about
     how to overcome their specific learning difficulties.

505. Margalit, M., and S. Shulman. 1986. Autonomy percep-
     tions and anxiety expressions of learning disabled
     adolescents. *Journal of Learning Disabilities*
     19:291-93.

        Forty male students enrolled in the sixth and
     seventh grades were divided into two groups. The
     boys in one group were learning disabled while the
     boys in the other group were not. The study was
     conducted in order to examine autonomy levels and
     anxiety expressions of learning disabled adolescents.
     The State-Trait Anxiety Inventory and the Autonomy
     Multiple Choice measure were administered to each

person. The adolescents who were learning disabled
demonstrated lower levels of autonomy when the source
of the decisions concerned parents or peers. High
and stable anxiety levels were also found in this
group. The results pinpointed the dilemma that
arises from excessive support and the training and
endeavors to attain autonomy.

506. Margalit, M., and I. Zak. 1984. Anxiety and self-
      concept of learning disabled children. *Journal of
      Learning Disabilities* 17:537-39.

      The purpose of this study was to compare anxiety
      levels and self-concepts between two groups, 100
      learning disabled and 118 non-disabled children,
      ranging in age from six through thirteen years old.
      The results show that the children with learning
      disabilities clearly have higher levels of anxiety
      and lower self-concepts and personal satisfaction.

507. Mastropieri, M.; T. Scruggs; and J. Levin. 1985. Mne-
      monic strategy instruction with learning disabled
      adolescents. *Journal of Learning Disabilities* 18:94-
      100.

      The purpose of this study was to see if mnemonic
      strategy instruction could help learning disabled
      students. Fifty-five children were taught about the
      hardness levels of minerals. The group consisted of
      ten ninth grade students with learning disabilities
      and forty-five non-disabled seventh graders. The
      three procedures used in teaching were: (1) keyword-
      pegword mnemonic, (2) free study, and (3) a question-
      ing procedure. The study revealed that the mnemonic
      students significantly out-recalled the free study
      and questioning students regardless of the individual
      student's achievement level.

508. Mayer, C. 1974. *Understanding young children: Learning
      development and learning disabilities*. Urbana, Ill.:
      University of Illinois Press.

      This booklet designed for parents and teachers
      describes aspects of development and learning in
      young children and characteristics of learning dis-

abilities. Such characteristics include poor eye-hand coordination, perseveration, poor visual memory skills, and poor self image. Mayer suggests the following for helping learning disabled children: the use of a multisensory approach, step-by-step learning, and the reduction of distraction.

509. McConaughy, S.H. 1986. Social competence and behavioral problems of learning disabled boys aged 12-16. *Journal of Learning Disabilities* 19:101-6.

Parents' reports on social competence and behavioral problems were obtained for fifty-three learning disabled boys. As in the author's study on boys age eight to eleven, the L.D. boys age twelve to sixteen showed lower levels of social competence and more behavioral problems compared with normative samples. The results of the two studies demonstrate the existence of serious and resistant problems in social competence and behavior among learning disabled boys. The scores of the boys age twelve to sixteen often were so low they fell in the clinical range. Both studies indicate a strong need to develop programs that address the social-emotional needs of L.D. children.

510. McConaughy, S.H., and D.R. Ritter. 1985. Social competence and behavioral problems of learning disabled boys aged 6-11. *Journal of Learning Disabilities* 18:547-53.

The authors did a study on social competence and behavioral problems of 123 L.D. boys age eight to eleven. On an average the L.D. boys had significantly lower levels of social competence including participation in activities, social involvement, and school performance. On the behavioral problem scales, the L.D. boys had significantly higher scores for "externalizing" and "internalizing" problems including problems related to depression, uncommunicativeness, obsessive-compulsive behaviors, social withdrawal, hyperactivity, aggressiveness, and delinquency.

511. McGrady, H.J. 1985. Administrative support for main-
      streaming learning disabled students. *Journal of
      Learning Disabilities* 18:464-66.

          This study highlights the administrative commit-
      ment and support necessary for the success of the
      Parallel Alternate Curriculum or PAC Program. The
      goal of the program is to enable learning disabled
      students to survive in mainstream classes by changing
      the behaviors of teachers, not students, through
      staff development. Key administrative elements in-
      clude: start with a solid commitment to the concept
      by regular and special education administrators;
      hire competent, dedicated teachers; and provide fi-
      nancial and psychological support to the staff on a
      long-term basis.

512. McHugh, L.M. 1982. Similarities among diagnostic and
      prescriptive decisions made by reading specialists
      and LD, Title I, and fourth-grade teachers. *Journal
      of Learning Disabilities* 15:216-20.

          The study compares the diagnostic and prescrip-
      tive decisions made by reading teachers, LD teachers,
      Title I teachers, and classroom teachers about a
      child experiencing difficulty in reading. Results
      were that the subjects made similar diagnostic and
      prescriptive decisions with the exception of deter-
      mining the child's reading level. All tended to
      recommend easier instructional materials than the
      classroom teacher did.

513. McLeod, T., and S.W. Armstrong. 1982. Learning dis-
      abilities in mathematics--skill deficits and remedial
      approaches at the intermediate and secondary level.
      Learning Disability Quarterly 5:305-10.

          A total of 114 junior-high, middle-grade, and
      high school learning disabilities teachers responded
      to a questionnaire that the researcher distributed
      concerning various aspects of mathematics disabili-
      ties experienced by their students. The most common
      areas reported included the following: division of
      whole numbers, basic operations involving fractions,
      decimals, percent, fraction terminology, multiplica-
      tion of whole numbers, place value, measurement, and

mathematic terminology in general. The study found
that most often teachers used adaptations of mainstream texts, followed by commercial as well as
teacher-made materials in endeavoring to teach their
children. Respondents indicated a need for a commercial mathematics program that would be systematic
and have extended practice.

514. Mercer, C.D., and A.R. Mercer. 1981. *Teaching students
with learning problems*. Ohio: Charles E. Merrill.

The first part of this book deals with planning
instruction, choosing and developing materials, and
developing social-emotional goals. The major part
of the text is devoted to teaching academic skills
with specific chapters devoted to assessment and
followed by a chapter discussing the teaching of
specific skills.

515. Miletic, A. 1986. The interpersonal values of parents
of normal and learning disabled children. *Journal
of Learning Disabilities* 19:362-66.

One hundred thirty-six parents of normal and
learning disabled children were asked to complete a
forced-choice questionnaire in order to discover
repetitive patterns in the parents' value orientation
systems. When compared with fathers of "normal"
boys, fathers of boys who were learning disabled
scored higher on Independence and Leadership and
lower on Conformity and Support. Mothers of learning
disabled boys favored authoritative attitudes while
mothers of learning disabled girls valued conformity
and sources of emotional and group support.

516. Miller, M. 1984. Social acceptability characteristics
of learning disabled students. *Journal of Learning
Disabilities* 17:619-21.

A study was done to examine social acceptability
among learning disabled children. A group of 332
elementary students were selected. The youngsters
were a mixture of learning disabled and normal children. The study revealed that students with learning
disabilities were less accepted by normal children

in a social situation. However, there was a more
positive attitude towards L.D. children than towards
children with other kinds of handicaps. It was found
that these positive attitudes were seen more in the
very young grades one to two or in the older grades
five to six.

517. Montague, M., and C.S. Bos. 1986. The effect of cog-
      nitive strategy training on verbal math problem solv-
      ing performance of learning disabled adolescents.
      Journal of Learning Disabilities 19:26-33.

      This study investigated the effect of a cogni-
      tive strategy on verbal math problem solving perform-
      ance. Six learning disabled adolescents were used
      in the study. The cognitive strategy was an eight-
      step process designed to enable students to read,
      understand, carry out, and check verbal math prob-
      lems. During treatment students received strategy
      acquisition training, strategy application practice,
      and testing. Overall, the students improved in their
      two-step problem solving performance. Maintenance
      and generalization of the strategy were evident.

518. Moore, S.R., and R.L. Simpson. 1984. Reciprocity in
      the teacher-pupil and peer verbal interactions of
      learning disabled, behavior-disordered, and regular
      education students. *Learning Disability Quarterly*
      7:30-38.

      Reciprocal interactions of learning disabled,
      behavior disordered, and regular education students
      were researched in this study. The interactions of
      fifteen students from each of the above three groups
      and their peers, teachers, and classroom aides were
      observed using a behavior observation instrument.
      The instrument was designed to monitor (1) frequency
      of fourteen target behaviors, (2) the direction of
      the interaction (given to and received from), and
      (3) status of the party involved in the interaction.
      As indicated by the correctional analysis, negative
      peer-student interactions were reciprocal. In con-
      trast, neither positive or negative student-teacher
      interactions nor positive student-peer interactions
      were reciprocal. The research also showed that
      behavior-disordered, learning disabled, and regular

students responded to the other groups in a similar manner.

519. Pany, D., and J.R. Jenkins. 1978. Learning word meanings: A comparison of instructional procedures. *Learning Disability Quarterly* 1:21-32.

The effects of three instructional strategies on the reading comprehension of six nine- through 11-year-old learning disabled students in a resource program were compared. The students' recall of word meanings and facts from a story were measured using three different treatment conditions: meanings from context, meanings given, and meanings practiced. The results showed that as emphasis on direct instruction of word definitions increased so did performance on vocabulary measures.

520. Patten, M.D. 1983. Relationships between self-esteem, anxiety, and achievement in young learning disabled students. *Journal of Learning Disabilities* 16:43-44.

Eighty-eight kindergarten through sixth grade learning disabled children placed in regular classrooms with resource help were tested individually by a certified learning disabilities teacher. Significant relationships were found among (a) self esteem and mathematics, reading recognition, and general information achievement scores for the total group and females, (b) self-esteem, reading recognition, and general information achievement scores for males, (c) general anxiety and general information achievement scores for the total group and for males, and (d) general anxiety and self-esteem for the total group and males.

521. Pearl, R., and T. Bryan. 1982. Mothers' attributions for their learning disabled child's successes and failures. *Learning Disability Quarterly* 5:53-57.

The mothers of eighteen elementary L.D. students completed a questionnaire concerning the reasons for their children's successes and failures in reading, social interaction with other children, and solving puzzles. Their responses were compared with those of

mothers of non-disabled children. The results indicated that mothers of L.D. children viewed their
children's successes less positively and their failures more negatively than did mothers of normal children. These negative views were exactly the same as
those held by the children themselves about their
own performances. The findings indicate that these
mothers may inadvertently be communicating to their
children that their negative attitudes about their
own abilities and self worth are correct. The study
suggests that parents take an active role in expressing to their children that they do not believe that
their failures mean a lack of ability. Instead,
parents must point out areas in which the children
generally do well and thus help to prevent and overcome these detrimental feelings of inadequacy and
hopelessness. It is important to note that this
particular study was unable to determine whether the
attitudes of the mothers of these L.D. children were
more the cause or the result of their children's
poor performance. Further investigation into parents' perceptions and behaviors toward their L.D.
children is recommended.

522. Pearl, R.; T. Bryan; and A. Herzog. 1983. Learning
disabled and nondisabled children's strategy analyses
under high and low success conditions. *Learning
Disability Quarterly* 6:67-74.

This study focuses on the effects of strategy-
producing deficits that L.D. children seem to exhibit. It has been observed that L.D. children may
not in all cases actually lack the individual skills
necessary to perform a given task, but instead may
be unable to pull together all the necessary skills
into a working strategy to obtain desired results as
normal children do. One possible reason for this
inability to produce strategies may involve the type
of internal message that L.D. children communicate
to themselves about the reasons for their performance. This study involved learning disabled (L.D.)
and non-learning disabled (N.L.D.) children in a
bowling game to record their high and low game scores
and compare their attitudes and game strategies.
The results showed that the L.D. children tended to
attribute their failing scores to bad luck or to
other factors over which they had no control--a help-

less attitude. Regarding successful scores, the
L.D. children remembered fewer of their successes,
exaggerated the number of their failures, and attributed whatever successes they did experience to sheer
luck rather than ability. The N.L.D. children, however, attributed their own low scores to a lack of
effort and were more motivated to try harder in order
to succeed the next time. Furthermore, they learned
from their mistakes and went on to develop a sophisticated strategy to help obtain success.

523. Phipps, P. 1984. Regular classroom teachers look at
LD classrooms. *Academic Therapy* 19:599–605.

Eight regular class teachers visited special
education classes for learning disabled students.
These regular class teachers noted both the L.D.
students' constant need for approval and the success
of high expectations and realistic goals set for the
children. These eight teachers also showed great
admiration for the work of the special education
teachers.

524. Pullis, M. 1985. L.D. students' temperament characteristics and their impact on decisions by resource
and mainstream teachers. *Learning Disability Quarterly* 8:109–22.

Twenty special education resource teachers and
163 regular education teachers rated 412 learning
disabled first to sixth graders. The ratings were
for school competence and the temperament characteristics for task orientation, adaptability, and reac-
tivity. The teachers had to indicate the monitoring,
behavior management, and instructional strategies
used with each student. Analyses showed that temperament characteristics, especially task orientation,
significantly influenced teacher decisions.

525. Riedlinger-Ryan, K.J., and C.M. Shewan. 1984. Comparison of auditory language comprehension skills in learning disabled and academically achieving adolescents. *Language, Speech, and Hearing Services in the Schools* 15:127-36.

   Thirty adolescents, half of whom were learning disabled, were tested for auditory language comprehension. The results showed that seventy-three percent of the learning disabled group scored lower than the control group in one or more of these various tests. The authors emphasize that recognizing auditory comprehension problems is very important in teaching the learning disabled.

526. Ritter, D.R. 1978. Surviving in the regular classroom: A follow-up of mainstreamed children with learning disabilities. *Journal of School Psychology* 16:253-56.

   In this study twenty L.D. children of elementary school age who were assessed before being mainstreamed were reassessed after being mainstreamed for one year. The results showed that learning gains in reading and math during the year that the children were mainstreamed were similar to those gains found during the year they had been enrolled in a special L.D. program. The study concludes that regular classroom instruction alone may be insufficient for mainstreamed children and that supplemental programming seems necessary if prior rates of academic learning are to be maintained.

527. Rogers, H., and D.H. Saklofske. 1986. Self-concepts, locus of control and performance expectations of learning disabled children. *Journal of Learning Disabilities* 18:273-77.

   Forty-five learning disabled (L.D.) and forty-five normally achieving (N.A.) children were used to examine general and academic self-concepts, general and academic locus of control beliefs, and academic performance expectations. The L.D. children had significantly lower self-concepts, more external locus of control orientations, and lower performance expectations. This study also showed a significant

difference between experienced resource room students
(E.L.D.) and students newly enrolled in resource
room (N.L.D.). The N.L.D. had higher expectations
for future success than the E.L.D. children.

528. Rose, M.; B. Cundick; and K. Higbee. 1983. Verbal
      rehearsal and visual imagery: Mnemonic aids for
      learning disabled children. *Journal of Learning
      Disabilities* 16:352-54.

      This study compared the effects of two mnemonic
      aids taught to learning disabled children. Thirty
      children were divided into three groups: rehearsal,
      imagery, and control. Both mnemonic aids improved
      comprehension and retention in reading over the con-
      trol group. The authors suggest that mnemonic train-
      ing become part of the classroom instruction.

529. Rose, T., and P. Furr. 1984. Negative effects of il-
      lustrations as word cues. *Journal of Learning Dis-
      abilities* 17:334-37.

      The purpose of this study was to investigate
      the effects of illustrations on the reading perform-
      ance of learning disabled students. The topic of
      utilizing illustrations has been a source of great
      debate for many years. Advocates of illustrations
      have argued that they help to motivate children to
      read, improve clarity, and reduce vagueness. Crit-
      ics, however, claim that illustrations and visual
      cues only distract L.D. children's attention and pre-
      vent them from acquiring word recognition skills,
      thus interfering with their reading progress. The
      study involved teaching words both with and without
      picture cues to L.D. boys in elementary school. The
      results indicated that picture cue illustrations did
      indeed interfere with the acquisition of new words
      presented in isolation for handicapped readers, while
      the absence of pictures significantly increased and
      hastened their acquisition of new words. Due to the
      apparent adverse effects of using illustrations with
      L.D. students, the study suggests that L.D. teachers
      should de-emphasize illustrations when teaching words
      in isolation and focus the learner's attention only
      on the relevant characteristics of the word itself.
      These suggested modifications to instructional ap-

proaches might allow a student to read earlier from
a wider variety of non-illustrated materials, such
as newspapers.

530. Ryan, M.; D. Miller; and J. Witt. 1984. A comparison
      of the use of orthographic structure in word discrim-
      ination by learning disabled and normal children.
      Journal of Learning Disabilities 17:38-40.

          The purpose of this study was to compare learn-
      ing disabled children to normal children in their
      ability to discriminate between real words (ortho-
      graphically correct) and nonsense words (orthograph-
      ically incorrect). A group of forty-five L.D. stu-
      dents and forty-five normal students were shown pairs
      of letter patterns. Within each pair, one word was
      real and the other was a nonsense word. The object
      was to have the children pick out the legitimate
      word from the pair. After identifying twenty pairs
      of words, the children were administered the reading
      section of the Wide Range Achievement Test (WRAT).
      The results suggest that L.D. children in grades two
      to four are deficient in their ability to discrim-
      inate between orthographically legitimate and illegit-
      imate words as compared to normal children of the
      same grades. These results also correlated with
      their performance on the WRAT test. This suggests
      that there is a significant relationship between
      knowledge of orthography and word decoding skills.

531. Salend, S.J., and S. Salend. 1986. Competencies for
      mainstreaming secondary level learning disabled stu-
      dents. *Journal of Learning Disabilities* 19:91-94.

          A research study done on 334 regular and ele-
      mentary educators resulted in a list of necessary
      social skills for mainstreaming. The research in-
      cluded a questionnaire rating thirty-six skills as
      to importance for success in the mainstream. The
      authors feel the list of important skills makes rat-
      ing possible mainstreamed candidates easier as mas-
      tery of the specified skills would facilitate main-
      streaming. They also suggest that having a list of
      competencies bridges the communication gap between
      special ed. and regular ed.

532. Samuels, J.S., and N.L. Miller. 1985. Failure to find
      attention differences between learning disabled and
      normal children on classroom and laboratory tasks.
      Exceptional Children 51:358-75.

           This study compares laboratory tasks of atten-
      tion among learning disabled and normal boys from
      grades three, five, and six. The tasks were visual,
      with and without distraction. The same students
      were also examined for on task behavior in the class-
      room. Findings showed no differences between learn-
      ing disabled students and normal students on the
      tasks, and no difference in sustained attention.
      There were also no differences in on task behavior
      between the groups. The authors note that attention
      was enhanced in special education classes over regu-
      lar classes, in small groups of nine or less over
      larger groups, and in teacher directed over indepen-
      dent activities.

533. Schumaker, J.B. 1982. Social interaction of learning
      disabled junior high students in their regular class-
      rooms: An observational analysis. *Journal of Learn-
      ing Disabilities* 15:355-58.

           The purpose of this study was to compare the
      social interaction of learning disabled students in
      a regular classroom environment. Forty-seven pairs
      of learning disabled and non-disabled students were
      observed. An extensive recording system was used
      throughout the entire observation period. The re-
      sults showed that the learning disabled students did
      not appear to be socially separated in the classroom.

534. Schumaker, J.B.; J.S. Hazel; J.A. Sherman; and
      J. Sheldon. 1982. Social skill performances of
      learning disabled, non-learning disabled, and delin-
      quent adolescents. *Learning Disability Quarterly*
      5:388-397.

           This study compared learning disabled adoles-
      cents' performances on eight general social skills
      to two other groups of adolescents: a group of non-
      handicapped members of a high school band and a group
      of "court-adjudicated" juvenile delinquent adoles-
      cents who had been referred by their probation offi-

cers for social skills training. The social skills
were tested individually by the use of role-playing
situations. The results showed that the non-learning
disabled adolescents performed significantly more
appropriately than the other two groups on seven of
the eight skills. The eight social skills consisted
of: giving positive feedback, giving negative feedback, accepting negative feedback, resisting peer
pressure, negotiating conflict situations, following
instructions, conversation, and personal problem
solving. In resisting peer pressure, the boys and
girls who had learning disabilities were found to
perform significantly better than the group designated as delinquents. The results of the study point
to an urgent need for social skills training at the
secondary level.

535.   Scruggs, T.; M. Mastropieri; J. Levin; and J. Gaffney.
       1985. Facilitating the acquisition of science facts
       in learning disabled students. *American Educational
       Research Journal* 22:575-86.

           Fifty-six L.D. students were presented materials
       describing minerals of North America and had to learn
       three associated attributes: the mineral's hardness
       level, its color, and its common use. The students
       were randomly assigned to four different methods of
       study--direct instruction, mnemonic instruction,
       reduced-list direct instruction, and free study.
       Results strongly supported past findings that learn-
       ing was superior in the mnemonic instruction condi-
       tion (memory-enhancing strategy). Mnemonic instruc-
       tion has been found to result in dramatic increases
       in learning and retention for L.D. and E.M.R. stu-
       dents.

536.   Serwer, B.; B. Shapiro; and P. Shapiro. 1973. The
       comparative effectiveness of four methods of instruc-
       tion on the achievement of children with specific
       learning disabilities. *Journal of Special Education*
       7:241-49.

           Sixty-two first graders, high risk learners,
       were assessed before and after remediation in lan-
       guage arts and arithmetic. The children were as-
       signed to a direct remediation group (Distar Reading

Method), an indirect group (training given by a perceptual-motor specialist), a combined group (dividing time between direct and indirect method) or the control group. Results showed small differences among the groups, but statistically the indirect or combined group did better.

537. Shapiro, A.H. 1986. Projection of body image and printing the alphabet. *Journal of Learning Disabilities* 19:107-11.

A direct nonverbal measure of body image was conducted upon 242 children who were not experiencing letter reversals and thirty-two children who were reversing letters. Using a figure outline wall chart upon which a four-dot grid had been placed, children were asked to point to the location on the chart that matched the site the experimenter had twice tapped them on the back. An analysis of incorrect responses showed that the causes were due to inattention to directional cues. An analysis of the data collected showed that the subgroup of children who were letter reversers also persistently reversed their body sides, thus suggesting a processing mirror-image disturbance. The author proposes remedial strategy.

538. Shelton, T.; A. Anastopoulos; and J. Linden. 1986. An attribution training program with learning disabled children. *Journal of Learning Disabilities* 18:261-65.

This research was done to determine if altering causal attribution for failure would help learning disabled students with learned helplessness to deal with failure more effectively. An experimental reading situation was provided for 16 "helpless" learning disabled students split into an attribution training group and an assessment control group. The results showed that trained subjects demonstrated greater reading persistence and increased effort. Attribution training did not however promote increases in self-esteem.

539. Shepherd, M.; L. Gelzheiser; and R. Solar. 1985. How
good is evidence for a production deficiency among
learning disabled students? *Journal of Educational
Psychology* 77:553-61.

    This study was conducted to investigate produc-
tion deficiency as a trait of L.D. children. Learning disabled children and adolescents performed two
tasks that called for and studied the use of three
mnemonic strategies--categorical organization during
study, clustering during recall, and elaboration.
L.D. students did not differ from their nonhandicapped peers in categorical organization but
showed less clustering skills at recall. Fewer L.D.s
used elaboration. These skills prove to be weak to
moderate correlates of academic achievement for both
groups. The study questions whether students should
be recommended for special education based on a char-
acterization of L.D. students as production deficient.

540. Siperstein, G.N., and M. Goding. 1985. Teachers' behavior toward learning disabled and non-learning
disabled children: A strategy for change. *Journal
of Learning Disabilities* 18:139-44.

    Study to determine the importance of teachers'
behavior in setting social climate of classroom.
The study did pre- and post-intervention measurements
on the behaviors of teachers towards specific L.D.
and non-L.D. children in the classroom. Although
the amount of teacher initiation towards the students
remained the same--more for the L.D. student--the
quality of teacher initiation did change to a more
positive method. If goal is the social acceptance
of L.D. children, then teacher behavior towards L.D.
children must be as a positive role model. Suggestions in the article are not to change teacher attitudes in general towards disabled children, but to
concentrate on specific attitudes towards specific
children.

541. Slife, B.; J. Weiss; and T. Bell. 1985. Separability of metacognition: Problem solving in learning disabled and regular students. *Journal of Educational Psychology* 77:437-45.

This study tested the effects of metacognitive factors in problem solving to determine whether metacognition is a separate factor from cognition. Elementary learning disabled students in math were matched to regular students on the basis of I.Q., math performance, and achievement scores. L.D. students prove to be weak in two areas of metacognition with respect to their knowledge of their problem solving skills and ability to monitor their problem solving performance. The study suggests that a math deficiency is due to poor metacognition. Personality and motivational factors must also be considered.

542. Smith, C.R. 1985. Learning disabilities: Past and present. *Journal of Learning Disabilities* 18:513-17.

This article examines some factors involved in the learning successes of the learning disabled student. Learning disabled students enter classrooms with unusual patterns of strengths and weaknesses. Successful learning depends on modifications educators and parents make in settings and assignments. These modifications should take into account the student's achievement, physiological makeup, and personality traits.

543. Stevenson, D.T., and D.M. Romney. 1984. Depression in learning disabled children. *Journal of Learning Disabilities* 17:579-82.

One hundred three students ranging in age from eight to thirteen years old were evaluated from a Children's Depression Inventory. Fourteen percent of the scores were estimated at or above the critical cut-off point. When the scores of children who were the most depressed were compared to those who were the least depressed, certain points were revealed. Learning disabled children who were the most depressed had a lower self-esteem, shared feelings of neuroticism, and were over-sensitive.

544. Strawser, S., and C. Weller. 1985. Use of adaptive
      behavior and discrepancy criteria to determine learn-
      ing disabilities severity subtypes. *Journal of
      Learning Disabilities* 18:205-12.

            The study investigates the hypothesis that when
      scores from intelligence, achievement, language, and
      process assessment measures are used along with
      adaptive behavior severity groupings, a more accurate
      description of learning disabled subtypes and sever-
      ity can be obtained than that provided by ability/
      performance discrepancy alone. L.D. children ages
      eight to eleven years were administered the WISC-R,
      the Peabody Individual Achievement Test, the Clinical
      Evaluation of Language Functions, the Developmental
      Test Visual-Motor Integration, and the Test of
      Psycholinguistic Abilities. Teachers used the
      Weller-Strawser Scales of Adaptive Behavior on the
      sample. Three groups were then identified on the
      basis of severity. The results suggest that severity
      is more appropriately determined by adaptive behavior
      assessment than by discrepancy between ability and
      academic or processing performance.

545. Swanson, H.L. 1978. Memory development in learning
      disabled children: Evidence from nonverbal tasks.
      Journal of Psychology 100:9-12.

            The purpose of this study was to test the devel-
      opmental memory lag hypothesis. Twenty-two learning
      disabled children were evaluated by means of two and
      three dimensional nonverbal tasks. Among the find-
      ings were that age-equivalent recall in primacy and
      recency positions reflected patterns similar to those
      of normal children, and that there were constant
      age-related differences in nonverbal recall among
      subjects. Results suggest that the developmental
      memory lag interpretation has been confounded with
      learning disabled children's generalized verbal def-
      icits.

546. Test, D., and W. Heward. 1983. Teaching road signs
      and traffic laws to learning disabled students.
      Learning Disability Quarterly 6:80-82.

            This study evaluated the effectiveness of a

special driver education unit that was developed to
teach learning disabled teenagers the skills necessary to pass the written Ohio Motor Vehicle test in
order to obtain a temporary driving permit. All
information contained within four sections of the
motor vehicle digest was broken down and presented
to the students using the Visual Response System
(VRS). This technique utilizes individual desktop
overhead projectors to project student responses to
the teacher as well as to classmates. It uses various instructional stimuli to enhance learning and
motivation and incorporates three positive features
into the unit: a high rate of student response to
ensure learning; immediate feedback to student responses; and use of peers' responses as models. The
results indicate that this was a successful approach
for L.D. students since those students who took the
written test passed the exam. The study also offers
simple modifications to this technique in order to
make it more feasible for regular classroom use (e.g.,
holding up file cards with student responses or re-
arranging student desks in a circle).

547. Thorpe, H.W., and K. Sommer-Borden. 1986. The effect
      of multisensory instruction upon the on task behav-
      iors and word reading accuracy of learning disabled
      children. *Journal of Learning Disabilities* 18:279-
      86.

          This investigation consisted of four experiments
      to study the effects of multisensory instruction upon
      word reading accuracy and on task behavior. The
      study was done on seven-, eight-, and nine-year-old
      learning disabled students. Visual and auditory
      instruction with and without praise was compared to
      a program combining visual auditory, kinesthetic,
      and tactile instruction, also with and without teach-
      ers' praise. First, all programs increased reading
      accuracy when compared to pretest scores. Results
      of the four treatment programs revealed that the
      least effective was visual auditory alone. Visual
      auditory with praise was the most effective.

548. Vallecorsa, A., and L. Henderson. 1985. Spelling instruction in special education classrooms: A survey
of practices. *Exceptional Children* 52:19-24.

      The participants in this study were twenty-three
special education teachers of learning disabled students. The purpose of the study was two-fold: 1) To
investigate special education teachers' knowledge
and ability to differentiate between supported and
unsupported methods of spelling instruction. The
findings showed for the most part that these teachers
were reasonably well informed. However, unsupported
methods were often mistakenly labelled as supported
techniques. This suggests that special education
teachers may have some misconceptions about appropriate methods of spelling instruction. From this it
was decided that these teachers would benefit from
inservice training designed to improve their knowledge of valid and effective methods of spelling instruction. 2) To examine how often special educators
reported utilization of supported and unsupported
techniques in their spelling instruction. Results
showed that these teachers used most of the validated
methods on a regular basis. However, it was found
that these teachers often used many of the unsupported methods as well, thus wasting valuable time
on activities that were unproductive to spelling
achievement.

549. Valletutti, P. 1983. The social and emotional problems
of children with learning disabilities. *Learning
Disabilities, An Interdisciplinary Journal* 2:17-29.

      This article deals with the social and emotional
needs of the learning disabled student. Included in
this research are the following: difficulties in
understanding non-verbal communication, rejection,
impulsivity, negative moods, and difficulty in role-
taking. The findings conclude that teacher education
should increase emphasis on teaching social skills
and enhancing emotional development.

550. Wanat, P.E. 1983. Social skills: An awareness program with learning disabled adolescents. *Journal of Learning Disabilities* 16:35-39.

The purpose of this study was to investigate the usefulness of an in-school social skills program with learning disabled adolescents. Thirty L.D. students were divided into experimental and control groups. The first group took part in a sixteen-week social skills awareness program that met five days a week for one hour per day. Although no significant differences were found on grade averages, there were significant enough social differences to conclude that support should be given to social skills awareness programs in L.D. classrooms. The author stresses the importance of the L.D. teacher not only being familiar with a student's achievements and I.Q. scores but also understanding and appreciating the student as a social being.

551. Weiner, S. 1980. How to help children with learning disabilities--"I'm not dumb, am I?" *Childhood Education* January:156-69.

The author describes classroom scenes involving four learning disabled youngsters and their difficulties in processing information. Suggestions are made to utilize children's strengths in order to remediate weaknesses. She includes a checklist for teachers as an aid to identifying the learning disabled child in the regular classroom.

552. Weiss, E. 1984. Learning disabled children's understanding of social interactions of peers. *Journal of Learning Disabilities* 17:612-15.

This study examined learning disabled children's interpretation of their own social interaction. Physically aggressive, learning disabled boys were compared to normal boys exhibiting appropriate behavior. The results showed that there were no significant differences between the aggressive and non-aggressive boys. However, learning disabled boys detected feelings of unfriendliness from other children within a social setting.

553. Wilgosh, L. 1984. Learned helplessness in normally
      achieving and learning disabled girls. *Mental Re-
      tardation and Learning Disability Bulletin* 12:64-70.

          Sixty fourth grade girls, half of whom were
      learning disabled, took part in this study. Help-
      lessness effects were stronger for the learning dis-
      abled girls than for normally achieving girls. This
      study was compared to an earlier one with boys of
      the same age and ability that suggested the possibil-
      ity of sex differences determining effectiveness of
      helplessness alleviation procedures.

554. Ziegler, R.G. 1981. Child and context: Reactive adap-
      tations of learning disabled children. *Journal of
      Learning Disabilities* 14:391-93.

          The author explains that as the degree of mis-
      match increases between the child's abilities and
      the material that the child is expected to master,
      the child must adapt to this difficulty. He postu-
      lates three stages of psychological adaptation to the
      distress: (1) an initial reaction of quiet withdrawal
      or active response, (2) disengagement, and (3) de-
      fensiveness. The implications of these behaviors
      for both the classroom teacher and the clinician are
      discussed and case illustrations are presented.

CHAPTER VI:
BRAIN DAMAGE

Although some researchers group brain damage with learning disability because both disorders display similar components, we are restricting the term brain damage to those disabilities that can be verified through neurological or psychological evaluations. By limiting the term to neurological
impairment that can be proven conclusively, we are attempting
to eliminate some of the disturbing imprecision resulting
from labeling and the use of medical jargonese. The term
learning disabled applies to children whose behavior resembles
that of brain damaged individuals, but who cannot, with cer-
tainty, be called brain damaged. Basically, the distinction
is between organic (verifiable) and behavioral (conjectural)
factors. Unfortunately, the use of the neurological term
brain damage carries with it a host of negative undertones.
It implies some degree or other of hopelessness because of
the irreversibility of neuronal damage. In actual point of
fact, however, there are a great many techniques, procedures,
and programs for brain damaged students.
    The primary causes of brain damage are genetic, congeni-
tal, accidental, and/or traumatic. Regardless of specifics,
it comes as a totally disrupting element in the life of the
child and his/her family. The child may need the services of
one or more medical specialists and may be impaired for a
short period of time or for the remainder of his/her life.
The child also may become intellectually impaired (mentally
retarded) as a consequence or develop strange behavioral patterns. It is fair to say that the lives of all involved are
forever changed as a consequence of brain damage.
    Strauss and other early investigators studied the impact
of brain injury on the behavior and development of mentally
retarded children. In the course of observation of retarded
children, Strauss discovered different behavior in some children in the perceptual and cognitive spheres, which he assumed
to be the consequence of brain damage. He postulated that a
brain damaged child is one who either received an injury to,
or suffered an infection of, the brain before, during, or

after birth. As a result, such a child may also have motor
defects, disturbances in thinking and perception, and/or emotional behavioral difficulties. Because these disturbances
would be expected to prevent or impede the normal learning
process, he proposed special educational methods in order to
remedy these handicaps.

Strauss' theoretical views, in part at least, stemmed
from the studies of other researchers, such as Head and
Goldstein, who worked with brain injured adults during the
First World War. Frequently young soldiers demonstrated a
loss of intelligence after they had undergone damage to the
brain following cerebral infectious diseases, serious concus-
sions, or skull fractures. After surgical recovery, their
behavior was observed to be peculiar and many of their previous skills were lost or extremely impaired. Strauss noted
these same kinds of behavioral and skills defects in many
children who were considered to be mentally retarded. He
theorized that virtually the same type of behavior and loss
of skills were present in the group of mentally retarded children who, although they showed no indications of any kind of
gross neurological involvement, did have a history of brain
injury. This led to a new classification, exogenous mental
deficiency, that could be applied to children who had deficient intelligence, a history of brain injury, minor neurological symptoms, and conspicuous organic behavior.

Strauss used three criteria to determine brain injury in
children:

(1) No history of mental retardation in the family.
Strauss felt that it was important to rule out endogenous or
genetic abnormalities of the brain, such as familial mental
retardation. He was only concerned with the child who had
damage to an otherwise normal brain.

(2) A history of neurological impairment. This refers
to evidence in the medical history of brain injury that occurred before, during, or after birth.

(3) Slight neurological signs. This relates to soft
signs, rather than hard signs of neurological abnormalities.
For example, awkwardness of gait or the inability to perform
fine motor skills are considered as soft signs.

In Strauss' thinking, a child could be diagnosed as
brain-injured without hard evidence of any of the three biological criteria. As Strauss observed specific behavior patterns in his original subjects known to have brain injury, he
presumed that children who exhibited the same characteristic
behavioral patterns suffered brain injury at some time.

The following are among the characteristics Strauss noted
in the children he categorized as brain injured:

(1) Perceptual disorders--When looking at a picture, the

child with perceptual disorders sees parts instead of wholes, or sees figure-ground distortions that may confuse the background with the foreground. An example of seeing an object as a whole rather than as unrelated parts is the identification of a letter. When asked to identify the capital letter "A" the child with a perceptual problem may perceive 3 unrelated lines rather than the whole letter "A."

(2) Perseveration--A child with perseverative behavior continues an activity once it has started and has difficulty changing to another. A child can also exhibit perseverative emotional behavior. An emotional reaction like laughter or crying may persist for hours and hours. Research has shown that this reaction may not be controlled by the will of the brain-injured child, but comes about as an emotional reaction caused by the stimulation of certain parts of the brain not associated with cognitive consciousness. The emotional outburst seems to be driven by outside forces so the child doesn't act rationally.

(3) Conceptual disorders--A child with conceptual disorders is unable to organize materials and thoughts in a normal manner. This disorder affects the child's cognitive abilities. Reading and listening skills are affected, and the child experiences much confusion.

(4) Behavior disorders--Children with behavior disorders exhibit hyperactivity and distractibility. Strauss defined distractibility as a "constant fluctuation in thinking" and stated that "there is an undue fixation of attention upon irrelevant external stimuli." The child has difficulty focusing his attention as he is so easily distracted by the slightest change in his environment. The child who exhibits hyperactivity, according to Strauss, is "unable to inhibit his impulses" and is driven "to boisterous talking, shouts, uncontrolled laughter, running about the room, etc." This is the child whom the teacher describes as unresponsive to correction. Punishment and scoldings are not effective.

Another important point to add here is that often what Goldstein terms a "catastrophic reaction" occurs in brain injured children. The child will burst into explosive crying when confronted with a difficulty. The child's reaction is a "state of helplessness and complete despair upon being confronted with a situation that he can't solve.

Furthermore, Strauss maintained that the catastrophic reaction could come about even if the task required by the child is not "beyond the child's level of knowledge or established ability."

Several factors can be manipulated by the classroom teacher in order to produce optimum effects. The teacher can control the physical setting, time, amount of work given to

the child, difficulty level of material, language, and interpersonal relationship.

Controlling the physical setting would be conducive to
learning because the teacher can modify space by the use of
partitions, screens, quiet corners, etc. In addition, the
teacher can remove any distracting stimuli in the room so
that the child can learn to focus his attention more on his
work. Strauss stresses the importance of a nondistracting
school environment. The work can be distributed in various
ways in an effort to shorten the time required to complete
the work. The material chosen for the child can be modified
to meet his/her performance level.

Language can also be altered so that the child will
clearly understand the teacher's directions. Moreover, the
language should not exceed the child's level of understanding.
The goal is to enhance the child's learning, not hinder it.
Simplifying the language, reducing the directions, maintaining
visual contact with the child, and speaking in a slow manner
are all techniques suggested to help the brain injured child
learn.

It is evident that the rapport between the teacher and
the child is very important. More learning is likely to take
place if a positive, warm relationship exists between pupil
and teacher. Furthermore, the child's self-image is enhanced
through a good pupil-teacher relationship. Janet Lerner suggests specific "therapeutic principles" that should be used
by the teacher to help the brain injured child develop a better self-concept of himself/herself.

555. Aviezer, Y., and S. Simpson. 1980. Variability and instability in perceptual and reading functions of brain-injured children. *Journal of Learning Disabilities* 13:327-33.

Thirty-four children diagnosed as brain-injured and enrolled in a school for brain-injured children and forty children in regular classes took part in the study. The results indicate that while both older and younger brain-injured children display instability in various perceptual areas, young brain-injured children appear not to differ in this respect from their normal peers. Only in the case of older brain-injured children is such instability of diagnostic significance.

556. Blackman, S., and K.M. Goldstein. 1982. Cognitive styles and learning disabilities. *Journal of Learning Disabilities* 15:106-15.

The authors review research relating the cognitive style dimensions of field dependence and reflection impulsivity to underachievement, process deficits (minimal brain dysfunction), and hyperactivity. Basically, better performance was associated with field independence and a reflective cognitive style. The importance of modifying the learner's cognitive style and matching the learning environment to the learner's cognitive style are also examined.

557. Bochner, S. 1977. Doman-Delacato and the treatment of brain injured children. *Australian Journal of Mental Retardation* 4:4-7.

Research on the effectiveness of the Doman-Delacato method for brain damaged children is reviewed in this article. The author concludes that there is no evidence to support claims on the effectiveness of the Doman-Delacato techniques and that on the contrary there is growing concern about negative effects of these methods, particularly on parents involved in the program.

558. Borenstein, R. 1984. Unilateral lesions and the Wechsler Adult Intelligence Scale-Revised: No sex

differences. *Journal of Consulting & Clinical Psychology* 52:604-8.

This study tested sex differences previously reported in WAIS-R scores (Verbal I.Q. vs. Performance I.Q. discrepancies) in male patients with unilateral lesions by administering the WAIS-R to thirty-one subjects (sixteen males--mean age 42.6 years and fifteen females--mean age 38.4 years) with right hemisphere lesions and to thirty-two subjects (seventeen males--mean age thirty-two years and 15 females--mean age 40.7 years) with left hemisphere lesions. Results show that both males and females had expected discrepancies between Verbal I.Q. and Performance I.Q.

559. Brannigan, G.G., and R.G. Young. 1978. Social skills training with the MBD adolescent: A case study. *Academic Therapy* 13:401-4.

The case study of a thirteen-year-old boy with minimal brain damage illustrates the use of a social skills training program that concentrated on rebuilding a damaged self-image by identifying maladaptive behaviors and providing alternatives.

560. Brenner, A. 1982. The effects of megadoses of selected B complex vitamins on children with hyperkinesis: Controlled studies with long-term follow-up. *Journal of Learning Disabilities* 15:258-59.

This study suggests that the hyperkinetic cerebral dysfunction syndrome is multifactoral. A significant number of cases are caused by vitamin deficiency or pharmacologic dependency.

561. Broadhead, D., and G.L. Rarick. 1978. Family characteristics and gross motor traits in handicapped children. *Research Quarterly* 49:421-29.

The work examined the association between selected family characteristics and some gross motor traits of 481 children (six to thirteen years old) diagnosed as either educable mentally retarded or minimally brain injured. Data were obtained for

each of the seven gross motor tasks of the modified
AAHPER (American Association for Health, Physical
Education and Recreation) Youth Fitness Battery.
Questionnaires completed at home provided details of
the educational and occupational status of the head
of household and the number of children in each family. One of the findings was that high quality gross
motor performance tended to be associated with larger
families and with lower status occupation and education.

562. Brown, T., and M. Wynne. 1982. An analysis of attentional components in hyperactive and normal boys.
Journal of Learning Disabilities 15:162-63.

Attentional performance was examined in hyperactive and normal ten- to fourteen-year-old boys.
Findings were interpreted to suggest that while activity levels of hyperactive children may diminish
at adolescence, hyperactive adolescents continue to
be impulsive and impaired in attention, and that the
three hypothesized components of attention are independent of intelligence.

563. Carter, J.L., and P.K. Miller. 1971. Creative art for
the minimally brain injured children. *Academic Therapy* 6:245-52.

The authors believe the present methods (as of
1971) designed to increase perceptual-motor coordination of slow learning/minimally brain injured children are based on methods that discourage children
from solving small problems and help them to avoid
major ones. They tried a creative art activity that
they call pleasurable and rewarding. Based on test
results (Frostig Development Test of Visual Perception), they claim significant gains were made in
each subtest.

564. Clements, S.D., and M. Barnes. 1978. The three Rs and
central processing training. *Academic Therapy*
13:535-547.

The authors discuss the theories and principles
underlying central processing training for children

with specific learning disabilities and minimal brain
dysfunction. Assumptions of central processing
training are critiqued, three potential problem areas
(including over-fascination with the actual training
activity) are cited, and conclusions from research
on the topic are discussed. The intervening factor
of maturation is analyzed. The authors conclude
that there is no inherent remediation magic in central processing training activities.

565. Cotterell, G. 1973. Jeremy learns to read. *Special
      Education* 62:26-29.

        A seven and one-half-year-old boy took part in
an individualized instructional program. Jeremy was
dyslexic and exhibited hyperactive destructive behavior. There was a family history of severe reading
problems. Phonics, writing, programmed reading,
recall of sound units, and topic books made and illustrated by Jeremy were part of the program. In
two years Jeremy gained four and one-half years'
progress in reading.

566. Crichton, J. 1985. My very special sister Suzy. *Sev-
      enteen* 44:88-90.

        This article discusses the conflicts that the
sibling of a brain damaged child goes through. While
she loved Suzy, valued the abilities that she had,
and took great umbrage when somebody belittled her,
the author did not always have the patience needed
to handle her. This in turn caused guilt feelings.
In order to resolve her conflicts, she had to realize
that her reactions were normal and that she neither
could nor had to be the perfect sister all the time.

567. Cunning, J. 1976. Emotional aspects of head trauma in
      children. *Rehabilitation Literature* 37:11-12.

        This article surveyed the effects of head trauma
on several domains including speech difficulties,
intellectual deficits, and motor function.

568. Daryn, E. 1961. Problems of children with "diffuse brain damage": Clinical observation on developmental disturbance. *Archives General Psychiatry* 4:299-306.

    Among 170 children between the ages of three and fifteen referred to a mental health clinic for treatment without suspicion of organicity, eighty-four were found to have "diffuse brain damage" on close psychological and neurological examination. No history of encephalitis was found in any case. A congenital defect may have been the cause. An improvable maturational lag seemed to be involved. The microsymptoms found in skull x-rays were similar to those of mongoloids. Acknowledgement of the organic condition is important for treatment.

569. Dubnick, B. 1976. An investigation of knowledge among counselors, educators, educators in clinical psychology and psychiatrists regarding selected aspects of brain damage. *Dissertation Abstracts International* 37:131.

    This dissertation reports on selected aspects of brain damage as discussed by educators, educators in clinical psychology, counselors, and psychiatrists.

570. Ellis, H.; E. Ellis; and G.T. Warren. 1984. Can you imagine feeling that way about your own helpless kid? Mixed feelings about new opportunities. *Exceptional Parent* 14:45-50.

    This article discusses the emotional trauma that the parents of Jimmy, a brain-damaged child who was unable to communicate, went through. The problems ran from feelings of guilt and other conflicting emotions to marital difficulties. They were first plagued by these emotions when they had to decide whether to keep him at home or to institutionalize him. Years later, they came upon a computer device that would enable Jimmy to communicate. The father went into withdrawal and depression because he could not bring himself to get the device for his son, but could not bear the guilt of feeling that he was holding him back. Ultimately he went to a therapist and

he and his wife now look forward to a more productive
life for Jimmy.

571. Eno, L., and J. Deichmann. 1980. A review of the
      Bender Gestalt Test as a screening instrument for
      brain damage with school-aged children of normal
      intelligence since 1970. *Journal of Special Educa-
      tion* 14:37-45.

          The authors review recent literature regarding
      the effectiveness of the Bender Visual-Motor Gestalt
      Test in screening for brain damage in school-aged
      children of normal intelligence who display learning
      problems. Problems with research of this type and
      various administrations and scoring methods are dis-
      cussed. All methods reviewed significantly discrim-
      inate between groups of brain-damaged and unimpaired
      children. No method, however, provides successful
      predictive rates high enough to warrant the use of
      the Bender as the sole diagnostic instrument in in-
      dividual cases.

572. Erasmus, J.A. 1976. Minimal brain dysfunction: Fact
      or fancy. *Phoenix Journal* 9:3-6.

          Examined are medical and educational issues
      related to the causes and treatment of minimal brain
      dysfunction (MBD) in children. Etiological theories,
      incidence, biochemical aspects, and drug therapy are
      discussed. The following categories of MBD are de-
      scribed: the purely hyperactive child; the congenital
      dysemotional child; the child with perceptual prob-
      lems; the child with motor insufficiency; the child
      with speech, language, and communication problems;
      and the child with reading and spelling disability.

573. Erickson, M.T. 1977. Reading disability in relation
      to performance on neurological tests for minimal
      brain dysfunction. *Developmental Medicine and Child
      Neurology* 19:768-75.

          To analyze the relationship between neurological
      test performance and chronological age, mental age,
      and I.Q. 155 second grade students were given an
      intelligence test, an oral reading achievement test,

and a series of items assessing minimal brain dysfunction (MBD). Correlational analyses indicated
that about half the MBD items were significantly
related to mental age and I.Q. score. From the first
sample, three groups of reading disabled children
were identified on the basis of objective criteria.
Statistical comparisons between the reading disabled
groups and control groups, matched for sex and I.Q.
showed no differences on the neurological test items
for minimal brain dysfunction. Results seem to con-
tradict the current view that learning disabled children are neurologically impaired.

574. Freeman, R.D. 1976. Minimal brain dysfunction, hyperactivity, and learning disorders: Epidemic or epi-
sode? *School Review* 85:5-30.

The author reviews literature on the etiology
of hyperkinesis and the use of stimulant drugs for
the treatment of hyperkinetic children. He points
out the ambiguities and confusions in diagnosis and
treatment of hyperactivity and recommends an examination of the social and ideological influences on
medical diagnosis and treatment of the disorder.

575. Gallagher, J.J. 1962. Changes in verbal and non-verbal
ability of brain-injured mentally-retarded children
following removal of special stimulation. *American
Journal of Mental Deficiency* 66:774-81.

Examined the effect of eliminating special tutoring procedures in a group of institutionalized
mentally-retarded brain-injured children who had had
tutoring from one to two years. The author suggests
the professional worker can be cautiously optimistic
regarding the possibility of small gains in ability
of some retarded children given special stimulation.
These gains are not necessarily lost when the stimulation is removed.

576. Gardner, L. 1976. Review: Is brain damage a useful
concept? *Child Care, Health and Development* 2:395-
411.

The author cites evidence that supports the

concept of brain damage: data from persons who have
suffered brain impairments as adults, studies of
persons having well-known clinical conditions such
as cerebral palsy as children, and the pioneering
work of Strauss and Lehtinen on physically normal-
appearing but learning retarded children. The causes
of brain damage may be prenatal, natal, or postnatal.
The author suggests the term specific learning disorders and lists hyperactivity, perceptual-motor
impairments, emotional lability, clumsiness, poor
coordination, and attention disorders as behavioral
and learning difficulties associated with brain damage.

577. Hebb, D.O. 1976. Physiological learning theory. *Journal of Abnormal Child Psychology* 4:309-14.

The relationship between physiological learning
theory and the school aged child with minimal brain
damage is explored. The author points out: attention
or "concentration" requires control of activity in
those excess neurons that are not necessary for a
task at hand; the control is probably not a great
inhibitory suppression but may be a recruiting
process, a function of complex perceptual and associative learning that begins with early experience;
inhibition, however, may still be of crucial importance as a sharpener of associative mechanisms, and
the child with minimal brain damage may have suffered
a selective loss of inhibitory neurons.

578. Heckleman, R.G. 1984. Splinter intelligence, "I am
sure he can do better!." *Academic Therapy* 19:409-12.

People assume that a child can do as well in
every area as he does in any area. In the case of
the brain-injured child, this may not be so. Areas
in which variations in ability can occur include,
but are not limited to, expressive speech, interpre-
tive speech, and motor control. Most remediation
aimed at a poorly functioning cerebral area is a
waste of the teacher's time and is frustrating to the
student. His assignments should be adjusted to fit
the best of what his splinter intelligence can offer.

579. Heilburn, A.B., Jr. 1962. Issues in the assessment of organic brain damage. *Psychological Report* 10:511-15.

The importance of various problems in assessing brain damage is related to research goals. The major problems encountered when the goal is to maximize accuracy of selection of brain-damaged or nonbrain-damaged are contrasted with those that arise when the goal is a theoretical one of increasing knowledge of brain-behavior relationships. The author also discusses research methods.

580. Hersher, L. 1978. Minimal brain dysfunction and otitis media. *Perceptual and Motor Skills* 47:723-26.

The frequency of otitis media among twenty-two hyperactive children (ages seven to thirteen years) with learning disorders was compared with the frequency of otitis media in a sample of 772 normal matched-age children. A significantly higher percentage of hyperactive children (fifty-four percent) had more than six episodes of otitis media than was found in the normal group (fifteen percent). Thirty-six percent of hyperactive children had more than 10 cases compared to five percent in the normal sample.

581. Jacobs, W.J. 1976. *Any love notes today?* Evergreen, CO: Learning Pathways.

The personal experiences of a teacher of eight educationally handicapped children with minimal brain dysfunction are related. Teaching methods are presented in descriptive dialogue form.

582. Kaslow, W., and J.C. Abrams. 1979. Differential diagnosis and treatment of the learning disabled child and his/her family. *Journal of Pediatric Psychology* 4:253-64.

The symptoms of learning disability, hyperkinesis, or minimal cerebral dysfunction are viewed as expressions of ego disturbances. Suggestions for habilitation are aimed at aiding both the child and the family to deal with the deficits in adaptive fashion. Interventions are predicated on differential diagnosis and based on a continuum of possibilities, including educational strategies and therapy with both the child and the family.

583. Langhorne, J.E., and J. Loney. 1979. A four-fold model for subgrouping the hyperkinetic/MBD syndrome. *Child Psychiatry and Human Development* 9:153-59.

The key finding of the study was that the presence or absence of aggressive symptomatology differentiated in a group of 846 12-year-old hyperkinetic/minimal brain dysfunction (MBD) boys on a number of important measures at initial referral during treatment with methylphenidate, and at subsequent five-year followup. When the sample was sorted into high and low aggression groups, several findings emerged that would otherwise have been hidden. Furthermore, there were no significant interactions between aggression (control deficits, negative affect, aggressive interpersonal behavior) and hyperactivity (judgment deficits, hyperactivity, inattention).

584. Leoine, M. 1962. Discrimination in diffuse brain damage. *American Journal of Mental Deficiency* 67:287-300.

Diffuse brain-damaged students demonstrated significantly poorer discrimination sensitivity than emotionally disturbed and normal controls in three studies employing different techniques as well as different groups of males and females. Discrimination sensitivity was found to correlate significantly with intelligence, particularly in the brain-damaged students. The author suggests that discrimination, as a basic organismic process, warrants careful investigation since it is reasonable to suspect that deficiency in discrimination has consequences for more complex psychological functions.

585. Levine, M., and G. Spivack. 1962. Adaption to repeated exposure to the spiral visual after-effect in brain damaged, emotionally disturbed, and normal individuals. *Perceptual and Motor Skills* 14:425-26.

   In a series of trials, normal and emotionally disturbed students showed a decrease in duration of Spiral Visual After-effects sooner than brain-damaged students. Normal and emotionally disturbed groups increased frequencies of failure to report SVA in later trials; the brain-damaged group did not show this tendency. The authors conclude that brain-damaged students show a different adaption pattern to SVA.

586. Martin, S. 1977. Developmental drama for brain damaged children. *Communication Education* 26:208-13.

   This article offers recommendations for using developmental drama including: discussion of organization of the play environment, leaders, and play groups; sensory-awareness games, movement-mime projects, and story dramatizations; and video tape utilization for play evaluation.

587. Mattis, S.; H. Joseph; and I. Rapin. 1975. Dyslexia in children and young adults: Three independent neuropsychological syndromes. *Developmental Medicine and Child Neurology* 17:150-63.

   Children eight to eighteen years old were divided into three groups: those with brain damage who could read (N31), those with brain damage with dyslexia (N53), and those without brain damage who were dyslexic (N29). Tests were given and no difference was found between the dyslexic groups. Language disorder, articulation and graphomotor dyscoordination, and visuo-perceptual disorder were found among the great majority of children who had dyslexia.

588. Milich, S., and J. Loney. 1979. The factor composition
      of the WISC for hyperkinetic/MBD males. *Journal of
      Learning Disabilities* 12:491-95.

           The study explored the intellectual functioning
      of ninety hyperkinetic, minimally brain damaged boys
      (mean age twelve years) by means of an analysis of
      student test performance in relation to the factor
      composition of the Wechsler Intelligence Scale for
      Children (WISC). Results from factor analysis indi-
      cated that poor performance on those subtests loading
      on the inattention factor plays an important role
      when accounting for the WISC performance of hyper-
      active children.

589. Millichap, J.G. 1975. *The hyperactive child with min-
      imal brain dysfunction: Questions and answers.* Chi-
      cago, IL: Year Book Medical Publishers.

           Directed to physicians, parents, and teachers,
      the book presents information on children with hyper-
      active behavior and minimal brain dysfunction. Ques-
      tions and answers relate to the following topics:
      definitions and frequency; etiology; symptoms, signs,
      and syndromes; speech and language disorders; dys-
      lexia and other specific learning disorders; pediat-
      ric neurology examination and the electroencephalo-
      gram; neuropsychologic tests; hearing and vision
      tests; differential diagnosis; general treatment and
      educational management; drug therapy, diets, and
      other remedies: prognosis and prevention; and re-
      search goals. Five case studies conclude the text.

590. Nelson, G. 1975. Learning to be: A look into the use
      of therapy with Polaroid photography as a means of
      recreating the development of perception and the
      ego. *Art Psychotherapy* 2:159-64.

           A therapist conducted art therapy sessions with
      a five-year-old emotionally disturbed and minimally
      brain damaged boy using a Polaroid camera to deter-
      mine the effectiveness of the camera in limiting and
      recording what the child perceived. Results indi-
      cated the following: the child's verbal expression
      improved, immediate feedback was present, photograph

ing people was initiated, and the ability to tolerate frustration developed.

591. Newcomer, P., and D. Hammill. 1973. Visual perception of motor impaired children: Implications for assessment. *Exceptional Children* 39:335-37.

   The aim of this study was to see if the Bender Visual Motor Gestalt Test for Children gave a significant number of incorrect diagnoses in measuring visual perception. Ninety motor impaired children, ages five to twelve, were given the Bender Test and the Motor Free Test of Visual Perception. The tests showed that the greater the children's impairment, the poorer the scores. The tests also showed that the students tended to function appropriately for their chronological age on the motor free test regardless of their degree of impairment.

592. Ottenbacher, K. 1979. Hyperactivity and related behavioral characteristics in a sample of learning disabled children. *Perceptual and Motor Skills* 48:105-6.

   The study examined the prevalence and characteristics of hyperactive behaviors in a sample of sixty-four learning disabled and twelve minimal brain damaged children (mean age twenty-one months). Students were evaluated by their teachers on eleven categories of behavior. Analysis showed that behavioral characteristics associated with hyperactivity did not differentiate among the students. Teachers rated poor motor coordination as the outstanding trait of the sample.

593. Peters, J.E. 1974. Minimal brain dysfunctions in children. *American Family Physician* 10:115-23.

   Minimal brain dysfunction (MBD) is discussed in terms of definition, syndrome types, etiology, diagnosis, and management. Signs of MBD are said to include the following: rapid decay of attention, distractibility, problems in pattern perception, inability to keep a plan in mind, hyperactivity, impulsiveness, labile emotions, disorders in language

development, disturbance in directionality, and poor
motor coordination. The author also reviews the
effects of different drugs in treating MBD children.

594. Pollack, C. 1962. Sleep-learning as an aid in teaching
     reading to a brain-injured boy. *Journal of Mental
     Deficiency* 8:101-7.

           After presenting a review of ten studies demon-
     strating some positive effects of sleep-learning,
     including one partially successfully attempt to teach
     speech to an aphasic child, the author cites a case
     study of a seventeen-year-old boy with an I.Q. of
     seventy-one. The boy, a non-reader with "an organic
     brain syndrome of a developmental character," was
     tested on two sets of words to assure equal diffi-
     culty. Both tests were consciously learned; the
     experimental list was sleep-learned in addition.
     Errors and number of attempts were scored. A sig-
     nificant gain was found in the accuracy of synthe-
     sizing words as well as in the number of attempts
     with which words were attached. Auditory material
     is learned during sleep. A Pavlovian theory is of-
     fered.

595. Rappaport, J.L. 1976. Hyperactivity in open and tra-
     ditional classroom environments. *Journal of Special
     Education* 10:285-90.

           Classroom observations and teacher ratings of
     hyperactivity in thirty boys were done as part of a
     one-year follow-up program in a clinical hyperactive
     study. Comparison was made between subjects in
     "open" and "traditional" rooms for hyperactive behav-
     ior and academic gains. Most of the boys were re-
     ceiving a stimulant drug. There were no significant
     academic differences, but the boys in open classroom
     environments showed a more significant decrease in
     teacher rated hyperactivity, suggesting that perhaps
     the traditionally structured environment is a less
     desirable placement for moderately hyperactive boys.

596. Reitan, R.M. 1960. The significance of dysphasia for intelligence and adaptive abilities. *Journal of Psychology* 50:355-76.

   The relationship between language functions and adaptive intelligence was studied using three groups (N=32 in each) including students with brain damage but no organic language dysfunction, and students who were hospitalized for various reasons but with no evidence of brain damage. The brain-damaged groups performed more poorly than the controls on all measures with the exception of the non-dysphasic group on the verbal Wechsler subtest. The results suggested that intact language functions are less important for thinking and adaptive intelligence than is generally believed, since the dysphasics compared so well with undysphasic brain-damaged students on all measures.

597. Ribner, S. 1978. The effects of special class placement on the self-concept of exceptional children. *Journal of Learning Disabilities* 11:319-23.

   The self-concept of 386 minimally brain damaged children (eight to sixteen years) in special classes was compared with that of ninety-six children with similar disabilities who were in regular classes. The study revealed that students in regular classes had significantly lower self concepts in school adequacy but not in general competence. When compared with normal students, both groups of brain damaged students had significantly lower self concepts in school adequacy, but only students in regular classes held significantly lower self concepts than normal students in general competence. No relationship was found between self-concept and length of stay in special classes.

598. Rutherford, W.L. 1975. Teaching the brain-damaged child to read. *Reading Clinic* 1:13-15.

   Suggestions for teaching the brain damaged child basic reading skills are offered to regular classroom teachers. Suggestions include reducing the distractibility of a brain damaged child, fitting instructional tasks to the child, providing immediate rein-

forcement, combining whole word and part-to-whole
teaching methods, and stressing reading for meaning.

599. Salili, F., and R. Hoosain. 1985. Hyperactivity among
     Hong Kong Chinese children. *International Journal
     of Intercultural Relations* 9:177-85.

        Classroom teachers evaluated over 600 males and
     females in order to discover the incidence of hyper-
     activity in Chinese children. Males were more hyper-
     active, and the sex differences were similar to Amer-
     ican findings. An overall decrease in hyperactive
     symptoms toward adolescence also was found.

600. Schoen, S.F. 1986. Decreasing noncompliance in a se-
     verely multihandicapped child. *Psychology in the
     Schools* 23:88-94.

        In modifying the noncompliant behavior of an
     emotionally disturbed six-year-old boy with brain
     damage, the findings indicate that the most effective
     treatment is increasing the density of instructional
     commands and reinforcing discrete compliant re-
     sponses.

601. Schwethelm, B., and G. Mahoney. 1986. Task persistence
     among organically impaired mentally retarded chil-
     dren. *American Journal of Mental Deficiency* 90:432-
     39.

        An attempt was made to determine the goal-
     directed persistence of forty-four organically im-
     paired children. The results indicated that chil-
     dren's persistence was associated significantly with
     their relative ability to perform the tasks.

602. Selz, M., and R.M. Reitan. 1979. Neuropsychological
     test performance of normal, learning disabled, and
     brain-damaged older children. *Journal of Nervous
     and Mental Disease* 167:298-302.

        The performance of seventy-five brain damaged,
     learning disabled, and normal children age nine to
     fourteen years was compared on thirteen neuropsycho-

logical test measures to determine the nature of the
differences between the groups. Analysis of variance, supplemented by DZ tests, indicated a significant difference beyond the .01 level on eleven measures and beyond the .05 level on one measure. A
discriminant analysis based on weighings of the
thirteen measures yielded eighty percent correct
classification of students—a finding in agreement
with the result of the multivariate analysis of variance. The results indicated that these psychological measures were individually sensitive to differences among the three categories of students and, as
a group, were capable of classifying children at a
level far exceeding chance.

603. Simensen, R.J., and J. Sutherland. 1974. Psychological
assessment of brain damage: The Wechsler Scales.
Academic Therapy 10:69-81.

The authors discuss efforts to find a clearly
defined pattern of subset responses for identifying
children with neurologically based learning disorders
and review research concerning use of the Wechsler
scales as a means of indicating cerebral movement.
They conclude that there is inconsistency and general
disagreement among research findings regarding the
value of the Wechsler Intelligence Scale for Children
in diagnosing and assessing brain damage.

604. Sortini, A.J. 1961. Rehabilitation of brain-damaged
children. *Volta Review* 63:101-5.

Speechreading and auditory training are useful
for the child who is brain-damaged. Clinicians
should try to establish relationships with such a
child. Lauretta Bender's designation of difficulties
in patterned motor behavior, severe anxiety, and the
need for human support are useful. Problems in
teaching speechreading stem from short retention
span in addition to the neuromuscular impairment.
Suggestions on how to deal with practical problems
in working with the cerebral palsied child are offered. The author advocates a holistic approach
that emphasizes using what works.

605. Spivack, G. 1962. A note on generality of discrimina-
     tion deficiency in life-long brain damage. *American
     Journal of Mental Deficiency* 67:473-74.

     Data on relationship between performance of
     brain-damaged children on a visual and auditory dis-
     crimination task are reported. Results support the
     notion that there is a general discriminatory defi-
     ciency in life-long brain-damaged individuals.

606. Stein, C.L.E., and J. Goldman. 1980. Beginning reading
     instruction for children with minimal brain dysfunc-
     tion. *Journal of Learning Disabilities* 13:219-22.

     The study involving sixty-three children (six
     to eight years old) compared the effects of two read-
     ing programs, the Palo Alto Reading Program and
     DISTAR, on primary grade children with reading prob-
     lems. Results indicated that use of an operant read-
     ing program (DISTAR) was more effective than the
     Palo Alto program.

607. Steinberg, M., and J. Rendle-Short. 1977. Vestibular
     dysfunction in young children with minor neurological
     impairment. *Developmental Medicine and Child Neurol-
     ogy* 19:639-51.

     Two aspects of vestibular functioning, post-
     rotary nystagnus and head righting with and without
     vision, were compared in forty-four randomly selected
     preschool children and twenty-five preschool children
     referred for minimal neurological impairment. Re-
     sults showed that alteration in post-rotary nystagmus
     and abnormalities in head righting are frequently
     found in children of normal intelligence with educa-
     tional or behavioral problems.

608. Tarnopol, L., and M. Tarnopol. 1979. Motor deficits
     that may cause reading problems. *Journal of Learning
     Disabilities* 12:522-24.

     The authors postulate that dysfunctions in the
     cortical sensorimotor area of the brain that controls
     internal speech may adversely affect the learning of
     reading, writing, spelling, and arithmetic, espe-

cially in children who are first learning these
skills. Correlations between arithmetic scores and
copying geometrical designs are attributed to any
underlying, unstable relationship between visual
stimuli and their evoked brain wave responses in
many cases. Other learning skills may be affected
in a similar manner.

609. Taylor, D.C., and I.A. McKinlay. 1979. What kind of
thing is "being clumsy"? *Child: Care, Health and
Development* 5:167-75.

Aspects of "clumsy" behavior are examined in
terms of its use as a specific diagnostic entity
regarding the condition of the central nervous system
(CNS). Clumsiness is seen to be dependent on CNS
integrity, maturational level, and state (continuum
of arousal between deep unconsciousness and extreme
wakefulness), as well as on rehearsal of the activity.

610. Touliatos, J., and B.W. Lindholm. 1975. TAT need
achievement and need affiliation in minimally brain-
injured and normal children and their parents. *Journal of Psychology* 59:49-54.

Need for achievement and for affiliation were
compared in the families of sixteen minimally brain
injured and sixteen normal children (eight to thirteen years old). Thematic Apperception Test (TAT)
type cards were used to measure the requirements of
parents and children. Results revealed that achievement motivation was lower in minimally brain injured
students and their mothers than in normal students
and their mothers. In addition, the achievement
needs of mothers of brain injured students were positively related to their children's behavior, while
the fathers' achievement needs were negatively related.

611. Whaley-Klahn, M.A., and J. Loney. 1977. A multivariate
      study of the relationship of parental management to
      self-esteem and initial drug response in hyperki-
      netic/MBD boys. *Psychology in the Schools* 14:485-
      492.

           The authors examine the relationship between
      the judge rated and self and spouse reported parent-
      ing characteristics of the mothers and fathers of
      eighty-three hyperkinetic/MBD (minimal brain dysfunc-
      tion) boys (four to twelve years old), the rated
      self esteem of the boys at the time, and their clin-
      ical response to central nervous system medication.
      Among findings were that the direction of the rela-
      tionships is such that mothers of children with more
      profound esteem deficits did not describe themselves
      as too strict, were rated higher in the direction of
      hostility, listed fewer self reported shortcomings,
      and described their husbands as too demanding; and
      that fathers of the lower self esteem boys tended
      not to describe themselves as too demanding.

612. Wiener, G. 1966. The Bender Gestalt Test as a predic-
      tor of minimal neurologic deficit in children 8 to
      10 years of age. *Journal of Nervous and Mental Dis-
      ease* 143:275-280.

           This study was designed to relate types of
      Bender-Gestalt impairment to minimal neurological
      deficit. Data was gathered about 417 premature and
      405 full term children, eight to ten years old,
      matched according to race, sex, and economic status.
      The data of history and neurologic evaluations were
      applied to a nineteen-variable, unweighted scale
      used as an operational definition of minimal neuro-
      logical deficit. Analysis of data showed low but
      significant correlation of each of the Bender-Gestalt
      variables with the neurologic deficit scale and the
      birth weight. Seven individual Bender-Gestalt vari-
      ables correlated. Twenty-two with a scale score
      related to presumed minimal brain damage. Gross
      distortions and inability to produce angles and
      curves seemed to be independent predictions.

613. Zentall, S.S. 1986. Effects of color stimulation on
      performance and activity of hyperactive and non-

hyperactive children.   *Journal of Educational Psychology* 78:159-165.

Investigated the effects of color stimulation on hyperactivity with elementary school age children (sixty-six hyperactive and eighty normal). Findings reveal that stimulation added early or late to a sustained attention task could normalize the performance of hyperactive children and reduce their activity. When the task involved acquisition of new information, stimulation added late reduced the activity of the hyperactive children.

CHAPTER VII:
SPEECH AND LANGUAGE IMPAIRMENTS

Speech and language impairment is an area that is particularly difficult to categorize. If we were to place it under
"Physical Disabilities," we would be only partially correct.
When we refer to speech defects caused by difficulty in articulation on account of cleft palate or hearing impairment or
severe malocclusions or dysarthria (associated with cerebral
palsy), we are clearly showing the organic or neurological
basis of the problem. However, when we see evidence of speech
defects that are caused by environmental factors, such as
anxiety and arrested mental development, we would be compelled
to emphasize that retarded language development is closely
linked to those psychological factors that inhibit or retard
normal growth and development.
There is a close and obvious relationship between mental
retardation and speaking proficiency. Those who have lower
intelligence levels also tend to have a lesser ability to
acquire language. However, it is erroneous always to make
the assumption of lower intellectual functioning when poor
speech is found. The causes are diverse, and they must be
viewed as clues to the understanding of a child who is having
difficulty in one area of his/her development.
Speech impairment is defined in PL 94-142 as a communication disorder, such as stuttering, impaired articulation, a
language impairment, or a voice impairment, that adversely
affects a child's educational performance. The speech impaired will lack fluency, have articulatory difficulties, and
have difficulty in comprehending or verbalizing symbols. A
combination of conditions will result in communication problems.
Speech impairment refers to disorders of articulation
and fluency. Language impairments refer to disorders in comprehending or expressing the rules and symbols of the language
itself. The most common speech defects are in articulation--
distortions of sounds, addition and/or omission. Fluency
disorders refers to the uneven flow of speech--with stuttering, needless drawn out words, hesitation, and unnecessary

interjections in sentences. Voice disorders relate to hoarseness or huskiness, breathy, highly nasal sounds, or squeakiness. Vocal quality refers to vocal pitch and intensity.

Language disorders relate to a lack of comprehension or expression. Phonemes are sounds within a language. Morpheme is a minimum set of units, unified in a group or structure for meaningful language. Syntax is the set of grammatical rules for placing words in a sentence. Semantics includes vocabulary, concepts, and word relationships. Delayed speech might refer to a slight retardation in the ability to communicate. Delayed language may relate to brain damage.

Speech disorders are present in the mentally retarded, the hearing impaired, the learning disabled, children with a cleft palate, and normal children. The mentally retarded exhibit the most intensive language and speech difficulties. The hearing impaired have the most difficulty with articulation, voice and language. It has been found that ten to fifteen percent of the children who have the more serious speech defects also have other physical disabilities. Visually and aurally handicapped children have a higher rate of speech defects than normal children. Emotional problems also affect children's speech patterns, particularly in the case of stuttering.

Normal language and speech development begin at birth and follow a maturational cycle. If by the age of five or six the child mispronounces many words and if he has difficulty communicating with others, he should be taken for a consultation to a speech therapist. An intellectual assessment and a psychological assessment should be made in order to determine the causes of the child's defective speech pattern. When a diagnosis has been made, a program of remediation should be initiated as early as possible.

The most frequently encountered type of exceptional child in the schools is one with some type of speech or language impairment. Language disorders usually refer to disorders in comprehending or expressing verbally the symbols and grammatical rules of language. The most common type of speech disorder is an articulation impairment by which is meant disorders of both the motor production and phonological rules of language. Research indicates that by the age of four, children have developed adequate skills in articulation. By the age of nine biological maturation alone can no longer result in improvements in sound production. Another type of speech disorder is a fluency disorder, or dysfluency. Stuttering is the most common of these dysfluencies. Determining whether a child has a dysfluency is dependent mostly on personal evaluation by a speech clinician. The identification of a stutterer is based not only on observation of dysfluent speech but also on the speaker's self-concept. The cause of stuttering has been debated. Disagreement is voiced in whether there is a biological predisposition to stuttering or if it is environmentally caused.

Voice disorders are another type of speech disorder. An individual may change the pitch of his voice in the middle of speaking. Other variations include speaking through the nose and speaking with a very raspy voice. Treatment is usually the domain of the speech clinician. However, there are several things that a classroom teacher can do to help the child along with his therapy. The teacher should have a conference with the clinician in order to find out what is being done and how he/she can help. A teacher is usually the first person to recognize a child's speech or language problem. Stuttering is quite easy to identify on a very basic level, although it's up to the clinician to decide if in fact this is a dysfluency. If a child exhibits a communication disorder the teacher must be very careful not to bring it to the attention of the class because this may exacerbate the problem. The teacher should discourage teasing of the child. If a child must go to a special remediation class the timing of the class should be made with the idea of it being inconspicuous. Teachers may help reinforce the therapy.

Speech therapy has been administered to children in the public school system since the 1920s. Prior to this period, speech therapy was included in programs for children who were residing in hospitals and institutions. The currently intervening years have witnessed a rapid rise in the number of speech specialists in the schools.

Classroom teachers play a vital role in furthering their students' speech and language development, both as part of a team working toward that end and separately within the classroom by setting good speech standards, by demonstrating understanding and support to those children with specific linguistic problems, and by being in the best position to identify and refer those students needing special attention to the proper professional specialists.

In closing, bear in mind that children with expressive linguistic and speech problems need a relaxed classroom setting that is conducive to oral participation, effective speech, and language models; ample and sufficient time to process given information and to respond; appropriate and adequate verbal cues or prompts; and continual encouragement and positive reinforcement for speaking.

614.   Allen, K.E.   1980.   The language impaired child in the
        preschool: The role of the teacher.   *Directive
        Teacher* 2:6;8-10.

            Implications of the incidental teaching model
        and the communication-interaction model for classroom
        intervention with young language impaired children
        are examined.   Child initiation is the essential
        feature of incidental learning, while the communi-
        cative-interaction model stresses the role of the
        teacher as facilitator.   Illustrations for each model
        are given.

615.   Anderson, D.E., and R.O. Coleman.   1980.   Language en-
        hancement in the developmentally delayed child
        through a cognitive/receptive mode.   *Child: Care,
        Health and Development* 6:35-46.

            Over a two-year period, sixteen language im-
        paired and developmentally delayed English children
        (mean age 4.9), were provided with eight weeks of
        concentrated instruction in five language areas
        (nouns, verbs, adjectives, prepositions, and syntax).
        Instruction consisted of regulated verbal stimulation
        without overt attempts to elicit expressive language.
        Responses by the students were in the form of motor
        behavior, through picture/object identifications.
        Results indicated a marked increase in the number of
        stimuli to which these children could provide approp-
        riate responses at the end of the eight-week instruc-
        tional period.   The gains were maintained for three
        months after termination of instruction and so the
        learned material was considered to have become part
        of these children's verbal repertoire.

616.   Andrews, G.; P.M. Howie; M. Dizsa; and B.E. Guitar.
        1982.   Stuttering: Speech pattern characteristics
        under fluency-inducing conditions.   *Journal of Speech
        and Hearing Research* 25:208-16.

            Speech samples were collected from three adult
        male stutterers under six baseline conditions and
        fifteen conditions believed to increase fluency.
        After moments of stuttering and filled pauses had
        been deleted from the samples, a speech pause analy-
        sis technique developed by Goldman-Eisler was used

to measure the following speech pattern characteristics: mean phonation duration (i.e., the duration between pauses), pause proportion, articulation rate, fluent speech rate, mean sentence length, and percentage of syllables stuttered. Greater than fifty percent reduction in stuttering occurred in all but three conditions (speak and write, relaxed, alone with cards). Greater than ninety percent reduction occurred under prolonged/DAF speech, singing, chorus reading, shadowing, slowing, syllable-timed speech, and response contingent stimulation. The data were examined for evidence of speech pattern characteristic changes that were associated with reduced stuttering. Lengthened mean phonation duration occurred consistently under four conditions: chorus reading, shadowing, singing, and prolonged/DAF. Slowed speech (lower overall rate, lower articulation rate, or increased pause proportion) occurred consistently in seven conditions: prolonged/DAF, slowing, syllable-timed speech, arm swing, speak and write, relaxed, and singing. Only in prolonged/DAF speech did lengthened phonation duration occur in conjunction with slowed speech. The results of this exploratory study suggest that stuttering may be reduced under different conditions by means of different strategies. Lengthened phonation and slowing were the predominant strategies used in those conditions investigated in this study. The results are consistent with those of effective treatment techniques. Theoretical accounts of the association between change in fluency and change in speech pattern characteristics are discussed.

617. Appelman, K. 1975. The conditioning of language in a nonverbal child conducted in a special education classroom. *Journal of Speech and Hearing Disorders* 40:3-13.

The purpose of this study was twofold: 1) to assess the feasibility of conducting speech conditioning sessions within a preschool classroom, and 2) to examine the process of transfer of learned verbalization from these sessions to classroom free-time.

The results indicated that the former was not only feasible, but effective. A nonverbal boy, enrolled in a special education preschool was taught to imitate reliably six words in forty-six fifteen-

minute sessions. Furthermore, the child's use of
spontaneous whole words during the rest of the classroom day seemed to be responsive to the contingencies
of the speech sessions.

618. Baltaxe, C.A. 1984. Use of contrastive stress in normal, aphasic, and autistic children. *Journal of
Speech and Hearing Research* 27:97-105.

Studies in child language have shown that contrastive stress appears to be an early developing
device to mark the topic-comment distinction, and
thus is important for the acquisition of pragmatic
knowledge. This study examined the use of contrastive stress by autistic children with mean-length-of-
utterance (MLU) scores between 1.9 and 4.1 morphemes.
Normal and aphasic subjects at similar MLU levels
served as contrast groups. The contrastive stress
task required that the subjects verbally assess the
counterfactual nature of a presupposition in a yes-
no question. Toy manipulation was used to elicit
the desired responses in a play situation. Listener
judgment served as the basis for analyzing results.
Although all subject groups were able to perform the
task, differences were seen in the number of correct
responses and the patterns of stress misassignment.

619. Bedwinek, A.P. 1983. The use of PACE to facilitate
gestural and verbal communication in a language-
impaired child. *Language, Speech, and Hearing Services in Schools* 1:2-6.

Promoting Aphasics' Communicative Effectiveness
(PACE) is a treatment technique that simulates natural face-to-face conversation while providing for
the use of multimodality communication. In this
case study, PACE techniques were used with a five-
year and four-month Down's syndrome child to facilitate simultaneous use of verbal and gestural communication.

620. Berk, S.; D.S. Doehring; and B. Bryans. 1983. Judg-
      ments of vocal affect by language-delayed children.
      Journal of Communication Disorders 1:49-56.

         Judgment of vocal affect was studied in nineteen
      language-delayed children and nineteen children with
      normal language. The children responded to utter-
      ances spoken in an angry, sad, or happy tone of voice
      by pointing to a picture of an angry, a happy, or a
      sad face. The language-delayed children made signif-
      icantly fewer correct judgments. The normal children
      judged all three emotions quite accurately, whereas
      the langauge-delayed children were very poor in judg-
      ing sadness and showed a bias for judging all three
      emotions as anger. The language-delayed children
      tended to improve with age, but age trends in normal
      children were obscured by near-perfect performance
      of many children.

621. Bernstein, L.E., and R.E. Stark. 1985. Speech percep-
      tion development in language impaired children: A 4-
      year follow-up study. *Journal of Speech and Hearing
      Disorders* 50:21-29.

         This study was an attempt to see if perceptual
      defects can be associated with specific language
      impairments. A group of specifically language im-
      paired children (SLI) were matched with a group of
      non-SLI children on tests of speech perception and
      language ability given over a four year period. The
      authors found perceptual deficits do cause specific
      language impairments.

622. Bromley, K., and C.C. Cavallaro. 1983. Teachers' per-
      ceptions of language skills necessary for mainstream-
      ing. *Journal of Child Communication Disorders* 6:91-
      101.

         This study compared kindergarten and preschool
      teachers' perceptions of the language skills most
      necessary for mainstreaming kindergarten placement
      of handicapped children. A high correlation was
      observed between mean rankings of skills by both
      groups of teachers. Moderate and low correlations
      existed between the a priori skill sequence and mean
      rankings of kindergarten and preschool teachers re-

spectively. Improving these teachers' knowledge of
language development might be one way to better provide for the special needs of handicapped children
who are making the transition between preschool and
kindergarten.

623. Bryen, D.N., and D.G. Joyce. 1984. Language intervention with the severely handicapped: A decade of research. *The Journal of Special Education* 19:7-55.

The authors examined forty language intervention
studies published during 1970 to see if they applied
current linguistic thinking in their programs and to
determine the degree of success in increasing communication competence. They found that only a little
over one-third of the studies succeeded in increasing
communication competence in severely handicapped
subjects. They also found that those involved in
these programs lagged behind current thinking in
clinical experience and research.

624. Casby, M.W., and K.F. Ruder. 1983. Symbolic play and
early language development in normal and mentally
retarded children. *Journal of Speech and Hearing
Research* 3:404-11.

This study investigated the relationship of
early language development and symbolic play behaviors in normal and mentally retarded children. Forty
children served as subjects: twenty normal and twenty
trainable mentally retarded children, ten each at
MLU stage pre-1 and MLU stage 1. The MLU stage pre-
1 children demonstrated significantly more restricted
symbolic play than did the MLU stage 1 children regardless of developmental status. A Pearson product-
moment correlation between MLU and mean symbolic
play score showed a high positive correlation between
the two variables. Symbolic play that involves the
use of one object to represent another was found to
be a strong correlate of early language development.

625. Cavallaro, C.C., and L.M. Bambara. 1982. Two strategies for teaching language during free play. *Journal*

of the Association for the Severely Handicapped 7:80-92.

An incidental teaching procedure (using natural opportunities for instruction) was more effective than a question-labeling procedure (using open questions) in increasing the rate and variety of two-word requests produced by a severely langauge-delayed preschooler during free play. The rate of spontaneous production was lower than expected.

626.   Chapman, K.; L.B. Leonard; L.E. Rowan; and A.L. Weiss. 1983. Inappropriate word extensions in the speech of young language-disordered children. *Journal of Speech and Hearing Disorders* 48:55-62.

The purpose of this study was to determine the frequency of inappropriate word extensions in the spontaneous speech of young language-disordered children, and how these extensions should be characterized. Inappropriate word extensions were identified and tested, first in a production task, and then in a comprehension task for nine language-disordered children (age 2:8 to 3:4). The results indicated that the percentage of inappropriate word extensions seen in the speech of these children was comparable to that seen in normal children at the same level of linguistic development. As with normal children, these inappropriate word extensions reflected varying levels of lexical knowledge. The findings of this study are discussed in terms of their clinical applicability for lexical training with language-disordered children.

627.   Courtright, J.A., and I.C. Courtright. 1979. Imitative modeling as a langauge intervention strategy: The effects of two mediating variables. *Journal of Speech and Hearing Research* 22:389-402.

Imitative modeling was compared with mimicry in teaching grammatical rules to thirty-six 3-6 year old language impaired children. Results confirmed earlier findings which suggested that modeling strategies were superior to mimicry. In addition, it was found that neither reinforcement nor third person models significantly increased the teaching effectiveness of modeling techniques.

628. Courtright, J.A., and I.C. Courtright. 1983. The per-
      ception of non-verbal vocal cues of emotional meaning
      by language-disordered and normal children. *Journal
      of Speech and Hearing Research* 26:412-17.

      The study compared language-disordered (N=49)
      in ability to interpret emotional meaning from vocal
      cues of adult speakers. Findings indicated that
      language-disordered children were less accurate in
      identifying vocal cues of emotion than were normal
      children, although their error pattern was not sig-
      nificantly different.

629. Culatta, B. 1980. Language processing skills: The
      hidden prerequisite. *Education Unlimited* 2:52-54.

      Intended for the teacher of handicapped chil-
      dren, the article describes some symptoms of language
      processing difficulty. Prerequisite skills for lan-
      guage comprehension are reviewed and characteristics
      that can help identify children with receptive lan-
      guage difficulties are listed.

630. Culatta, B.; J.L. Page; and J. Ellis. 1983. Story
      retelling as a communicative performance screening
      tool. *Language, Speech, and Hearing Services in
      Schools* 14:66-74.

      This study investigated the use of a story re-
      telling task as a mechanism for screening integrated
      communicative performance. Comparisons were made
      between story retelling performance and performance
      on two standardized screening tools for kindergarten.
      Results suggest that story retelling is a more strin-
      gent measure of integrated communicative performance.

631. Donahue, M.; R. Pearl; and T. Bryan. 1932. Learning
      disabled children's syntactic proficiency on a com-
      municative task. *Journal of Speech and Hearing Dis-
      orders* 47:397-403.

      The purpose of this study was to investigate

learning disabled children's syntactic proficiency
during a task requiring them to convey information to
a listener (in a social context). Oral language
samples were collected by having learning disabled
and normally achieving children in grades two, four,
six, and eight participate in a referential communication task. The length and syntactic complexity of
the children's descriptions were assessed. Learning
disabled children in all grades were found to produce
shorter mean t-units and shorter mean main clauses
than non-disabled children. Although learning disabled children's linguistic problems have previously
been characterized as subtle, these findings suggest
that their productive language deficits may be significant enough to interfere with even the informal
and simple conversations characteristic of communication among peers and family members.

632.   Ekeiman, B., and D.M. Aram. 1983. Syntactic findings
       in developmental verbal apraxia. *Journal of Communi-
       cation Disorders* 16:237-250.

       This article is about the analysis of spontane-
ous language samples of eight children (four to
eleven years old) diagnosed with developmental verbal
apraxia (motor speech disorder), which revealed that
at least some of the errors could not be attributed
to motor-speech and/or phonologic limitations but
rather indicated concomitant syntactic disorders.

633.   Elbert, M.; D.A. Dennsen; and T.W. Powell. 1984. On
       the prediction of phonologic generalization learning
       patterns. *Journal of Speech and Hearing Disorders*
       49:309-17.

       The study was an attempt to determine whether
correlations exist between children's misarticulation
of consonant clusters and certain facts that influence generalization learning patterns. It was found
that although all subjects could generalize there
were differences in their learning patterns. Explanations are given for these differences. Essentially
they emanate from each individual's phonologic knowledge and the interactions with the consonant clusters
themselves.

634. Filer, P.S. 1981. Conversations with language delayed children: How to get them talking. *Academic Therapy* 17:57-62.

    The classroom teacher can contribute to the language delayed child's language development through language interaction strategies. It is important that teachers recognize the child's language level. Structured interaction strategies include prompting, echoing, expansion interaction, re-casting sentences, and expatiation of modeling interactions.

635. Flynn, P.T. 1983. Speech-language pathologists and primary prevention: From ideas to action. *Language, Speech, and Hearing Services in the Schools* 14:99-104.

    Speech-language pathologists can help prevent communication disorders by helping to promote disability awareness, focusing on good health, limiting noise pollution, and helping to prevent injuries due to vocal misuse. Activities for each aspect are suggested.

636. Folkins, J.W., and R.N. Linville. 1983. The effects of varying lower-lip displacement on upper-lip movements: Implications for the coordination of speech movements. *Journal of Speech and Hearing Research* 26:209-17.

    Upper-lip and lower-lip movements were transduced in the inferior-superior dimension in five normal-speaking subjects during four tasks. In task 1, visual feedback was used to manipulate the maximum displacement of the lower lip during speech. The upper lip elevated significantly less for the opening gesture when the amount of opening from the lower lip was increased. The upper lip moved to significantly lower positions for bilabial closure when the distance to be moved by the lower lip was increased. In task 2, the same procedures were followed with a bite block between the teeth. The bite block did not significantly change the interactions between lips for the opening gesture. The interactions were larger for bilabial closure with the bite block. In task 3, different vowels instead of visual feedback

were used to manipulate lower-lip displacement. The
relations between lips were similar to those in task
1. In task 4, it was shown that these relations
between lips are not found in nonspeech lower-lip
movements. The interactions between lips are discussed in relation to models of speech motor control,
including spatial targets, mass-spring systems, and
planned trajectories.

637.   Fuchs, D.; L.S. Fuchs; and D.R. Garwick. 1983. Test
performance of language handicapped children with
familiar and unfamiliar examiners. *Journal of Psychology* 114:37-46.

Investigated the importance of examiner familiarity to children's performance on tasks requiring
high or low levels of symbolic mediation. Thirty-
four handicapped preschoolers were examined within a
repeated-measures crossover design, once by one of
two familiar classroom teachers and once by one of
four strange teachers. Students performed significantly better with familiar than with unfamiliar
examiners on high symbolic mediation tasks; no such
differential performance was obtained on low symbolic
mediation items. Findings are related to efforts to
identify procedural and situational variables in
assessment, uncontrolled by present standard test
administrations, that may preclude children's optimal
performance.

638.   Fujiki, M., and B. Brinton. 1983. Sampling reliability
in elicited imitation. *Journal of Speech and Hearing
Disorders* 48:85-89.

This study examined the number of trials necessary to obtain sampling reliability in elicited imitation. An examiner-constructed elicited imitation
test was administered to fifteen language-disordered
subjects, sampled from the age range of 5.6 to 6.6
years. All test sentences were controlled for
length, syntactic construction, and semantic content.
The test instrument contained multiple occurrences of
sixteen syntactic structures. For each of these
forms, subject performance on one, three, five, and
seven trials was compared with performance on ten
trials. It was observed that sampling reliability

increased as the number of trials increased, but as few as three repetitions provided reliable data.

639. Gilbert, S.F. 1979. Early-childhood education for the developmentally delayed: Diagnosis, intervention, and evaluation. *Language, Speech, and Hearing Services in Schools* 10:81-91.

This article describes the referral, diagnostic, interventive, and evaluative procedures used in a self-contained behaviorally oriented noncategorical program for preschool children with speech and language impairments and other developmental delays. The program is said to follow a verbal-didactic model with emphasis on parent involvement and behavior modification. The floor plan and daily schedule are described. Among four appendixes are lists of formal and informal diagnostic measures used.

640. Hall, P.K., and J.B. Tomblin. 1977. A follow-up study of children with articulation and language disorders. *Journal of Speech and Hearing Disorders* 43:227-41.

Eighteen language-impaired and eighteen articulation-impaired children were followed up with respect to communication skills and educational performance thirteen to twenty years after their initial contact with the speech and hearing clinic. The study found that these subjects had the same impairments, but to a lesser degree than when they began the program.

641. Handleman, J.S. 1981. Transfer of verbal responses across instructional settings by autistic-type children. *Journal of Speech and Hearing Disorders* 46:69-76.

The generalization of verbal behavior by autistic-type children was assessed across different settings. Autistic subjects (five males aged five, six, and seven, and one female aged twelve) who learned responses to common questions under two training conditions were probed to determine transfer of learning to a novel instructional environment. Four subjects demonstrated only low rates of generalization irrespective of the original training conditions.

642.   Hurford, A.   1980.   How peer tutors can help.   *Special
       Education: Forward Trends* 7:23-26.

       A program of peer tutoring for language and
       speech handicapped primary English schoolchildren
       is described.   The tutors were trained for ten to
       fifteen minutes once a week for eight weeks, and
       then began working with their language impaired
       peers.   Results indicated that the program has prom-
       ise, as most children demonstrated improvement in
       conversational skills.

643.   Johnston, J.R.   1982.   Narratives: A new look at commu-
       nication problems in older language-disordered chil-
       dren.   *Language, Speech, and Hearing Services in the
       Schools* 13:144-55.

       The author briefly reviews four specific per-
       spectives on narrative structure and uses a case
       study to illustrate how these perspectives can pro-
       vide useful insights into the language behavior of a
       language-disordered child.

644.   Johnston, J.R., and S.E. Weismer.   1983.   Mental rota-
       tion abilities in language-disordered children.
       Journal of Speech and Hearing Research 26:397-403.

       Normal and language-disordered children in the
       first and third grade (matched for sex and cognitive
       level) were asked to decide whether two geometric
       arrays were similarly ordered.   Language disordered
       children did not differ from normal children in ac-
       curacy of judgment or require more training trials.
       They did, however, respond more slowly.

645.   Kaczmarek, L.A.   1982.   Motor activities: A context for
       language/communication intervention.   *Journal of the
       Division for Early Childhood* 6:21-35.

       Three types of language skills (receptive, func-
       tional expressive, and descriptive expressive) are

discussed in terms of how they can be integrated
into typical gross and fine motor activities for
language delayed preschoolers.

646. Klein, H.B., and C.C. Spector. 1985. Effect of syllable stress and serial variability in polysyllabic
production of speech-delayed children. *Journal of
Speech and Hearing Disorders* 50:391-97.

This study attempted to learn the effects of
syllable stress and position in polysyllabic words
on the performance of speech-delayed children. The
continuous speech patterns of eight mild to moderate
speech delayed children, ages 5:2-6:11, were recorded
and studied. The authors found increased use of
reduced stress syllables that occur early in a sequence. They also found that syllables with reduced
stress were often associated with atypical errors.

647. Langdon, H.W. 1983. Assessment and intervention strategies for the bilingual language-disordered student.
Exceptional Children 50:37-46.

The article discusses the following topics:
language acquisition, development, and disorders in
bilingual individuals; instruments to assess first
and second language skills of bilingual students;
determination of a language disorder in a bilingual
population; and intervention techniques used by the
author, in her experience working with Puerto Rican
and Mexican-American students.

648. Levine, S.C., and S. Carey. 1985. Up front: The acquisition of a concept and a word. *Journal of Child
Language* 9:645-57.

The purpose of this study was to determine the
order in which two and three year old children learn
the concepts of the words "front" and "back."
Thirty-six children took part in this study. The
authors found that knowing the concept of "front"
and "back" precedes knowing the words themselves and
that "back" is usually known before "front."

649. Liles, B.Z., and M.D. Shulman. 1980. The grammaticality task: A tool for language assessment and language
intervention. *Language, Speech, and Hearing Services
in Schools* 11:260-66.

The usefulness of the grammaticality task (judgment as to the correctness of a sentence) as a clinical tool is discussed by presenting the task as a
method of eliciting a language sample. Data from a
pilot study (N=37 language-disordered children, aged
5:4 to 6:7) support the validity of the procedure.
Clinical observations elaborate the application of
the procedure and implications for management are
discussed.

650. Litowitz, B.E., and F.A. Novy. 1984. Expression of
the part-whole semantic relation by 3- to 12-year-
old children. *Journal of Child Language* 11:159-78.

This study investigated the expression of the
part-whole semantic relation by children three to
twelve years of age. Controlling both task format
and dimensions associated with experimental stimuli,
the verbal responses of two age groups of children
were analyzed. While results revealed the part-whole
semantic relation expressible by even the youngest
children, age-group comparisons indicated that the
older children preferred its use significantly more
often. The part-whole semantic relation was also
observed to take several linguistic forms, the selection of which varied as a function of age, task format, and type of experimental stimuli. Findings are
discussed relative to issues concerning research
methodology, the elicitation and assessment of children's semantic knowledge, and cognitive developmental theory.

651. Mattes, L.J. 1982. The Elicited Language Analysis
Procedure: A method for scoring sentence imitation
tasks. *Language, Speech, and Hearing Services in
Schools* 13:37-41.

Elicited imitation tasks are frequently used as
a diagnostic tool in evaluating children with communication handicaps. This study presents a scoring
procedure that can be used to obtain an in-depth

descriptive analysis of responses produced on elicited imitation tasks. The Elicited Language Analysis
Procedure makes it possible to systematically evaluate responses in terms of both their syntactic and
semantic relationships to the stimulus sentences
presented by the examiner. Response quality measures
are also included in the analysis procedure.

652. McCauley, R.J., and L. Swisher. 1984. Psychometric
review of language and articulation tests for preschool children. *Journal of Speech and Hearing Disorders* 49:34-42.

Thirty language and articulation tests developed
for use with preschool children were reviewed using
ten psychometric criteria appropriate to norm-
referenced tests. Half of the reviewed tests met no
more than two criteria, and only three tests met
over four criteria. Most frequently unmet criteria
were those requiring empirical evidence of validity
and reliability. Implications are drawn regarding
the current status of norm-referenced language and
articulation tests for preschool children.

653. McDermott, R.P., and T.A. Jones. 1984. Articulation
characteristics and listeners' judgments of the
speech of children with severe hearing loss. *Language, Speech, and Hearing Services in Schools*
15:110-26.

This study investigated selected articulation
characteristics of eight- to twelve-year-old children
with severe hearing impairment and the relations
between these characteristics and judged adequacy of
spontaneous conversational speech. The thirty experimental children, although variable in articulation
performance, presented significant problems in ap-
proximating the adult phonological code. The mean
number of test errors observed in the hearing-
impaired children most closely approximated the errors of normal-hearing three and one-half-year-old
children of the standardization sample. Errors were
primarily of the substitution type in the final word
position. Target phonemes most-to-least vulnerable
to error were (a) affricates, (b) fricatives,
(c) glides, (d) plosives, (e) vowels and diphthongs,

and (f) nasals. Frequency and consistency measures showed high-to-moderate correlations with judged adequacy of conversational speech.

A multiple regression analysis yielded an R of .92 and indicated that the number of defective test items accounted for eighty-four percent and vowel-diphthong errors for four percent of the variance in judged adequacy of conversational speech. The correlational analyses support the usefulness of a single index such as that derived from a comprehensive articulation test for the purpose of quantifying the degree to which a speaker is judged to be deficient in "general speech adequacy" by listeners in the environment.

654. McGee, S.R.; J.M. Hutchinson; and P.N. Deputy. 1981. The influence of the onset of phonation on the frequency of disfluency among children who stutter. *Journal of Speech and Hearing Research* 24:269-72.

This study was designed to assess the effects of on-off voice adjustments on the frequency of stuttering in children. Essentially this is a replication of the experimental paradigm used by Adams and Reis (1971, 1974) with adult stutterers who were asked to read two passages: one contained a normal distribution of voiced and voiceless sounds; the other contained nearly all voiced sounds. The latter passage was associated with less stuttering and more rapid adaptation. In this study, fifteen childhood stutterers in the third through the seventh grades were asked to read these same passages. Contrary to the previous results with adults, however, the children did not stutter less nor adapt more rapidly with the all-voiced passage. These results are discussed with reference to previous literature and to the influence of pausing.

655. Meline, T.J., and L.J. Sanders. 1978. Imitation, comprehension, and spontaneous production of main verbs by normal and language disordered children. *Acta Symbolica* 9:63-76.

The performance of twenty-five normal children (two to four years old), and twenty-five language disordered children (six years old), with mean

lengths of utterance between 3.5 and 4.5 morphemes,
was compared on linguistic tasks. Information was
collected from four tasks of linguistic knowledge of
main verbs, namely, comprehension, spontaneous production, elicited imitation of shorter sentences,
and elicited imitation of longer sentences. Results
indicated that some comprehension tests may overestimate children's linguistic knowledge, and that
spontaneous production and elicited imitation procedures are equally capable of estimating children's
linguistic knowledge for main verb forms; however,
length of sentences to be imitated is a critical
consideration.

656. Menary, S.; S.E. Trehub; and J. McNutt. 1982. Speech
discrimination in preschool children: A comparison of
two tasks. *Journal of Speech and Hearing Research*
25:202-207.

Four-year-old children were tested for their
discrimination of the following word pairs: rope/
robe, seat/seed, pick/pig, ice/eyes, and mouse/mouth.
Two discrimination tasks were used: a picture-
pointing task that typifies discrimination tasks
currently in use with young children, and an operant
technique that exemplifies procedures used in the
testing of infants. Both discrimination tasks
yielded roughly comparable levels of performance.
All word pairs were found to be discriminable, but
performance on seat/seed and mouse/mouth was inferior
to that on the other word pairs. In a limited sampling of production data, misarticulations were observed in the final consonants of ice, eyes, mouse,
and mouth.

657. Minskoff, E.H. 1982. Sharpening language skills in
secondary learning-disabled students. *Academic Therapy* 18:53-60.

Since the nature of language demands changes
with age, language instruction must also change.
The five advanced areas of language training--vocab-
ulary, listening comprehension, making conversation,
abstract language, and adjusting language to differing social situations--all require a systematic,
step-by-step teaching approach, utilizing an induc-

tive teaching method and role playing. The teacher
uses the inductive method to lead the students to
discover underlying meanings and rules governing
verbal behavior. Role playing is used to give students practice in applying these rules to simulated
situations. Finally, the teacher encourages students
to use these advanced language skills in their verbal
interactions at home, school, play, and work.

658. Muma, J.R. 1977. Language intervention strategies.
      Language, Speech, and Hearing Services in Schools
      8:107-120.

          Comparisons are drawn between natural language
      learning and language intervention concerning con-
      tent, sequencing, pacing, and reinforcement context.
      The Lockean and Rousseauean philosophies of interven-
      tion as respective precursors of behaviorism and
      psychosociolinguistic orientations are compared.
      Six specific intervention strategies are presented
      in terms of basic principles, underlying assumptions,
      applications and limitations. The six strategies
      are: first, language learning; second, language
      learning intermodality transfer; third, language
      rehabilitation; fourth, systematic extension of avail-
      able repertoire; fifth, spontaneous exploration; and
      sixth, variation of available verbal repertoire.

659. Nataraja, N.P., and M. Jayaram. 1982. A new approach
      to the classification of voice disorders. *Journal
      of the All-India Institute of Speech & Hearing* 13:21-
      28.

          Reviews various classification systems for voice
      disorders. Many such systems are not descriptive
      nor are they based on the etiology of the disorder
      or the therapeutic procedures to be employed. A new
      approach to classification is proposed in which a
      good voice is defined as one that has optimum fre-
      quency as its fundamental frequency. There are sev-
      eral objective methods of finding fundamental and
      optimum frequencies.

660. Nippold, M.A., and S.H. Fey. 1983. Metaphoric under-
      standing in pre-adolescents having a history of lan-

guage acquisition difficulties. *Language, Speech, and Hearing Services in Schools* 14:171-180.

This study was designed to investigate metaphoric understanding and its relationship to a cognitive task of combinatorial reasoning in preadolescent children ($\bar{x}$ age = 10:7) who were diagnosed as language impaired during their preschool years. Although the children performed as well as a group of normal preadolescents ($\bar{x}$ age = 10:8) on certain tests involving literal aspects of language and on a nonverbal intelligence test, they were deficient in their understanding of metaphoric sentences and in performing the cognitive task. This result suggests that children who as preschoolers exhibit difficulty in acquiring language may at a later time have difficulty dealing with figurative aspects of language.

661. Panagos, J.M., and P.A. Prelock. 1982. Phonological constraints on the sentence productions of language-disordered children. *Journal of Speech and Hearing Research* 25:171-77.

The effects of phonological and syntactic structure on the sentence productions of language-disordered school children (mean age = 6:2 years) were investigated. Phonological complexity in lexical items disrupted syntactic performance in a quantitative fashion. Whereas the syntactic constructions determined the patterns of errors, added phonological complexity simply increased the errors within the patterns. The causal interrelationships between children's syntactic and phonological disorders are discussed in terms of a theory of general organizational deficit.

662. Partyka, C.M., and J.D. Kresheck. 1983. A comparison of categorization skills of normal and language-delayed children in early elementary school. *Language, Speech, and Hearing Services in Schools* 14:243-51.

This study compared the categorization skills of first-grade children representing three levels of expressive language development. Each group of twelve children (normal, mild-moderate delay, and

severe delay) was tested on seven different categorization tasks. The results indicated a significant
difference in categorization skills between the children with normal expressive language development and
each of the two expressive language-delayed groups.
Differential results for the three language groups
are discussed.

663. Phatate, D.D., and H. Umano. 1981. Auditory discrimination of voiceless fricatives in children. *Journal
of Speech and Hearing Research* 24:162-69.

Auditory discrimination of the voiceless fricatives / f s/ was studied in 200 subjects between
the ages of four and six and a half years. In the
test task the subject was asked to remember one of
the sounds and then to indicate each time this sound
was presented. Two types of errors were analyzed.
An error of omission was a failure to identify the
remembered sound, and this type of error did not
change with age. An error of commission, a failure
to discriminate between the remembered sound and one
of the other voiceless fricatives, decreased with
age. The results are interpreted as support for a
theory of the development of auditory perception of
speech in which discrimination of some properties in
speech, such as relatively weak spectral cues and
second formant transitions, have to be learned by a
child.

664. Prelock, P.A., and J.M. Panagos. 1980. Mimicry versus
imitative modeling: Facilitating sentence production
in the speech of the retarded. *Journal of Psycholinguistic Research* 9:565-78.

Criticisms of imitative language training led
to the development of the modeling method for language acquisition of retarded children. The methods
of mimicry and imitative modeling are evaluated as
teaching approaches. The imitative modeling group
learned to express three-word sentences, to apply
information processing strategies, to express language structure, and to process sentence production
for conversational purposes. Multidimensional learning was best facilitated by the modeling rather than
the mimicry procedures.

665.   Prizant, B.M.   1983.   Language acquisition and communi-
       cative behavior in autism: Toward an understanding
       of the "whole" of it.   *Journal of Speech and Hearing
       Disorders* 48:296-307.

            There have been few attempts to bring a sense
       of cohesion to the varied communicative symptomatol-
       ogy evident in autism because much of the research
       literature has been product oriented rather than
       process oriented and has focused on language struc-
       ture rather than function.   This discussion reviews
       symptomatology of autistic communication in reference
       to "gestalt" versus "analytic" modes of cognitive
       processing, language acquisition, and language use.
       Based on research on language behavior of normal and
       autistic children, specific issues are considered,
       including a reconsideration of echolalic behaviors,
       patterns of social interaction, and patterns of
       cognitive-linguistic development in autism.

666.   Revelle, D.M., 1971.   Aiding children with specific
       language disability.   *Academic Therapy* 4:391-97.

            The author describes methods used to help chil-
       dren with a specific learning disability achieve
       sufficient proficiency in writing to be able to func-
       tion in school up to the secondary level and in daily
       living.   Among such methods are: going from the sim-
       ple to the complex, giving children ample practice,
       and maintaining a pleasant atmosphere.

667.   Ribner, S.; L. Becker; S. Marks; P. Kahn; and F.
       Wolfson.   1983.   A validation study of the elementary
       and advanced screening tests of the Clinical Evalua-
       tion of Language Functions.   *Language, Speech, and
       Hearing Services in Schools* 14:215-22.

            The elementary and advanced screening tests of
       the Clinical Evaluation of Language Functions (CELF)
       were administered to children recommended for special
       education classes in the New York City school system.
       The children were also evaluated by speech/language
       specialists and were rated by them on the extent of
       their language deficit.   The CELF scores were then
       compared to the ratings of the language specialists.
       The findings indicate that the CELF tests did not

consistently identify children requiring therapeutic
help nor those with language deficits and the scores
also exhibited considerable variability.

668. Ritterman, S.I.; S. Zook-Herman; R.L. Carlson; and S.W.
      Winde. 1982. The pass/fail disparity among three
      commonly employed articulatory screening tests.
      Journal of Speech and Hearing Disorders 47:429-33.

          This study compared children's performances on
      three screening tests of articulation. The Templin-
      Darley Screening Test of Articulation, the Screening
      Deep Test of Articulation, and the Predictive Screen-
      ing Test of Articulation were administered to ninety-
      one first graders ranging in age from 5:6 to 7:0
      years of age. Comparisons were made in terms of the
      number of individuals failed. Results indicated
      that while there was no significant difference be-
      tween the numbers of individuals failing each test,
      there was poor correlation between the tests in terms
      of the particular individuals failed. Of the eleven
      children failing one or more of the tests, only one
      failed all three. Results are discussed in terms of
      their clinical implications.

669. Rom, A., and L.S. Bliss. 1983. The use of nonverbal
      pragmatic behaviors by language-impaired and normal-
      speaking children. *Journal of Communication Disor-
      ders* 16:251-56.

          Play was the only behavior that distinguished
      among six nonverbal pragmatic behaviors for three
      groups: twenty language impaired subjects (mean age
      four years) and two control groups equated with the
      experimental subjects by age and mean length of ut-
      terance. No significant differences were observed
      for distance, physical contact, vocalization, look-
      ing, and smiling.

670. Roth, F.P. 1984. Accelerating language learning in
      young children. *Journal of Child Language* 11:89-107.

          To examine the effects of direct intervention
      on language learning, eighteen children ranging in
      age from 3:6 to 4:6 were systematically taught lin-

guistic structures still beyond their developmental
grasp. Four types of relative clause sentences were
trained using a toy manipulation task. Solid improvement was found in the performance of subjects
in the two experimental conditions between the pre-
and post-test phases. No significant improvement
was demonstrated by the control condition subjects.
This successful outcome is viewed as demonstrating
that the language learning process is somewhat independent of cognitive development.

671. Schwartz, E.R., and C.B. Solot. 1980. Response patterns characteristic of verbal expressive disorders.
Language, Speech, and Hearing Services in Schools
11:139-44.

The authors examine the need to analyze free
expression as part of an overall expressive language
evaluation in school aged children. Use of the Social Adjustment B subtest of the Detroit Tests of
Learning Aptitude is advocated for this purpose.
Seven language characteristics are identified that
may help in recognizing disorders of self-expression.
Of the three identified groups of language impaired
children, those whose communication skills are
grossly within normal range but whose answers in
class are brief or circumlocutious are particularly
vulnerable to associated school problems.

672. Schwartz, R.G.; K. Chapman; B.A. Terrell; P.A. Prelock;
and L.E. Rowan. 1985. Facilitating word combinations in language impaired children through discourse structure. *Journal of Speech and Hearing
Disorders* 50:31-39.

The authors wanted to study the influence of
adult-child discourse structure on the use of early
word combinations in language impaired children. A
group of ten children between the ages of 2:8 and
3:4 took part in the study. Eight of the children
were the experimental group. The other two were the
controls. The eight were exposed to multi-word constructions instead of simple language. The experimental group ended up using more multi-word constructions than the control group.

673. Scofield, S.J. 1978. The language-delayed child in
      the mainstreamed primary classroom. *Language Arts*
      55:719-23.

          What the teacher can do to attend to the special
      needs of the language delayed student mainstreamed
      into the primary classroom is the focus of this arti-
      cle. Characteristics of the language delayed child
      are reviewed and three theoretical strands in the
      empirical literature on language intervention are
      outlined. Three kinds of intervention are described:
      systematic instruction, experience with a range of
      language functions, and provision of opportunities
      for spontaneous speech.

674. Shadden, B.B. 1983. Videotape applications in prag-
      matic intervention with language-impaired children.
      Journal of Child Communication Disorders 6:71-84.

          Problems in developing pragmatic-based language
      intervention programs are discussed in this article
      and some theoretical applications of client-directed,
      context-bound video playback are described. Specifi-
      cally, the author suggests that the use of video
      systems to record children's behaviors in natural
      settings and the playing back of these recordings to
      children themselves can enhance therapeutic acquisi-
      tion and expansion of pragmatic, communication-
      oriented skills. Observations from an experimental
      language project seem to support this hypothesis,
      though the need for further clinical research is
      stressed.

675. Shriberg, L.D. 1980. An intervention procedure for
      children with persistent /r/ errors. *Language,
      Speech, and Hearing Services in Schools* 11:102-10.

          This article describes a diagnostic teaching
      procedure for use with children who have persistent
      /r/ errors. Rationale for the procedure includes a
      two-category typology of children with persistent
      /r/ errors and an analysis of articulatory gestures
      associated with a child's attempts to say /r/ cor-
      rectly. The five step intervention procedure con-
      sists of forty-five-minute sessions involving both
      assessment and diagnostic teaching.

676. Shriberg, L.D., and J. Kwiatkowski. 1982. Phonological
disorders I: A diagnostic classification system.
Journal of Speech and Hearing disorders 47:226-41.

Presents data to support the validity and util-
ity of a diagnostic classification system for persons
with phonological disorders. Rationale for the classification system is developed from current reviews
of issues and concepts in phonology and classification systems. The system proceeds from a worksheet
for reduction of phonological and other assessment
data through five hierarchical levels of classification entries. The system will accommodate lower-
level elaboration of etiological subgrouping, pending
appropriate research. A retrospective classification
study of forty-three children with delayed speech is
described. Procedural details relating classification procedures to two companion papers (Shriberg
and Kwiatkowski, 1982a, 1982b) are provided.

677. Shriberg, L.D., and J. Kwiatkowski. 1982. Phonological
disorders II: A conceptual framework for management.
Journal of Speech and Hearing Disorders 47:242-56.

Proposes conceptual framework for management of
phonological disorders. The framework includes a
ten-element system for describing the structure of
management programs and invokes a diagnostic classification system for determining appropriate management content. Data from three serial studies of
management structure describe the effectiveness,
efficiency, and clinician acceptance of four modes
of management: drill, drill play, structured play,
and play. Review of past, present, and future content of management programs emphasizes the central
role of individual differences among persons with
phonological disorders.

678. Shulman, M.D., and B.Z. Liles. 1979. A sense of grammaticality: An ingredient for language remediation.
Language, Speech, and Hearing Services in Schools
10:59-63.

There is a need for training children with language disorders to judge correctness or incorrectness
of sentences that reflect error patterns. Such judg-

ments are seen as an integral part of language remediation. The author cites several studies of language disordered children.

679. Silverman, E.M., and K. Van Opens. 1980. An investiga-
      tion of sex-bias in classroom teachers' speech and
      language referrals. *Language, Speech, and Hearing
      Services in Schools* 11:169-74.

      One hundred and thirty-three kindergarten
      through sixth grade classroom teachers in four school
      districts completed questionnaires designed to deter-
      mine whether they would be more likely to refer a
      boy than a girl with an identical communication dis-
      order. The teachers were found to be equally likely
      to refer a girl as a boy who presented a disorder of
      articulation, language, or voice, but they were more
      likely to refer a boy for speech-language remediation
      who presented the disorder of stuttering.

680. Singh, S.; M.E. Hayden; and M.S. Toombs. 1981. The
      role of distinctive features in articulation errors.
      Journal of Speech and Hearing Disorders 46:174-83.

      Articulation errors of 1,077 children of various
      ages, etiologies, and sexes were taken from several
      standardized articulation tests. The Singh and Singh
      (1976) distinctive feature system was used to produce
      profiles for each subgroup for consonant phonemes in
      the initial, medial, and final word positions. Dis-
      tinctive features were used with different degrees
      of importance causing hierarchial orders among the
      features. The hierarchy of features established in
      this study was consistent with that found in previous
      studies. It was more pronounced for the initial
      position than for the medial and final positions,
      and for the younger age groups as compared with the
      older groups. In addition, the feature hierarchy
      for the articulation-disordered group was more dis-
      tinct than that for the language group. Females
      revealed a generally superior performance to males,
      but this superiority was in general not statistically
      significant. Findings are discussed as to their
      relevance in the overall application of a phonologi-
      cal theory to speech production strategies.

681. Smith, J. 1979. Classroom help for the non-verbal and
      speech delayed child. *Early Years* 10:74-76.

      Describes activities for encouraging and improv-
      ing speech in nonverbal and speech delayed children.
      Outlines informal testing procedures for such areas
      as auditory discrimination and self concept, and
      suggests activities that include using stories that
      contain repetition.

682. Steckol, K.F., and L.B. Leonard. 1979. The use of
      grammatical morphemes by normal and language-
      impaired children. *Journal of Communication Disor-
      ders* 291-301.

      Grammatical morpheme usage of ten normal chil-
      dren (two to three years old) and ten language im-
      paired children (four to six years old), matched at
      their different levels of mean utterance length, was
      examined. Language impaired students displayed less
      grammatical morpheme usage than normal students with
      equivalent mean utterance length. No use of alterna-
      tive features of semantic importance by the language
      impaired students was noted, suggesting that no
      unique patterns for acquiring language were in opera-
      tion. Instead, it appeared that the language im-
      paired students may have attached less communicative
      significance to grammatical morphemes.

683. Thal, D.J., and T. Goldenberg. 1981. Programming di-
      versity of response: A method for teaching flexibil-
      ity of language use. *Journal of Childhood Communica-
      tion Disorders* 5:54-65.

      Describes a program that was designed to teach
      diversity of response to two language disordered
      students (six years old) who used language in an
      inflexible and uncreative manner. The method in-
      cluded modeling a particular part of speech and then
      reinforcing correct production, but only if a number
      of different words were used. The authors suggest
      that the approach to therapy outlined here may be
      particularly useful for teaching more creative and
      flexible language use to children who continue to
      need more structure than can be provided in a natu-
      ralistic setting.

684. Toombs, M.S.; S. Singh; and M.E. Hayden. 1981. Marked-
      ness of features in the articulatory substitutions
      of children. *Journal of Speech and Hearing Disorders*
      46:184-91.

          This study concerns an analysis of articulatory
      substitutions of 801 students using markedness theory
      and a distinctive feature model (Singh & Singh,
      1976). The 556 male and 245 female students ranged
      in age from three to seven years and were diagnosed
      as evidencing an articulatory disorder or a linguis-
      tic delay. Significantly more feature substitutions
      moved from marked to unmarked values than from un-
      marked to marked values (p < .05, binomial distribu-
      tion). The study proposed a hierarchy of distinctive
      features in terms of markedness rather than in terms
      of features per se. The applications of articulatory
      and acoustic data to phonological theory and the
      implications of the findings to speech treatment are
      discussed.

685. Wall, M.J., and F.L. Myers. 1982. A review of linguis-
      tic factors associated with early childhood stutter-
      ing. *Journal of Communication Disorders* 15:441-49.

          This paper summarizes recent thinking on several
      aspects of early childhood stuttering. It examines
      the concept of fluency and reviews research that
      traces the acquisition of fluency in young children
      and its relationship to language acquisition. Other
      topics considered are the relationship of normal
      childhood nonfluencies to early stuttering, stutter-
      ing as it relates to language acquisition, and psy-
      cholinguistic influences on stuttering in young chil-
      dren.

686. Wallace, G., and G.C. Canter. 1985. Effects of per-
      sonally relevant language materials on the perform-
      ance of severely aphasic individuals. *Journal of
      Speech and Hearing Disorders* 50:385-89.

          The authors tested the theory that severely
      aphasic individuals perform better with personally
      relevant materials than with non-personal materials.
      Twenty-four severely aphasic adults were tested in
      four language areas. They performed significantly

better with personally relevant materials in all
areas tested.

687. Waller, M.; R. Sollod; E. Sander; and E. Kunicki. 1983.
Psychological assessment of speech- and language-
disordered children. *Language, Speech, and Hearing
Services in Schools* 14:92-98.

Recent evidence indicates a high prevalence of
psychological problems among children with articulation and language disorders. The article reviews
these findings and draws implications as to the role
of the speech-language pathologist in behavior problem identification, referral, and therapy. For the
screening of relevant behavior traits, a battery of
psychological tests, including both parent-teacher
questionnaires and child performance measures, is
suggested and discussed.

688. Warren, S.F.; R.J. Mc Qugarter; and A.K. Rogers-Warren.
1984. The effects of mands and models on the speech
of unresponsive language-delayed preschool children.
Journal of Speech and Hearing Disorders 49:43-52.

The effects of the systematic use of mands (non-
yes/no questions and instructions to verbalize),
models (imitative prompts), and specific consequent
events on the productive verbal behavior of three
unresponsive, socially isolate, language-delayed
preschool children were investigated in a multiple-
baseline design within a classroom free play period.
Following a lengthy intervention condition, experimental procedures were systematically faded out to
check for maintenance effects. The treatment resulted in increases in total verbalizations and nonobligatory speech (initiations) by the subjects.
Subjects also became more responsive in obligatory
speech situations. In a second free play (generalization) setting, increased rates of total child
verbalizations and nonobligatory verbalizations were
observed for all three subjects, and two of the three
subjects were more responsive compared to their base-
lines in the first free play setting. Rate of total
teacher verbalizations and questions were also higher
in this setting. Maintenance of the treatment effects was shown during the fading condition in the

intervention setting. The subjects' MLUs increased
during the intervention condition when the teacher
began prompting a minimum of two-word utterances in
response to a mand or model.

689. Watson, B.U., and R.W. Thompson. 1983. Parents' per-
      ception of diagnostic reports and conferences. *Lan-
      guage, Speech, and Hearing Services in Schools*
      14:114-120.

      Questionnaires were used to evaluate fifty-nine
      parents' reactions to and understanding of diagnostic
      information from written reports and conferences in
      a clinic for speech, learning, language, and hearing
      problems.

690. Weber, J.L.; W.V. Kushnir; and S.E. Weber. 1982. A
      comprehensive approach to assessment and treatment
      of severe developmental speech and language disor-
      ders. *Journal of Learning Disabilities* 15:8-14.

      Discusses comprehensive approach to assessment
      and treatment of severe developmental speech and
      language disorders based on clinical experience with
      sixty-nine children between two and one-half and
      seven years of age. Assessment involves the integra-
      tion of many variables, including differentiation
      between linguistic competence versus performance,
      diagnosis, familial and environmental factors, and
      pragmatics. Suggest framework for treatment that
      distinguishes therapy goals from therapy styles.
      The decision regarding choice of goals and styles is
      based on an integrative assessment, with the result
      that the treatment plan is appropriately designed
      for each individual.

691. Weismer, G., and M. Elbert. 1982. Temporal character-
      istics of "functionally" misarticulated /S/ in 4- to
      6-year-old children. *Journal of Speech and Hearing
      Research* 25:275-287.

      This paper reviews instrumental studies of
      "functional" misarticulations in children and reports
      on an experiment involving acoustic measures of the
      duration of normally articulated and misarticulated

/s/. Three subject groups (n=7 in each group) included normally articulating adults, normally articulating children, and children who misarticulate the /s/ sound. Multiple repetitions of nonsense sequences containing /s/ were obtained from each subject, and group and individual subject comparisons were based on means, standard deviations, and the derived coefficient of variation associated with /s/ duration. Results indicate that /s/ durations of misarticulating children are significantly more variable than those of normally articulating children, and that this difference is more striking in /s/-stop clusters than in the case of singleton /s/. The possibility is raised that the variability differences between the two child groups may reflect differences in speech motor control capabilities. The authors suggest that such control differences should predict temporal variability differences between the two child groups for sounds that are articulated correctly by children in both groups. In addition, these variability differences should be observed for the spectral dimension of speech sound production, since this measure is sensitive to control of articulatory configuration.

692. Weiss, A.L.; L.B. Leonard; L.E. Rowan; and K. Chapman. 1983. Linguistic and nonlinguistic features of style in normal and language-impaired children. *Journal of Speech and Hearing Disorders* 48:154-64.

This study explored language-learning styles described in recent investigations of early child language. Eight children, four normally-developing and four language-impaired, were classified as "referential" or "expressive" speakers on the basis of their lexical distribution. For both the normal and language-impaired children, linguistic features suggested in the literature as correlating to one or another language-learning style were found to exist in clusters consistent with the children's pattern of lexical distribution. In addition, analyses of videotaped samples coded for the focus and context of the normal and language-impaired children's play behaviors revealed object-based and social-interaction-based activities that were generally consistent with the children's lexical distribution.

693. Weiss, M.A., and M.R. Duffy. 1979. Oral language disorders in children: Identification and remediation.
Journal of Clinical Child Psychology 8:206-11.

    Describes childhood language disorders and their
    potential negative impact on the child's academic
    and psychological functioning. Early identification
    of the problem, such as a failure to consistently
    respond to sound at one year, is of utmost impor-
    tance. Discusses diagnostic and remediation strate-
    gies, including a listing of tests and possible place-
    ments.

694. Westby, C.E. 1980. Assessment of cognitive and language abilities through play. *Language, Speech, and
Hearing Services in Schools* 11:154-68.

    Details ten-stage symbolic play language scale
    and relates it to the language concepts and struc-
    tures associated with each developmental play stage.
    The assessment can determine if a child should be
    given priority for receiving language remediation
    and what communicative functions, semantic concepts,
    and syntactic structures would need to be taught.
    The scale is a simple observation form, and relevant
    definitions are appended.

695. Willems, S.G.; L.J. Lombardino; J.D. MacDonald; and
R.E. Owens. 1982. Total communication: Clinical
report on a parent-based language training program.
Education and Training of the Mentally Retarded
17:293-98.

    A model for training parents to teach total
    communication to their language-disordered children.
    Five severely language-disordered children and their
    parents participated in a ten-week sign training
    program. Group parent teaching sessions were con-
    ducted in four phases and individual training was
    provided on a weekly basis. All children showed
    substantial gains in their use of productive lan-
    guage. The authors discuss guidelines for designing
    similar training programs.

CHAPTER VIII:
ORTHOPEDIC AND OTHER PHYSICAL IMPAIRMENTS

Unlike the exceptional children whose cognitive functioning is either superior or inferior to that of their normal peers, children with physical impairments are not limited in their intellectual capabilities, but suffer and encounter barriers to learning due to physical factors. Cerebral palsy children comprise the largest number of the physically disabled in need of special education. Other subgroupings include epilepsy, diabetes, chronic medical illnesses, muscular dystrophy, spina bifida, hemophilia, sickle-cell anemia, and various cardiac conditions. PL 94-142 defines physical impairments as those caused by congenital anomaly (e.g., clubfoot, absence of a limb), by disease (e.g., poliomyelitis), and from other causes, such as cerebral palsy and amputations.

Today, children who are orthopedically and physically impaired are provided with instruction within the regular classroom whenever possible. To comply with the provisions of PL 94-142, new school buildings are being designed to accommodate the physically handicapped. In older buildings many architectural barriers have been eliminated in order to enable the physically impaired to be more mobile. The installation of ramps and elevators, the widening of doors to permit the passage of wheelchairs, the lowering of water fountains, and the provisions of specially equipped bathrooms are some of the many changes which have been made.

Mainstreaming of the physically handicapped student does provide experiences that are beneficial. As students in a regular normal class, the physically handicapped would not lose instructional time due to specialized programs and they would learn to cope with stressful situations and relationships. They would be able to seek assistance from their nonhandicapped peers when needed, and they would provide the nonhandicapped with empathetic experiences. Contacts between the two could lead to a better understanding and appreciation of one another within the classroom and outside in the community as well.

The educational programming for physically handicapped

children needs to involve special educators, psychologists,
doctors, social workers, physical therapists, and speech and
language therapists. The goal of educating these individuals
should include the mastery of daily living skills, self-
awareness, academic growth, and interpersonal relations.
Many physically handicapped individuals have multiple handicaps. Quite often it is difficult to assess their intelligence because their multiple handicaps make standard testing
procedures inadequate. However, task analysis and observations are valuable and reliable in assessing abilities, and
once evaluation is made, ways of reaching the educational
goals must be invented. Personal development can be fostered
by activities designed to increase independent thought and
therefore increase self-concept. Acquisition of academic
skills will be a great help to these children in helping them
to understand the world they live in. They must learn to
accept their handicapping situations especially in the social
realm. Teachers should help foster a philosophy of life
within these children as they will continually encounter stum-
bling blocks. Vocational counseling and training is of great
importance to their future. In the end it is very difficult
to prescribe specific interventions for educating these children because of the wide range of problems involved and their
ever changing needs. The curriculum must be flexible. Sensitivity and an optimistic approach will go a long way in
smoothing the bumps in the road ahead.

The primary role of the teacher working with the physically impaired should be that of a supportive and accepting
educator, neither patronizing nor inflexible. The teacher
must plan individualized programs of instruction if needed
and warranted and learn to accept a great deal of absenteeism
(due to medical conditions, medical and clinic visits, and
programs of specialized therapy). At times, the teacher may
need to administer medications to students or remind them to
see the school nurse. But of all of the requirements needed
by the teacher for success, perhaps the most important and
fundamental one is the adoption and exhibition of a maximally
positive attitude toward these particular children, so that
they can develop a positive outlook toward themselves.

Further, when working with this population, teachers
must be fully aware of the physical capabilities and physical
limitations of their charges. Also, completion of assigned
tasks should be emphasized. Tasks assigned to individual
pupils should be completed by the pupils themselves, as this
will lead to feelings of self-esteem. In the pursuit of the
goal of self-esteem and independence, the teacher should first
make sure that all expectations are realistic. The next step
is to provide an environment that is conducive to functioning

with a motor handicap. For example, the entire classroom
should be accessible for all wheelchair-bound children, including aisles, desks, and closets. For those who can profit
from them, parallel bars and railings should be installed in
the room. Tools, too, can be made useful for the instruction
of students with physical difficulties; typewriters and computers can be suitably modified, if need be.

Finally, the orthopedically impaired children as well as
other handicapped youngsters need encouragement from their
classroom teachers. They need to explore their attitudes
toward themselves, including social, sexual, academic, and
vocational potentials. They need to express their feelings of
happiness, sadness, anger, and other emotions. Teachers and
therapists must provide opportunities for these children to
explore their feelings, including those related to family
life, human sexuality, and death education. These children
need to know that it is normal to experience many feelings.
These children also should be provided with opportunities to
teach them how to deal with frustration and disappointment.

696. Agrawal, K., and U. Dhar. 1983. Causal attribution
      and disability. *Journal of Psychological Researches*
      27:81-86.

        This study examined thirty-two normal and
      thirty-two disabled (seventeen orthopedically handi-
      capped and fifteen blind) students to assess whether
      levels of ability and/or effort or environmental
      factors determined success or failure in a variety
      of success/failure experiences; e.g., good jobs,
      personal popularity, losing an election, serious
      illness. Data indicate that self-attribution was
      more apparent in success than in failure experience.
      Normal students showed lower self-attribution scores
      compared to disabled students. Orthopedically handi-
      capped students showed lower self-attribution than
      the blind students who had a higher belief in them-
      selves and had a greater tendency to attribute suc-
      cess and failure to self, rather than to societal
      forces or to luck. Results confirm a general human
      tendency to attribute failures to others rather than
      to oneself.

697. Alvin, J. 1965. *Music for the handicapped child*. New
      York: Oxford University Press.

        Discusses musical sensibility in the handicapped
      and contribution of music to a child's general, emo-
      tional, intellectual, and social maturation. Recom-
      mends forms and types of music for listening and
      creating and describes music and musical movement
      for children who are maladjusted, cerebral palsied,
      and physically handicapped.

698. Anton, B.S., and G. Dindia. 1984. Parental perception
      of cognitive abilities of children with cerebral
      palsy. *Psychological Reports* 54:987-90.

        The literature compared the parental perception
      of their children's intellectual ability with actual
      level of functioning. Included in the study were
      thirty-nine children ranging in age from four years
      of age to nine years of age. All thirty-nine chil-
      dren had cerebral palsy. The students took standard-
      ized intelligence tests and the parents took the
      Academic scale of the Developmental Profile - II.

The results indicated that the students' parents' perceptions of intellectual functioning were highly correlated with actual ability. It was also found that parents of younger cerebral students tended to overestimate the cerebral palsy child's cognitive abilities.

699. Arnold, J. 1984. Values of exceptional students during early adolescence. *Exceptional Children* 51:230-34.

This study administered an eleven-item, rank order values inventory to 104 sixth and ninth grade exceptional adolescents in five diagnostic categories (physically handicapped, emotionally handicapped, and hearing impaired), and to 101 nonexceptional adolescents. Results indicate the two main groups have similar value hierarchies. Both ranked good education, freedom, family security, and true friendship among their top five values, and equality, exciting life, and sense of accomplishment least important. Comparison of ranking to those from different, nonexceptional adolescent populations shows that demographic factors may influence value patterns more than handicapped conditions. Exceptional and nonexceptional students did differ significantly on good education and freedom.

700. Arundel, G. 1982. What is the least restrictive environment for physically handicapped students? *Educational Horizons* 60:31-33.

Because of the need for special assistance, extra time and rest, mainstreaming the physically disabled student may actually result in a more restrictive school experience and decreased individualized instruction. The author suggests that the requirement P.L. 94-142 may be misinterpreted to the student's disfavor.

701. Bachman, W., and K. Law. 1961. Manuscript writing with the cerebral palsied child. *Exceptional Children* 27:239-45.

This report describes an attempt to apply techniques of teaching writing developed by various dis-

ciplines to teaching writing to the multiply handicapped cerebral palsied child. The techniques used
included those recommended for teaching writing to
the cerebral palsied child with hand involvement and
those recommended for teaching writing to the child
with perceptual difficulties and no motor involvement. The group consisted of three boys and six
girls ranging in age from seven to nine. Of the
three children listed as having known eye defects--
two had glasses which they seldom wore. Their intelligence ranged from severely retarded (1) educable
(2) dull normal (4) borderline (2) and normal (1).
The aim of this project was to integrate the two
techniques of teaching writing: that used to teach
the cerebral palsied child with hand involvement and
that used to teach the child with perceptual difficulties. One of the major advantages of the presentation was the initial evaluation of the group's
level of readiness, and allowing the students to
begin on a level that would guarantee success.

702.   Banham, K.M. 1978. Measuring functional motor rehabil-
       itation of cerebral palsied infants and young chil-
       dren. *Rehabilitation Literature* 39:111-15.

            Provides two experimental forms of an observa-
       tional checklist to evaluate functional motor per-
       formance in cerebral palsied infants three to thirty
       months of age and thirty to sixty months of age.
       The checklists each contain fifty behavioral items
       to be rated by the evaluator as either true, rarely
       true, or false. Checklist one evaluates functional
       movement of the head, trunk, arms, hands, legs and
       feet; checklist two, for older children, evaluates
       bodily functions and posture, self help using arms
       and hands, and locomotion using arms and legs. The
       checklists are seen to allow for greater latitude in
       judging equality of performance than the earlier
       Motor Rehabilitation Scale.

703.   Banham, K.M. 1983. Left-handed preschool children
       with orthopedic disabilities. *Rehabilitation Liter-
       ature* 44:23-26.

            This study compared mental development of left-
       handed vs. right-handed preschool age children, all

having orthopedic disabilities. The sample was 332
children (mean age four years two months) assessed
over a ten-year period using the Cattell Infant Intelligence Scale. Results indicate that left-handed
students were definitely slower in developing speech
and language skills than right-handed students.
They also had lower I.Q.s, both on the general mental
ability scales and on the verbal items of the scales.
Students with cerebral palsy had lower general and
verbal I.Q.s than those with orthopedic disabilities.

704.   Barden, J. 1970. Furniture in the classroom. *Special
Education* 59:11-13.

The author describes furniture specifically
designed for the cerebral palsied student, but which
can also be utilized by the nonhandicapped student.
Included in the grouping is an L-shaped desk, a table, two typing tables, and an aqual chair which is
used in hydrotherapy. All of the furniture is ad-
justable in height and angle.

705.   Beail, N. 1983. Physical disability: The self and the
stereotype. *International Journal of Rehabilitation*
6:56-57.

The article cites studies of people who have
been placed in a stigmatized category. Studies show
that group members reject general identification
with society's stereotype of their group. The present study investigated this phenomenon in thirty
eighteen- to fifty-seven-year old physically disabled
students who compared their perceptions of themselves
with their perceptions of their societal stereotype.
Results show that students rejected general identification with the stereotype of the disabled.

706.   Belgrave, F. 1984. The effectiveness of strategies
for increasing social interaction with a physically
disabled person. *Journal of Applied Social Psychology* 14:147-61.

This study investigated the effectiveness of
strategies by a physically disabled person to increase the willingness of fourteen female undergrad-

uates to engage in social interaction. Students
chose the amount of time to be spent listening to
music vs. social interaction with another person before and after learning that the other person was
disabled. The student witnessed, via "closed circuit" TV (actually videotaped), a brief interaction
between the male and another female in the waiting
room from which she had just come. Results show
that changes in preference for social interaction
were significantly more positive in conditions attentive to others' typical activities and athletic activities.

707. Berel, M. 1978. Teaching mathematics to a multihandicapped girl: A case study. *International Journal of
Rehabilitation Research* 1:71-79.

Describes the teaching of basic mathematics to
a severely multihandicapped girl with cerebral palsy
who was extremely hyperactive, distractable, somewhat
retarded, and had no speech; all of these factors
contributed to her learning disability which was
compounded by coming from a bilingual home. The
article also describes her progress in individual
psychoeducational therapy sessions in which a method
called "chaining" or association patterning was used
to facilitate her learning.

708. Blumberg, L. 1973. Case for integrating schooling.
Exceptional Parent 3(4):15-17.

The author, a college senior with cerebral
palsy, believes based on her own experiences that
most physically handicapped children should be integrated into regular classes. She claims that the
mechanical problems such as navigating steps or the
inability to write can be overcome. She further
claims that the physically handicapped get short-
changed in academics because their physical therapy
takes away from academic class time. She points out
that the advantages of attending regular classes are
making neighborhood friendships and the development
of a self concept based on functioning in a nondisabled world. In her own case, other children
rarely ridiculed her and were willing to help when
she needed assistance.

709.   Burden, P. 1983. Exceptional and normal children's
       descriptions of themselves. *Education* 104:204-5.

           In this study, twenty-one sixth, seventh, and
       eighth graders classified as being physically handi-
       capped, learning disabled, or emotionally disturbed,
       and twenty-one normal sixth, seventh, and eighth
       graders were asked to evaluate themselves on the
       Personal Attribute Inventory for Children (PAIC).
       Strikingly few variations in self-perception were
       reported. All four groups were found to be statis-
       tically independent on forty-five of the forty-eight
       descriptions presented on the PAIC. Furthermore,
       when the exceptional students were grouped together
       and compared with normal students the two groups
       were found to be statistically independent on forty-
       three of the forty-eight adjectives on the PAIC.
       Results suggest that the negative stereotypes of
       exceptional children held by themselves and non-
       handicapped peers, as reported previously, may not
       readily be adopted by the exceptional children them-
       selves. They tend to rate themselves as highly, and
       sometimes higher than, comparable children sent to
       special schools for the handicapped.

710.   Carlsen, P. 1975. Comparison of two occupational ther-
       apy approaches for treating the young cerebral palsy
       child. *American Journal of Occupational Therapy*
       29:267-72.

           Two occupational therapy approaches (facilita-
       tion and functional) were compared during a six-week
       period on the overall development of twelve cerebral
       palsied children from one to five years old. The
       Denver Developmental Screening Test and Bayley Motor
       Scale were administered to subjects before and after
       treatment. Results showed that subjects receiving
       treatment based on facilitation of gross motor inte-
       gration showed greater developmental gains than sub-
       jects receiving fine motor adaptive and self-care
       activities.

711. Carr, J. 1983. Educational attainments of spina bifida children attending ordinary or special schools. *Special Education Forward Trends* 10:22-24.

> Twenty-two spina bifida children in special and regular classes were tested and compared and it was found that children in special schools were behind in mathematics, but that there was no significant difference in reading.

712. Cassity, M. 1981. The influence of a socially valued skill on peer acceptance in a music therapy group. *Journal of Music Therapy* 18:148-54.

> To determine influence of a socially valued skill (playing the piano) on the performer's peer acceptance in a music therapy group, thirteen physically handicapped preadolescents were introduced as music therapy student observers. The performer participated as a group member for five one-hour sessions without playing the piano. Group members were then asked to rank each other according to three questions selected from the affective domain. The next condition was altered by having the performer play the piano at the end of each lesson. Following this, the same sociometric test was given. The two conditions (five sessions of nonperformance) were then repeated to constitute an ABAB complete reversal design. The Friedman Two-Way Analysis of Variance indicated that the performer's status or rank position significantly changed over the four experimental conditions. The remaining students failed to obtain significant gains in status.

713. Caston, D. 1981. *Easy to make aids for your handicapped child*. London, England: Souvenir Press.

> The book instructs parents, teachers, and caretakers, to make simple aids for everyday living. Illustration and text focus on buying wood, using tools, etc. Actual step-by-step plans detail fifty aids and devices such as a floor seat, baby chair, back rest, seesaw, toilet conversion, etc.

714. Cecconi, C.M.P., and S.P. Rothenberg. 1980. Model
      instructional program for mainstreaming handicapped
      children. *Physical Therapy* 60:1022-25.

           A study was conducted in order to test the ef-
      ficacy of an instructional program that was created
      to teach normal children about cerebral palsy. The
      program was presented to seventeen first grade chil-
      dren which resulted in a significant increase in the
      students' knowledge of cerebral palsy over the con-
      trol group. A discussion follows on the results of
      the study in regard to placement of the handicapped
      children by physical and occupational therapists.

715. Cheong, L.M. 1980. The impact of mainstreaming on the
      handicapped child. *Special Education in Canada*
      54:30-32.

           The child's anxiety about attempting new experi-
      ences is depicted as a major problem in mainstreaming
      the physically disabled child. The article discusses
      the impact of social as well as physical barriers.

716. Chinn, R.H., Jr. 1976. *Each step of the way.*
      Johnstown, Pennsylvania: Mafex Associates.

           The author, a cerebral palsied young man, re-
      lates the story of his life. Particular emphasis is
      placed on the personal problems he encountered during
      adolescence and early adulthood. He also relates
      his activities with the United Cerebral Palsy Associ-
      ation, his experiences in school, his family rela-
      tionship, social life, and religious convictions.

717. Cohen, J. 1980. Classroom business venture: Career
      education for physically disabled students. Unpub-
      lished doctoral dissertation. Washington, D.C.:
      Special Education Program.

           Describes classroom business ventures (CBV) for
      the physically disabled in fifth, sixth, and seventh
      grades. A CBV is a simulated business situation
      where students with teaching guidance plan and orga-
      nize its operation toward the eventual goal of the
      distribution of the product or service they them-

selves have decided upon. A checklist for planning
and implementing the CBV is included.

718. Cotton, E. 1974. Improvement in motor functioning
      with the use of conductive education. *Developmental
      Medicine and Child Neurology* 16:637-43.

          Two cerebral palsied boys (nine and eleven years
      old) at a British residential school were helped to
      improve grasp, balance, and motor function through a
      structured program of conductive education based
      upon methods developed by Peto. The children used
      speech to express their intentions to move and then
      carried out a rhythmic movement while they counted
      from one to five. The teacher (conductor) broke up
      motor tasks into basic elements in order to set goals
      the boys could achieve. Each successful movement
      was used by the conductor to motivate the students
      to improve motor functioning.

719. Cunningham, C. 1977. Problems in diagnosis and manage-
      ment of children with cerebral palsy and deafness.
      Developmental Medicine and Child Neurology 19:474-84.

          This paper reports on the problems in the diag-
      nosis, management, and educational placement of ten
      children with cerebral palsy and deafness. There
      were serious problems in the study, including delays
      in diagnosis, frequent changes in schools and serv-
      ices to the children, and unsatisfactory student
      progress.

720. Davies, H.B. 1960. Factors rendering the cerebral
      palsied child capable or incapable of benefitting
      from formal education. *Cerebral Palsy Bulletin* 2:28-
      33.

          The author believes that cerebral palsy children
      benefit best from formal education if they have aver-
      age intelligence and aptitude and good drive, accom-
      panied by incentive and adequate learning and physi-
      cal aids. Because of the wide range of individual
      differences and peculiar learning difficulties, edu-
      cation must be largely individual. A lowered capac-
      ity for intellectual activity in cerebral palsied

children is the principal limiting factor to learning, but this is not indicative of their ultimate
potential.

721. Diamond, L.J., and P.K. Jaudes. 1983. Child abuse in
      a cerebral-palsied population. *Developmental Medi-
      cine and Child Neurology* 25:169-74.

          Of eighty-six cerebral-palsied children (six
      months-eight years old) in one care center, seventeen
      had been abused. Eight of these children's cerebral
      palsy was a result of abuse. The findings suggest a
      high incidence of child abuse among children with
      cerebral palsy. There is also a "double indication"
      for abuse, both as a cause and result of cerebral
      palsy.

722. Eddy, C. 1972. No fingers to play a horn. *Music Edu-
      cators Journal* 58:25-26.

          In this article, a music teacher recalls the
      request of a sixth grade child who in spite of his
      handicap, the absence of fingers, wished to play a
      musical instrument. The child's successful musical
      career was attributed to the positive attitude of
      his parents.

723. English, W.R. 1971. Combatting stigma towards physi-
      cally disabled persons. *Rehabilitation Research and
      Practice Review* 2:19-27.

          The author introduces guidelines that will aid
      in the elimination of discriminatory attitudes
      towards the physically handicapped. Suggestions
      include: the increase of contact between the disabled
      and non-disabled, the use of the mass media to give
      the public a more realistic view of the disabled,
      and the organizing of pressure groups to help repeal
      legislation that restricts the lives of the disabled.

724. English, W.R. 1971. Correlates of stigma towards phys-
      ically disabled persons. *Rehabilitation Research
      and Practice Review* 2:1-17.

            The article reports on a study to assess social
      attitudes and their correlation to the physically
      handicapped. Among such correlates of stigma were:
      sex, socioeconomic status, age, education, disabil-
      ity, religion, and occupation. The results of the
      research indicate that persons with a high self-
      concept, a less aggressive personality, and low lev-
      els of anxiety were most accepting of the physically
      handicapped.

725. Ereckson, T. 1982. Access to laboratories and equip-
      ment for the physically disabled. *Journal for Voca-
      tional Special Needs Education* 4:26-28.

            Describes attitudinal as well as architectural
      barriers to laboratories and equipment for physically
      disabled students. Diagrams a model for decision
      making in providing accessibility that takes into
      account general access to school buildings, access
      to vocational education labs, and access to equip-
      ment. Recommends a five-step implementation sched-
      ule.

726. Fair, D.T., and J.W. Birch. 1971. Effect of rest on
      test scores of physically and non-handicapped chil-
      dren. *Exceptional Children* 38:335-36.

            A study was performed on both physically handi-
      capped and non-handicapped students taking the Ad-
      vanced Stanford Achievement Test to determine the
      effects of a rest period between sections of the
      test. The authors conclude that only the handicapped
      students benefitted from the inclusion of a rest
      period.

727. Farrow, A. 1973. The Farrowgraph finds a way. *Special
      Education* 62:14-16.

            A device has been developed that allows severely
      physically handicapped children to draw the maps
      required for geography study. The need for such a

device was pointed out by a study that found that
only students not severely disabled in the upper
limbs were being taught geography. The ability to
draw maps can help to decrease the gap between the
handicapped and the nonhandicapped. The device is
also appropriate for art work and lettering by the
handicapped.

728.   Feldman, W.S.; J. Kathleen; and J.W. Varni. 1983. A
       behavioral parent training program for single mothers
       of handicapped children. *Child Care, Health & Devel-
       opment* 9:157-68.

            A study was done on the single mothers of forty-
       four ten-year-olds with congenital physical disor-
       ders. The mothers participated in a nine-week
       parent-training program developed to instruct them
       in the systematic utilization of behavioral tech-
       niques to enable them to teach their children self-
       help skills and to reduce behavioral problems. Find-
       ings suggest the potential of behavioral parent-
       training techniques in facilitating functional inde-
       pendence in physically handicapped children, as well
       as providing single parents with increased feelings
       of being able to systematically contribute to their
       children's physical and psychosocial development.

729.   Fenton, E. 1980. An assessment of academic achievement
       and school adjustment of handicapped students in
       regular versus special school setting. Unpublished
       doctoral dissertation. Claremont CA: Univ. of Cali-
       fornia.

            Physically handicapped secondary students (n=20)
       in regular school settings showed significantly
       greater academic achievement than physically handi-
       capped children (n=20) placed in special school set-
       tings. Students in special settings, however, were
       significantly better adjusted (as measured on the
       Quality of School Life Scale) to school life than
       students in regular settings.

730.   Field, T.; S. Roseman; L.J. de Stefano; and J. Koewler.
       1982. The play of handicapped preschool children
       with handicapped and nonhandicapped peers in inte-

grated and nonintegrated situations. *Topics in Early Childhood Special Education* 2:28-38.

Investigated whether children with sensorimotor handicaps follow the same developmental sequence--interaction with adults, toys, and peers--as nonhandicapped children (Exp. I; nonintegrated condition). The play of handicapped children in the presence and absence of normal children was also investigated (Exp. II; integrated condition). Students were thirty-six handicapped (cerebral palsy, Down's syndrome, mental retardation, and hearing and speech deficits) and twelve normal children, aged two and one-half to four years. Overall results indicated that more prosocial, child-directed and less teacher-directed, teacher-initiated behavior occurred for handicapped students when playing with normal students. Although normal students continued to relate more frequently to their own classmates, handicapped students appeared to watch and make as many social overtures to their normal peers as to their own classmates. The direction of effects suggests that normal preschoolers continue to play as if undisturbed by the addition of less developed children and that handicapped children appear to make the greater effort to assimilate themselves into the ongoing stream of activity.

731.   Foulds, R. 1982. Applications of microcomputers in the education of the physically disabled child. *Exceptional Child* 49:112-118.

Microcomputers can serve as expressive communication tools for severely physically disabled persons. Features such as single input devices, direct selection aids, and speech synthesis capabilities can be extremely useful.

732.   Frith, G., and R. Eduards. 1981. Misconceptions of regular classroom teachers about physically handicapped students. *Exceptional Child* 48:182-84.

To identify teachers' misconceptions and concerns about physically handicapped students, questionnaires were administered to forty-six regular classroom teachers who had never interacted with

physically handicapped students (Group 1) and to
thirty-two regular classroom teachers who had or had
had physically handicapped students in their programs
(Group 2). Differences were found between perceived
concerns of teachers who had and teachers who had
not taught the physically handicapped. The major
concern expressed by most of Group 1 teachers involved toileting responsibilities while the major
concern of Group 2 teachers was lack of materials.

733. Gay, M.G. 1965. A preschool program for children with
      cerebral palsy. *Children* 12:105-8.

          A child with cerebral palsy approaching nursery
      school confronts stricter entrance requirements than
      the regular student. This article reviews a pre-
      school center with few conditions for exclusion.
      Neither lack of toilet training nor achievement on a
      standardized test are used as reasons to exclude the
      student. The article outlines a typical day that
      could be adapted to a public school program. A typ-
      ical day in one of the program's classes would con-
      sist of 1) learning the skills needed to undress,
      2) free play, 3) a group activity, 4) a milk and
      cookie period, 5) nap time, 6) active group play,
      7) quiet activity, 8) learning to dress. The policy
      of the school reflects a positive attitude in dealing
      with cerebral palsied children. Until the child has
      had an opportunity to fail, they believe there is no
      basis for rejecting a child because of deficits.
      The article emphasized that the inconveniences to
      adults of a liberal screening policy are greatly
      outweighed by the benefits to the child.

734. Goodman, L. 1973. The efficiency of visual-motor
      training for orthopedically handicapped children.
      Rehabilitation Literature 34:299-304.

          A random sample of forty-four cerebral palsy
      and skeletally deformed children were divided into
      control and training groups. Both groups were ex-
      tensively pre-tested. The training group was then
      given the Kephart, Getman and Kane visual-motor
      trainings. Retesting showed no difference between
      the two groups. The author concludes that such
      training provides no benefit for the children.

735. Grand, S.A.; J.E. Bernier; and D.C. Strohner. 1982.
      Attitudes toward disabled persons as a function of
      social context and specific disability. *Rehabilita-*
      tion Psychology 27:165-74.

           A study was done on 191 nondisabled eighteen-
      to sixty-four-year-olds who completed the Disability
      Social Relationship Scale, which includes social
      situation subscales of work, dating, and marriage,
      and disability subscales of amputee, epilepsy, cere-
      bral palsy, and blindness. Results reveal signifi-
      cant differences across social situations and among
      specific disabilities, as well as a significant in-
      teraction between social situation and disability.
      Thus, situational context affects attitudes toward
      disabled persons.

736. Harper, D.C. 1980. School adjustment and degree of
      physical impairment. *Journal of Pediatric Psychology*
      5:377-83.

           Studied teachers' ratings of the school behavior
      of children with either cleft palate or cerebral
      palsy and with either mild or severe physical dis-
      figurement. The total sample of 124 children (mean
      age 170 months) were individually matched in terms
      of sex, age, I.Q., grade level, and socioeconomic
      status. On the Behavior Problem Checklist, the cleft
      palate children displayed more impulsivity (conduct
      problem dimension) than the cerebral palsy group.
      Children with a mild degree of physical impairment
      (of either type) displayed greater inhibition of
      impulse (personality problem dimension) than severely
      impaired children. The data suggest that type of
      disability and degree of impairment affect different
      modes of behavioral expression. Also discusses the
      relationship of school behavior to physical disabil-
      ity and degree of functional impairment.

737. Hartley, N. 1974. Symbols for diplomats used for chil-
      dren. *Special Education in Canada* 48(2):5-7.

           The article talks about Charles Bliss's symbol
      system created for use with cerebral palsied and
      severely handicapped children who are non-verbal.
      The Bliss system is based on the Chinese approach of

taking basic concepts and using them to build up
sets of related ideas. The article points out that
users of sign language can often communicate across
language barriers more effectively than users of
verbal language systems.

738. Harvey, D., and P. Greenway. Congruence between mother
      and handicapped child's view of the child's sense of
      adjustment. *Exceptional Child* 29:111-16.

            Compared the responses of twenty-two nine to
      eleven year old physically handicapped Australian
      children to selected items on the Piers-Harris Self
      Concept Scale for Children with their mothers' re-
      sponses to equivalent items of the Personality Inven-
      tory for Children. The direction of the responses,
      whether children were more or less positive in self-
      evaluation than mothers perceived them to be, was
      analyzed with respect to sex of child, type of school
      attended, and diagnosis of handicap (cerebral palsy
      or spina bifida). Only diagnosis of handicap was
      significantly related to the tendency for children
      to be either less or more positive in response to
      the items than their mothers, with cerebral palsy
      children more positive and spina bifida children
      consistently less positive in direction. Possible
      explanations are considered with particular reference
      to the children's views regarding peer relationships.

739. Haskill, S.H. 1971. Programmed instruction for physi-
      cally handicapped children: Some educational and
      sociological implications. *British Journal of Mental
      Subnormality* 17:117-24.

            This article examines the attitudes of teachers
      towards the use of programmed instruction for the
      physically handicapped. The author includes the
      attitudes of three teachers in relation to the use
      of programmed instruction. The first teacher finds
      the programmed instruction to be beneficial for his
      students with mixed handicaps. The second teacher
      complains that the machine does not provide for the
      individual needs of his cerebral palsied students.
      The third teacher dislikes the rigidity of the pro-
      grammed instruction.

740. Hedrich, V. 1972. Applying technology to special edu-
      cation. *American Education* 8:22-25.

          The author briefly discusses special Federal
      funds that were received by the Seattle public
      schools Special Education program. The funds went
      to a neurophysiologist, an electrical engineer, and
      an electronics technician. Their job was to work as
      a team to help solve educational problems inherent
      in cerebral palsy. Two electromechanical aids are
      mentioned: a lightweight plastic prototype model
      helmet that was used to help stabilize the head move-
      ment of a young cerebral palsied girl, and an arti-
      ficial sensory device designed to help a young C.P.
      girl learn to move and control her damaged arm. The
      author concludes that early motor development is an
      important prerequisite for late learning and that
      parents should acquaint themselves with their child's
      needs.

741. Herron, C.J. 1970. Some effects of instrumental music
      training on cerebral palsied children. *Journal of
      Music Therapy* 7:55-58.

          Four cerebral palsied subjects were given indi-
      vidual lessons twice a week for twelve weeks to ex-
      amine the possibility of improving muscular coordina-
      tion through instruction in a musical instrument.
      Evaluation was based on writings by the investigator,
      a panel of evaluative judges, and the Belwin Singing
      Achievement Test. Results showed improvement in
      muscular coordination and breath supports in all
      subjects with musical performance achievement varying
      according to the severity of muscular dysfunction
      and mental retardation.

742. Hilland, J.A. 1975. Towards acceptance of the physi-
      cally disabled. *Rehabilitation Digest* 6:9-11.

          This article focuses on the problems the physi-
      cally handicapped have gaining acceptance in society.
      Quotations from disabled people illustrate society's
      non-acceptance of them and their handicaps. It is
      clear that integration or segregation of the physi-
      cally handicapped person must be made by the person
      himself. Changes in attitude toward the handicapped

can only come about through increased exposure to
the handicapped in a normal setting.

743. Hoop, W. 1965. Listening comprehension of cerebral
palsied and other crippled children as a function of
two speaking rates. *Exceptional Children* 31:233-40.

This study attempted to determine the amount of
learning that would take place among cerebral palsied
children and noncerebral palsied crippled children
compared under conditions of listening to a normal
speaking rate (175 wpm) and a rapid rate (275 wpm).
There were significant differences between the two
groups on the comprehension test of the selection
presented at 175 wpm but, contrary to expectations,
the samples did not differ significantly on comprehension of the selection presented at 275 wpm.

744. Howe, J.A. 1984. Putting cognitive psychology to work
teaching handicapped children to read. *School Psychology International* 5:85-90.

This article describes a computer-based approach
to teaching word-decoding skills to mildly mentally
and physically handicapped children. The program is
based on a cognitive model of the process underlying
reading. The apparatus is a computer-controlled
slide projector and a touch-sensitive screen. In
learning initial letters, the student is asked to
say aloud the name of the object shown, trace around
the letter given, and answer questions that require
a forced choice between alternate letters. Four
initial consonants are taught in conjunction to establish criteria for success. Good results were
obtained in a preliminary study of students who had
about twenty-five hours of contact time over eighteen
months.

745. Huberman, G. 1976. Organized sports activities with
cerebral palsied adolescents. *Rehabilitation Literature* 37:103-6.

Based on scientific investigation of exercise
physiology and psychological and social benefits,
there is a need for organized sports activities and

contests for cerebral palsied persons. The author proposes a blueprint for an international meet emphasizing individual programs in which overall fitness training, agility, endurance, strength, speed, and coordination are encouraged.

746. Hunsinger, K. 1976. A simple headstick for cerebral palsied children. *American Journal of Occupational Therapy* 30:506.

Describes a headstick designed for cerebral palsied children and tested for use primarily with Blissymbol communication boards, but also useful as a typing aid and in other appropriate activities. Includes instructions for making the headband and headstick attachment.

747. Jones, R.L. 1974. Correlates of orthopedically disabled children's school achievement and interpersonal relationships. *Exceptional Children* 41:191-2.

This study was undertaken to determine if impaired mobility and physical dependency affect academic achievement and interpersonal relationships. 102 orthopedic disabled children, ages six to sixteen were involved in the study. All of the subjects were given the Bialer Locus of Control Scale. Teachers completed questionnaires on each pupil. The study found that impaired mobility and physical dependency did not affect achievement or teacher-rated interpersonal relationships.

748. Junkala, J. 1982. Cognitive styles of students with cerebral palsy. *Perceptual and Motor Skills* 55:403-40.

The study showed that fourteen-year-old cerebral palsied students' cognitive styles were qualitatively similar to those of non-handicapped students, although the extraocular movement of some students appeared to affect the classifications of cognitive style to which they were assigned by data.

749. King, A.J. 1975. Integration goes beyond the class-
      room. *Special Education in Canada* 49:4.

           The author questions the value of spending large
      amounts of money on programs for the physically hand-
      icapped because such programs must be accompanied by
      changes in housing, employment, transportation, the
      delivery of services, and recreation in order for
      them to be beneficial.

750. Klein, J.W., and L.A. Randolph. 1974. Placing handi-
      capped children in head start programs. *Children
      Today* 3:7-10.

           Children with various handicaps were integrated
      with non-handicapped children in a Head Start pro-
      gram. Crippled and orthopedically handicapped chil-
      dren were included in the group. The integration of
      the handicapped and the non-handicapped children
      proved to be beneficial for both when the curriculum
      was individualized.

751. Kohring, C., and V.S. Tracht. 1978. A new approach to
      a vocational program for severely handicapped high
      school students. *Rehabilitation Literature* 39:138-
      46.

           In order to more accurately and realistically
      assess the severely handicapped individual's voca-
      tional potential, a study was undertaken of ninety-
      two severely handicapped high school students who
      participated in a pioneer Goodwill program. The
      students were from two high schools, one comprised
      of fifty-one percent cerebral palsied students, the
      second of a group of deaf and hearing impaired stu-
      dents. The program consisted of three phases: (1)
      orientation, testing (including intelligence, abili-
      ties, interests, objective and/or projective person-
      ality measures, the Hester Evaluation System, and
      the Singer/Graflex System), and information gather-
      ing; (2) group discussion, practice in filling out
      application forms, and individual conferences; and
      (3) "hands-on" work experience at one of Goodwill's
      training areas. While the program illustrates that
      a community agency and a public education institution
      can work well together, it does not provide for the

necessary follow-up, including the aspect of assuring parental cooperation, or failing that, development of sufficient maturity and motivation in the student to face the inevitable difficulties of finding a job.

752. Kuhn, G.G. 1974. Individually molded seat-shells for severely handicapped persons. *Inter-Clinic Information Bulletin* 13:1-6.

    This article discusses the new technique that has been developed for the creation of individually molded seats for severely handicapped patients. The advantages of the molded chair are as follows: conformity to individual anatomical requirements, the avoidance of pressure points, and optimal correction of deformity.

753. Leach, G. 1982. Making science more accessible. *Special Education: Forward Trends* 9:13-15.

    The author describes and illustrates aids and adaptations for science classes serving severely physically handicapped students. Also offers guidelines on presentations, school made aids (such as a trolley), and use of microscopes.

754. Luepker, E.T. 1980. Mainstreaming the child who is physically handicapped. *Education Unlimited* 2:17-21.

    Guidelines for teachers on ways in which they can help the mainstreamed orthopedically handicapped child. Included is information on the ways and means of assisting parents and other professionals, preparing and acquainting the child with schedules, as well as preparation for hospitalization.

755. Maner, R.A. 1979. Young children's responses to a physically disabled storybook hero. *Exceptional Children* 45:326-30.

    This study sought to determine if identification with an affinity for a storybook hero are functions of physical status. Similar groups of children aged four to seven years (127 students, one group dis-

abled) were randomly assigned to one of two storybook treatments telling of two boys' friendship.
One version depicted both boys as nondisabled (control); the other depicted one boy as disabled (experimental). Questions were asked to determine whether
the hero's disability affected students' identification with or choice of him as a friend. Significant
differences appeared between responses to the two
groups and again when sex was isolated as a variable.
Disabled males identified less willingly with the
disabled hero than did disabled females, and preferred friendship with the nondisabled hero. Nondisabled males identified with the nondisabled hero,
but preferred friendship of the disabled hero, while
nondisabled females rejected him as a friend.

756. Marinoff, S.L. 1973. When words are not enough--video-
      tape. *Teaching Exceptional Children* 5:66-73.

          Discusses the use of videotapes with cerebral
      palsied children as an evaluation measure in cases
      where standardized tests fail to indicate growth, as
      an ongoing source of relevant teaching materials for
      teachers and students, and as a way of bringing par-
      ents to a realistic comprehension of their children.
      Benefits of tapes are that they are said to speed-up
      recognition of methods that work and those that do
      not. Also examines strategies for taping children
      at various times to capture early language or gross
      motor development. Parents can help stimulate memo-
      ries in cerebral palsy by showing tapes to children.

757. Martin, J.F. 1976. Behavior modification and cerebral
      palsy. *Journal of Pediatric Psychology* 1:48-50.

          Defines cerebral palsy and reviews the litera-
      ture on the use of behavior modification in disorders
      of this type. Stresses the importance of an inter-
      disciplinary approach.

758. Martin, J.E., and D.A. Sachs. 1973. The effect of
      visual feedback on the fine motor behavior of a deaf

cerebral palsied child. *Journal of Nervous and Mental Disease* 157:59-62.

This article deals with the effects of visual feedback on the fine motor behavior of an 11-year-old, cerebral palsied female. There were five metal tips that were connected to the child's fingertips. The child was told to touch a light box with each finger in sequence. Amber lights were lit sequentially at random intervals in the noncontingent visual feedback. The lights were also lit sequentially contingent upon correct finger touches in the contingent visual feedback condition. It was found that the performance of the child was best in the contingent visual feedback condition and during latter practice sessions. The article shows that practice and feedback play a role in fine motor performance.

759. Mearig, J.S. 1974. The assessment of intelligence in boys with Duchenne muscular dystrophy. *Rehabilitation Literature* 40:262-74.

Studies of intellectual ability in boys with Duchenne muscular dystrophy have not taken into account the various confounding dimensions of intelligence testing. Data presented in these studies differ from those in most previous studies and do not support the hypothesis of a verbal deficit.

760. Meyers, L.S.; C.L. Coleman; and L.M. Morris. 1982. Conservation training of three cerebral palsied children. *Bulletin of the Psychonomic Society* 20:14-16.

Three six- to eleven-year-old severely physically disabled cerebral palsied children participated in conservation training. Students were performing below age level compared with the normal population at the outset of the training. A training procedure emphasizing the verbal rule of conservation and minimizing the motor demands of the task resulted in rapid acquisition of trained tasks and generalized mastery of two nontrained conservation tasks. During the longest tested interval of nine weeks, both trained and generalized mastery were retained. The authors suggest that conservation can be acquired

and retained with little motor involvement in the
original learning.

761. Mischel, M.H. 1978. Assertion training with handi-
     capped persons. *Journal of Counseling Psychology*
     25:238-41.

          This study investigated the effects of assertion
     training in five handicapped college students and
     five handicapped discharged rehabilitative medicare
     outpatients. Students were matched on self-reported
     assertiveness and were assigned to one or two groups:
     (a) treatment students who received assertion train-
     ing, and (b) waiting-list control students who re-
     ceived no treatment for five weeks and then received
     assertion training. Behavioral role playing, self-
     respect, and activity budget, pre- and post-test
     measures revealed that assertion training students
     reported significantly greater gains in assertive
     behavior and showed greater improvement in perform-
     ance on seven criterion measures than did control
     students.

762. Myers, P. 1965. A study of language disabilities in
     cerebral palsied children. *Journal of Speech and
     Hearing Research* 8:129-36.

          In this study the Illinois Test of Psycholin-
     guistic Abilities was administered to sixty-eight
     spastic, twenty-four athetoid, and thirty-two normal
     children. Results showed that spastic children in
     general can be expected to be inferior to athetoid
     children on language tasks at the representational
     level but superior on tasks involving the automatic-
     sequential level.

763. Neely, M.A., and M.W. Kosier. 1977. Physically im-
     paired students and the vocational exploration group.
     Vocational Guidance Quarterly 26:37-44.

          The effects of the two-hour structured Voca-
     tional Exploration Groups were studied on self-
     ratings of fifty-four physically impaired (PI) stu-
     dents relative to effects on eighty-nine nonhandi-
     capped (NH) high school students. Groups of about

five students attended sessions in counselors' of-
fices and completed pre-session and follow-up ratings
of the personal importance of work satisfaction and
interest-skill variables. Analysis of variance
showed no sex or group differences in movement of
ratings. Chi-square analysis showed most variation
resulting form the girls' ratings. PI girls tended
to change ratings more than NH girls or boys. PI
students tended to change ratings more at follow-up
than NH students.

764. Ostring, H., and S. Nieman. 1982. Concept of self and
the attitude of school age CP children towards their
handicap. *International Journal of Rehabilitation
Research* 5:235-37.

Studied thirty three- to thirteen-year-old cerebral palsy children (CP) and thirty-four ten- to
twelve-year-old physically healthy children to investigate (a) the relationship between self-concept and
attitudes towards cerebral palsy, and (b) the relationship between attitude toward the handicap and
self-esteem on the one hand and school achievement
and school adjustment on the other. Students completed the Rorschach, the Coopersmith Self-Esteem
Inventory, and the Children's Seashore House Picture
Test. Results show that both groups had similar
body images. Acceptance of the dependence brought
about by the handicap and its integration into the
self-concept were essential for positive self-concept
and self-esteem of the CP students. Age and intelligence seemed to correlate with the degree of adjustment to the handicap. A positive attitude of the CP
students toward their handicap and good self-reliance
had a statistically significant correlation with good
school achievement and school adjustment. To the
control group, school was an institution requiring
performance, but to the CP children it had manifold
emotional meaning.

765. Palmer, J. 1980. A career education program for students with physical disabilities. *Career Development
for Exceptional Individuals* 5:13-24.

The Human Resources School Career Education
program (designed to improve and maintain positive

self-concept, build decision making skills, and
broaden career awareness) was evaluated with 230
kindergarten through twelfth grade physically disabled students from the HRS and two comparison
groups. Students were administered the Nowicki-
Strickland Locus of Control Scale for Children,
Piers-Harris Children's Self-concept Scale, and the
attitude component of the Career Maturity Inventory.
Among findings were that the HRS students are more
externally controlled, less career mature, and have
higher self-concepts than their able bodied peers.

766. Reese, K. 1981. Teaching chemistry to physically hand-
      icapped students. *American Chemical Society* 4:12-14.

      The manual provides information on teaching
      techniques and services as well as materials, equip-
      ment, and publications for teaching chemistry to
      physically handicapped students. Section I addresses
      the classroom in terms of common needs, lecture/dis-
      cussion techniques, and special arrangements. Sec-
      tion II covers the laboratory with general guidelines
      and guidelines for serving students with impaired
      mobility.

767. Rich, Y. 1984. Perceptions of school life among phys-
      ically disabled mainstreamed pupils. *Educational
      Research* 26:27-32.

      This study examined the perceptions of school
      life among seventy-five nine- to ten-year-old physi-
      cally disabled pupils learning in regular classrooms
      in Israel. Three groups (twenty-five per group) of
      pupils--extremely short, diabetic, and orthopedically
      impaired--corresponding to Goffman's categorization
      of stigmatized persons, responded to the Israeli
      Quality of School Life Scale. Significant differ-
      ences between the groups were found on four of the
      seven subscales. Short students as compared to or-
      thopedically impaired students were more satisfied
      with social aspects of schooling but reacted less
      positively to their teachers. Diabetic students
      were also less satisfied with their teachers than
      were orthopedically impaired students, and demon-
      strated relative dissatisfaction with affective com-
      ponents of schooling.

768. Roberts, M.C.; A.Q. Johnson; and W.B. Beidleman. 1984.
The role of socioeconomic status on children's per-
ceptions of medical and psychological disorders.
Journal of Clinical Child Psychology 13:243-49.

The purpose of this study was to determine if
socioeconomic background would affect attitudes of
children toward imaginary peers who were described
as suffering from various forms of medical or psychological disorders. The results indicate that socioeconomic status accounts for little of the variance.
The study also found that children have a greater
understanding of the course and nature of medical
illnesses and less sophistication with regard to
psychological disorders.

769. Sandowski, C. 1979. The handicapped adolescent.
School Social Work Journal 4:3-13.

Physically handicapped adolescents and their
families face special social-emotional problems,
including those produced by negative social attitudes
and the effects of separation (hospitalization or
institutionalization). Special challenges facing
persons with cerebral palsy, spinal cord injury, and
muscular dystrophy are noted, and suggestions are
made for social workers dealing with physically handicapped persons.

770. Serow, R., and K. O'Brien. 1983. Performance of handicapped students in a competency testing program.
Journal of Special Education 17:149-155.

Data from the North Carolina Competency Test
were used to compare scores of 1,652 nonhandicapped
and 108 handicapped senior high school pupils. Students were compared on initial minimum competency
testing (MCT) performance, participation in remediation, improvements in subsequent MCT, and eligibility
for receiving high school diplomas. Nonhandicapped
students generally fared better than handicapped on
all measures. However, sharp differences were found
across categories of exceptionality, with results
for learning-disabled and physically impaired students approaching those of the non-handicapped
sample.

771. Sethi, M., and A. Sen. 1981. A comparative study of
orthopedically handicapped children with their normal
peers on some psychological variables. *Personality
Study & Group Behavior* 1:83-95.

This study examined the intelligence, creativity, self-concept, and frustrations of twenty eight-
to twelve-year-old orthopedically handicapped children, and compared them with twenty age-matched normal controls. Although the intelligence levels of
the handicapped students were the same as those of
normals, their creativity scores differed significantly, with normals demonstrating more creative
powers. Handicapped students had better self-concepts,
as compared with the normal children.

772. Tew, B. 1983. The relationship between spina bifida
children's intelligence test scores on school entry
and at school leaving. *Child: Care Health and Development* 9:13-17.

This preliminary report for Wechsler scores
taken at five, ten, and sixteen years, indicates
that for the majority of spina bifida children reliable predictors regarding intellectual status at
sixteen years of age can be made upon entry to
school.

773. Wisely, D., and S. Morgan. 1981. Children's ratings
of peers presented as mentally retarded and physically handicapped. *American Journal of Mental Deficiency* 86:281-86.

Third and sixth grade children (N=160) were
shown slides and tapes presenting target children as
either physically nonhandicapped and nonretarded,
physically handicapped only, mentally retarded only,
or physically handicapped and mentally retarded.
All children were rated more favorably by third graders than sixth graders and more favorably by boys
than girls. Physically handicapped target children
were rated more favorably than were nonhandicapped
children on behavioral intentions measures but were
not rated differently on an attitude scale; retarded
children were also rated more favorably than were
nonretarded children on the former measures but less
favorably on the attitude scale.

CHAPTER IX:
EMOTIONAL AND BEHAVIORAL IMPAIRMENTS

If a child in class is chronically unhappy or withdrawn
or is extremely aggressive toward his teachers and peers and
if no close relationships have been developed, the child may
be emotionally disturbed. Emotional impairment is widespread.
It is noncategorical in that it can happen to anybody, regardless of race, religion, sex, socioeconomic status, and so
forth. Emotional disturbance has been defined for classroom
teachers, administrators, and other educational personnel by
PL 94-142 as a condition exhibiting one or more of the following characteristics over a long period of time and to a marked
degree, which adversely affects educational performance: an
inability to learn that cannot be explained by intellectual,
sensory, or health factors; an inability to build or maintain
satisfactory interpersonal relationships with peers and teachers; inappropriate types of behavior or feelings under normal
circumstances; a general pervasive mood of unhappiness or
depression; or a tendency to develop physical symptoms or
fears associated with personal or school problems.
The etiology of emotional disturbance usually involves
the interaction of multiple factors rather than a one-to-one
relationship between single cause and single effect. Several
factors have been suggested as important in the development
of the emotionally disturbed personality, including the possibility of genetic causation. According to some, the physical status (i.e., drugs, alcohol, and maternal infections)
and psychological attitude of the expectant mother (i.e.,
anxiety and depression) may affect the developing fetus.
There also is a correlation between the physical development
of the child in later childhood and emotional and psychological responses in the adolescent period. Additionally, the
importance of early family interactions in explaining emotional problems has been widely researched.
At rock bottom, there are two groups of children that
are identified as emotionally impaired--hyperactive-aggressive
children, and those who are fearful and withdrawn. Children
who are hyperactive-aggressive have difficulty functioning in

a normal school setting. Because they are very easily distracted, they rarely complete a given task, have difficulty
following directions, and are disruptive. Very few of these
kinds of children have an above average I.Q., and most are
academically retarded; there is a direct correlation between
emotional disturbance and academic achievement. The second
group of children are most fearful, and they fail to relate
to others and to their environment. Those few children who
are exceedingly withdrawn and who cannot relate at all are
called autistic or schizophrenic, and such individuals are
typically institutionalized. The remainder, generally termed
neurotic, tend to exhibit high levels of anxiety and emotion.
Feelings of misery, insecurity, inferiority, and dissatisfaction with life are often present. Neurotic children may also
be phobic, depressed, and obsessive and compulsive; often
their functioning tends to be self-defeating and self-
damaging.

Vital in the teaching of the emotionally impaired child
is the establishment of a good teacher-student relationship.
The emotionally deviant child may exhibit aggressive, hostile
behavior; may have temper tantrums; may employ foul and ob-
scene language; or may be violent toward others in the class.
The teacher must be able to contend with these types of behavior, understand the causes, but never condone them. This
attitude on the part of the teacher is referred to as differential acceptance. Outbursts of hostility and violence need
to be understood and viewed as an outgrowth of that hate and
pain that the child feels at the moment of rage.

It often is difficult for the child to remain in class
all day; if emotional outbursts or acting-out behavior occur,
the crisis teacher will need to be called in to remove the
child from class until the particular crisis has been re-
solved. (Removal from the classroom and being able to speak
to the crisis teacher will help relieve the tension.) The
teacher also must be intuitive--he/she needs to be tuned into
nonverbal clues in order to prevent crises. The student must
be made to feel that he/she is a winner. Thus, the educator
must provide meaningful and successful learning experiences.

In order to alter a child's behavior pattern, an intervention program must be implemented. To implement a successful instructional program, initial instruction must be focused
on the individual child. Group instruction is then introduced
only when the child is ready and able to work with others.
The physical arrangement of the classroom will need to include
individual task areas as well as cooperative group problem-
solving areas. Time periods for completion of tasks must be
very flexible, and successful completions must be amply rewarded. At some point, these extrinsic rewards will eventu-

ally be replaced by intrinsic feelings of self worth.

Strategies to modify the educational curriculum for emotionally impaired children include approaches as diverse as behavior modification and psychoeducational, ecological, and psychodynamic alterations. It is apparent, then, that the total program for educating these children is one that will pick aspects of treatment from many different theories of personality and methods of teaching. There are no static techniques or methods that will solve all problems for all teachers. Special educational materials are not necessarily the answer to the children's problems. Rather, it is the teacher's ability to incorporate suitable and appropriate methods and materials, assimilating them through personal and flexible means, that will ensure the greatest success.

Teachers should not expect an emotionally or behaviorally impaired child to demonstrate typical behavior throughout the school day. These children may display functionally sound behavior for some periods of time. Educators should not be too quick to judge children and hurry them back to regular classes. An entire look at the total environmental level of functioning is needed. Should the severity of the problem be too great to be dealt with, then a suitable referral will need to be made for psychotherapeutic and/or psychiatric intervention.

There is no question that working with emotionally impaired pupils is an exceedingly difficult task. In effect, frequently the teacher is working with psychotherapeutic principles, such as building up low levels of self-esteem. The difficulties and challenges are many, but the rewards also are deeply gratifying. If an emotionally disturbed youngster can be helped to change his/her life pattern so that he/she can function adequately in society, then in effect a life has been saved.

774. Algozzine, B.   1976.   The disturbing child: What you
      see is what you get?   *Alberta Journal of Educational
      Research* 22:330-33.

           In this study teachers were asked to make check-
      list ratings on emotionally disturbed children.   The
      results showed that regular teachers were far more
      perturbed by what they found than special education
      teachers.

775. Algozzine, B.   1981.   Effects of label-appropriate and
      label-inappropriate behavior on interpersonal rat-
      ings.   *Exceptional Child* 28:177-82.

           The relationship between the diagnostic label
      either emotionally disturbed (ED) or learning dis-
      abled (LD) assigned to a child and the type of behav-
      ior exhibited by that child was investigated with a
      group of advanced undergraduate students.   Four label
      and behavior conditions were simulated and analyzed.
      Analysis of results suggested that label-inapprop-
      riate behavior (i.e., LD child with ED behavior) was
      more disturbing and less accepted than label-approp-
      riate behavior (i.e., ED child with ED behavior).
      Implications of the study were discussed with regard
      to labeling theory and teacher training practices.

776. Algozzine, B., and L. Sherry.   1981.   Issues in the
      education of emotionally disturbed children.   *Behav-
      ioral Disorders* 6:223-27.

           Focuses on three major problems related to help-
      ing disturbed children: assessment practices, the
      nature of emotional disturbance, and the treatment
      of emotional problems.   Because of the wide range of
      theoretical backgrounds of practitioners in the field
      and because of non-standardized practices in defin-
      ing, identifying, placing, and treating disturbed
      children, these issues continue to cause widespread
      disagreements among professionals when implementing
      treatment programs.   There is an urgent need for
      objectively defining emotional problems and ratio-
      nally designing programs to meet individual child
      requirements.

777. Anderson, D.R. 1981. Documentation and change in prob-
      lem behaviors among anxious and hostile-aggressive
      children enrolled in a therapeutic pre-school prog-
      ram. *Child Psychiatry and Human Development* 11:232-
      40.

          Utilized a relatively simple, straightforward
      procedure to identify and document changes in problem
      behaviors among twenty-three children enrolled in a
      therapeutic preschool program. Results of two out-
      come measures indicated a significant overall reduc-
      tion in problem behaviors for the total group. When
      subgroups of anxious and hostile/aggressive children
      were considered, however, there was a significantly
      greater probability that anxious children would bene-
      fit more from the program than hostile/aggressive
      children. The article stresses the need to consider
      subgroups of patients when documenting treatment
      effectiveness and discusses the advantage of building
      documentation techniques into the record-keeping
      system.

778. Anderson, D.R. 1983. Prevalence of behavioral and
      emotional disturbance and specific problem types in
      a sample of disadvantaged preschool-aged children.
      Journal of Clinical Psychology 12:130-36.

          The primary objectives of this study were to
      document the prevalence of emotional disturbance and
      behavioral problems in preschool-aged children who
      were disadvantaged economically. In this study 462
      Head Start children were rated by their teachers.
      As a result 31.6% of the children were rated as ex-
      hibiting emotional or behavioral problems at such a
      level as would indicate a need for further diagnostic
      study. The discussion focuses on the necessity for
      diagnostic and intervention services among disadvan-
      taged children.

779. Anderson, N., and R.T. Marrone. 1977. Group therapy
      for emotionally disturbed children: A key to affec-
      tive education. *American Journal of Orthopsychiatry*
      47:97-103.

          Outlines the practical aspects of the operation
      of a therapeutic program for children in public

schools with severe emotional problems. The authors discuss the merits of the group therapy approach in relation to other modalities, and set out ground rules for the operation of groups by teachers.

780. Auger, T. 1975. Differences in child symptom ratings among teachers and parents of emotionally disturbed children. *Psychological Reports* 36:867-73.

Fifty-five behavioral descripters were rated in terms of their importance for child mental health by sixty-seven elementary school teachers, special educators, and parents of emotionally disturbed children. Among the findings was that special educators attached significantly greater importance to personality problems than did parents. The parents attached significantly greater importance to socialized delinquency behaviors than did special educators.

781. Ballow, B. 1979. Definitional and prevalence problems in behavior disorders for children. *School Psychology Digest* 8:348-54.

Definitions of behavior disorders in children are far from standardized. This lack of a precise vocabulary continues to plague both research and clinical practice. Confusion about definitions and differences in identification procedures have led to widely varying prevalence figures. School administrators estimate the prevalence of behavior disorders to be in the two percent to three percent range while teachers and school psychologists report that fifteen percent to thirty percent of the school population are in need of special attention for behavioral maladjustment. The article also deals with the significance of environmental intolerance and the instability of many behavior problems over time.

782. Barnette, S.M., and L.G. Parker. 1982. Suspension and expulsion of emotionally handicapped: Issues and practices. *Behavioral Disorders* 7:173-79.

Questionnaires were sent to fifty state agencies to investigate the legal status of suspension and expulsion procedures for emotionally handicapped or

behaviorally disordered students. Court decisions
that involved the suspension or expulsion of a behaviorally disordered student were included for discussion. In addition, the survey of existing practices
used by state education agencies was summarized.
Implications for programming and disciplinary actions
were formulated based on both the court decisions
cited and the existing state policies that address
this area of exceptionality. Among findings were
that of the twenty-six responding states, nine states
reported procedures specifically designed for disciplinary action for emotionally handicapped students.
Policies of specific states are mentioned.

783.   Barr, K.L., and R.L. McLowell. 1972. Comparison of
       learning disabled and emotionally disturbed children
       on three deviant classroom behaviors. *Exceptional*
       Children 39:60-63.

            This study put forth the hypothesis that there
       would be no significant difference in the observed
       frequency of three deviant behaviors--out of seat,
       negative physical contact, and vocalizations--between
       the emotionally disturbed and learning disabled.
       Sixteen children were the subjects. Half were dis-
       turbed, the other half learning disabled. The hy-
       pothesis was rejected on all except out of seat be-
       havior. The emotionally disturbed were found to have
       a much higher frequency of negative physical contact
       and vocalizations.

784.   Beare, P. 1981. Mainstreaming approach for behavior-
       ally disordered secondary students in a rural school
       district. *Behavioral Disorders* 6:209-18.

            The study assessed the efficacy of a systematic
       program of intervention designed to facilitate a
       goodness of fit between thirty-eight problem second-
       ary level students and a rural school system. Two
       control groups were utilized, one group consisting
       of 224 nontarget students attending Middleville
       junior-senior high school, the other 225 students
       attending a neighboring community high school. The
       intervention program involved teacher inservice, the
       implementation of a teacher staffed advocacy program,
       and the founding of a crisis teacher program. Pre-

and post-evaluation of students' school morale showed
no significant changes in target group attitude
toward school. Evaluation of behavioral reaction
toward school as measured by dropout rate and attend-
ance did show definite improvement. Implications of
the study are that teachers may be effective advocates for problem students when assisted by trained
personnel. A pressing need for more environmentally
based intervention components outside school was
strongly indicated.

785. Berkman, I.P., and L. Rosenblum. 1982. Serving high
school students in need: A look at restrengthening
the linkage between the school and community referral
sources. *Adolescence* 17:465-70.

Communication between professionals in the community (such as therapists) and in the schools is
necessary to serve secondary students with emotional
disturbances. Cooperation may be enhanced through
direct contact on an ongoing basis and through commitment on the part of both school and community
professionals.

786. Birnbrauer, J. 1981. The effects of vicarious prompting on attentive behavior of children with behavior
disorders. *Child Behavior Therapy* 3 (1):27-41.

Assessment of ten children with behavior disorders in two classrooms as to the effect of using
vicarious (subtle and indirect) prompting on their
attentive behavior. Room 1 was responsive to vicarious prompting using social reinforcement. Room 2
did not respond at all.

787. Bloom, R., and L. Hopewell. 1982. Psychiatric hospitalization of adolescents and successful mainstream
reentry. *Exceptional Children; Special Education and
Pediatrics: A New Relationship* 48:352-57.

A group of eighty-eight adolescent patients at
a state mental hospital were followed up six months
after discharge to determine the percentage of those
successful in remaining in the mainstream as opposed
to those who were readmitted. The article discusses

the potential of education to interrupt the rehospi-
talization "revolving door." Forty-three percent of
the adolescents had been hospitalized. Those who
were able to remain in the mainstream had returned
to school and/or lived with one biological parent,
and/or had a shorter hospitalization prior to discharge.

788. Brendtro, L.K., and P.R. Stern. 1967. A modification
      in the sequential tutoring of emotionally disturbed
      children. *Exceptional Children* 33:517-21.

             Previous research has indicated that the primary
      intervention in special classes for the disturbed is
      sequential tutoring. In this method the teacher
      provides individual attention by rotating from stu-
      dent to student. The authors discuss a number of
      limitations of this approach and suggest as an alter-
      native method of individualizing the instructional
      procedure a modified sequential involving system.

789. Brooks, M.L. 1981. Evaluation of emotionally disturbed
      primary school age boys and girls by mental health
      workers and educators. *Journal for Special Educators*
      17:344-351.

             Mental health workers (N=128) and educators
      (N=372) rated the degree of emotional disturbance and
      needed treatment of four modified case histories.
      Among conclusions were that there were no statisti-
      cally significant differences between the two groups
      in perceived emotional disturbance and that both
      groups realized the need for professional help.

790. Buckalew, L.W., and Patricia B. Buckalew. 1983. Behav-
      ioral management of exceptional children using video
      games as reward. *Perceptual and Motor Skills* 56:580-
      83.

             This study found that free time to play a popu-
      lar video game was a powerful reinforcer for excep-
      tional children with emotional problems. The tradi-
      tional reinforcers, such as candy and toys, were not
      nearly as effective.

791. Byrne, E., and C. Cunningham. 1985. The effects of
      mentally handicapped children on families--A concep-
      tual review. *Journal of Child Psychology and Psychi-
      atry* 26:847-64.

            To study the effects of mentally handicapped
      children upon families three categories were devised
      based on the underlying conceptions which appear to
      guide them. The first were families most vulnerable
      to the stress of child. The second category empha-
      sizes the material and practical problems. The last
      stresses the competence of families and describes
      the resources used to develop coping strategies.
      Links drawn between the three categories provide a
      basis for future research.

792. Byrnes, D. 1984. Forgotten children in classrooms.
      The Education Digest 50:50-54.

            This study involved twenty-six children who
      were passive, shy, and compliant. These children
      had a tendency to become invisible. They were un-
      happy, had low self esteem, and viewed themselves as
      failures. The author suggests that the schools and
      teachers become the special support that these chil-
      dren often do not get at home.

793. Calhoun, G., Jr., and R.N. Elliott, Jr. 1977. Self
      concept and academic achievement of educable retarded
      and emotionally disturbed pupils. *Exceptional Chil-
      dren* 43:379-80.

            A three-year study was conducted using fifty
      educable mentally handicapped and fifty emotionally
      disturbed students. Half of each group were main-
      streamed and half of each group were placed in spe-
      cial classes. The data showed that students who
      were mainstreamed achieved significantly more than
      the students in special classes.

794. Campbell, N.; R. Campbell; and H.C. Goymer. 1981.
      Academic contracting with emotionally disturbed chil-
      dren. *Psychological Reports* 48:605-6.

            In this study sixteen nine- to eleven-year-old

males were given contracts stating that if they completed their academic studies, they would be dis-
missed from the classroom early. The results demonstrated increased academic performance in the contingency management program. Also, inappropriate
behavior diminished.

795. Chalk, J. 1975. Sanctuary units in primary schools.
      Special Education/Forward Trends 2(4): 18-20.

          This article describes the program of special
      sanctuary-type classes that remove disturbed and
      disturbing students (in nursery through secondary
      school) from the regular classroom. Includes reports
      on the benefits of the units and some aims and objec-
      tives. The author concludes that the value of the
      units is proven and that they deserve consideration
      by schools planning additions to their support serv-
      ices.

796. Chamberlin, R.W. 1976. The use of teacher checklists
      to identify children at risk for later behavior and
      emotional problems. *American Journal of Diseases of
      Children* 130:141-45.

          This article concludes that teacher checklists
      are reliable and valid indicators of a child's cur-
      rent school functioning but are not very accurate at
      predicting behavior in other settings or the develop-
      ment of future behavior problems. The primary care
      physician could provide the teacher with information
      on the child's development and neurological status,
      home behavior, and family situation to help the
      teacher decide which children to refer for more thor-
      ough evaluation. Follow-up studies suggest that many
      behavioral disturbances seen in preschool settings
      are transient situational disturbances that could be
      adequately managed through behavior modification
      techniques, or simply through the passage of time.

797. Charny, I.W. 1960. Communication between psychothera-
      pist and teacher in treatment of the severely dis-
      turbed child. *Mental Hygiene* 43:40-47.

          The need for establishing an effective working

relationship between the child psychotherapist and
the patient's teacher is developed through the presentation of several case examples. Such a relationship requires effective communication, mutual respect, and understanding between therapist and
teacher. Results of such a relationship are in the
interest of better therapeutic outcomes although
they may require a change in the original treatment
plan.

798. Clarizio, H.   1985.   Cognitive behavioral treatment of
childhood depression. *Psychology in the Schools*
22:283-301.

There has been a recent interest in childhood
depression. Models for the treatment of childhood
depression arise largely from the treatment of adult
depression because the two seem to be alike. Very
little is known about the treatment of children.
The cognitive approach seems to be the selecting
intervention, though the approaches of the school
psychologists are also discussed.

799. Clements, J.E., and D.B. Tracy.   1977.   Effects of touch
and verbal reinforcement on the classroom behavior
of emotionally disturbed boys. *Exceptional Children*
43:453-54.

This study compared the effectiveness of tactile
and/or verbal reinforcement on arithmetic task performance of ten emotionally disturbed boys (ages
nine to eleven). Consistently higher results were
indicated when both tactile and verbal reinforcers
were used simultaneously.

800. Cline, R.   1981.   Principals' attitudes and knowledge
about handicapped children. *Exceptional Children*
48:172-74.

In this study data was gathered from ninety-one
principals in a large metropolitan school district
of 92,000 kindergarten through twelfth grade students
on their attitudes towards and knowledge of handicapped children. Six categories were used: mentally
retarded, emotionally disturbed, learning disabled,

mild, moderate, and severe handicaps. It was found that principals with ten or fewer years of experience were more knowledgeable than principals with more than ten years of experience. It was also found that the presence or absence of a special program or class did not affect the principal's attitude toward or knowledge of handicapped children.

801. Cobb, D.E., and J.R. Evans. 1981. The use of biofeedback techniques with school aged children exhibiting behavior and/or learning problems. *Journal of Abnormal Psychology* 9:251-81.

   The article reviews forty-four studies that investigated the efficacy of biofeedback techniques in treating childhood behavioral and learning disorders. Although the data suggest that children can learn voluntary control over a variety of physiological processes, methodological flaws make it impossible to specify the mechanisms responsible for such learning. Further, the data do not suggest that biofeedback techniques are superior to more conventional treatments in remediating learning or behavioral disorders. Suggestions for future research focus upon the elimination of methodological weaknesses, the use of more stringent diagnostic criteria, and the use of more sophisticated biofeedback equipment and procedures.

802. Coleman, M.C., and J. Gilliam. 1983. Disturbing behaviors in the classroom: A survey of teacher attitudes. *Journal of Special Education* 17:121-29.

   One hundred thirty-nine first through sixth grade teachers were the subjects of this survey study. They all read a vignette of hypothetically emotionally disturbed students and responded to an attitudinal survey. Teachers responded far more negatively toward the aggressive student, were most concerned about mainstreamed students, and less concerned about special education students.

803. Cooke, P. 1981. Children with emotional and behavioral
      problems. *Australian Journal of Remedial Education*
      13:4-6.

          Reviews research on the social perception of
      emotionally and behaviorally disordered students.
      Students who view their social world in a unidimen-
      sional manner should be helped to analyze situations,
      discover alternatives, and lengthen their attention
      span.

804. Cooney, J. 1985. An ethical approach to teacher refer-
      ral of children for individual counseling. *Elemen-
      tary School Guidance and Counseling* 19:198-202.

          This paper is an eight-step outline on how the
      parent, teacher, and counselor can best work together
      to help the child that is referred to the counselor.
      There should be a collaborative effort between the
      adults who have concern for the child.

805. Cowen, E.L. 1979. The evaluation of an intervention
      program for young schoolchildren with acting-out
      problems. *Journal of Abnormal Psychology* 7:381-96.

          Describes the rationale and nature of a program,
      the Primary Mental Health Project, to train nonpro-
      fessional child aides for helping interactions with
      young acting out school children (N = 234). Pe/post
      teacher measures of children's problems and compe-
      tencies, aid measures of problem behavior, and school
      mental health professionals' change in behavior esti-
      mates were used to evaluate the program's effective-
      ness. Children seen by trained aides showed signifi-
      cantly greater reductions both in acting out problems
      and in overall maladjustment than did similar chil-
      dren seen by comparable aides who did not have addi-
      tional training, or by the same aides before train-
      ing. Discusses implications for optimizing outcomes
      both in the specific school intervention project in
      question and in other, broader types of clinical
      interventions.

806. Csapo, M. 1981. Educational provisions for emotionally
      disturbed children in British Columbia status report.

British Columbia Journal of Special Education 12:357-67.

The results of two surveys gave some indication of the proper mode in the provision of services for emotionally disturbed children in the Province of British Columbia. There is a trend towards individualized solutions to children with problems.

807. Curley, J.F., and R. Pabis. 1978. Cognitive deficiencies in emotionally disturbed children. *Journal of Psychology* 98:145-58.

The cognitive development of 120 emotionally disturbed and 120 normal children (six to twelve years old) were examined. Results of the Southern Illinois University Test (a test of Piagetian classification concepts) indicated significant main effects for age, sex, and emotionality factors. Emotionally disturbed students scored lower than normal students and exhibited an inferior rate of cognitive skill development.

808. Dehouske, E.J. 1982. Story writing as a problem-solving vehicle. *Teaching Exceptional Children* 15:11-17.

Story writing helps handicapped and normal students develop a meaningful approach to daily experiences through fantasy production. Benefits of such an approach with emotionally disturbed adolescents have included increased abilities of students to examine problem situations, conceptualize alternatives, and understand potential consequences.

809. Demers, L.A. 1981. Effective mainstreaming for the learning disabled student with behavior problems. *Journal of Learning Disabilities* 14:179-88.

The program was developed to minimize the classroom disruptions that often occur when a behavior problem student (nine to thirteen years old) from a special education homeroom is placed in the mainstream. The program also was designed to encourage on-task performance and work completion both in the homeroom and mainstream settings through reinforcement for points earned during the day. Behavior change was the primary goal; it follows that academic progress frequently occurs as a result of increased task completion. Length of time in the program varied for each student from one to three years. The program initially was supportive and highly structured, but according to program design, the pupil gradually became more self reliant and less dependent on the system. Consequently, a transitional return to the regular class or to a less restrictive educational environment could be shaped gradually. The program was most effective when used in its entirety. Some teachers, however, were more comfortable and have found some success by using modified versions or isolated aspects of the program.

810. Dolce, R. 1984. Being a teacher of the behavior disordered. *Education* 105:155-159.

This teacher discusses her first experience of teaching a class of emotionally disturbed children. The advice she offers is to be honest and consistent. Children should accept personal responsibility. Use a good reward system. Parents are a very important resource. These children crave praise. Have a good sense of humor. And, results take time.

811. Donahue, T.R. 1978. Television's impact on emotionally disturbed children's value systems. *Child Study Journal* 8:187-96.

In this study emotionally disturbed children in institutions were given various behaviorally ambiguous situations in which they were asked how they, their best friends, and parents would act under those situations. Also, they were asked to indicate the "right" behavior. This study concluded that regular violence was engaged in by these children's favorite T.V. character. Also, these children did not see their own patterns of behavior to be more antisocial than most children shown on T.V. Finally, the children indicated more violent responses for themselves, favorite T.V. characters, and best friends than for all of the other categories.

812. Durlak, J.A. 1980. Comparative effectiveness of behavioral and relationship group treatment in the secondary prevention of school maladjustment. *American Journal of Community Psychology* 8:327-29.

The prediction that behavioral intervention would be more effective and efficient than relationship intervention after ten weeks of treatment was supported by teachers' ratings of the classroom adjustment of 119 children in the first, second, and third grades. Children in the behavioral groups improved most, followed by children in the relationship groups, followed, in turn, by a group of untreated controls who did not change over time. Furthermore, more children were successfully terminated from the behavioral program than from the relationship program after ten weeks. Program terminators in each intervention maintained their treatment gains over a four month follow-up period. Generally, however, each intervention was more successful for children with moderate rather than severe school maladjustment, and the more maladjusted children showed relatively modest improvement in classroom behavior even with additional treatment.

813. Edelbrock, C. 1981. Vocational-technical training for emotionally disturbed adolescents. *Journal of Teaching Exceptional Children* 14:75-79.

The Alternative Vocational School in Connecticut services ninety adolescents identified as acting out, emotionally disturbed, or socially maladjusted students in a program emphasizing behavior management and discipline. Five components of the school are administration, job preparation and placement, clinical services, vocational-technical training, and learning disabilities instruction.

814. Elias, M.J. 1983. Improving copying skills of emotionally disturbed boys through television based social problem solving. *American Journal of Orthopsychiatry* 53:61-72.

In this study children were involved in working through problem situations on videotapes. These tapes (ten were selected) were shown two times a

week for five weeks to 109 boys, ages seven to fifteen years, who were enrolled in special education
classes at a residential treatment center. A pre-
test, post-test and follow-up design were used.

815. Fagen, S.A., and N.J. Long. 1976. Teaching children
self-control: A new responsibility for teachers.
Focus on Exceptional Children 7(8):1-11.

This article covers self-control curriculum
topics including teacher training, curriculum development, characteristics of a successful primary prevention program, structure of self-control, and an
overview of a self-control curriculum. The self-
control curriculum in special education is seen as a
means of preventing emotional and learning problems
in children through instruction of personal skills
leading to self-directed behavior with responsibility.

816. Fagen, S.A., and N.J. Long. 1979. A psychoeducational
curriculum approach to teaching self-control. *Behavioral Disorders* 4:68-82.

This article outlines the Fagen-Long curriculum
that has as its purpose the development of self-
control skills in emotionally disturbed youngsters.
Self-control will reduce the frequency of disorderly
conduct. The curriculum consists of eight areas
that are each subdivided into units.

817. Fleece, L. 1981. The use of a contingent observation
procedure to reduce disruptive behavior in a preschool child. *Journal of Clinical Psychology* 10:128-
30.

Investigates the use of a contingent observation
procedure to effect reductions in disruptive behavior
and increases in appropriate social behavior in a
five-year-old kindergarten student. The procedure
can be divided into the following four components:
behavioral instruction, modified timeout, modeling,
and contingent social reinforcement. Large reductions in intrusive-aggressive and noncompliant behavior were observed after implementation of the proce-

dure. Anecdotal reports from the student's teacher
suggested improved social behaviors over the course
of the experiment. Although methodological limitations hampered clear interpretations of the data,
type of modeling instruction (general vs. specific
individual) did not seem to affect results. Results
of the study supported the effectiveness of the contingent observation procedure and suggested that it
is applicable to a wider range of children than was
previously established.

818.   French, D.C., and G.A. Waas. 1985. Behavior problems
       of peer-neglected and peer-rejected elementary-aged
       children: Parent and teacher perspectives. *Child
       Development* 56:246-52.

       Eight hundred seventy eight- and eleven-year-
old children who were either rejected, neglected, or
popular students were studied to determine what their
status had to do with their behavior in class and in
their home. Both parents and teachers completed
behavior checklists. The results of the study showed
that rejected children had more behavior problems
than neglected and popular children. There was very
little difference between the behavior problems of
the neglected and the popular students. The authors
recommend that clinicians and researchers concentrate
on understanding and remediating the problems of
rejected children.

819.   Fritsch, R.E. 1980. Screening behavior problem chil-
       dren: Let's make it a team effort. *Learner in the
       Process* 2:43-51.

       The classroom teacher's role in screening chil-
dren with possible behavior problems includes conducting direct and indirect observations of the students. Direct observation of the students' classroom
interactions can be done through continuous recording, interval recording, and time sampling. Indirect
observation is accomplished through behavior rating
scales and checklists. Counselors and special educators then conduct direct and indirect observations
and a team decision about referral is made.

820. Fuller, G.B., and R.E. Rankin. 1984. Personality dif-
      ferences between learning disabled and emotionally
      impaired children. *School Psychology Review* 13:221-
      24.

         A study was made to determine the differences
      among learning disabled, emotionally impaired, and
      regular education students on the basis of personal-
      ity characteristics. Using the Children's Personal-
      ity Questionnaire as an evaluation tool, the results
      of this study showed that while learning disabled
      and emotionally impaired differentiated from the
      regular students, they were in no sense abnormal or
      severely disturbed. Further results of this study
      showed that some of these children may require a
      fairly strong external source of orientation and
      structural environment (EI), while others may do
      better in an independent learning situation (LD).

821. Good, C.; B.F. Eller; R.S. Spangler; and J.E. Stone.
      1981. The effect of an operant intervention program
      on attending and other academic behavior with emo-
      tionally disturbed children. *Journal of Instruc-
      tional Psychology* 9:25-33.

         In this study five males (aged twelve to four-
      teen yrs.) were selected randomly from a class of
      emotionally disturbed students. Various aspects
      affecting students' behavior such as tangible rein-
      forcers, social praise, and different types of sched-
      uling were studied. The reinforcers used were atten-
      tion from the teacher, social praise, tokens, and
      charting. Results agreed with previous findings
      that changes in behavior can be affected through the
      systematic application of reinforcers.

822. Green, L. 1976. Face two special fears. Educating
      the emotionally disturbed adolescent. *Devereux Forum*
      11:37-44.

         This article, intended for special educators,
      discusses characteristic fears of the emotionally
      disturbed adolescent. The child's fear of giving up
      the past and the educator's fear of insisting that
      the adolescent face the reality of his aging are
      focal points of the discussion. Two of the five

points of reference from which to view adolescent
growth are that it is a time when group relations
are most important and that it is a time to seek
individual status.

823.   Gresham, F.M. 1984. Social skills and self efficacy
       for exceptional children. *Exceptional Children*
       51:253-259.

       This article points out that mainstreaming ef-
       forts have been faulty due to the emphasis of these
       programs. Although development of academic skills
       is necessary for mainstreaming, there must be an
       effort made to develop the social skills of handi-
       capped children to enable them to socialize both
       with their classmates and society. Because of hand-
       icapped children's inability to gain social accept-
       ance with their peers, they may find themselves in an
       unwelcome environment, thus jeopardizing their abil-
       ity to learn.

824.   Gruber, J.J., and M. Noland. 1977. Perceptual-motor
       and scholastic achievement relationships in emotion-
       ally disturbed elementary school children. *Research
       Quarterly* 48:68-73.

       The article examines the relationships between
       the mental and motor development of sixty-one emo-
       tionally disturbed elementary school children. The
       analysis of results of the Wide Range Achievement,
       five physical fitness items, and four arm and leg
       coordination measures indicated no relationship be-
       tween academic achievement, fitness, and coordina-
       tion.

825.   Harris, J.; S. King; J. Reifler; and L. Rosenberg.
       1984. Emotional & learning disorder in 6-12 year
       old boys attending special schools. *Journal of the
       American Academy of Child Psychiatry* 23:431-37.

       Four hundred emotionally disturbed children and
       three hundred normal children were compared by two
       special schools. Teachers used a checklist to make
       the comparisons. The purpose of the study was to
       show an association between academic underachievement

and psychiatric problems in children. The findings
were that the children in school for emotionally
disturbed are more seriously disturbed than learning
disabled on all scales. The emotionally disturbed
are more socially withdrawn, self-destructive, inat-
tentive, nervous, and over-reactive. Both groups
need new programs in reading since they are far behind in that area.

826. Haskins, R. 1985. Public school aggression among children with varying day-care experience. *Child Development* 56:689-703.

Children with varying amounts and types of day-
care experience were followed over their first two
or three years of public schooling. Teachers noted
aggressiveness and compliance of the children.
Children who had attended a cognitively oriented day-
care program beginning in infancy proved to be more
aggressive than all other groups of children who had
attended day-care. Aggression among these children
did decline over time and the children were not difficult to manage.

827. Haubrich, P.A., and R. Shores. 1976. Attending behavior and academic performance of emotionally disturbed
children. *Exceptional Children* 42:337-39.

Five elementary-aged children in a residential
treatment center for emotionally disturbed children
were investigated to determine the relationship of
attending behavior to academic production. Attending
behavior was controlled by using study cubicles.
Contingent reinforcement procedures were used to
control academic performance. When cubicle and reinforcement conditions were compared, the reinforcement
condition produced significantly higher rates of
attending.

828. Hewett, F.M. 1967. Education engineering with emotionally disturbed children. *Exceptional Children*
33:459-67.

An engineered classroom design based on the
behavior modification model has been developed and

used in institutional and public schools. It attempts to provide a setting for implementation of a
hierarchy of educational tasks, meaningful rewards
for learning, and an appropriate degree of teacher
structure. The classroom, students, and techniques
are described.

829. Hogan, P.T. 1981. Phototherapy in the Educational
Setting. *Arts in Psychotherapy* 8:193-99.

Phototherapy, the use of photography as a treatment tool, is said to be valuable in working with
students with emotional disturbances by helping them
cope with their feelings and perceptions of themselves. Seven group exercises are cited that include
work on interactions, positive feelings, and fantasy.

830. Hoover, J. 1984. Behavioral intervention program for
remediating mild emotional/behavioral problems in
rural county elementary schools. *Education* 104:287-
90.

This model approach is designed to meet the
problems in rural county elementary schools where
there are large distances between school districts,
a low incidence of children with serious emotional/
behavior problems, and limited funds. The purpose
of the program is both to be preventive, to remediate
mild or moderate emotional/behavior problems in elementary classrooms. It emphasizes a consultive team
approach that utilizes the knowledge and skills of a
special educator teacher and/or school psychologist,
a behavioral specialist, and a regular classroom
teacher.

831. Hulbert, C.M. 1977. A teacher-aide programme in action. *Special Education: Forward Trends* 4:27-31.

This supplement to an article on the theory of
introducing nonprofessionals into ordinary schools
to work with disadvantaged or emotionally vulnerable
children describes a teacher aide program tested in
six English schools. Teacher aides were employed to
work with children who were psychologically at risk
by means of a compensatory nurturing approach and

behavior shaping techniques. The following program
components are discussed: selection of aides, role of
aides, training of aides, and parental and teacher
involvement. Problems are identified, including
teachers' anxieties about dividing students' loyal-
ties, differences in experience and attitude among
teachers, and difficulties in time and space limitations. Staff are reported to have evaluated the
project favorably.

832. Janes, C.L., and V.M. Hesselbrock. 1978. Problem chil-
      dren's adult adjustment predicted from teachers'
      ratings. *American Journal of Orthopsychiatry* 48:300-
      9.

      Teacher ratings of 187 children (four to fifteen
      years old) seen at a guidance clinic were compared
      to interview-based ratings of social adjustment nine
      to fifteen years later. When followed up, children
      who were described as failing to get along with oth-
      ers were seen to be relatively disturbed. Differ-
      ences were found between teacher-rated behavior pat-
      terns relating to later social adjustment for boys
      and those for girls. This study concluded that,
      especially if focused on the child's peer relation-
      ships, teacher ratings can be useful predictors of
      adjustment.

833. Kaltern, N.M., and G. Marsden. 1977. Children's under-
      standing of their emotionally disturbed peers. II.
      Etiological factors. *Psychiatry* 40:48-54.

      Thirty-one fourth and sixth grade students were
      presented five vignettes. Four vignettes depicted
      boys with emotionally disturbed behavior, and one
      vignette depicted a normal boy. Each boy was experi-
      encing a situational problem. The objective was to
      determine the students' concepts of etiology or
      causes of behavior. An analysis of interview re-
      sponses regarding the development of such disturbed
      behavior indicted that factors other than severity
      of emotional illness seemed to determine how the
      students perceived the etiology. There was a lack
      of agreement among the students, even within the
      same grade, on their views of etiology for each cen-
      tral figure.

834. Kaplan, H.K., and I. Kaufman. 1978. Sociometric status
      and behaviors of emotionally disturbed children.
      Psychology in the Schools 15:8-15.

          In a residential treatment center, behavior
      checklists and sociometric data were correlated on
      twenty emotionally disturbed children (six and one-
      half to thirteen and one-half years old). Behaviors
      found to relate significantly (and negatively) with
      sociometric status pertained mainly to physical and
      verbal aggression and to intrusive acts. Behavior
      incidence in groups identified as high, average, and
      low in status were also studied.

835. Karper, W. 1981. The use of exercise in alleviating
      emotional disturbance: A review of the literature.
      Journal for Special Educators 18:61-72.

          Karper examines studies that claim that exercise
      provides tension release. He reviews the concepts
      of "time out" and self mastery and shows how studies
      have demonstrated that exercise can produce organic
      change in emotionally disturbed as well as normal
      people. He recommends further research in this area,
      particularly using people with different types of
      emotional disturbances.

836. Kauffman, J.M. 1980. Where special education for dis-
      turbed children is going: A personal view. *Excep-
      tional Children* 46:522-524.

          This article relates problems in the definition
      of emotional disturbance and the requirement of vari-
      ous services for all children identified. Conse-
      quently, Public Law 94-142 is likely to result in
      suppressed rather than expanded services to mildly
      disturbed students. Attending to the problem of
      behavioral deviance via a legal approach is of ques-
      tionable wisdom. The field of special education is
      turning toward forces often external to special edu-
      cation.

837. Kavale, K.A., and A. Hirshuren, 1980. Public school
      and university teacher training programs for behav-
      iorally disordered: Are they compatible? *Behavioral*

Disorders: Posture on Issues and Programs for Children with Behavior Problems 5:151-55.

Presents findings from a survey on thirty-three public school programs for behaviorally disordered children indicating that a majority considered their theoretical focus to be behavioral. Another portion of the survey, however, indicated that the pragmatic approaches to treatment fund in public school behavior disorders programs cover techniques reflecting a wide variety of theoretical models. Consequently, there exists a mismatch that prevents maximum effectiveness in both teacher training and service delivery for behaviorally disordered children. Concludes that university teacher training programs should reflect a more eclectic stance by carefully synthesizing assorted theoretical components into a composite that meets the diverse pragmatic demands of public school programs for behaviorally disordered children.

838. Kohn, M. 1967. Individualized teaching with therapeutic aims of disturbed preschool children. *American Journal of Orthopsychiatry* 37:341-42.

Reports on the development of a Competence Scale and a Symptom Checklist for rapid identification of emotionally disturbed children, and the testing of a new therapeutic approach—namely, individualized teaching and therapeutic aims.

839. Lanunziata, L.J. 1981. Teaching social skills in classrooms for behaviorally disordered students. *Behavioral Disorders* 6:238-46.

Selected procedures of instruction from Social Skills in the Classroom were applied to class related social behaviors of four elementary and intermediate level behavior disordered students. Four classroom teachers identified two social behaviors of one student in each of their classrooms using the categories and operational definitions included in this curriculum. Data for seven behaviors were collected and analyzed. Teachers were trained to define and measure target behaviors during an in-service workshop and in classroom training. Social modeling, contracting, and social reinforcement were the teaching strategies employed as specified in Stephens' curriculum. Improvement occurred in all targeted behaviors. Functional relationships between teaching strategies and changes in the targeted behavior were established in four of the targeted behaviors.

840. Lavietes, R. 1962. The teacher's role in the education of the emotionally disturbed. *American Journal of Orthopsychiatry* 32:854-62.

The teacher of emotionally disturbed children must function in a way that integrates typical educational rules with a special clinical role. She/he must be supervised both by an educator and by a clinician. Observations made at the Godmothers' League Day Treatment Center and School for Emotionally Disturbed Children are presented to illustrate differences between goals and methods used with normal children and emotionally disturbed children.

841. Lawrenson, G.M., and A.J. McKinnon. 1982. A survey of classroom teachers of the emotionally disturbed: Attrition and burnout factors. *Behavioral Disorders* 8:41-49.

A survey of thirty-three teachers of emotionally disturbed children revealed that there was a high attrition rate. Difficulty with administration was the major reason for leaving and for job dissatisfaction; teachers' major satisfaction involved relationships with students; and teachers remaining on the job had more degrees and greater administrative support.

842. Leone, P. 1984. A descriptive follow-up of behaviorally disordered adolescents. *Behavioral Disorders* 9:207-14.

This article is a follow-up study concerned with societal adjustment. It found that the successful graduates of programs for the disturbed had serious deficits in academic skills. Out of the fourteen students only four were not employed, attending school or training.

843. Lerner, B. 1985. Self-esteem and excellence: The choice and the paradox. *American Educator* Winter:10-16.

    According to the article, self-esteem in the child is the key to success. Excellence, or even competence, cannot be achieved until self-esteem is raised. Teachers must give priority to the task of raising the child's self-esteem, and each child must be accepted as he/she is.

844. Leventhal, M.B. 1980. Dance therapy as treatment of choice for the emotionally disturbed and learning disabled child. *Journal of Physical Education and Recreation* 51:33-35.

    A dance therapist describes the role of dance therapy in treating emotionally disturbed or learning disabled children, distinguishes dance therapy from creative dance, and describes a five-part session in dance therapy. Emphasis is on the importance of the child-therapist relationship.

845. Levinson, C. 1982. Remediating a passive aggressive emotionally disturbed pre-adolescent boy through writing: A comprehensive psychodynamic structured approach. *Pointer* 26:23-27.

    The article is an account of the author's work in a remedial reading department with John, a pre-adolescent, passive aggressive student at the Rose School (Washington, DC) for emotionally disturbed children. The case posed the dual problem of working with the passive aggressive dynamic within a curriculum that would meet John's emotional and academic needs. The case provides an example of blending teaching skills with psychological insights.

846. Livingston, R. 1985. Depression illness and learning difficulties; Research needs and practical implication. *Journal of Learning Disabilities* 18:518-19.

    There is substantial evidence that Major Depressive Disorder (MDD) and LD are associated in several ways and there is much research to do to clarify

this association. Educators should be aware of the
signs of MDD--sad expression, change in activity
level, social isolation, uncharacteristic fighting
or arguing. They must also learn how to treat and
react when MDD signs are observed. For many students
it wouldn't make a difference if they are diagnosed
EH or EH/LD, but MDD requires a very specific treatment. A wrong diagnosis can be very harmful to the
child.

847. Lubin, M. 1982. Responding to the disturbed child's
      obscure reparative and communicative wishes: Mutual-
      ity in the special education of a vulnerable and
      explosive early adolescent boy. *Residential Group
      Care & Treatment* 1:3-20.

           This article deals with an emotionally disturbed
      adolescent boy (fifteen years old) in a residential
      treatment center. The author discusses his interac-
      tions with the boy through various classroom set-
      tings. The student and teacher are involved in a
      very positive relationship that is a hallmark of the
      teacher's philosophy.

848. Luchow, J.; T. Crowl; and J. Kahn. 1985. Learned help-
      lessness: Perceived effects of ability and efforts
      on academic performance among EH and LD/EH children.
      Journal of Learning Disabilities 18:470-74.

           The Intellectual Achievement Responsibility
      Questionnaire, which measures perceived locus of
      control of academic outcome, was given to twenty-
      eight EH and twenty-five LD/EH. Results of the
      between-group revealed that EH and LD/EH were compa-
      rable with respect to their attitude of their per-
      sonal responsibility for success. EH children took
      a more personal responsibility for failures than did
      LD/EH. Results of the within-group comparison re-
      vealed that EH attributed success more toward their
      ability than to effort, but their failure was attrib-
      uted to a lack of ability and lack of effort. It
      seems that the two groups have different views toward
      their academic performance. Therefore these differ-
      ent views should be taken into account in helping
      them overcome learned helplessness.

849. Marling, C. 1985. Perceptions of the usefulness of
      the I.E.P. by teachers of learning disabled and emo-
      tionally disturbed children. *Psychology in the
      Schools* 22:65-67.

          This report used questionnaires given out to
      teachers of emotionally disturbed and learning dis-
      abled children to determine the usefulness of Indi-
      vidualized Education Program (I.E.P.). Most teachers
      responded that I.E.P. doesn't affect them in their
      daily lesson planning, but does give them a general
      background understanding of their students. Teachers
      also responded that they very rarely check the
      I.E.P., nor is it accessible to the teachers. The
      study concludes that teachers feel that unless I.E.P.
      is used on a daily basis it isn't worth the time it
      takes to fill out the I.E.P.

850. Marsden, G., and N.M. Kalter. 1976. Children's under-
      standing of their emotionally disturbed peers. *Psy-
      chiatry* 39:227-38.

          The reactions of thirty-one fourth and sixth
      graders to five vignettes, depicting one normal and
      four emotionally disturbed boys, were recorded to
      gather data on how children understand their emotion-
      ally disturbed peers. The findings indicated that,
      like adults, fourth and sixth graders do discriminate
      the behavior of normal children to that of emotion-
      ally disturbed children. The children also made
      distinctions, like those made by clinicians, among
      degrees of disturbed behavior. Their perceptions of
      emotional disturbance were, for the most part, sep-
      arate from their like or dislike for the disturbed
      peers.

851. Maughan, B.; G. Gray; and M. Rutter. 1985. Reading
      retardation and antisocial behavior: A follow-up
      into employment. *Journal of Child Psychology and
      Psychiatry* 26:741-58.

          Four groups of boys, with and without reading
      retardation and with and without behavioral distur-
      bance, were explored in childhood, secondary school,
      and the early work years. The majority of retarded
      readers appeared to leave school early. Unstable

work records and depressed skills characterize those with behavioral problems.

852. Meeks, J.W. 1982. Reading needs of the emotionally disturbed child: An institutional view. *Journal for Special Educators* 18:17-20.

     An examination of twenty-seven adolescent students in a private psychiatric center was conducted to determine a similarity in characteristics, academic deficits, and special learning problems of ED children. Findings indicted that most problems occurred between third and seventh grade. The majority of students were one or more years below grade level in reading. Structured remediation was recommended.

853. Morgan, S.R. 1984. Counseling with teachers on the sexual acting-out of disturbed children. *Psychology in the Schools* 21:234-43.

     Explores subconscious meanings and motivations as well as explanations for various types of sexual acting-out behavior. Includes guidelines for discussions with teachers.

854. Morgan, S.R. 1984. Development of empathy in emotionally disturbed children. *Journal of Humanistic Education and Development* 22:70-79.

     This study demonstrated that the humanistic/psychoeducational model was more effective in developing empathy among disturbed children than the behavioral/learning model. Also examines help-giving behavior, self-control, and responsibility.

855. Morris, J.D., and D. Arrant. 1978. Behavior ratings of emotionally disturbed children by teachers, parents and school psychologists. *Psychology in the Schools* 15:450-55.

     Emotional disturbance in a group of 104 disturbed children was rated by parents, schools, psychologists, and teachers. Teachers were found to be most severe in their judgments.

856. Morse, W.C.   1976.   The helping teacher/crisis teacher
      concept. *Focus on Exceptional Children* 8(4):1-11.

          Reviews the concepts of the crisis teacher for
      emotionally disturbed elementary school students and
      the helping teacher as a special education resource
      person. The author traces the erosion of this help-
      ing teacher program, seeing mandatory legislation as
      the cause of the schools' inability to formulate the
      program clearly and make it effective. The author
      notes that the helping teacher format is a natural
      medium for assisting teachers in the present public
      school system.

857. Murphy, L., and S. Ross.   1983.   Student self-control
      as a basis for instructional adaptation with behav-
      iorally disordered children. *Behavioral Disorders*
      8:237-43.

          The authors review the literature and point out
      that academic instruction receives less attention
      than managing social behavior when dealing with be-
      haviorally disordered children. They suggest using
      student's individual self-control levels as a major
      determinant for individual planning. They also sug-
      gest pairing degree of self-control with individual
      methods of instruction. If external control is nec-
      essary, then individual tutoring is used. If a child
      has greater control then the instructional strategy
      would be matched to that particular self-control
      stage. The authors hope to stimulate more research
      in the pairing of teaching method and self-control.

858. Neumann, P.   1984.   What do you say to a child in tears?
      Instructor 94:52-54.

          This article offers various reasons why teachers
      are unable to offer comfort to a child in emotional
      pain. Teachers are experts in dealing with academic
      problems but find themselves ill-equipped to deal
      with emotional pain that a child may have. The
      author suggests ways of dealing with this problem:
      (1) recognition of feeling; (2) validation of feel-
      ing; (3) release of feeling; (4) acceptance of feel-
      ing. If at all possible allow the child to make his
      own decision because just in case the teacher made

the wrong decision the child will carry a grudge
against the teacher.

859. Northcutt, J.R.W., and G.B. Tipton. 1978. Teaching
      severely mentally ill and emotionally disturbed ado-
      lescents. *Exceptional Children* 45:18-26.

      The writers of this article feel that the
      teacher of the emotionally disturbed is not only an
      educator but a therapist in kind: the teacher must
      make the educational setting therapeutic. They
      stress the importance of teacher training with regard
      to scheduling and intervening. Every facet of every
      moment of the day must be considered as a way of
      making "academic tasks therapeutic tools."

860. O'Rourke, R.D. 1977. Troubled children. A new design
      for learning. *Teaching Exceptional Children* 9:34-35.

      Examines a teacher-designed school day and ex-
      plains new ways of programming. Integrating academ-
      ics with mental and physical relaxation aid social
      development of emotionally disturbed children.

861. Ostrower, C., and A. Ziv. 1982. Soft reprimands and
      self control as ways of behavior modification in the
      classroom. *Israeli Journal of Psychology & Counsel-
      ing in Education* 15:21-28.

      This study compared two behavior modification
      methods. Subjects were thirty-seven boys and twenty-
      seven girls in seventh and eighth grades at a school
      for socially disadvantaged and emotionally disturbed
      children. One method instituted a "soft-reprimand"
      issued by the teacher. The other method instituted
      record keeping by the disruptive pupil of his/her
      own disruptions. Results showed more disruptive
      behavior in the self-control group than in the soft
      reprimand group.

862. Paget, K.D. 1980. On the relationship between the
      creative and social-emotional development of emotion-

ally handicapped children. *Journal of Clinical Psychology* 36:977-82.

The article examines the relationship between the creative and social-emotional development of seventy-eight emotionally handicapped children, six to twelve years of age. Would changes in social-emotional development over the course of treatment correspond to changes in creativity? The children were rated on their mastery of social-emotional objectives and were given similar forms of a creativity test at the beginning and at the end of eight weeks. Results indicate a significant relationship between changes in social-emotional status and creativity.

863. Paget, K.D. 1982. The creative abilities of children with social and emotional problems. *Journal of Abnormal Child Psychology* 10:107-12.

Responses of seventy-eight emotionally disturbed children on the Torrance Tests of Creative Thinking were compared to those from a standardization sample. Subjects were close to the average in ability to arrive at different ideas, experienced difficulty in producing original ideas, and were substantially below average in the other areas of creativity. Presenting particular difficulty for the disturbed children was the area of elaboration; that is, the addition of details to ideas.

864. Pastor, D.L., and S.M. Swap. 1978. An ecological study of emotionally disturbed preschoolers in special and regular classes. *Exceptional Children* 45:213-17.

This study sought to identify the effect of setting on behavior among four emotionally disturbed preschool boys. Written records were kept on the youngsters. It was evident from observations that the special education setting proved more successful in working with these young boys.

865.   Paul, L.   1985.   Where are we in the education of emo-
       tionally disturbed children?   *Behavioral Disorders*
       10:145-51.

            The thesis of this paper is that there is a
       tremendous need to develop the areas of technique in
       working with emotionally disturbed. At the same
       time, some of the most significant breakthroughs in
       special education have taken place specifically in
       working with this population. Another point devel-
       oped in this thesis is that the area of emotional
       handicap has very little to do with pedagogical
       roots, but more to do with philosophical and psycho-
       logical roots. This can be a distinct advantage
       toward the development of skills for working with
       emotionally disturbed children because the trend of
       the country is to shy away from pedagogy and embrace
       philosophy and psychology. This article also dis-
       cusses the history, strength, and challenges that
       exist in the field of emotionally disturbed children.

866.   Pelletier, G., and C. Lessard.   1981.   Educational dif-
       ferentiation and integration.   The viewpoint of teach-
       ers in Quebec.   *Apprentissage et Socialisation* 4:149-
       59.

            This article examined the point of view of teach-
       ers on varied teaching methods and their opinions on
       eventually mainstreaming emotionally disturbed and
       learning disabled students. It was found that the
       majority of the teachers supported some mainstreaming
       for children with learning difficulties. However,
       they felt insecure about their abilities to meet
       such a challenge. One variable found in the research
       that explained many variations in opinion was that
       French-speaking teachers were more supportive of
       mainstreaming than English-speaking teachers.

867.   Peretti, P.; D. Clark; and P. Johnson.   1984.   Effect
       of parental rejection on negative attention-seeking
       classroom behaviors.   *Education* 104:313-17.

            This study sought to determine the effect of
       parental rejection on the negative attention-seeking
       behavior of students. It also wanted to examine
       which parent's rejection would have more of an effect

on their children's negative behavior. The results
showed a significant relationship between parental
rejection and negative seeking behavior, particularly
when the rejection came from the father. Teachers
should therefore not take students' negative-seeking
behavior to heart and realize its cause. Remediation
may require that student and parents be involved in
a therapeutic process.

868. Phillips, K.M. 1981. Aggression and productiveness in
      emotionally disturbed children in competitive and
      non-competitive recreation. *Child Care Quarterly*
      10:148-56.

      An observation of twelve ED children during
      competitive, semi-competitive, and non-competitive
      recreation. More aggression was found during compet-
      itive recreation. More productive behavior was found
      after non-competitive recreation. Girls expressed
      more verbal than physical aggression, but there was
      no difference in boys' expression.

869. Pierce, L., and H. Klein. 1982. A comparison of parent
      and child perceptions of the child's behavior. *Be-
      havioral Disorders* 7:69-74.

      Twenty-three behaviorally disturbed children
      (aged seven to sixteen) and their parents completed
      a behavioral description form. A significant level
      of agreement was found on very few items, indicating
      that children and parents see the child's behavior
      differently.

870. Prieto, A.G., and H.Z. Stanley. 1981. Teacher percep-
      tion of race as a factor in the placement of behav-
      iorally disordered children. *Behavioral Disorders*
      7:34-38.

      One hundred nineteen regular and special educa-
      tion teachers judged placement in a class for emo-
      tionally disturbed students more appropriate for
      Mexican-American students than white students when
      they were given a fictitious case study of an eight-
      year-old child functioning slightly below grade level
      with mild behavior problems.

871.   Resnick, R.J.   1978.   The primary teacher and the emo-
       tionally disabled child.   *Education* 98:387-91.

           This article aids the elementary school teacher
       in detecting an emotional handicap.   It describes
       common problems and explores strategies and inter-
       ventions through anecdotal data.

872.   Rich, H.L.   1979.   Classroom interaction patterns among
       teachers and emotionally disturbed children.   *The
       Exceptional Child* 26:34-40.

           This article discusses a study that was done on
       classroom interaction patterns.   At the conclusion
       of the study it was found that the quality of class-
       room environments is primarily shaped by dominating
       behaviors rather than by nurturant or facilitative
       relationships.   Also included in this article is a
       discussion of teacher managerial/instructional behav-
       iors and the impact of varied student behaviors.

873.   Riester, A.   1984.   Teaching the emotionally disturbed
       student.   *Pointer* 28(3):13-18.

           This article provides guidelines for meeting
       the needs of emotionally disturbed students.   It
       deals with programming and intervention strategies.
       There is also a focus on structuring the classroom
       environment, managing troublesome behavior, and
       teaching pro-social skills.

874.   Rose, T.   1984.   Effects of previewing on the oral read-
       ing of mainstreamed behaviorally disordered students.
       Behavior Disorder 10:33-34.

           A study was made to determine what effect two
       previewing methods had on oral reading: (a) listening
       preview whereby the instructor read quietly to the
       student while the student followed along quietly in
       the book; (b) silent previewing whereby the student
       read quietly the passage he would have to read out
       loud.   Results indicated that the listening preview
       had a higher rate of words read correctly than the
       silent previewing.   However, neither preview method
       reduced the rate of errors.   In view of the cost

efficiency of these preview methods, the authors
highly recommend them and in particular the listening
preview.

875. Salvador, M.; P. Chamberlain; and P. Graubard.   1967.
      A project to teach learning skills to disturbed,
      delinquent children. *American Journal of Orthopsy-*
      chiatry 37:558-67.

         The intervention curriculum and teaching method-
      ology appeared to be quite effective in changing the
      learning behavior of disturbed, delinquent children.
      This change was achieved by focusing not on behavior,
      but on cognitive growth. With these children, as in
      the general field of learning disabilities, the un-
      derlying correlates of the disability must be reme-
      diated before successful teaching of the skill per
      se can be accomplished.

876. Schloss, P.J.; R.A. Sedlak; E.D. Wiggins; and D. Ramsey.
      1983.   Stress reduction for professionals working
      with aggressive adolescents. *Exceptional Children*
      49:349-54.

         Relaxation training and systematic desensitiza-
      tion techniques were used to reduce stress. A sample
      of fourteen professionals and paraprofessionals who
      work with severely behaviorally disordered adoles-
      cents were assigned to an experimental or control
      group. The experimental group was instructed in
      relaxation training and systematic desensitization.
      The control group participated in restraint training
      and other aggression management activities. The
      experimental group appeared to show a significant
      reduction in stress.

877. Scott, D.   1982. *Helping the maladjusted child: A guide*
      for parents and teachers. Englewood, N.J.: Prentice-
      Hall.

         Intended for professionals, students, and par-
      ents, the book describes types, causes, and treat-
      ments of maladjustment in children and adolescents.
      Maladjustment is first defined and distinguished
      from other types of unusual or undesirable behavior.

Next, it examines issues of the child's separation
from the mother in early childhood and deprivation
of mother love. Six case studies are then provided
that detail three major reactions to deprivation--
withdrawal, hostility, and avoidance. Discusses
countermeasures to deprivation including temporary
refuge for the child, professional work with parents
during child's absence, and aims and forms of temporary residential care (including school discipline).
Four main family oriented situations that produce
maladjustment are discussed in detail including child
fear of loss of the preferred or only parent. Suggests to parents and teachers ways of treating such
reactions to deprivation as hostility and avoidance
compulsion. Then suggests approaches (with illus-
trative case studies) to treating two handicaps of
temperament.

878. Scruggs, T.; M. Mastropieri; and L. Richter. 1985.
      Peer tutoring with behaviorally disordered students:
      Social and academic benefits. *Behavioral Disorders*
      10:283-93.

      Reviews the effects of tutoring programs for
      behaviorally distorted children and concludes that:
      (a) students involved as tutees almost invariably
      gain knowledge of the context being tutored;
      (b) tutors gain academically if the material being
      tutored is appropriate to serve this purpose;
      (c) tutors and tutees alike appear to benefit so-
      cially in areas directly involving the tutoring in-
      tervention; (d) students do not appear to benefit
      from tutoring interventions with respect to global,
      social or self-concepts measures. Although the re-
      sults of tutor programs for behaviorally disordered
      programs have been impressive, teachers are advised
      to monitor the results and effectiveness of the pro-
      gram closely.

879. Sherry, M., and M. Franzen. 1977. Zapped by zing:
      Students and teachers develop successful problem
      solving strategies. *Teaching Exceptional Children*
      9:46-47.

      The zing curriculum for emotionally disturbed
      junior high school students is an innovative curric-

ulum put together by students and teachers that
stresses strategies for coping. Co-operative productive thinking is the direction the authors feel
certain will provide for more appropriate education
of this population.

880. Slavin, R.E. 1977. Student team approach to teaching
      adolescents with special emotional and behavioral
      needs. *Psychology in the Schools* 14:77-84.

          This article discusses the effect of the Teams-
      Games-Tournament (TGT) on thirty-nine adolescents
      with special emotional and behavioral needs. The
      TGT is an instructional technique involving student
      teams and learning games, mutual attraction, helpful-
      ness, task interaction, and time on task. The stu-
      dents were assigned to two treatments (TGT or indi-
      vidualized instruction) and their interaction and
      task behaviors were recorded on a five-category be-
      havioral observation scale. The students were also
      administered a five-item sociometric instrument.
      The results confirmed the hypothesis that TGT would
      exceed individualized instruction on the students'
      attraction to one another, frequency of peer tutor-
      ing, and percent of time on task. TGT students dis-
      tributed among six new classes were still interacting
      with their peers both on and off task more than the
      control students when a followup was performed five
      months later.

881. Smith, C.R. 1978. Trends in programming for emotion-
      ally disturbed and chronically disruptive pupils.
      Iowa Perspective 4:1-8.

          The paper focuses on trends in the areas of
      emotional disabilities (ED) related to identifica-
      tion, programming considerations, and general deliv-
      ery issues. An increase in the number of children
      identified as ED has affected the need for more pro-
      grams and personnel for this group and for public
      awareness of the disability. Touches on other trends
      such as the use of observation as a means of identi-
      fication and the use of educational rather than medi-
      cal or psychiatric terminology. Discusses six pro-
      gramming considerations including the mandated indi-
      vidualized educational program, an increasing aware-

ness of the importance of education in the lives of
children, the mandated need for accountability, a
growing uniformity in program evaluation, mainstreaming, and more intensive and extensive training of
teachers.

882. Smith, C.R.   1980.   One look at aggression in the classroom. *Iowa Perspective* 6:1-6.

The author defines classroom aggression, deals
with possible explanations as to why such behavior
occurs, looks at misconceptions related to classroom
aggression, and points out items that need to be
looked at when analyzing classroom aggression. Two
types of aggression--hostile and instrumental--are
considered. Determinants of aggression are seen to
include social, environmental, situational, and individual factors. Among the misconceptions regarding
classroom aggression are that aggression is a drive
that must be released through some process and the
best educators can do is channel the means by which
this is done, and that frustration is the primary
cause of aggression and always leads to aggression.
Suggestions include the following: take a look at
the type of aggression seen in pupils, take steps
accordingly, look at many different possible causes,
and remember that the teacher's behavior is important.

883. Smith, C.R.   1981.   The effects of disturbed adolescents
on their teachers. *Iowa Perspective* 6:15-21.

The difficulties faced by teachers of disturbed
and disruptive adolescents. Depicts situations in
which the teacher experiences anxiety and reacts in
inappropriate ways. Also discusses long-term effects
of dealing with these students such as anger at co-
workers, envy of students, and retreat into professional neutrality.

884. Smith, D.E.P.   1981.   Is isolation room time-out a punisher? *Behavioral Disorders* 6:247-56.

The commonly held assumption that time-out intervention, as represented by use of an isolation

room, constitutes a punisher is disputed on empirical
and theoretical ground. Consistent, unemotional use
of time-out, without ancillary punishers, is shown
to result in typical extinction curves (rather than
the steeper gradient of punishment curves) for both
autistic and mentally impaired children with widely
different abrasive behaviors. Such curves ordinarily
result from withdrawal of either a positive or a
negative reinforcer. But "maladaptive" classroom
behaviors are thought to be maintained by negative
reinforcement, the reduction of stress (an aversive
stimulus) following aggression. Thus, extinction of
"maladaptive" behavior will result from withdrawal
of the aversive stimulus (i.e., escape from class-
room-induced stress). Dangers of punishment and the
therapeutic value of reduced environmental stimulation are pointed out.

885. Smith, J., and S. Johnson. 1981. Serving troubled
      youth: Quality progress. *Pointer* 26:39-41.

      Describes three approaches to the problems of
      troubled and disturbed youths: therapeutic discussion
      groups with mental health professionals; a resource
      room model based on W. Glasser's reality therapy in
      which students earn points for responsible behavior
      and task completion; and an integrated approach to
      drug and alcohol abuse.

886. Stowitschek, C. 1982. Behaviorally disordered adoles-
      cents as peer tutors: Immediate and generative ef-
      fects on instructional performance and spelling
      achievement. *Behavioral Disorders* 7:136-8.

      An investigation of the effects of peer tutoring
      on twelve behaviorally disordered adolescents who
      were directly trained by their teachers (control
      group) and a similar population not directly trained
      by teachers (non-control group). Learner performance
      on daily spelling tests increased with the use of
      peer instruction. All peer tutors eventually used
      record keeping and graphing strategies of control
      group.

887. Tisdale, P.C., and R.E. Fowler. 1983. The effects on
      teachers' perceptions of the prevalence of emotion-
      ally disturbed children and youth. *Education*
      103:278-80.

          This study's primary objective was to determine
      the effects of labels on teachers' perceptions of
      the prevalence of emotionally disturbed children and
      youth in the regular classroom setting. An estima-
      tion was required of the teachers to categorize emo-
      tionally disturbed pupils according to severity:
      mild, moderate, and severe. The study found that
      labels did have an effect on teachers' perceptions
      of the prevalence of emotionally disturbed children
      in the regular classroom.

888. Trippe, M.J. 1963. Conceptual problems in research in
      educational provisions for disturbed children. *Ex-
      ceptional Children* 29:400-6.

          What is urgently required is concentrated atten-
      tion to changes that can be brought about in troubled
      children based upon considerations of their total
      life situation that are relevant for educational
      planning. Determined efforts are required to discern
      meaningful relationships between the variety of dif-
      ficulties to which children are prone and the provi-
      sions that might be made for them by the school,
      rather than continuing to make an inappropriate sys-
      tem work by establishing special classes for 'dis-
      turbed' children.

889. Vacc, N.A. 1972. Long term effects of special class
      intervention for emotionally disturbed children.
      Exceptional Children 39:15-24.

          The purpose of this study was to evaluate the
      effectiveness of separating emotionally disturbed
      youngsters for special education. The question is
      whether they fare better than the disturbed child
      that remains in the regular class. The subjects
      were thirty-two elementary school children all of
      whom were classified emotionally disturbed and
      matched for intelligence. Half of them were in reg-
      ular classes and half in classes for the disturbed.
      The findings suggest that there is no significant

difference in achievement, and the author questions
the placing of emotionally disturbed children in
special classes in light of this.

890.   Vacc, N.A., and N. Kirst.   1977.   Emotionally disturbed
       children and regular classroom teachers.   *Elementary
       School Journal* 77(4):309-17.

          Reviews literature on the value of mainstreaming
       as opposed to special classes for emotionally dis-
       turbed children.   A survey of 149 regular class teach-
       ers resulted in reports that teachers believed the
       education of emotionally disturbed children in spe-
       cial classes is superior to the education provided
       for them in a regular class.   Also reported is that
       emotionally disturbed children in a regular class
       would be detrimental to the non-handicapped students,
       and that regular teachers in a regular class setting
       would find emotionally disturbed children unmanage-
       able.

891.   Walker, H.M., and H. Hops.   1979.   The CLASS program
       for acting out children: R and D procedures, program
       outcomes and implementation issues.   *School Psychol-
       ogy Digest* 8:370-81.

          Describes the CLASS (Contingencies for Learning
       Academic and Social Skills) program for acting out
       children in the primary grades.   Explains the re-
       search and development process used at the Center at
       Oregon for Research in the Behavioral Education of
       the Handicapped to develop, test, and validate the
       package; provides an overview and guidelines for the
       package; and considers implementation problems and
       potential responses.

892.   Warger, C.L., and M. Trippe.   1982.   Preservice teacher
       attitudes toward mainstreamed students with emotional
       impairments.   *Exceptional Children* 49:246-52.

          Student teachers (N = 113) completed question-
       naires about mainstreaming emotionally disturbed
       (ED) students.   Results indicated generally positive
       attitudes, despite recognition of some behaviors as
       disturbing.   Further, they asserted that their skills

were sufficient to deal with the mainstreamed setting.

893.   Webster, R.E. 1981. Vocational-technical training for
       emotionally disturbed adolescents. *Teaching Excep-
       tional Children* 14:75-79.

       The Alternative Vocational School in Connecticut
       services 90 adolescents identified as acting out,
       emotionally disturbed, or socially maladjusted in a
       program emphasizing behavior management and disci-
       pline. The five components of the school are admin-
       istration, job preparation and placement, clinical
       services, vocational-technical training, and learning
       disabilities instruction.

894.   Whitaker, M. 1985. Creativity and emotionally dis-
       turbed children: Teaching ideas. *Pointer* 29:18-20.

       The author of this article points out that EH
       children have very poor self-concepts. Teachers of
       EH must plan activities that help disturbed children
       learn that they are unique human beings and have an
       unlimited potential. These activities must be set
       up to achieve success and to help the children under-
       stand that being different is acceptable. The author
       provides a list of creative activities that are all
       fun and easy to do.

895.   Williams, R.P. 1982. The ED primary student: An ap-
       proach that works. *Academic Therapy* 18:217-23.

       The author describes the Cavendish school pro-
       gram in London, England, that serves severely emotion-
       ally disturbed children seven to twelve years old.
       Noted among program characteristics are a small en-
       rollment; only two one-half hour daily academic peri-
       ods with the rest of the day devoted to various ac-
       tivities such as play, recess or lunch; daily meet-
       ings attended by the whole school; and an emphasis
       on physical activity. Among the factors seen to be
       most critical to the school's success are immediate
       response to a school crisis; use of the student
       "Court" to settle disputes; and use of play, games,

and sports as integral parts of the students' behavioral and social education.

896. Wood, F.H., and R.H. Zabel. 1978. Making sense of
      reports on the incidence of behavior disorders/
      emotional disturbance in school-aged populations.
      Psychology in the Schools 15:45-51.

          Reviews estimates of the incidence of emotional
      disturbance/problem behavior in school aged children
      and concludes that schools should anticipate a need
      for alternative programming for the two to three
      percent of their students predicted to have recurrent
      or persistent problems in adjusting to school situa-
      tions. Evidence also suggested a need to assist
      teachers in dealing with the stresses created by the
      high incidence of transient behavior affecting
      twenty-five to thirty percent of the total school
      population.

897. Wright, L. 1985. Suicidal thoughts and their relation-
      ship to family stress and personal problems among
      High School seniors and College undergraduates.
      Adolescence 20:575-80.

          This study investigated incidence of suicidal
      thoughts (STs) among twenty percent of high school
      seniors and ninety percent of college students and
      the relationship between STs and drinking, drug prob-
      lems, family stress, and delinquency. The study
      shows that those who have STs were more likely to
      view themselves as having a drinking or drug problem,
      family conflict, or poor relationship with parents.
      The results of this study suggest that family coun-
      selling should be stepped up in order to avoid STs
      in our educational system.

898. Wynne, M. 1984. Preparing teachers for emotionally
      disturbed children: A psychoeducational teacher-
      training approach. *Pointer* 29:11-15.

          Explains the content and structure of a psycho-
      educational approach toward the teaching of teachers
      the ability to teach self-control. This program
      develops the skills and understanding of the teacher

in a number of areas including: (1) an understanding
of normal child development and the importance of
psychoeducational teaching for emotionally disturbed
children; (2) positive teacher-child relationship
through communication skills; (3) teacher's confidence to therapeutically manage students' surface
behavior; (4) management of stress to prevent conflict from getting out of hand; (5) clear understanding of cognitive and affective components of self-
control; (6) sensitive diagnostic skills to understand each child's affection and cognitive strengths;
(7) techniques to build students' self-esteem as
they acquire academic knowledge.

899.   Yard, G.J., and R.L. Thurman. 1982. Seizure disorders
       and emotionally disturbed children and youth: An
       inservice training model. *Behavioral Disorders* 7:86-
       90.

       Project SAFE (Seizure Assimilation For Educa-
       tors) was designed as a pilot project to train edu-
       cation personnel in the various aspects of seizure
       management in emotionally disturbed students. The
       project training program, utilizing a pretest/post-
       test design, compared the knowledge levels of thirty-
       three educators on seizure disorders and their man-
       agement. Results were found to be statistically
       significant, indicating that teachers had little
       knowledge of seizure disorders and their management,
       and that Project SAFE was an effective education
       training project.

900.   Yaseldyke, J.E., and G.G. Foster. 1978. Bias in teach-
       ers' observations of emotionally disturbed and learn-
       ing disabled children. *Exceptional Children* 44:613-
       15.

       This study tested two hypotheses in which
       seventy-five elementary school teachers were asked
       to view a videotape of a normal fourth grade boy.
       The teachers were divided into three groups. One
       group was told that the child was normal, the other
       two were told that the child was emotionally dis-
       turbed or learning disabled. All the teachers were
       given behavior checklists to fill out after viewing
       the video. This study demonstrated that the percep-

tions and expectations of teachers are adversely affected by knowledge of labels.

Mainstreaming is a movement in education to teach exceptional children together with normal children while providing
any needed special education. The impetus for this concept
was PL 94-142, which mandates that handicapped children be
given appropriate public education in the least restrictive
environment. Three factors are understood in terms of mainstreaming children: (1) that the handicapped children will be
placed with their peers; (2) that they will require special
needs satisfaction which will be met within the regular classroom; and (3) that in this least restrictive environment they
will be able to interact socially as much as they can with
their regular classmates. Essentially, mainstreaming is providing the most appropriate education for each child in the
least restrictive setting. It looks at the educational needs
of children instead of clinical or diagnostic labels, and it
serves to unite the skills of general education and special
education so that all children will have equal educational
opportunity. Mainstreaming is not any wholesale return of
all exceptional children in special classes to regular
classes, nor does it ignore the need of some handicapped children for a more specialized program than can be provided in
the general education program.
    The underlying goal of mainstreaming is to integrate all
children into the "real" world, and not isolate them in an
artificially structured setting. The thinking along this
line is that if a child cannot function among his/her peers,
then how will that child be able to function in society at
large?
    Mainstreaming can be accomplished totally or partially--
the whole day can be spent in the regular classroom, or just
selected periods. If children are being considered for mainstreaming, the class(es) that they go to should be chosen
with great care. If this is not done, they have little chance
of success in a mainstream class. Among the factors that
must be considered is the style of didactic presentation. If
a lot of the instruction is lecture or through group work,

special direction may be required. If the child has to take
notes or read from the chalkboard and he/she cannot read or
write well, special assistance will be needed. Perhaps the
child can photocopy someone else's notes, or perhaps a peer
tutor can read the homework questions or the textbook. Other
variables that may play a role include whether or not the
mainstreamed class will provide clear and consistent routines,
and the emotional support that the child is likely to receive
during and after the transfer.

Staff development programs are essential to insure success. A discussion of possible teaching problems, teaching
strategies and goals, as well as ways of promoting acceptance
and understanding by the other children in the classroom are
among the topics that ought to be covered. Classrooms must
accommodate the disabled children's needs, and careful planning and modifications are essential.

Much of the impetus for mainstreaming came from the deinstitutionalization movement for the mentally retarded and
the emotionally ill in the 1970s. It may strain credulity,
but our institutions were originally conceived of as a merci-
ful solution to the plight of these groups, who at the time
were subject to abuse, neglect, and imprisonment. Bearing
this in mind, we should be wary of the rosy picture that is
painted of mainstreaming. As a matter of fact, deinstitutionalization of orthopedically and sensorily handicapped children
preceded the thrust for the retarded and mentally ill, and
integration into the regular class was practiced sporadically.

Another impetus for mainstreaming was the belief that
race, socioeconomic class, and personality were often used as
excuses for special education placement by educational personnel. Still another impetus was the consequence of past failures in special education. For example, hearing impaired
children have scored below level in academic achievement for
over fifty years (from 1921-1975). Thus, integration, even
on a part-time basis, is viewed as desireable. However, despite the potential for greater success, mainstreaming also
can cause greater stress, as the handicapped child becomes
more acutely aware of his/her limitations and has to compete
with those who are not as disadvantaged, or not disadvantaged
at all. The result may be a negative self-image and a feeling
of failure, which is self-defeating. Therefore, carefully
designed guidance and support programs and services are essential. The decision to "mainstream" must be based upon the
individual needs of the individual child--it is not a panacea.

Further, for regular teachers mainstreaming usually means
extra efforts, requiring a broad range of tolerance for and
acceptance of behavioral and academic differences, and forming
a new working bond with the field of special education. For

special education teachers it might mean watching while exceptional learners struggle in a competitive educational situation where individuation and supportive encouragement is not always present. It may also mean trying to establish working relationships with less-than-enthusiastic regular teachers. And for the exceptional student it might mean being more vulnerable and more subject to stress situations, but it also might mean being viewed as less special and less isolated. Most of all, it might mean more stimulation with the right kind of language and behavioral role models to emulate.

As one trades off isolation and labeling stigmata for a more normal educational environment with many unknowns, it is hardly ever possible to say that mainstreaming is "good" or "bad." But the range of options available for providing a better education for exceptional students is wider. However, successful integration of the handicapped requires careful planning, commitment, and cooperation. Teachers have to be more resourceful in using a greater variety of methods in their instruction. They must have proper materials (e.g., large print or braille books, large pencils, typewriters, lap trays) and they need to rearrange their classrooms and traffic patterns to accommodate these children. Individualized teaching, learning centers, and a maximum of flexibility will be needed. Teachers will have to work with paraprofessionals and special education personnel, so that much time will be spent on organization and in keeping records, with some autonomy lost. For many teachers, these are negative features. Only small class sizes, compensatory time for the paper work and regularly scheduled released time for consultations, together with teaching assistance, can make mainstreaming work. Translating theory to practice is often a difficult step. How effectively mainstreaming will be implemented remains to be seen. However, none can fault its goals or lofty ideals.

901. Adey, S. 1983. A strategy for integration. *Special Education: Forward Trends* 10(2):27-28.

    Based on her experiences the author describes necessary factors for successful integration of children with hearing and visual impairments. She suggests that planning must include the physical set up, commitment of staff, school organization, and parents' involvement.

902. Allen, K.E. 1981. Curriculum models for successful mainstreaming. *Topics in Early Childhood Special Education* 1:45-55.

    Discusses different curriculum models used for successful mainstreaming. These include open-educational, language-based, cognitive (Piaget), behavioral, Montessori and developmental-interaction models. An effective mainstreaming program must take into consideration such aspects as the role of the teacher, learning through imitation, physical arrangements, and inter-disciplinary programming. Before making a choice of which model to use the benefits and disadvantages should be weighed.

903. Almond, P. 1979. Mainstreaming: A model for including elementary students in the severely handicapped classroom. *Teaching Exceptional Children* 11:135-39.

    Using the concepts of normalization, mainstreaming, and individualized instruction, a big brother/sister program was developed in which sixteen handicapped autistic children, four to fifteen years old, were tutored by nonhandicapped elementary students. Among results of the program were increased understanding and acceptance of the autistic children.

904. Ames, L.B. 1982. Mainstreaming: We have come full circle. *Childhood Education* 58:238-40.

    The article traces past and present trends in mainstreaming and discusses chronological grouping and grading as a kind of mainstreaming. The author advocates special classes for children with special needs, as opposed to mainstreaming, and favors Devel-

opmental Placement in which the developmental level
is the basis for placement.

905. Anderson, B.R. 1973. Mainstreaming is the name for a
new idea: Getting the problem child back into a regular classroom. *School Management* 17:28-30.

Describes a program to mainstream handicapped
children with support from a learning resource center
in a New Jersey middle school. The LD teacher consultant encouraged the design of a variety of educational programs to deal with problems and a community
organization to improve educational services. The
center is manned by three special education teachers
and an assistant, resulting in financial savings.
Children are reported to gain from this mainstreaming
program--due partly to the cooperation of regular
teachers. The community organization is actively
involved.

906. Anderson-Inman, L. 1981. Transenvironmental programming: promoting success in the regular class by maximizing the effect of resource room instruction.
Journal of Special Education Technology 4(4):3-12.

Transenvironmental programming is a data based
approach for promoting regular class success for
handicapped students by carefully programming resource room instruction. The article describes an
experimental study with a twelve-year-old student
with behavior problems and academic deficiencies
that supports the efficacy of the approach.

907. Arundel, G. 1982. What is the least restrictive environment for physically handicapped students? *Educational Horizons* 60:115-17.

Because of the need for special assistance,
extra time, and rest, mainstreaming the physically
disabled student may actually result in a more restrictive school experience and decreased individualized instruction. The author suggests that the requirements in P.L. 94-142, the Education for All
Handicapped Children Act, for placement in the least

restrictive environment may be misinterpreted to the student's detriment.

908. Beech, M.C. 1983. Simplifying texts for mainstreamed students. *Journal of Learning Disabilities* 16:400-2.

Author suggests that difficulty in readability and with concepts in textbooks can be reduced for mainstreamed students by simplifying content, sentences, and vocabulary. Included guidelines from psycholinguistic research and an example of a simplified test.

909. Blacher, J., and A.P. Turnbull. 1983. Are parents mainstreamed? A survey of parent interactions in the mainstreamed preschool. *Education and Training of the Mentally Retarded* 18:10-16.

In an interview with eighty-two parents of mainstreamed preschoolers about their interactions with other parents, parents of handicapped preschoolers said they interacted equally often with parents of nonhandicapped and handicapped children. Parents of nonhandicapped children said they interacted more with parents of nonhandicapped children. Results proved there is still room for mainstreaming of parents.

910. Blacher-Dixon, J. 1981. Mainstreaming at the early childhood level: Current and future perspectives. *Mental Retardation* 19:235-41.

Presents an updated review of preschool mainstreaming. Reviews topics such as rationale, program outcomes, child outcomes, teacher variables and effects on parents. The effects of mainstreaming on severely handicapped children are largely unknown.

911. Blackhurst, A.E. 1982. Competencies for teaching mainstreamed students. *Theory into Practice* 21:139-43.

Reviews three major studies on the competencies needed by regular educators for instructing mainstreamed handicapped students. The author considers

the competencies identified by each study and points
out that the majority are competencies that good
teachers should possess, whether or not they teach
mainstreamed students. Explains competencies related
directly to mainstreaming such as legal mandates,
characteristics of exceptional students, integration
approaches, and relationships with specialists,
rather than specific teaching methods.

912. Boersma, F.J.; J.W. Chapman; and J. Battle. 1979.
      Academic self-concept change in special education
      students: Some suggestions for interpreting self-
      concept scores. *Journal of Special Education* 13:433-
      42.

         Studied changes in academic self-concept. The
      Student's Perception of Ability Scale measured
      changes in fifty severely learning disabled students
      and eighteen educable mentally retarded students in
      special education classes and in eighty-three chil-
      dren in the regular classroom. The subjects were
      eight to twelve years old and were studied for a
      one-year period. The results showed that full-time
      placement in special education classes increased
      academic self-concept, especially in reading, spell-
      ing, and confidence.

913. Bond, J., and A. Lewis. 1983. Reversing a sentence
      for life. *Special Education: Forward Trends* 9(4):11-
      13.

         This article discusses stages in transferring
      mentally retarded students in England from special
      schools to mainstream classes. The stages include:
      discussion with class teachers, evaluations, main-
      stream school selection, teacher visitations, discus-
      sion with parents, use of mainstream school's mate-
      rials at the special school, placement in mainstream
      school, and follow-up visits.

914. Brulle, A.R. 1983. A comparison of teacher time spent
      with physically handicapped and able-bodied students.
      Exceptional Children 49:543-45.

         This article observed and charted the behaviors

of sixteen teachers who had day-to-day contact with twenty-three physically handicapped, mainstreamed high schoolers. The conclusions were that teachers spent more time with the handicapped students.

915. Campbell, N.; J. Dobson; and J. Bost. 1985. Educator perceptions of behavior problems of mainstreamed students. *Exceptional Children* 51:298-303.

One hundred five educators involved in this study were mainly regular classroom teachers, but also comprised counselors, administrators, special educators, and librarians. In general, they appeared to view student behavior problems as more serious when exhibited by nonhandicapped or physically handicapped students than when exhibited by mentally handicapped students. However, the same educators recommended more authoritarian behavioral treatments for nonhandicapped than for physically handicapped students. This study revealed that educators need to develop the attitudes and skills necessary for behavior management in the mainstreamed school environment.

916. Carden-Smith, L.K., and S.A. Fowler. 1983. An assessment of student and teacher behavior in treatment and mainstreamed classes for preschool and kindergarten. *Analysis and Intervention in Developmental Disabilities* 3:35-57.

Data were collected in mainstreamed and treatment classrooms on the rate and form of problem behaviors to classify conditions under which eleven children, aged 3.3 to 6.3 years and referred for special services due to learning and behavior problems, differed from regular classmates.

917. Carpenter, D.; L.B. Grantham; and M.P. Hardister. 1983. Grading mainstreamed handicapped pupils: What are the issues? *Journal of Special Education* 17:183-88.

Issues in grading mainstreamed handicapped students include the definition of grades, who reads grades, what grades mean, how grades can be a fair comparison of students, and the fairness of a

separate-but-equal policy. Grades can show progress,
effort, competence or comparison with others, but
they are not useful if the message that was intended
is not the message received.

918. Clarkson, M.C. 1982. *Mainstreaming the exceptional
      child: A bibliography.* San Antonio, TX: Trinity
      University Press.

The text provides information on 3,122 books,
journal articles, theses, dissertations, government
documents, proceedings, pamphlets, and other materials (1964-1981) on mainstreaming of handicapped children. The bibliography was drawn from searches of
the Educational Resources Information Center (ERIC)
database. Entries include information on author,
title, data, source and pagination, along with ERIC
document number if appropriate. Citations are organized alphabetically by author's last name according
to eight areas of exceptionality: general, gifted,
hearing impaired, learning disabled and emotionally
disturbed, mentally handicapped, physically handicapped, speech handicapped, and visually handicapped.
A subject index is provided.

919. Clements, C.B., and R.D. Clements. 1984. *Art and main-
      streaming: Art instruction for exceptional children
      in regular school classes.* Springfield, Illinois:
      Charles C. Thomas.

Suggestions for providing art instruction to
mainstreamed handicapped and gifted children. Each
of seven conditions is discussed in terms of how the
individual learns and how he/she can profit from
mainstreamed instruction. The following conditions
are considered: behavior disorders, educable mental
retardation, trainable mental retardation, severe
mental retardation, learning disorders and hyperactivity, hearing impairments, blindness, neurological
and orthopedic handicaps and giftedness.

920. Cohen, S.B. 1983. Assigning report card grades to the mainstreamed child. *Teaching Exceptional Children* 15:86-89.

This article studies the problems involved in grading mainstreamed students. The suggested solutions include: communication between regular class and resource teachers, use of a combination of feedback and scores, use of individualized education performance objectives, and emphasis on individual assessment.

921. Cruikshank, W.M. 1974. The false hope of integration. *Slow Learning Child* 21:68-83.

An evaluation of effective special education and integrated programs. Administrators who forced misplacement of children for self-convenience and regular class teachers and special educators who were accomplices in educational mismanagement point to one of the reasons that special education (SE) is under attack. Colleges are encouraged to instruct educators to teach to the disability rather than to its consequences. Recommends that SE be improved through screening and review by citizen boards. What is needed are qualified teachers, acceptance of the child at his developmental level, administrative decisions to reduce class sizes, and commitment to maximizing the achievement of every child.

922. Davis, W.E. 1980. Public school principals' attitudes toward mainstreaming retarded pupils. *Education & Training of the Mentally Retarded* 15:174-78.

Studied the perceptions of 345 Marine Public School principals toward mainstreaming handicapped children according to their type and the level of their handicap. Mentally retarded students were viewed as having the least chance for successful mainstreaming. Even those students who were only mildly retarded were seen as having poor chances for successfully being integrated into the regular classroom.

923. Elias, L. 1983. Jason goes to kindergarten. *Excep-
      tional Parent* 13:55-58.

           This study relates the experiences of a Down's
      Syndrome child mainstreamed into a regular kinder-
      garten class and points out the benefits of the least
      restrictive environment, such as cost effectiveness.
      Also looks at the attitudes of the teacher, special
      education aide, and principal.

924. Frostig, M. 1980. Meeting individual needs of all
      children in the classroom setting. *Journal of Learn-
      ing Disabilities* 13:158-161.

           Discusses the conditions that need to be met
      for mainstreaming to be effective. Explores instruc-
      tional methods, the needs of exceptional children,
      classroom management, and the use of outside help,
      as well as future directions of mainstreaming.

925. Garvey, M. 1982. CAI as a supplement in a mainstreamed
      hearing-impaired program. *American Annals of the
      Deaf* 127:613-16.

           Article describes how CAI (computer assisted
      instruction) can be incorporated into subject areas
      in special classes and resource rooms for hearing
      impaired secondary students. CAI supplements lan-
      guage, vocabulary reading, and math instruction. The
      method includes development of software programs by
      the school staff.

926. Giordano, B. 1983. Would you place your normal child
      in a special class? *Teaching Exceptional Children*
      15:95-96.

           This article discusses how the placement of a
      nonhandicapped young girl in a preschool program for
      handicapped children benefited the nonhandicapped
      child. The girl served as a model child for the
      handicapped class and thus gained social skills and
      understanding.

927. Goodspeed, M.T., and B. Culotta. 1982. Professors' and teachers' view of competencies necessary for mainstreaming. *Psychology in the Schools* 19:402-7.

    Teacher competencies necessary for mainstreaming were compared for eleven categories by thirty-seven college professors and sixty-four classroom teachers. In all cases, teachers thought the competency was more important than did the professors. Significant differences between groups were found on twenty-six of the seventy-five items. There was a four-point difference in rank-order assigned by the two groups in goal-setting and curriculum development (viewed as more important by the professors), and communication and assessing students' needs (viewed as more important by the teachers).

928. Gottlieb, J. 1982. A point of view. *Education and Training of the Mentally Retarded* 17:79-82.

    In this article the author raises issues concerned with the appropriateness of mainstreaming for educable mentally retarded students, including students mainstreamed, reasons for the placement, how long they should be in mainstream settings, and daily experiences of mainstreaming. Also discusses the need to examine how children are educated.

929. Graham, R.M. 1980. *Teaching music to the exceptional child: A handbook for mainstreaming.* Englewood Cliffs, NJ: Prentice-Hall.

    The book is intended to help educators use music in the education of handicapped children. An initial chapter focuses on the contributions of music to mainstreaming and reviews the history of music education for the handicapped in the U.S. Assessment, establishment of long term goals and short term instructional objectives, and parental involvement are among topics considered in the chapter on individualized education programs. Guidelines for mainstreaming in the music program address general problems (such as short attention span and sensory needs) and implications for particular handicaps.

930. Greenbaum, J.; M. Varas; and G. Markel. 1980. Using
      books about handicapped children. *Reading Teacher*
      33:416-19.

           Discusses the use of appropriate books about
      handicapped children that can aid in some of the
      problems caused by mainstreaming and suggests methods
      for evaluating the books. An annotated bibliography
      is included in the article.

931. Gresham, F.M. 1983. Social skills assessment as a
      component of mainstreaming placement decisions.
      Exceptional Children 49:331-36.

           Author recommends that the use of social skills
      be assessed in order to make placement decisions
      regarding mainstreaming. When assessing many fac-
      tors, the use of social skills should be included as
      a component. Further suggests that social skills
      information may be more important in making a deci-
      sion to mainstream than IQ or achievement.

932. Gugerty, J. 1981. Modifying tools and equipment to
      serve mainstreamed vocational students. *Career De-
      velopment for Exceptional Individuals* 4:96-99.

           Describes considerations for modifying or ad-
      justing equipment for the mainstreamed student and
      lists administrative, curricular, and instructional
      decisions involved in serving mainstreamed students
      in vocational education.

933. Hamre-Nietupski, S. 1981. Integral involvement of
      severely handicapped students within regular public
      schools. *Journal of the Association for the Severely
      Handicapped* 6:30-39.

           The authors contend that in addition to regular
      school placement, systematic efforts to promote posi-
      tive interactions between severely handicapped stu-
      dents and their nonhandicapped peers must be made.
      Formal and informal methods for promoting integra-
      tion, directed toward both school staff and students,
      are designed to assist teachers of the severely han-
      dicapped in systematically integrating their students

into the regular school milieu. Among such procedures are the following: presenting inservice sessions to special and regular education faculty, arranging for severely handicapped to use as many
school facilities as possible, involving parents in
plans to integrate their child, associating with a
team of teachers, arranging for flexible individual
programming and team teaching among special education
classes, offering an "open door" visitation policy
for special education classrooms, and involving severely handicapped students in school jobs.

934. Handleman, J.S. 1984. Mainstreaming the autistic-type
child. *Exceptional Child* 31:33-38.

This article discusses mainstreaming as it per-
tains to autistic children as opposed to any other
type of exceptional child, such as the mentally retarded or mildly retarded. It suggests that mainstreaming is very important for the autistic child
as for any other child with special needs. In order
to modify the situation, one must adopt a regulariza-
tion approach, together with strategies to gain more
normalized settings for greater success. Due to the
specific needs of every individual autistic child,
the transition process must be well planned and programmed for each child.

935. Hart, L.; J.M. Hill; S. Healy; and S.A. Fagen. 1983.
Objectives and types of inservice training for mainstreaming. *Pointer* 28:25-28.

The Montgomery County Public Schools in-service
training program describes the in-house evaluation
of the school coordinator. The position of the coordinator was set up to help local schools and teachers training in relation to the mainstreaming of handicapped students. Includes in-service objectives,
in-service activities, and an evaluation of the progress made to date by the coordinator.

936. Henfield, P., and M. Stieglitz. 1981. Comparisons of
      parent and teacher attitudes toward mainstreaming.
      Albertson, NY: Human Resources Center.

           Two hundred eighty-two parents and 121 teachers
      were surveyed on academic and social issues related
      to mainstreaming handicapped students. Teachers and
      parents represented four different educational set-
      tings: a minimally mainstreamed public school, a
      heavily mainstreamed public school, a special school
      for students with disabilities, and a reverse main-
      streamed school (a special school that also enrolls
      nonhandicapped students). Regular school parents
      and teachers had the greatest agreement in responses,
      generally believing that their children and students
      were appropriately or very independent for their
      ages. Both expressed strong support for mainstream-
      ing despite concerns about the number and nature of
      disabilities. More parents than teachers felt that
      only teachers with special education training should
      teach disabled students.

937. Hewett, F.M. 1980. *Planned positive peer interaction:
      An approach for facilitating the integration of ex-
      ceptional learners in regular classrooms.* Washing-
      ton, DC: Office of Education.

           The report outlines achievements of a twenty-
      seven-month project designed to develop and implement
      a curriculum approach for increasing peer acceptance
      and interaction of mainstreamed exceptional students.
      Project efforts include development of classroom
      observation procedures and the use of those proce-
      dures to observe twenty mainstreamed classrooms;
      interviews with teachers and graduate students in
      special and regular education; and development of a
      curriculum. The curriculum was evaluated in four
      different settings serving severely language handi-
      capped and otherwise disabled children in main-
      streamed settings. Among findings were that slower
      and shy children needed coaching with an adult to
      become skilled at the games before being paired with
      another child and that adults needed to model and
      reinforce clear and positive communication between
      students during the tasks. Dissemination activities
      include the presentation of teacher workshops and
      preparation of manuals explaining the curriculum.

Among appendixes are sample teacher interviews and results from a list of behaviors associated with students' poor social skills.

938. Hite, M. 1981. Toward a least restrictive environment. *Learner in the Process* 3:3-6.

Proposes a step-by-step process to eliminate restrictive elements that are found in every class-room before a least restrictive environment (as defined by P.L. 94-142, the Education for All Handicapped Children Act) can be possible for any child. Reports on results of a study involving seventy-six administrators and teachers to test the process for identifying restrictive elements.

939. Horne, M.D. 1983. Attitudes of elementary classroom teachers toward mainstreaming. *Exceptional Child* 30:93-98.

Examines the attitudes toward mainstreaming of 139 elementary classroom teachers taking an intro-ductory course in special education. Investigates additionally how they felt about Public Law 94-142. The findings show there is a great need for compre-hensive in-service training programs for these regu-lar teachers to understand special education and mainstreaming needs.

940. Humphrey, M.J.; E. Hoffman; and B.M. Crosby. 1984. Mainstreaming learning disabled students. *Academic Therapy* 19:321-27.

Suggestions to increase the success of learning disabled students in a mainstream setting. Examines altering the environment and teaching and testing methods. Acceptance of individual differences, ac-knowledgement of each student's worth, and outlets for classroom tensions all facilitate learning.

941. Johnson, A.B. 1981. Teacher's attitudes toward main-streaming: Implications for inservice training and

program modifications in early childhood. *Child Care Quarterly* 10:134-47.

Inservice training for early childhood education teachers should focus on development of individualized education programs, behavior management, working with parents and volunteers, and working with the IEP team. The article also deals with the important topics of program modifications for facilitating mainstreaming and the use of support services.

942. Johnson, R. 1983. Integrating severely adaptively handicapped seventh-grade students into constructive relationships with nonhandicapped peers in science class. *American Journal of Mental Deficiency* 87:611-18.

This study discusses a successful method for mainstreaming forty-nine handicapped and forty-one nonhandicapped seventh grade children in science class. The finding of this study is that cooperative learning is more critical to the interaction of handicapped and nonhandicapped students than any individual learning condition.

943. Klein, V.W., and L.A. Randolph. 1974. Placing handicapped children in head start programs. *Children Today* 3:7-10.

Describes the integration of handicapped children into Head Start preschool classes as mandated by 1972 amendments to Head Start legislation. Illustrates national and Head Start distribution of disabled (including mentally retarded, deaf, speech impaired, visually handicapped, seriously emotionally crippled) and other health impaired children. Integrating handicapped and non-handicapped children is beneficial for both groups when curriculum is individualized.

944. Kunzweiler, C. 1982. Mainstreaming will fail unless there is a change in professional attitudes and institutional structure. *Education* 102:284-88.

This article discusses how teacher attitude,

teacher training, and structural changes in the institution affect mainstreaming. The research shows that the most important variable in achievement for mainstreamed students is the interaction between the mainstreamed students and their teachers and normal students in the class. The author feels there must be more exchange between the programs in college that train teachers for regular classes and those that train teachers for special classes. Institutional changes would include changes in classroom structure and the use of untapped resources and personnel.

945. Larrivee, B., and M.L. Bourque. 1981. Factor structure of classroom behavior problems for mainstreamed and regular students. *Journal of Abnormal Child Psychology* 9:399-406.

Thirty-five elementary school teachers completed behavior ratings of 876 students, including mainstreamed students, utilizing a group administered adapted version of Devereux Elementary School Behavior Rating Scale. The following five factors were defined: conduct problem, personality problem, adaptive classroom behavior, inadequacy-immaturity, and achievement anxiety. A similarity was found between the pattern generated by regular students' ratings and that by mainstreamed students.

946. Levine, M.H., and J.A. McColoum. 1983. Peer play and toys: Key factors in mainstreaming infants. *Young Children* 38:22-26.

This study examined ways that handicapped infants and toddlers can be mainstreamed with nonhandicapped children:
1. Placing handicapped near nonhandicapped children to facilitate an awareness of them as social beings.
2. Putting younger nonhandicapped children with older handicapped children depending on their level of development and maturity in behavior.
3. Having toys make interactions more common between handicapped and nonhandicapped infants.

947. Ley, D., and R. Metteer. 1974. The mainstream approach
     for the SLD child: A public school model. *Bulletin
     of the Orton Society* 24:130-34.

     Project Success mainstreams LD public school
     students (kindergarten through nine) through a class-
     room based delivery system in which a trained lan-
     guage therapist first demonstrates for a target
     classroom teacher, then team teaches with him, and
     finally withdraws into a supportive consultant role.
     The language arts program in the kindergarten empha-
     sizes systematic training in auditory skills, and in
     the elementary grades, a systematic phonics approach
     with multi-sensory input. Students are not permitted
     to experience failure in order to convince them that
     they can succeed. Three programs have been developed
     together with language arts to make sure that the
     child develops and is treated holistically as a per-
     son rather than a learning problem: motor perception
     training, curriculum modification, and parent demon-
     stration-participation workshops.

948. Lieberman, L.M. 1982. The nightmare of scheduling.
     Journal of Learning Disabilities 15:57-58.

     Discusses practical problems and situations
     such as moving handicapped children in and out of
     the regular classroom and special education classes.
     Problems include the facts that children spend too
     much time traveling between rooms, that teachers
     cannot keep track of their children's difficulties
     in scheduling, and that approaches tend to be incon-
     sistent.

949. Madden, N., and R.E. Slavin. 1983. Effects of coopera-
     tive learning on the social acceptance of main-
     streamed academically handicapped students. *The
     Journal of Special Education* 17:171-81.

     In this study, six classes of academically han-
     dicapped and normal-progress children were randomly
     assigned to study mathematics cooperatively or under
     a traditional classroom structure. Results indicted
     that cooperative techniques improved social accept-
     ance. Rejection of academically handicapped students
     was decreased, but friendships were not increased.

Academic achievement gains and increases in self-
esteem were found for the combined sample of students
in the cooperative learning treatment.

950. Meece, J.L. 1982. *A comparative study of the social
attitudes and behaviors of mildly handicapped children in two mainstreaming programs.* Washington, DC:
Office of Special Education.

The social outcomes of two mainstreaming programs were compared for twenty-four first- through
third-grade handicapped children. Students were
randomly assigned to one of two placements: a traditional resource room or an adaptive educational program. Placement differed in the amount of time students spent in an integrated setting, the instructional practices, and the opportunities for both
instructional and social interactions. Observational
data on classroom processes were analyzed to document
the distinguishing characteristics of the social and
academic environments in which the students were
placed. Differences were then examined in relation
to students' self reports of competence, friendship
patterns, and peer acceptance. Results revealed
that social outcomes varied markedly across the two
programs. More positive trends were uncovered in
the adaptive program where children were placed in
the integrated setting on a full-time basis, learning
assignments were matched to ability levels, itinerant
services were provided as much as possible within
the classroom, and opportunities to interact with
peers and form personal relationships were frequent.
Handicapped students in the adaptive education program had higher self-ratings of competence and received higher peer acceptance ratings than did handicapped students in the resource room program.

951. Meisels, S. 1977. First steps in mainstreaming. *Young
Children* 33:4-13.

Discusses the advantages and disadvantages of
integrating children with special and nonspecial
needs into the regular classroom. Some suggested
guidelines include: begin in-service courses, keep
an effective support system, have a school policy on
mainstreaming, arrange for consultants, make environ-

mental changes, and visit programs already in existence.

952. Michaelis, C.T. 1981. Mainstreaming: A mother's perspective. *Topics in Early Childhood Special Education* 1:11-16.

The mother of a preschool boy with Down's Syndrome discusses her experiences. She tries to keep
her child in the regular classroom rather than have
him placed in a special class. The article concludes
by stating that mainstreaming a child with special
needs should be considered only when the curriculum
and the facilities can deal with the needs of the
child.

953. Mlynek, S.; M.E. Hannah; and M.A. Hamlin. 1982. Mainstreaming: Parental perceptions. *Psychology in the
Schools* 19:354-59.

A survey was taken of 159 parents of learning
disabled, mentally retarded, or emotionally disturbed
children concerning their reactions to mainstreaming
handicapped children. The parents of learning disabled children were much more supportive of mainstreaming handicapped children than the parents of
mentally retarded and emotionally disturbed children.

954. Munroe, M.J. 1982. Individualizing the mainstream
classroom. *Pointer* 27:11-13.

This article emphasizes the importance of teaching style in linking cognitive with affective variables for mainstreamed handicapped students using
the Tuscon Interaction Model. Five aspects of the
model are depicted across three strands (response
opportunities, feedback, and personal regard). Even
with computer-assisted instruction the teacher's
role is still critical.

955. Munson, H.L.; J.K. Miller; and J. Berman. 1981. Helping handicapped students learn to work in a mainstream
environment. *Exceptional Child* 28:19-29.

The mainstreaming of handicapped students presents changes that are beneficial to the learning
experiences of the disabled. The authors discuss
how career and employment prospects can be enhanced
because they use school experiences to foster the
work task-learning maturation process. The discussion includes identification as a worker, evaluation
of worker traits, and development of work habits and
skills.

956. Nix, G.W. 1982. Mainstreaming: Illusion or solution?
*Association of Canadian Educators of the Hearing
Impaired* 8:7-14.

An examination of the system variables that led
to the collapse of the nineteenth century German
attempt to implement mainstreaming of hearing impaired children on each of a number of system-wide
bases. The current implementation of the mainstreaming of handicapped children is then examined on each
of the system variables. Striking parallels are
found, and the author concludes that unless the system variables are adequately addressed by current
practice history may well repeat itself.

957. Odom, S.L.; M. Deklyen; and J. Jenkins. 1984. Inte-
grating handicapped and non-handicapped preschoolers:
Developmental impact on non-handicapped children.
Exceptional Children 51:41-48.

This study was undertaken to examine the effects
of placing young non-handicapped into classes with
handicapped children. Sixteen non-handicapped students were randomly placed into four integrated special education classes, each with eight mildly to
moderately handicapped students. The control group
consisted of sixteen children matched for age and
sex who were assigned to preschools for non-handicapped. A battery of assessments given to both
groups at the beginning and the end of the academic
year showed no significant difference in performance
for non-handicapped students. The study concludes

that the placement of these students in classes where
the majority are handicapped does not interfere with
their normal development.

958. Odom, S.L., and M.L. Speltz. 1983. Program variations
in preschools for handicapped and nonhandicapped
children--mainstreamed versus integrated special
education. *Analysis and Intervention in Developmental Disabilities* 3:89-103.

This article reviews literature showing that
programs serving handicapped and nonhandicapped preschool children have been labeled inconsistently,
with few attempts to identify specific variables
that discriminate program types. Suggests the use
of the terms "integrated special education" (with a
high proportion of handicapped) and "mainstreamed"
(with a low proportion of handicapped).

959. Owens, M.F. 1981. Mainstreaming in the every child a
winner program. *Journal of Physical Education, Recreation and Dance* 52:16-18.

The Every Child A Winner Movement Education
Program focuses on movement tasks geared to needs of
individual students and thereby provides opportunities for success by mainstreamed handicapped children.

960. Payne, R., and C. Murray. 1974. Principals' attitudes
toward integration of the handicapped. *Exceptional
Children* 41:123-25.

A questionnaire was sent to 100 elementary
school principals (fifty urban, fifty suburban
schools), to determine attitudes towards regular
class placement of handicapped children. Some of
the conclusions indicated that 40.3% urban principals
and 71.4% suburban principals accepted the concept
of integration of handicapped children. Both groups
ranked inservice teacher training as the greatest
need for regular teachers in an integrative program.

961. Peck, C.A., and T.P. Cooke. 1983. Benefits of main-
     streaming at the early childhood level: how much can
     we expect? *Analysis and Intervention in Developmen-
     tal Disabilities* 3:1-22.

         The paper reviews research on early education
     of preschool handicapped and nonhandicapped children,
     conducted from 1971 to the present, to determine the
     effects of integration on developmental outcomes,
     peer interaction, and social attitudes toward the
     handicapped. Among conclusions drawn are that devel-
     opmental outcomes have not proved superiority for
     either segregated or integrated services.

962. Perlmutter, B.F. 1983. Sociometric status and related
     personality characteristics of mainstreamed learning
     disabled adolescents. *Learning Disability Quarterly*
     6:20-23.

         Analysis of sociometric ratings for 162 main-
     streamed tenth graders revealed that, while learning
     disabled students were generally less well liked
     than their peers, a subgroup of the disabled sample
     was very well regarded. Most of the remaining learn-
     ing disabled students were rated in the neutral
     rather than the disliked range.

963. Powell, J.V. 1978. Mainstreaming eight types of excep-
     tionalities. *Education* 99:55-58.

         Guidelines for mainstreaming the educable men-
     tally retarded, speech disordered, emotionally dis-
     turbed, physically handicapped, learning disabled,
     hearing impaired, visually handicapped, and gifted
     students. Also discusses the responsibilities of
     special education and regular classroom teachers.

964. Powers, D.A. 1983. Mainstreaming and the inservice
     education of teachers. *Exceptional Children* 49:432-
     39.

         The article presents a literature-based set of
     practical guidelines regarding mainstreaming in the
     areas of inservice method, format, planning, goals
     and objectives, location, scheduling, evaluation,

incentives, training personnel, school administration, and instructional materials.

965. Prillaman, D. 1981. Acceptance of learning disabled
      students in the mainstream environment: A failure to
      replicate. *Journal of Learning Disabilities* 14:344-
      46; 368.

           The purpose of this study was to determine the
      acceptance or rejection of twenty-eight learning
      disabled children in a mainstream environment with
      334 first to sixth graders based on the sociometric
      status of the students. The results showed that
      learning disabled are as accepted in the classroom
      as non-learning disabled children. The one area in
      which learning disabled children were different was
      in their high representation in the isolate/neutral
      category.

966. Ray, B. 1985. Measuring the social position of the
      mainstreamed handicapped child. *Exceptional Children*
      52:57-62.

           The purpose of this study was to determine
      whether mainstreamed special education students dif-
      fer significantly in social position on various in-
      struments for evaluation. Examines teacher rating
      scales, peer sociometric scales, and direct observa-
      tion as methods of evaluation. In respective order,
      the instruments found that handicapped children were
      perceived less socially acceptable by teachers,
      highly rejected by peers on sociometric measures and
      yet, equally likely to be observed in positive social
      interactions. The study calls for the reinterpreta-
      tion of past research since these findings conflict
      with past efforts.

967. Rodriguez, F. 1982. Mainstreaming a multicultural
      concept into special education: Guidelines for
      teacher trainers. *Exceptional Children* 49:220-27.

           A project at the University of Kansas has ana-
      lyzed, evaluated, and developed guidelines for multi-
      cultural emphasis in special education teacher educa-
      tion. The project has progressed from analysis of

the department curriculum to development of a workshop model. The format of the workshop model is
included in the article.

968. Rosensweig, J., and D. Vacca. 1983. The learning disabled student and social integration: Getting it to
work. *Academic Therapy* 18:275-83.

Describes a program to integrate learning-
disabled and nonlearning-disabled classmates. Some
of the goals of the program include: confronting
students' fears about being capable and intelligent
enough to correct incorrect information about the
nature of intelligence, to learn which factors affect
school achievement, and to encourage sensitivity
toward the handicapped persons.
Students became more familiar with the resource
room, staff, and watched a film of a multiply handicapped eleven-year-old boy. After the program was
completed, learning disabled students complained
significantly less about being ostracized.

969. Stafford, P.L., and L.A. Rosen. 1981. Mainstreaming:
Application of a philosophical perspective in an
integrated kindergarten program. *Topics in Early
Childhood Special Education* 1:1-10.

Examines the controversy over special or regular
preschool placement for handicapped children and
describes a university laboratory school approach at
Kent State University. Two full-day kindergarten
classes, composed of different proportions of handicapped and nonhandicapped children, were involved
in the project. Results revealed the need for both
a unified philosophy among staff regarding mainstreaming and the importance of integrating specialized
methods into the context of regular classrooms.

970. Salend, S.J. 1983. Using hypothetical examples to
sensitize nonhandicapped students to their handicapped peers. *School Counselor* 30:306-10.

This article presents a six-step model for gen-
erating hypothetical examples of what a handicapped
student might experience in a mainstreamed setting,

and preparing nonhandicapped students for this integration. Stages include determining student needs,
specifying environmental demands, identifying problems, translating and presenting hypotheticals to
the class, and brainstorming solutions.

971. Salend, S.J., and J. Johns. 1983. A tale of two teach-
      ers: Changing teacher commitment to mainstreaming.
      Teaching Exceptional Children 15:82–85.

      The case study describes how the positive behav-
      ior changes of a mainstreamed second grader with
      severe emotional problems resulted in similarly posi-
      tive changes in the attitudes and actions of two
      teachers toward mainstreaming. The authors propose
      that positive attitudes toward mainstreaming can be
      fostered in regular class teachers by helping them
      promote positive changes in the child who is main-
      streamed.

972. Schmelkin, L.P. 1981. Teachers' and nonteachers' atti-
      tudes toward mainstreaming. *Exceptional Children*
      48:65–68.

      The attitudes of special education teachers,
      regular teachers, and nonteachers toward mainstream-
      ing were assessed by means of a questionnaire. All
      groups had relatively positive attitudes towards
      mainstreaming as academically less costly than the
      other groups.

973. Schubert, M.A. 1984. Communication: One key to main-
      streaming success. *Exceptional Child* 31:46–53.

      Describes a consultation model that promotes
      effective communication between special education
      teachers and regular teachers working with the excep-
      tional child. No teacher is to assume the role of
      expert--rather all have specific skills and necessary
      knowledge. This model tends to more accurately re-
      flect the actual situation and discourages faculty
      members from appearing more knowledgeable than one
      another.

974. Schwartz, L.L. 1984. *Exceptional students in the mainstream.* California: Wadsworth.

> The text focuses on mainstreaming exceptional students. An introductory chapter reviews implications of P.L. 94-142. Subsequent chapters are devoted to separate disabilities, with information on characteristics, classification, identification, assessment, educational modifications, placement, and techniques for each. Disabilities include mental retardation, learning disabilities, hearing impairments, visual impairments, language handicaps, learning disabilities, hearing impairments, visual impairments, language handicaps, learning disadvantages (such as child abuse and neglect), cultural minorities, emotional problems, and social maladjustment. The final part addresses such concerns as teacher preparation and families of exceptional students.

975. Sigler, G.; W. Mabee; and L. Mabee. 1978. Children's attitude toward handicapped students as a result of mainstreamed settings. *Mental Retardation Bulletin* 6:92-97.

> This study assessed 180 sixth-graders in regular classrooms who were given the Attitude Toward Handicapped Individuals Scales and a stick figure report measure of self-concept. The results were that ATHI scores were non-accepting for all of the subjects. No significant relationship appeared between the type of educational setting and ATHI or between the length of time in educational settings and ATHI.

976. Silverman, M. 1979. Beyond the mainstream: The special needs of the chronic child patient. *American Journal of Orthopsychiatry* 49:62-68.

> Argues with Public Law 90-142's promotion of behaviorally disturbed children through mainstreaming. The author feels the needs and the rights of some behaviorally disturbed children are violated through mainstreaming due to the insistence on equality. Provides three examples to illustrate some of the difficulties caused by mainstreaming these children with special needs.

977. Sivage, C.R. 1982. Implementing PL 94-142: A case for
      organizational readiness. *Journal for Special Edu-*
      cators 18(2):29-42.

           A survey of 150 elementary schools was conducted
      to examine the organizational characteristics, not
      the characteristics of individual teachers, that
      facilitate or impede mainstreaming implementation.
      Individual variables were grouped into three cate-
      gories--communication/information variables, admin-
      istrator variables, and demographic variables. Among
      findings were that the variable with the highest
      correlation to effective mainstreaming implementation
      is goal clarity; schools with effective programs
      tend to be large; and effective mainstreaming pro-
      grams occur in schools where principals are seen as
      advocates of the program. The study concludes that
      successful implementation of mainstreaming depends on
      a systemwide approach that involves the whole school,
      from administrators to teachers.

978. Smart, R.; K. Wilton; and B. Keeling. 1980. Teacher
      factors and special class placement. *Journal of*
      Special Education 14:217-29.

           Examined the personal characteristics and atti-
      tudes of thirty-two regular class teachers. Half of
      these teachers recommended the transfer of a seven-
      to eight-year-old child from their class to a special
      class. Those teachers who did not refer children to
      special education classes were more in favor of main-
      streaming for children with low ability, and they
      had a higher proportion of low achievers in their
      classes.

979. Spencer, J., and J.G. Lutz. 1984. Mainstreaming or
      mainlining: A competency based approach to main-
      streaming. *Journal of Learning Disabilities* 17:27-
      29.

           Previous studies have shown that student behav-
      ior is even more important than academic performance
      in deciding whether or not a child is ready to be
      mainstreamed into a regular classroom. Similarly,
      other studies have detected a relationship between
      mainstreamed students' behavior and teachers' atti-

tudes toward the mainstreaming concept. With this
in mind, this particular study had 188 regular and
special education elementary teachers participate in
a thirty-six-item questionnaire that rated their
perceptions as to whether or not a specific social
skill was critical for success in the mainstream
setting. The results identified three main categories of critical social skills and competencies necessary for a student to possess in order to function
successfully in a regular classroom. These are:
interacting positively with other students, obeying
class rules, and displaying proper work habits.
This list of critical social behaviors is important
because it provides a mainstreaming criteria for
placement teams to use in determining whether or not
a student is ready for a regular classroom, or should
remain in a special program. If the team decides
that the student is not yet able to function in and
adapt well to the regular classroom, then these vital
social skills can be taught by the special educators
in order to expedite the student's readiness for
mainstreaming.

980. Stainback, W., and S. Stainback. 1981. A review of
research on interactions between severely handicapped
and nonhandicapped students. *Journal of the Association for the Severely Handicapped* 6(3):23-29.

The article reviews recent research concerning
interactions in integrated settings between severely
handicapped and nonhandicapped students. It also
examines studies that discuss interactions between
severely handicapped students and their mildly handicapped as well as nonhandicapped peers. Four topics
are addressed: the interactions that occur, the influence of those interactions on the students involved, the communicative characteristics of the
interactions, and ways of promoting interactions.

981. Stainback, W., and S. Stainback. 1982. Preparing regular class teachers for the integration of severely
retarded students. *Education & Training of the Mentally Retarded* 17:273-77.

Discusses the training needs of regular class
teachers as they prepare for the integration of se-

verely retarded students into their classrooms.
Also focuses on the identities of these retarded
students and the reasons they are being integrated.

982.   Stainback, W., and S. Stainback. 1983. A severely
       handicapped integration checklist. *Teaching Excep-
       tional Children* 15:168-71.

            This article presents a checklist for determi-
       ning the extent of integration of severely handi-
       capped students into regular school environments.
       The fourteen-item list is useful in identifying en-
       vironments that may need to be improved in anticipa-
       tion of the integration of severely handicapped stu-
       dents (i.e., cafeteria, assembly programs, recess,
       and school hallways).

983.   Stoner, M. 1981. Education in mainstreaming. *Clearing
       House* 55:39-42.

            Suggests activities to help teachers feel more
       comfortable with mainstreaming. Activities deal
       with teacher attitudes, empathy with students' spe-
       cial needs, and larger issues involving mainstream-
       ing.

984.   Strain, S. 1983. Generalization of autistic children's
       social behavior change: Effects of developmentally
       integrated and segregated settings. *Analysis and
       Intervention in Developmental Disabilities* 3:23-24.

            Four seven- to ten-year-old boys with autistic
       behavior were examined with behavioral and observa-
       tional measures in a peer mediated training, inte-
       grated generalization assessment, and a segregated
       generalization assessment setting. The results fa-
       vored the developmentally integrated condition for
       increasing positive social behavior.

985.   Streitmatler, J.L., and R.M. Santa Cruz. 1982. Main-
       streaming the institutional exceptional child.
       Pointer 27:14-16.

            Transition programs are critical when seriously

emotionally disturbed students from an institution
are placed in public schools. Communication and
long range planning were identified as major concerns
by public school and institutional teachers.

986. Tawney, J.W. 1981. A cautious view of mainstreaming
in early education. *Topics in Early Childhood Special Education* 1:25-36.

Discusses problems in the interpretation of
Public Law 94-142 and the definition of mainstreaming. The author feels mainstreaming has problems
within the current system relating to the poor quality of training of regular educators and their negative attitudes toward handicapped children. Additionally, there aren't relevant support services to
regular teachers.

987. Taylor, S.J. 1982. From segregation to integration:
Strategies for integrating severely handicapped students in normal school and community settings. *Journal of the Association for the Severely Handicapped*
7(3):42-49.

The author concludes from phone interviews and
site visits that there are many approaches to integrating severely handicapped students into school
and community settings. Examples cited include dis-
persal, planned interaction, provision of program
support and support for regular teachers, staff integration, parental support, and positive attitudes in
general.

988. Taylor-Hershel, D., and R.E. Webster. 1983. Mainstreaming: A case in point. *Childhood Education*
59:175-79.

Discusses some of the variables involved in
mainstreaming a three-year-old visually impaired
boy. The goals of the Montessori School that he was
mainstreamed to include self-determination, self-
teaching, and individual mobility. These goals contributed to his self-confidence, independence, and
academic and cognitive success.

989. Thompson, T.L. 1983. Communication with the handi-
      capped: A three year study of the effectiveness of
      mainstreaming. *Communication Education* 32:185-95.

           The results indicate that mainstreaming physi-
      cally handicapped children into regular classes is
      having some positive consequences. Nonhandicapped
      children participating in the mainstreaming program
      show more ability to communicate with the handicapped
      than those not participating in the program. Handi-
      capped children, however, are still not in the main-
      stream of classroom activities.

990. Tunick, R.H.; J.S. Platt; and J. Bowen. 1980. Rural
      community attitudes toward the handicapped: Implica-
      tions for mainstreaming. *Exceptional Children*
      46:549-50.

           Thirty-one rural nonfarmer adults and seventy-
      four rural farmer adults were given the Attitude
      Toward Disabled Persons Scale. The results showed
      that rural nonfarmers had more favorable attitudes
      toward the disabled than did rural farmers.

991. Turnbull, A.P. 1982. Mainstreaming in the kindergarten
      classroom: Perspectives of parents of handicapped
      and nonhandicapped children. *Journal of the Division
      for Early Childhood* 6:14-20.

           Telephone surveys of 101 parents of handicapped
      and nonhandicapped children in mainstreamed kinder-
      garten settings indicated a high level of agreement
      on the benefits and drawbacks of mainstreaming. The
      greatest benefits were identified as being related
      to social outcomes. The greatest drawbacks were
      identified in instructional areas.

992. Turnbull, A.P., and P. Winton. 1983. A comparison of
      specialized and mainstreamed preschools from the
      perspectives of parents of handicapped children.
      Journal of Pediatric Psychology 8:57-71.

           In this study mothers of fourteen handicapped
      children placed in specialized preschools and seven-
      teen handicapped children in mainstreamed preschools

were interviewed about factors influencing their
choice of schools. They also evaluated their child's
current preschool. Similarities and differences
were found in the perspectives of mothers toward
mainstreamed and special preschools. The major differences included greater emphasis by mothers of
mainstreamed students on exposure to normal peers
and the "real world" and greater emphasis by parents
of children in special schools on the need for professionals to assume responsibility for the education
of their child so they could relax and work.

993. Van Dominick, B. 1983. Special education resource
      programs. *Special Education in Canada* 57:4-5; 7-9.

         Resource programs are an outgrowth of recogni-
      tion that special classes have been largely ineffec-
      tive for many handicapped children. Resource teach-
      ers offer both direct and indirect services via as-
      sessment, programming, and consultation. Despite
      potential difficulties in maintaining gains in a
      mainstreamed child, resource rooms are cost effective
      and flexible.

994. Volkmann, C.S. 1978. Integrating the physically dis-
      abled student into the elementary school. *Education*
      99:25-30.

         Physically disabled students are encouraged to
      accept responsibility, feel needed in the classroom,
      and to develop basic skills through teacher strate-
      gies. Among the beneficiaries of these strategies
      are children with real illness, pseudo-illness, lim-
      ited vision or hearing, cerebral palsy, hyperactiv-
      ity, and problems with developmental growth have
      these strategies applied to them.

995. Wang, M., and E. Baker. 1985-1986. Mainstreaming pro-
      grams: Design features and effects. *The Journal of
      Special Education* 19:503-19.

         The goal of this study was to review and analyze
      the design features and efficiency of mainstreaming
      as an educational approach to serving disabled stu-
      dents. Eleven empirical studies of the effects of

mainstreaming published from 1975 through spring,
1984 were selected for analysis from a total pool of
264 studies. Findings showed that mainstreamed disabled students consistently outperformed nonmain-
streamed students. Selected design features found
in the extant effective-teaching literature to be
associated with programs designed to provide for
student differences were also found to be features
of mainstreaming programs that showed greater proportions of positive than of negative outcomes.

996. Warger, C.L., and M. Trippe. 1982. Preservice teacher
      attitudes toward mainstreamed students with emotional
      impairments. *Exceptional Children* 49:246-52.

          One hundred thirteen student teachers completed
      questionnaires about mainstreaming emotionally dis-
      turbed students. Results indicated generally posi-
      tive attitudes, despite recognition of some behaviors
      as disturbing. Further, they asserted that their
      skills were sufficient to deal with the mainstreamed
      setting. Implications for cognitive, affective, and
      behavioral components of preservice education are
      noted.

997. Westwood, P. 1982. Strategies for improving the social
      interaction of handicapped children in regular
      classes. *Australian Journal of Remedial Education*
      14:23-24.

          Teachers are a vital influence in fostering
      social interactions among handicapped and nonhandi-
      capped children. Classroom environments can be cre-
      ated in which competition is not a dominant element
      and in which children are grouped to encourage coop-
      eration. Careful monitoring and willingness to in-
      tervene on the part of the teacher are important.

998. Winnick, J.P., and J. Hurwitz. (Eds.) 1979. *The prep-
      aration of regular physical educators for mainstream-
      ing.* Washington, D.C.: Bureau of Education for the
      Handicapped.

          The monograph reports on a three-year project
      to develop competencies in physical education teach-

ers for dealing with mainstream exceptional students. Presents results of a survey of physical educators on the types of competencies needed to teach in mainstreamed settings. Adjustments made to the undergraduate physical education program at State University College at Brockport (New York) are illustrated, and twenty-three competencies associated with mainstreaming are set forth. Principles and guidelines for individualizing instruction are reviewed. The largest part of the monograph (nineteen papers) presents ways to integrate exceptional students in specific sports, including archery, backpacking, field hockey, golf, lacrosse, soccer, snow skiing, racquetball, tennis, and swimming. Two papers on evaluation of the mainstreaming sub-component conclude the volume.

999. Wood, J.W., and M. Carmean. 1982. A profile of a successful mainstreaming teacher. *Pointer* 27:21-23.

Cognitive and affective characteristics of a successful mainstreaming teacher are reported from a sample of administrators, regular classroom teachers, and special educators. Among the characteristics noted are love for children and a concern for their needs, positive attitudes toward and knowledge of special education and mainstreaming.

1000. Yecke, C. 1981. Pedigreeing your mainstreaming program. *Academic Therapy* 17:147-50.

Suggestions for encouraging teachers to become involved in mainstreaming programs. These include the presentation of demonstration lessons, sharing materials, inviting teachers to visit special education classes, and frequent consultations.

1001. Zigler, E., and S. Muenchow. 1979. Mainstreaming: The proof is in the implementation. *American Psychologist* 34:993-96.

Mainstreaming needs to be very closely monitored. The least restrictive environment, if not used carefully, is being compared to deinstitutionalization which in the authors' opinion leads to no

care at all. They feel research is needed to determine which children with which handicaps are best
able to benefit from mainstreaming. Mainstreaming
cannot succeed without appropriate teacher training
and support services.

AUTHOR INDEX

SUBJECT INDEX

Abacus, 268
Abuse (Child), 56, 721
Academic Contracting, 794
Academic Self-Concept Scale, 148
Acceleration, 115, 153, 670
Achievement, 443
  Academic, 214, 373, 729, 747
Adaptive Behavior, 32, 544
  Measures of, 38
Adjustment, 152, 329, 340
  School, 729
Administrators, 99
Adolescents, 27, 133, 143, 200, 367, 427, 455, 457, 475, 483, 488, 497, 505, 507, 525, 534, 699, 745, 769, 813, 876, 880, 883
Aggression, 826, 845, 868, 876, 882
Alphabet, 537
Anxiety, 452, 505, 506, 520
Aphasia, 686
Apraxia, 632
Arithmetic (see Mathematics)
Art, 90, 104, 358, 563, 919
Articulation, 653, 668, 680, 684
Assertion Training, 761
Attention, 31, 259, 494, 532, 827
  Deficits in, 469
Attitudes toward Disability, 735

Behavior Management (Modification), 359, 757, 790, 798, 817, 821, 861
Behavior Problems, 17, 37, 50, 157, 452, 463, 464, 509, 510, 518, 805, 809, 817, 818, 863, 945
Bender-Gestalt Test, 571, 591, 612
Biofeedback, 801
Blindisms, 219
Boehm Test of Basic Concepts, 323, 490
Books, 930
Braille, 230, 242, 278, 297
Brain Damage,
  Art &, 563
  Assessment of, 571, 579, 603
  Problems in, 568
  Rehabilitation in, 604
  Siblings &, 566
  Social Skills Training in, 559
Burnout, 218, 841

CAI, 925
Career Education, 40, 235, 297, 717, 765, 813
Cerebral Palsy, 698
  Assessment of, 719, 720, 748
  Education of, 733, 741, 760
  Language impairment in, 762
  Treatment of, 702, 710, 757
  Writing &, 701
Checklists, 796